The Origins of Modern Mexico

Laurens Ballard Perry,
General Editor

Outcasts in
Their Own Land

Mexican Industrial
Workers, 1906–1911

Rodney D. Anderson

Northern Illinois University Press   DeKalb 1976

About the artist: The scenes depicted on the jacket, frontispiece, and in the details throughout the book are from original artwork created by Mario Pérez Orona especially for the Origins of Modern Mexico series. Mario Pérez has exhibited his paintings, collages, and drawings in more than 25 exhibitions throughout Mexico in the past 15 years. He is a professor of painting, drawing, and graphics in the art department of the University of the Americas in Puebla, Mexico.

Library of Congress Cataloging in Publication Data

Anderson, Rodney D   1938–
    Outcasts in their own land.

    (The Origins of modern Mexico)
    Bibliography: p.
    Includes index.
    1.   Labor and laboring classes —Mexico — History.
2.   Strikes and lockouts — Mexico — History.   3.   Labor
and laboring classes — Mexico — Political activity — History.   I. Title.   II. Series.
HD8116.A525   301.44′42′0972   74–28896
ISBN 0-87580-054-8

Copyright © 1976 by Northern Illinois University Press
Published by the Northern Illinois University Press
DeKalb, Illinois 60115
Manufactured in the United States of America

ACKNOWLEDGMENTS

Parts of chapters 6, 7, and 8 appear in a different form in my article "Mexican Workers and the Politics of Revolution, 1906–1911," *Hispanic American Historical Review* 54 (February 1974):94–113, copyright 1974 by Duke University Press. Lines quoted from "The Heights of Macchu Picchu," p. vii, are from Pablo Neruda's *Canto general* (1950), in *The Penguin Book of Latin American Verse*, edited by E. Caracciolo-Trejo (Harmondsworth, Middlesex, England: Penguin Books Ltd., 1971), pp. 148–49, prose translation by Tom Raworth. Copyright Penguin Books Ltd.; selection and appendix, copyright E. Caracciolo-Trejo, 1971. Reprinted by permission of Penguin Books Ltd. and Carmen Balcells. Lines quoted from "Bruselas," p. 299, are from Pablo Neruda's *Tercera residencia* (1947), in *The Penguin Book of Latin American Verse*, edited by E. Caracciolo-Trejo (Harmondsworth, Middlesex, England: Penguin Books Ltd., 1971), p. 127, prose translation by Tom Raworth. Copyright Penguin Books Ltd.; selection and appendix, copyright E. Caracciolo-Trejo, 1971. Reprinted by permission of Penguin Books Ltd. and Carmen Balcells. Lines quoted from "A Worker Reads History," p. 3, are from Bertolt Brecht's *Selected Poems,* trans. H. R. Hays (New York: Grove Press, by arrangement with Harcourt, Brace Inc., 1959), p. 109. Reprinted by permission of Harcourt Brace Jovanovich, Inc. Photograph 1 is from Yamada, "The Cotton Textile Industry," p. 31. The remaining photographs are reproduced with the permission of the "Archivo Casasola," Bolivar 1106, the Federal District. Drawings 1, 2, and 3 are reprinted, by permission, from *José Guadalupe Posada: Ilustrador de la vida mexicana* (Mexico: Fondo Editorial de la Plástica Mexicana, 1963), pp. 378, 382, 439.

To my mother and father

Rise to birth with me, brother.

Give me your hand out of the deep
zone of your scattered sorrow.
You will not return from the depth of the rocks.

You will not return from subterranean time.
Your hardened voice will not return.
Your perforated eyes will not return.

Look at me from the depths of the earth,
tiller, weaver, silent shepherd.

Pablo Neruda, "The Heights of Macchu Picchu"

Contents

Illustrations

Preface

Set in Mexico early this century, this book tells a story of people—working men and women—caught up in harsh, relentless economic changes, changes which not only caused misery and hardship but which also appeared to the workers to erode their place in society, attacking their pride and self-esteem. The political rulers of Mexico, many of them men of high finance and business as well, brought industrial progress to Mexico, and with it had come the elements of a new social order.

The new order, in combination with already existing social and economic inequities, generated far-reaching changes in Mexican society. Large-scale agricultural interests continued the centuries-old process of encroachment on the lands of the villagers, but in a more systematic and effective way than ever before, producing a large number of landless rural people throughout the heavily-populated central states. In the towns and cities, factory-made goods slowly undermined those of the artisans, because hands and tools could not compete with machines. In the same way, the small, older factories could not compete with the newer, larger plants and were forced to replace their more relaxed industrial regimen with production systems run by cost-conscious managers, to the increasing misery of their workers. Finally, even the new economics proved to be defective, as the boom and bust character of the business cycle and the accompanying inflation added to the problems most working Mexicans were confronted with after the turn of the century.

Not being permitted to live a stable and secure existence, many workers protested their fate, demanding to share in the progress of their nation. They wanted adequate and secure material rewards for their labor and better working conditions; but more than that, they wanted to be considered somebody, to have a place in their society, to be treated with respect. What follows is the story of their struggle to achieve these ends.

The title of this study has undergone several changes. Initially I had in mind "Strangers in Their Own Land," a charge contained in a petition to the governor of the state of Veracruz signed by nine cotton mill hands. I personally liked it, because it portrayed a state of mind relevant to Mexican workers at the time and because it could be attributed to real people, and not simply to my attempt to dramatize their resistance. Yet when a flyer reached me announcing the publication of "Strangers in Their Own Land," a history of the Chicano by Albert Prago (Four Winds Press), I had no choice but to look for another title.

At one point I was considering some variant of "Workers on the Eve of Revolution." It seemed exciting to current taste and appealing to those who see the Mexican Revolution as a turning point in the history of modern Mexico. Yet in the end it did not feel right. All too often, it seems to me, "precursorism" robs the past of the meaning of its existence. By definition, it assumes the importance of people's lives to be in the effect they have on the future. Mexico happened upon a revolution in 1910, and whether or not it was inevitable is irrelevant. Few men acted as if they believed that a revolution was inevitable, and that is what is important. Instead, they lived out their lives from day to day *not* knowing what tomorrow would bring. The historian's hindsight is a valid perspective in the writing of history, but it is not history itself. I have tried to write a history that would have been believable to those who made it. If the attempt is in any way successful, I am satisfied.

Many people have aided and affected the writing of this book. David Ashton of Boston University taught me economics and introduced me to Latin America; it is an old but important debt. John Finan and Harold Davis taught me Latin American history. This book is, in a way, a culmination of the many beginnings made in those early years under their direction. Moisés González Navarro taught me about Mexican history and Mexican workers even before I met him and continued to give aid and encouragement in the decade that followed.

I owe a special debt of thanks to Jack Womack, who offered insight, asked hard questions, and suggested and criticized various parts of this manuscript and to Laurens B. Perry, who read this manuscript in its several drafts and made many important contributions in style and content.

To the friends and colleagues who read parts of this book, offering comments and suggestions, or who discussed questions of interpretation, I give my thanks: Barry Carr, Neil Betten, Helen Delpar, Tony Bryan, Heather Fowler Salamini, John Hann, John Hart, Michael Meyer, James P. Jones, Donald Horward, Darrell Levi, Steve Niblo, Nancyann Ropke, Jon Seymour, Paul Vanderwood, Dick Sinkin, William R. Walker, Dennis L. Hale, Mark Thompson, and Lyle Brown.

A note of special appreciation goes to Jorge Ignacio Rubio Muñé, and to the staff at the Archivo General de la Nación, especially José R. Guzmán and Luis Cortes Huerta; to the Colegio de México and Luis González y González, María del Carmen Velázquez, Silvio Zavala, Berta Ulloa, and Daniel Cosío Villegas; to María Teresa Gatouillat de Díaz for permission to use the General Porfirio Díaz Collection and to those at the University of the Americas who helped in the use of those materials: Laurens Perry, Joffre de la Fontaine, Errol Jones, and Steve Niblo; to the staff of the Hemeroteca Nacional for their assistance in pursuing worker-related periodicals, especially Gustavo A. Pérez Trejo and María del Carmen Ruiz Castañeda.

My thanks also to Arturo Romero Cervantes and to the staff of the Biblioteca de Hacienda; to Josephina González de Arellano, for use of the Archivo Espinosa de los Monteros at the Museo Nacional de Historia of the Castillo de Chapúltepec; to David Ramírez Lavoignet for permission to use the materials held by the Seminario de Historia Contemporanea de Veracruz; to Antonio Pompa y Pompa and the staff of the Biblioteca de Museo Nacional de Antropología e Historia; to Martín Quirarte and the staff at the Archivo Central de Secretaria de Relaciones Exteriores; to Alicia Reyes of the Capilla Alfonsina for permission to use the General Bernardo Reyes Archivo; to the staff at the Centro de Estudios de Historia Mexicana at Condumex, S.A.; to Fausto Marin-Tamayo at the Centro de Estudios Históricos de Puebla; to the staff at the U. S. National Archives; to Ann Lo and the staff of the Inter-Library Loan division of the Strozier Library, Florida State University; and to the staff of the Latin American Collection of the University of Texas Library, especially Nettie Lee Benson, whose aid to Mexicanists and whose love of Mexico are legendary.

I wish to thank Nicolas T. Bernal for his friendship and for his remembrances of Ricardo Flores Magón. I thank those in Mexico who aided in my research and in my understanding of their country and its people, especially María Teresa Dehesa y Gómez Farías, Fernando Leyva M., José O. Petricioli, Pablo L. Martínez, Gloria Grajales and Alicia Ortega Chamorro.

My thanks to Robert Clay for preparing the maps, to W. Scott Jessee for the charts and graphs, and to Larry Bloyd for his work on the bibliography, and to those who have typed the manuscript in its many drafts, for their patience and good humor, Kathy Meffert, Veronica Alexander, Sue Sullivan, Cheryl Jarnigan, and Matti Sims.

For financial support of various research trips to Mexico, I thank the U.S. Department of Health, Education and Welfare, the American Philosophical Society, the Florida State University Graduate Research Council, and my own Department of History of Florida State University.

I thank Bill and Judy Spruce, and Errol and Ellen Jones who offered their friendship and their homes in Mexico. A special thanks also to Lyle C. Brown for his valuable aid in my understanding of the *magonistas* and for his and his family's hospitality to me and to my family.

Finally, and most clearly, to my mother and father for their support and encouragement throughout the years; to Jim and Sharon for their love and the good times when they managed to lure me away from my work, and my regrets for the times they could not; and to Marti Trovillion Anderson, whose research-aid and editorial services were always efficient and whose belief was always sustaining—my affection. You are all here.

Introduction

". . . it is an injustice to be considered worse than an outcast in our own land."
—Letter to the editor of El Paladín, 13 March 1910, from certain "old weavers" of the Río Blanco mill near Orizaba, Veracruz.

They were mill hands, and the sentiment they expressed went to the core of their grievances with the owners and with their own society. They were invisible people, ignored, depreciated, and exploited by an entire generation of the nation's elite during the self-confident and prosperous gilded age that surrounded the turn of this century. Yet beginning in 1906, their grievances erupted into the major social issue of the day, forcing a reluctant society to acknowledge the existence of the labor unrest that had long been denied in Mexico.

No longer ignored, the men and women who made up Mexico's first generation of industrial workers demanded not only higher wages and better working conditions but respect from their fellow citizens as well. Most workers were willing to be a part of the developing industrial system, if the existing structure would satisfy their material needs and enable them to retain their self-respect. Too often, they explained, they were ill-treated by bigoted foreign supervisors and by callous bosses who regarded them as being no different from the machines they worked. Equally as humiliating, they were regarded as children or as savages or slaves, incapable of reason, who would work only if whipped and punished. They were human beings, they said, and citizens of a great Republic and should be treated as such.

Most industrial workers accepted the regime of General Porfirio Díaz, who had ruled their land since 1876, as the legitimate government, demanding only that the regime intercede in their conflicts with the employers. They were not asking for charity, they declared many times, but justice; that is, they were demanding to be treated as Mexican citizens with the corresponding political and social rights, rights which they firmly believed were guaranteed by the revered Constitution of 1857.

This study tells the story of those workers who protested the conditions under which they worked and lived, and of the issues they raised and the changes they demanded. It is also a story of how other groups within Mexico responded to the "labor question," as it was called, and of what stereotypes and attitudes nonworking-class people brought to their understanding of the workers' problems.

This book does not attempt to discuss systematically all industrial workers in Mexico; rather it concentrates on those industrial workers, urban craftsmen, and workers in allied occupations who demonstrated discontent, either through conflicts with their employers or through other behavior that gives evidence of their desire for change. Textile workers are given the most space in these pages, not because they were necessarily the most discontented but because their protests were widely documented and because the industrial process had affected the cotton textile mill hands longer than it had any other group of industrial workers, giving their protests a special significance in understanding Mexican labor history. Workers in other occupations that receive attention include those in the railroad, tobacco, and mining industries and those in several other industrial and craft pursuits.

There are important absences. The miners of Guanajuato, the mill hands of Guadalajara, Oaxaca, and Coahuila, and the smelter operators of Monterrey, to name a few, appear only marginally in this study, if at all. In some cases this is because of the lack of documentation, in others because of the absence of noticeable conflict, although neither situation means that such workers were necessarily contented. In short, although this study makes an effort to draw general conclusions about Mexican working men and women, vast areas of the history of Mexican working people are left to be explored. This book is just a beginning.

This book began in a graduate course on Latin American labor history at American University in the spring of 1965. I became interested in the revolutionary activities of the Mexican Liberal Party under the Flores Magón brothers prior to the Mexican Revolution and decided to do my doctoral research on what then appeared to me to be the decisive influence of the Liberals on the Mexican labor movement during the last decade of the Díaz regime. Through the years, the study slowly changed its nature and direction until it became what it is here.

Initial research in Mexico led me to believe that the relationship between Mexican workers and the Mexican Liberal Party was far less direct than had previously been assumed. Instead, I was drawn to the origins of the labor troubles of 1906 to 1911 period and the impact of the troubles on Mexican society. As time went on, especially after extensive research in the newspapers of the era, it became obvious to me that the labor problem during those years had been a far larger issue to many more Mexicans than accounts of the *Porfiriato* had ever indicated. Using the concept of a society facing a major social problem to organize the material into a manageable theme, I slowly developed the study around a number of research problems.

The most difficult questions proved to be the very basic ones: Who were the workers? How was the term "industrial" to be defined? Should artisans be included in the study? Could some workers be considered more "modern" in the way they viewed their work and their society?

The next problem was to describe the general conditions of life and work of Mexican workers in order to begin to understand what it was like to be an industrial worker during those years. The key question was not the conditions themselves as they appeared to me, but whether or not the workers protested such conditions, whether they saw themselves as being exploited by the developing industrial system. I needed also to know how those grievances changed over time, and why, and if there were any observable patterns of labor conflicts, and how such patterns were related to the social and economic forces unleashed by Porfirian industrial and commercial development. To deal with these questions, I broadened the study to include the nineteenth century in order to isolate the major factors influencing the nature and timing of the Mexican workers' response to their situation.

How did the workers go about their attempt to resolve their grievances and improve their situation? The answer to this question became the story not only of the rise of labor organizations but also of strikes, of petitions and spontaneous conflicts, and of the many ways in which the Mexican workers attempted to cope with their problems.

In addition, this study became a story of the workers' relationship with the major sources of potential relief—their employers, the federal government, and the political movements of 1909–1910. In essence, the questions asked were these: what were the goals of Mexican workers, and to what extent did they consider a radical reorganization of Mexican society necessary for them to obtain justice? Were many workers anarchists or syndicalists, either in formal ideology or in sentiment?

Given the workers' perception of their world, how were they and their problems perceived by other groups in Mexico? How did various governmental and nongovernmental elites react to the emergence of the labor problem in 1906? What were the influences governing and directing nonworking-class attitudes, policies, and actions toward workers? Specific institutions examined are the federal and state governments, the Catholic Church and its lay organizations, Mexican and foreign business concerns, and other social and political interests.

Finally, what was the workers' role in the Revolution of 1910? Where did workers actively participate in the overthrow of the old regime? What effect did the labor problem have on the demise of the Díaz government? It may well be that the fall of Díaz was more related to the problems of Mexican workers than has generally been acknowledged.

Yet of course the answers to these questions were not determined simply by the available data. Rather they developed out of my own perception and understanding of these materials, a process influenced by many factors. Certainly the most obvious is the work of other scholars that provided the insight and concepts which are the debts every scholar owes. Moisés González Navarro, Jean Chesneaux, Neil Smelser, Herbert Gutman, Jesse Lemisch, and John Womack wittingly and unwittingly inspired and prodded, helping me to understand what I had learned.

These influences were important, and I acknowledge them gratefully. Yet my response to what others had to say and my own perspective of the historical problem of the workers were not simply products of a logical, intellectual process. Clearly operating throughout this study were the subtle but pervasive mechanisms of my values and social origins. Few men escape their past; perhaps none do. And no doubt the very closeness of a young university scholar to the events and agonies of the last decade must surely have played a role here, unseen but basic to my changing intellectual and intuitive sense of the historical materials.

From these influences and probably others I do not clearly see comes a position that must be acknowledged here. Unmistakably and with no apologies, I have refused to adopt an attitude of disinterest toward the subjects of my study. Indeed, after ten years of association, I have formed an alliance of friendship and respect with the men and women who appear in the pages that follow. The historical truth of my account does not depend upon my interest or disinterest. Rather it depends upon conclusions reached in the continuing scholarly conversation about the situation of Mexican workers in the later years of the *Porfiriato*. In this study I offer my contribution to that conversation so that the reader may share what I believe and feel about those Mexican workers and come to his own conclusions.

Outcasts in Their Own Land

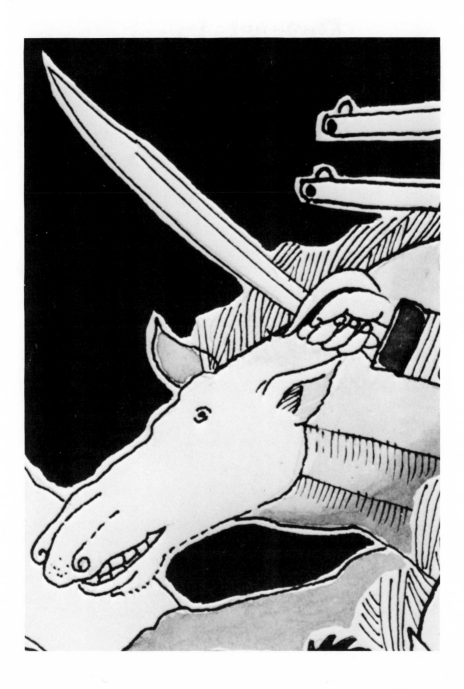

Chapter 1
The Workers of Anáhuac, 1521–1876

Who built the seven gates of Thebes?
The books are filled with names of kings.
Was it kings who hauled the craggy blocks of stone?
—Bertolt Brecht, from "A Worker Reads
History" in *Selected Poems*

Tenochtitlán lay in ruins. Once the capital of the powerful Mexica people, that great city had been destroyed by the men of Cortés and their Indian allies in seventy-five days of bitter fighting during the summer of 1521. In later years a historian recounting that siege told of an incident that took place in the last days of that struggle. The defenders had fought desperately but were being pushed back, block by block, toward the market district of Tlatelolco, their only remaining stronghold in the island-city they had once thought impregnable. During a lull in the fighting, a Mexica warrior watched helplessly from his own lines as the despised Tlaxcalans and the other Indian allies of the Spaniards leveled each building taken in the fighting. In his frustration and rage, he shouted "Go on! The more you destroy, the more you will have to build up again. If we conquer, you shall build for us and if your white friends conquer, they will make you do as much for them."[1] *And so it was.*

Within days after the last Mexica resistance had been overcome, the Spanish sent orders to all the towns within the Valley of Mexico. They were to supply men and materials for the rebuilding of Tenochtitlán. The towns and villages of the Valley responded willingly, since most had been held in subjugation by the Mexica and they were happy to be free of that burden. Texcoco, under the Spanish ally Ixtlilxochitl, contributed many skilled craftsmen and journeyman workers, for it was an important city and rejoiced at the fall of its former rival and

1. William H. Prescott, *Mexico and the Life of the Conqueror Hernando Cortés*, 2 vols. (New York: P. F. Collier and Son, 1900), 2:262.

master. From Coatepec came stonemasons, famous throughout the valley for the beauty and craft of their work. Chimalhuacán and Tepetlaoztoc sent their skilled carpenters and other artisans. From all quarters of the Valley they came, the workers of Anáhuac, to rebuild Tenochtitlán.[2]

It was not easy work. Having no beasts of burden, the workers carried the timbers on their own shoulders and hand-over-hand they hauled the heavy stones, salvaged from the ruined temples and shattered walls, to lay the foundations of the new city. Yet, as was their custom when laboring together on a common project, they sang and chanted as they went about their work. A Spanish friar noted that their songs and chants scarcely stopped day or night, "so great was the zeal which, in the early days, they brought to the building of the town."[3]

But in the months and years that followed, as the Indian craftsmen and workers built the public buildings and magnificent churches of New Spain, a different mood replaced the earlier sense of participation in a common enterprise. Observers noted that less and less often did the Indian craftsmen sing and chant at their work.[4] The town of Coyoacán gave open testimony to the changing mood when, barely three decades after the fall of Tenochtitlán, it brought suit against the heir of Cortés in order to recover the value of the materials and services it had provided for the rebuilding of the Mexica capital.[5] The Spanish had taken the work for granted, but, although they may have valued it cheaply then, the labor of the people of Anáhuac proved to be the most enduring of all the treasures won when the empire of the Mexica fell.

2. Charles Gibson, *The Aztecs Under Spanish Rule. A History of the Indians of the Valley of Mexico, 1519–1810* (Stanford, Calif.: Stanford University Press, 1964), p. 351; R. C. Padden, *The Hummingbird and the Hawk: Conquest and Sovereignty in the Valley of Mexico 1503–1541* (Columbus, Ohio: Ohio State University Press, 1967), pp. 225–26.

3. Toribio de Benavente (called Motolinía), *History of the Indians of New Spain*, ed. and trans. Elizabeth Andros Foster (Berkeley: Cortés Society, 1950), p. 42.

4. Gibson, *The Aztecs*, pp. 220–21.

5. Henry R. Wagner, *The Rise of Fernando Cortés* (Los Angeles, U.S.: The Cortés Society, 1944), p. 355.

Initially, the Spanish introduced few changes in the pre-Conquest system of agricultural labor, utilizing the existing forms of commercial exchange, tribute, common labor, and slavery to provide them with the necessary food, supplies, and services. In time, however, especially as the devastating epidemics of the sixteenth and early seventeenth centuries depopulated the once heavily-settled central plateau, many of the Indian villages lost large portions of their land to the great estates of their conquerers.[6]

The Europeans also needed the labor of the people of the central plateau to work the huge veins of silver that they soon discovered in the hills of the north, where few settled Indians lived. In the sixteenth century, this labor was obtained by forcing the towns of the central part of the country to send groups of workers to the north to work the mines. The trip was harsh, and because they had to provide for themselves on the way, many Indians died from hunger and exposure in the inhospitable regions through which they had to pass to reach the mines.[7]

Moreover, the dangers and the difficulties of their work were notorious, even then. Working in mines as deep as fifteen hundred feet, the miners dug their way precariously back into the hills, following the twisting, narrow veins of metal. They filled their buckets with 150 or 200 pounds of ore, then dragged it back to the central shaft, where they ascended the chicken ladders to the surface, still carrying their loads. But forced labor recruitment for the mines proved too inefficient from the Spanish point of view and was largely replaced by free wage laborers by the end of the colonial era. In order to attract workers, especially after the precipitous decline in Indian population between 1570 and 1650, wages were increased beyond the bare minimum that prevailed under the forced labor system.[8]

The Indian civilizations of pre-Conquest Mexico had developed a

6. Gibson, *The Aztecs*, pp. 224–56.

7. See Motolinía's description of mining labor in the early years, *History of the Indians*, p. 43.

8. Charles C. Cumberland, *Mexico: The Struggle for Modernity* (New York: The Oxford University Press, 1968), pp. 79–90; Silvio Zavala, *Ensayos sobre la colonización española en América* (Buenos Aires: Emecé editores, 1944), pp. 163, 169–71.

wide variety of arts and crafts, especially in the urban centers that bordered the great lake Texcoco where the Mexica had made their capital. The great market at Tlatelolco, the sister city of Tenochtitlán, astonished the Spaniards for the variety and quality of the goods exchanged there. Generally, each craft had its own market or its own stall within such traditional market places as Tlatelolco, Texcoco and Xochimilco. To have an idea of the extent of the lake, one should note that Xochimilco was located on a small island at the southern end of the lake, some fifteen miles from Tenochtitlán and some forty-five miles by water from the island town of Zumpango at the northern end of the lake.[9]

The towns around the lake had developed craft specialties over the years. Situated on the western shore just opposite Tenochtitlán, and an old rival, the town of Azcapotzalco was noted for its fine silver- and goldsmiths; Tepetlaoztoc was known for its carpenters; Coatepec and Texcoco were renown for stone masons, and Xochimilco for all kinds of woodworking. In the larger towns of the Valley of Mexico, the artisans lived in *barrios* made up of the families engaged in similar occupations and economic functions. In the *barrio* of Tepetenchi, in Xochimilco, lived the carpenters and sculptors, while the *barrio* of Huitznahuac in Tenochtitlán housed the fishermen of the city.[10]

Yet with the coming of the Spanish, European techniques and new products were introduced into the economy, profoundly altering the traditional crafts. Some trades were entirely new, such as sword making, glass blowing, tile making, blacksmithing, and the weaving of wool, requiring the assimilation of a completely foreign system of technology and production. Contemporary observers noted that this technological acculturation was facilitated by the existing high level of manual achievement of the Indian craftsmen and by their creativeness.[11]

Other crafts suffered a lingering death because the civilization on which they had been based no longer existed. The beautiful plume and feather crafts disappeared altogether, as they were too closely

9. Gibson, *The Aztecs*, pp. 352–53.

10. Manuel Carrera Stampa, *Los gremios mexicanos: La organización gremial en Nueva España, 1521–1861* (Mexico: Ibero Americana, 1954), pp. 250–51; Gibson, *The Aztecs*, pp. 349–52, 398–99.

11. Carrera, *Los gremios*, pp. 253–58; Gibson, *The Aztecs*, pp. 397–98.

tied to the defeated Indian aristocracy's political and religious functions. Some trades, particularly those that utilized precious metals, were too valuable to remain in Indian hands and came to be dominated by Spanish artisans. By the eighteenth century the once-famed Indian silversmiths of Azcapotzalco were reduced to casting bronze bells and making nails and door hinges. Most such skilled artisans of luxury goods (called *toltecas* in preconquest Anáhuac because their arts and methods were attributed to the Toltecs), who once worked for the wealthy and the powerful, were forced to adapt to a new medium or saw their position in their own craft slowly subverted by the cultural imperialism of their conquerors.[12]

Yet not all crafts changed significantly. The Spanish did not interfere with the production of the more inexpensive goods, and therefore many aspects of the more common Indian crafts remained intact throughout the colonial era. Pottery, for example, remained for the most part "Indian pottery." Northwest of the city of Mexico (as Tenochtitlán came to be called), the town of Cuauhtitlán produced its traditional fine ceramic ware on into the twentieth century. Indians of the central plateau used cotton and maguey fiber (the latter called *henequén*) for their cloth before the Conquest and continued to do so afterwards, although wool was introduced by the Spanish and was quickly adapted by the Indians as well. *Barrios* around Tlatelolco retained their pre-Conquest artisan specialization on into the late colonial period. Wherever old ways served a purpose of policy, wherever they were too unimportant to merit regulation or too remote to be affected by the changing institutional arrangements, they survived the Conquest. Forced to retreat to their lowest common component, many aspects of the Indian society retained for centuries their basic pre-Conquest character precisely because the society was repressed and despised, unable and even forbidden to change.[13]

Royal policy initially encouraged the full and free exercise of Indian trades. However, competition of Indian products with goods produced by immigrating Spanish artisans quickly led to the introduction of European-style guilds, called *gremios*, to protect the Spaniards

12. Gibson, *The Aztecs*, p. 350.
13. Ibid., pp. 335–37, 350–51, 398–99, 409.

from such competition. The *gremios* regulated wages, entrance into
the trade, advancement, and the quality of the finished product and
its price, and they in turn were regulated by the colonial government.
By the eighteenth century more than two hundred *gremios* worked
their trades in New Spain. Located mainly in the industrial towns and
cities of the Valley of Mexico and in a few of the larger provincial
capitals, many *gremios* were important and even prestigious institutions. It was not uncommon for *maestros* of the more important guilds
such as those of the gold- and silversmiths to be members of the town
cabildo, or municipal government. By strict regulation of production
and price, the members were generally sustained by their guilds in
hard times and enjoyed a certain amount of material security and
relative affluence in times of prosperity. Wages of the artisans of the
towns, for example, ranged from three to five *reales* per day in the late
eighteenth century, compared to one and one-half to two and one-
half *reales* for *peónes*; the differential had been even greater in the late
sixteenth and early seventeenth century.[14]

Although the guilds were initiated as purely Spanish institutions,
economic realities soon led to the integration of Indians and *mestizos* into
most fields. Few Spaniards who immigrated were willing to begin at
the apprentice level; hence the apprentices and the regular tradesmen, called *oficiales*, were by necessity often Indian and *mestizo*. Although certain trades excluded all but Spaniards, or at least required
the *maestros* to be *limpieza de sangre*, most trades simply could not
attract a sufficient number of Spaniards or their offspring (called
criollos) to enforce such a policy. The guilds, backed by official regulation and royal law, represented a relatively good life compared to the
opportunities in the mines and fields of New Spain.[15]

Yet the centuries of Spanish rule were ones of great economic
change in the western world, and Spain's colonial system could not
escape the consequences. As population grew in New Spain from the
mid-seventeenth century on and as commercial practices evolved,
some tradesmen such as the makers of cotton and woolen textiles and
shoemakers, who before had sold their wares and services directly to
their customers, were now forced to sell their merchandise through

14. Carrera, *Los gremios*, pp. 260–61, 264; Gibson, *The Aztecs*, pp. 250–52, 399.
15. Gibson, *The Aztecs*, pp. 399–402; Carrera, *Los gremios*, pp. 51–52, 264.

merchants and shopkeepers. As a result, their products gained a broader market, but in the process the guilds lost control of production and distribution and had virtually disappeared in these trades by the end of the eighteenth century. Aiding in the demise of these crafts were contraband imports from the more efficient capitalist-oriented shops of England, Holland, and France. In addition, the weaving and spinning trades had been subjected to competition from the domestic *obrajes*.[16]

The *obrajes*, introduced into New Spain in the 1530s with the woolen trade, were notorious urban sweatshops, which utilized hand-operated wooden looms. By the early seventeenth century, Mexico City had twenty-five such shops, the largest employing 120 workers and the average shop employing near 50. Concentrated in the woolen trades, whose market were urban and generally non-Indian consumers, the *obrajes* operated independently of the weaver guilds, often utilizing as laborers common criminals or Indians condemned as slaves. Anyone convicted of petty crimes could be contracted by the state to the owner of the *obraje* to work out his ten to fifteen year sentence. Free Indians were also contracted to fill the needs not taken care of by the bonded workers. The abuses and corruption that characterized such worker recruitment were notorious. Bonded or free, the workers often were forced to work, eat, and sleep in the shops, behind closed doors, some never emerging except in death. The colonial government forbade such treatment, of course, but the practice continued, although on a lesser scale from the eighteenth century on.[17]

Toward the end of the colonial era, most guilds were in trouble, unable to defend their members from the economic changes that were eroding their strength. The basic problems afflicting the guilds were the growth of the power of the merchants who marketed their goods, the competition from the more efficient industrially-produced goods from abroad, and the fluctuation in the business cycle as the colonies were irresistibly brought into the developing industrial

16. Carrera, *Los gremios*, pp. 265–66.

17. Gibson, *The Aztecs*, pp. 243–46. See Carrera, *Los gremios*, for a detailed bibliographic reference to *obrajes*. For *obrajes* in the city of Puebla, see Jan Bazant, "Evolución de la industrial textil poblana (1554–1845)" in *Historia Mexicana* 13 (abril–junio 1964): 482–92.

economy of Europe. One viceroy in the late eighteenth century was disgusted at the state of the trades in New Spain but blamed their decline on the vices and laziness of the native workers.[18] Of all the opinions held by other Mexicans to explain the misery and hardships of the Mexican worker, this one became the most common in the years ahead.

Most Spanish governmental ministers, true to their Bourbon ideal of progress and enlightenment, saw the guild as an institution out of the Middle Ages, weighing down the economic advance of the colony by standing for corporate control of production and price. The remaining guilds, therefore, came under increasing attack from official sources during the reforms of Charles III (1759–1788) and his successors. Laws were passed during the meeting of the *Cortes Extraordinarias de Cadiz* on 8 June 1813 enabling anyone to practice a trade without prior licensing or inspection by the guild or the state.[19] Meanwhile, the political ties with the mother country were slowly weakening. The once powerful Spain, like the Mexica before her, found Anáhuac not an easy land to rule.

Independence finally came to Mexico in 1821, after eleven years of bloody civil war, but the economic position of the guilds did not improve. Indeed, the new Republic accelerated the decline of the guilds by liberalizing import regulations and by confirming the colonial government's ban on the guilds' once important function of controlling prices and production. Even the strongest guilds, such as those of the gold- and silversmiths, declined in the early years of the Republic and finally passed out of existence sometime before mid-century.[20]

Yet long before the guilds disappeared, the industrial functions of the nation had been taken over by the artisan shops, using the hand labor of free artisans hired at a fixed wage, usually by the piece or by the day. The owner himself may have been the *maestro*, working side by side with his men.[21] Although the shop system guaranteed few of

18. Carrera, *Los gremios*, pp. 269–71. For an interesting comparison, see James Clayburn La Force, Jr., *The Development of the Spanish Textile Industry, 1750–1800* (Berkeley: University of California Press, 1965), Chapter 6 on Spanish guilds, pp. 88–108. Carrera, *Los gremios*, p. 269.

19. Carrera, *Los gremios*, pp. 272–75.

20. Ibid., pp. 276–77.

21. Ibid., pp. 284–88; Fernando Rosenzweig, "La industria," in Daniel

the material benefits of the earlier guilds, the resulting work patterns were often sufficiently personal and paternalistic to provide a congenial work environment.

Sharing the manufacturing work of the nation with the shops were the self-employed artisans. Often they worked at home, utilizing family labor and operating either as independent craftsmen or as artisans under contract to merchants. The self-employed artisans thus avoided becoming wage craftsmen or *jornaleros* (day laborers), but they lacked any of the security of the defunct guilds or even the likelihood of a steady income such as the shop artisans enjoyed in good times.[22]

Both the shop artisans and the self-employed craftsmen earned a precarious living in the first half century after Independence. Most suffered from import competition as well as competition from goods produced more efficiently by the *obrajes* and by the few mechanized factories established in Mexico after the 1820s.

The *obrajes* still flourished in the first several decades following independence from Spain, particularly in the woolen textile trades concentrated in the major urban centers of central Mexico, but convict labor and debt peonage had been replaced over the years by free day labor. While they competed with the artisan weavers of the area, they in turn suffered from the competition of lower-cost imported goods. In 1830 President Vicente Guerrero's defense against the rebellion of the Conservative general, Anastasio Bustamante, found no support among the textile *obrajeros* of Guadalajara. The Guerrero regime had permitted increased foreign imports of textile goods at the insistence of the larger merchant retail houses and to the misery of the *obrajes*.[23] In 1843 a group of artisans formed the *Junta de Fomento de Artesanos* in order to present a united front in their protest against foreign imports.[24]

In addition, under the guidance of Lucas Alamán, Bustamante's

Cosío Villegas, ed., *Historia moderna de México*, 10 vols. (Mexico: Editorial Hermes, 1956–71), vol. 7, *El Porfiriato: La vida económica*, by Nicolau d'Olwer et al., p. 322. (Hereafter, each volume of this series will be cited by its author or, if appropriate, the section title and author; e.g., Rosenzweig, "La industria.")

22. Carrera, *Los gremios*, p. 286.
23. Ibid., pp. 283, 288.
24. Diego G. López Rosado, *Historia y pensamiento económico de México: Co-*

chief minister, the government encouraged the importation of various kinds of industrial machinery and equipment in order to promote the establishment of modern, mechanized factories. Mechanized cotton looms, for example, were introduced in the early 1830s in the state of Puebla by Esteban de Antuñano at his mill, La Constancia Mexicana, and by Vicente Molina in his mill near the same city. The latter installed the Jacquard loom, the latest advance in power-driven textile machinery. Prior to the introduction of the mechanized factory, cotton textiles in Puebla had been produced by artisans working in their own homes. The power-driven looms quickly forced them out of business in the city and its environs.[25] By 1845 there were seventy-four textile "factories" in Mexico, according to one source.[26] Of these early mills, La Magdalena and Miraflores of the Federal District were the most modern, and even exhibited their products at the Paris Exposition in 1854.[27]

Despite such evidence of industrial progress, the years after 1821 had not proved to be peaceful ones for the Mexican Republic, and the political strife that characterized much of the period from 1821 to the 1850s did not encourage economic development much beyond this stage.

In order for any significant industrial development to take place, some form of political consensus had to be reached among the elites who ruled Mexico. In fact, however, the existing political structure

---

municaciones y transportes: Relaciones de trabajo, (Mexico: Universidad Nacional Autónoma de Mexico, 1969), p. 270.

25. Carrera, *Los gremios*, pp. 289–91. Bazant, "Evolución de la industrial textile poblana," pp. 495–504, 510–11.

26. Dawn Keremitsis, *La industria textil mexicana en el siglo XIX* (Mexico: Secretaría de Educación Pública, 1973), p. 58. Carrera, *Los gremios*, p. 291, lists 59 mills in 1843: Puebla had 21, Mexico (including the Federal District) 17, Veracruz 8, Durango 5, Jalisco 4, Queretaro 2, and Guanajuato and Sonora 1 each. For a statistical analysis of the Puebla cotton mills in 1843, see Jan Bazant, "Industria algodonera poblana de 1800–1843 en numeros," *Historia Mexicana* 14 (July–Sept., 1964): 131–43. See also Bazant, "Estudio sobre la productividad de la industria algodonera mexicana en 1843–1845," in *La industria nacional y el comercio exterior (1842–1845)* (Mexico: Banco Nacional de Comercio Exterior, 1962).

27. Keremitsis, *La industria textil*, p. 75.

had been so weakened by church-state conflicts and by regional, class, and personal interests that disputes between the competing liberal and conservative forces made political consensus impossible during those years.

In the decade and a half after the disastrous Mexican-American War (1846–1848), the struggle reached its peak. Catalyzed by the humiliating peace settlement of 1848, the Mexican political structure underwent a polarization that shattered the fragile truce arranged between the Liberal and Conservative camps during the war against the North Americans. The leadership of the Liberal movement was captured by a new generation of men angered by the defeat at the hands of the foreigners, yet now hardened and determined. Driven by their own private frustrations and ideals, they sought to build a nation independent of foreign domination and free of the ancient and traditional restrictions on the individual imposed by the inordinate powers, as they saw them, of the Church and the federal government.

By 1860 the Liberals had crushed the Conservative forces but were themselves temporarily ousted from power by invading armies of Napoleon III of France. The French-supported regime of Emperor Maximilian (1863–67) was overturned in 1867. However, the great Liberal, Benito Juárez, returned to Mexico City to preside over a nation divided by the effects of the armed struggles of the previous ten years. To make matters worse, the Liberals, united in adversity, soon broke into warring factions. Political stability appeared as remote as it ever had.

To make matters worse, the Restored Republic (1867–1876) was burdened by an economy which in many respects was inferior even in comparison to the colonial one. Save for the struggling cotton textile industry and several other factories of minor importance, manufacturing was still confined to artisans producing specialized goods by hand for local markets. In a few cases, Mexican artisans were noted beyond Mexico for their craftsmanship, as in the working of silver and the making of jewelry, but these were hardly the basis for a modern economy. The famous mines of the colonial era were producing far below their level attained under Spain, and indeed many were flooded and abandoned, victims of the violence and unrest of the first fifty years of independence. Roads were few and poor, and railroad track virtually nonexistent; high transportation costs discouraged interregional trade in everything but low-bulk, high-cost items. Economic activity was basically confined to the traditional markets established in the provincial capitals and in Mexico City, complemented by the markets of local handicraft specialties, often lingering remnants of the pre-Conquest cultures that refused to die. There were no private banks and few sources of investment capital except the traditional money lender, the *agiotista*, who loaned scarce capital at high and often exorbitant interest rates. There were few schools, public or private, and an over-abundance of highwaymen, beggars, and bandits.[28]

It is true that conditions improved somewhat in the brief span of nine years that made up the Restored Republic, yet serious attempts were never undertaken to resolve many of these problems because so much time and energy were devoted to the political intrigues that characterized most of those years. Juárez himself contributed to the political conflicts by refusing to step down, even after nearly fifteen years as the country's president. Given the increasingly hostile reaction from many in Juárez's own party to his maintenance of himself in power, it is understandable that when he died suddenly of a heart attack in July 1872, he left behind a volatile political situation.

At first Sebastian Lerdo de Tejada, president of the Supreme Court and Juárez's legal successor, easily gained the upper hand and was elected to a four-year term as president of the Republic. His major opposition came from General Porfirio Díaz, a hero of the Reform movement in the 1850s and of the struggle against the French. Díaz had unsuccessfully challenged Juárez several times for the presidency, and when Lerdo made evident his intention to seek reelection in 1876, Díaz announced again. His rebellion (its slogan was "effective suffrage and no reelection") attracted many dissident groups, and after a major military victory over the *lerdista* general, Ignacio Alatorre, Díaz marched into Mexico City in November 1876 to assume the leadership of an exhausted country.

Except for temporarily stepping down from 1880 to 1884, in *pro*

28. See the three volumes on the Restored Republic in the series *Historia moderna de México*, edited by Cosío Villegas.

forma homage to his earlier principle of no reelection, Porfirio Díaz ruled Mexico for the next thirty-five years. Those were years of progress and growth, as men of the times defined these terms, but they were also years in which little understood, irrevocable changes were working their way deep into the fabric of Mexican society.

Chapter 2
Mexican Workers and Industrial Progress, 1876–1905

"We are not seen as the free artisan of the nineteenth century but as the miserable slave of Antiquity."
—El Hijo de Trabajo, 1884.

Of the men who lived under the protection of the *Pax Porfiriana* and who profited from the order imposed by the regime, most found it easy to believe that the dramatic changes they saw in their lifetime were evidence that Mexico was experiencing a golden age, an era of peace and prosperity that they attributed to the strong but benevolent leadership of Porfirio Díaz. But for those who did not share in the benefits of this progress, the economic advances made during the *Porfiriato* served to remind them of promises that had not been kept. Great men of affairs had spoken of progress, but it had become a progress for other men, exacted at a harsh social cost paid by Mexican working men and women. What follows is a description and analysis of that "progress," including an examination of the patterns of industrial development from 1876 to 1911, a discussion of the social costs of economic growth, and a description of the organized response Mexican workers made to industrialization.[1]

Development of the Mexican Economy, 1876–1911

The icons of progress were everywhere. Railroad track spanned deep ravines and crossed rugged terrain once considered impassable. In

1. Today one almost automatically places quotation marks around the word "progress" to indicate a point of ironic question or disbelief. It is used in the text of this study, as it was used in the era being described, as a word meaning man's increasing technological domination over his environment, with the economic and social implications such a great process would entail.

1876 only 640 kilometers of track existed in the entire Republic; by 1910 the nation had 19,280 kilometers. Only the Yucatán peninsula still remained cut off from rapid land travel to the rest of Mexico.[2] Mexicans could now be in the United States in less time than it once took them to reach their own provincial capital from the towns of the interior.

Industrial production doubled from 1877 to the turn of the century, as great factories and mills were built and as mines, utilizing the latest techniques of extraction and smelting, supplied the raw materials for the industries of Europe and the United States. The Guanajuato Consolidated Mining and Milling Company, whose cyanide plant with its fifty steel tanks—capacity 2,300,000 gallons—was only one of many such facilities built in Mexico during the *Porfiriato*. Mexican textile mills near Orizaba, Veracruz, were among the largest and most modern in the world. The sugar plantations of Morelos were competitive with Hawaii and Puerto Rico, as world leaders. With the industrial progress came the expected monuments—street lamps and paved streets, libraries and theaters, and the arched public buildings worthy of a progressing nation. By all standards of the age, Mexico was well on her way to becoming a modern nation.

Mexicans often attributed those advances to Porfirio Díaz, whose strong leadership had brought peace to their land. When he came to power in those troubled years after the death of Juárez, Díaz had promised a weary nation that his administration would be one of "poca política y mucha administración." He would, he assured the country, govern as the representative of all Mexico and not of a particular region or political clique.[3] Many had trusted him then, and as the years passed, most Mexicans came to respect and venerate this man whose political talents, they believed, had created the foundation of national progress.

The Mexican government's early efforts to industrialize were directed by Matías Romero, head of the important Ministry of the

2. Francisco R. Calderón, "Los ferrocarriles," in d'Olwer, *La vida económica*, 7:516, 624.

3. John W. Foster to Secretary of State (Hamilton Fish), 19 February 1877, U.S., Department of State, *Papers Relating to the Foreign Relations of the United States, 1877* (Washington, D.C. 1862–), p. 398.

Treasury (*Hacienda*) in the first Díaz administration (1876–1880), who made efforts to encourage both foreign and domestic investment.[4] Initially, those efforts were only partly successful. In the 1870s, for example, major railroad concessions languished in Congress while the deputies heatedly debated the desirability of foreign investment, particularly American investment, in such a vital public utility as railroads.[5] The administration, still in the process of consolidating its political control, as well as of negotiating the difficult question of its foreign debt, was willing to remain in the background.

During the 1880s, however, General Manuel González (1880–1884) and then the reelected Díaz moved toward a more active facilitation of private economic activity. Tariff revisions in 1880, 1885, and 1887 reduced duties on certain raw materials and industrial equipment and increased the duties on many consumer products in order to encourage their manufacture in Mexico. The new Mining Code of 1884, the Mining, Agriculture, and Industry Act of 1886, the revision of the mining tax law in 1887, the abdication of the traditional national ownership of subsoil rights in favor of private ownership, the lowering of mineral taxes, and various tax exemptions given to a number of industries—all were designed to encourage foreign and domestic investment.[6]

European and American capitalists responded in large numbers, investing their surplus capital in business enterprises, from retail establishments to large-scale mineral exploitation. By the end of the *Porfiriato*, foreign investment accounted for 67 to 73 percent (according to two major calculations) of the total invested capital in the country. A large portion of it, perhaps between 50 and 60 percent, was invested during the last decade of the regime. United States' interests represented between 50 and 60 percent of the total foreign invest-

4. John W. Foster to William M. Evarts, 9 October 1878, U.S., Dept. of State, *Papers, 1878–79*, 1:636–54. See also Stephen R. Niblo, "The Political Economy of the Early Porfiriato: Politics and Economics in Mexico 1876–1880," (Ph.D. diss., Northern Illinois University, 1972), pp. 262–65.

5. U.S., Dept. of State, *Papers, 1879*, pp. 549–52, 636–54.

6. Carlos Díaz Dufoo, "Industrial Evolution," in *Mexico: Its Social Evolution*, ed. Justo Sierra, trans. G. Sentíñon, 3 vols. (Mexico: J. Ballesca & Co., 1900–04), 2:151–53; Marvin D. Bernstein, *The Mexican Mining Industry, 1890–1950* (Albany, N.Y.: State University of New York Press, 1964), pp. 18–19.

ment and upwards of 75 to 90 percent of the capital in mining.[7] Economic imperialism, whatever its vices or virtues, became even more pervasive and powerful than the earlier American and French attempts at political domination. Ultimately it came under attack, but for most of the *Porfiriato* foreign economic interests were welcomed by the political and economic elites of Mexico.

The most important development in the 1880s was the expansion of the railroads, almost entirely financed by foreign capital in conjunction with huge government concessions of land and tax incentives. In 1880 there were 1073 kilometers of track in Mexico. By 1884, with the completion of the Mexican Central's El Paso to Mexico City line, there were 5,731 kilometers, and by the end of 1890, 9,544 kilometers. In 1882 the Mexican National and the Mexican Central together carried 307,853 tons of freight; by 1890 they were carrying 1,182,564 tons.[8]

The railroad expansion had profound effects on the Mexican economy, and through economic change it affected all aspects of Mexican life. By cheapening the cost of transporting goods, men, and materials within the country, the railroads broadened the effective market for many products and thereby encouraged the expansion of domestic commercial and industrial enterprises. The large and efficient textile mills in Orizaba, Veracruz, and in the city of Puebla shipped their goods by rail to Mexico City, where they were purchased at wholesale and redistributed to the rest of the nation. Smaller, less modern mills generally sold their products in the surrounding countryside, but the railroads permitted the large Hércules mill in Querétaro, for example, to sell in Guanajuato and the mills of Coahuila to market their cloth and yarn in Zacatecas and Durango. By way of illustration of the cost savings involved in the expansion of the railroads, the cost of shipping a ton of cheap cotton textile goods from Mexico City to Querétaro declined from sixty-one dollars in 1877 to hardly three dollars in 1910. In addition, the railroads carried foreign

7. Luis Nicolau d'Olwer, "Las inversiones extranjeras," in d'Olwer, *La vida económica*, 8:1133–37, 1151–53, 1158–61.

8. Calderón "Los ferrocarriles," pp. 516–17, 540–41, 566–68. Matías Romero, *Mexico and the United States: A Study of Subjects Affecting Their Political, Commercial, and Social Relations, Made With a View of Their Promotion* (New York: G. P. Putnam and Sons, 1898), p. 197.

and domestic cotton, the latter particularly from the Laguna region of Coahuila, enabling the growth of textile production in areas where domestic sources of cotton were scarce.[9] Yet most of these effects and their attendant social changes only became significant in the 1890s, when Mexican industrial development reached full stride; the 1880s, paradoxically, were not good years for the Mexican economy.

Hurt by an American economy in recession, industrial production in the 1880s grew little if at all. Two key industries, textiles and tobacco, stagnated throughout most of the decade. By 1886–1887 the aggregate value of textile production was still under what it had been a decade before. The tobacco industry did not recover its 1877 level of production until 1894. Mineral production rose slowly through the seventies, stagnated from 1880 to 1883, and rose steadily throughout the remainder of the decade until the reversal of the poor years of 1889 and 1890. By 1890 the great bulk of Mexican industrial production was still largely confined to small factories of under a hundred workers, with a great many artisans working in shops or individually, using relatively rudimentary machinery.[10] Even in the textile industry, where the most mechanization had taken place, the average mill in 1893 employed only ninety-five workers.[11] The great surge of Mexican industrialization was yet to take place.

The recession of the last year of the decade continued on into the early 1890s, accelerated briefly by a precipitous drop in the world silver market in 1892. Mexico's foreign exchange rate was tied to

9. Rosenzweig, "La industria," pp. 314–15. Keremitsis, *La industria textil*, p. 162. Charles C. Cumberland, *Mexico*, p. 221. Mutsuo Yamada, "The Cotton Textile Industry in Orizaba: A Case Study of Mexican Labor and Industrialization During the Díaz Regime," (Master's thesis, University of Florida, Gainesville, 1965), pp. 42–43.

10. El Colegio de México, *Estadísticas económicas del Porfiriato: Fuerza de trabajo y actividad económicas por sectores* (Mexico: El Colegio de México, n.d., circa 1965), pp. 105–6. Matías Romero listed 3,771 factories in 1886, of which 3,175 were brewers of *aguardiente*, wines, and other alcoholic beverages, 146 soap manufacturers, 137 textile mills, 41 tobacco shops, 35 pastry shops, 28 match-making shops, 10 paper shops, 7 glass-blowing shops, and 192 noted as other (in Lino Medina Salazar, "Albores del movimiento obrero en México," *Historia y Sociedad* 4 (1965): 57.

11. Keremitsis, *La industria textil*, p. 207.

silver, and the nation's economy was hurt badly as prices of imports rose and foreign exchange earnings declined.[12] Yet it was this very crisis that marked the beginning of the period of Mexico's greatest industrial growth under Díaz.

Looking around for someone with sufficient experience in finance to handle the critical Ministry of *Hacienda* during the crisis, the president settled on José Y. Limantour. Although young, barely thirty-eight when he assumed the head of the Ministry in May of 1893, Limantour had acquired a considerable reputation as an economist and financier through his writing and his practical experience in business and banking. Moreover, he was a key member of the newly organized *La Unión Liberal*, whose members were bent on reforming Mexico's archaic economy. His appointment, therefore, served Díaz's political ends as well. With the energetic and able leadership of the new minister, Mexico soon pulled out of the recession. The public treasury even boasted of a budgetary surplus in mid-1894, and Mexico improved her international credit rating beyond everyone's expectations.[13] By 1895 the economy was undergoing an expansion of boom proportions.

Many existing firms expanded their plants and equipment in the 1890s, and increased the number of workers they employed. The cotton mill of Los Cerritos employed 180 mill hands in 1880; by 1907 the figure had risen to 690. An old woolen mill, San Ildefonso, operating near Mexico City, was reorganized by French capital in 1897, with new equipment being installed and several hundred more workers added to the payroll.[14]

New plants were common. French capitalists established *El Compañía Manufacturera Buen Tono*, a cigarette firm, in 1894. Its huge operations covered an entire city block in the Federal District, and it

12. Rosenzweig, "La industria," pp. 463–65.

13. José Yves Limantour, *Apuntes sobre mi vida pública (1892–1911)* (Mexico: Editorial Porrúa, 1965), pp. 12–17, 22–27; Jose C. Valadés, *El porfirismo: historia de un régimen*, 3 vols. (Mexico: Antigua Librería Robredo, de J. Porrúa e hijos, 1941–48)1:71; Rosenzweig, "La industria," pp. 463–72; William Dirk Raat, "Positivism in Díaz Mexico 1876–1910: An Essay in Intellectual History," (Ph.D. diss., The University of Utah, 1967), p. 187. Fernando Rosenzweig, "El comercio exterior," in d'Olwer, *La vida económica*, p. 641.

14. Keremitsis, *La industria textil*, p. 208. *The Mexican Yearbook, 1909–1910* (London: McCorguodale and Co., 1908, 1910), p. 425.

The Río Blanco cotton textile mill.

employed two thousand workers. A firm controlled by British capital under Sir W. H. M. Pearson built an electric streetcar system for the port of Veracruz, utilizing recently discovered oil and powered by the largest diesel and electric plant of its kind on the American continent. The *Compañía Industrial Jabonera de la Laguna*, founded in 1892, had a monthly capacity of seventy-five thousand seventy-five pound boxes of soap; its glycerine mill was the largest in the hemisphere, with a capacity of a thousand tons a year. At Monterrey, Guggenheim interests established the *Compañía Minera Fundidora y Afinadora*, a smelting and refining plant. Built to accommodate the firm's extensive mining operations in Mexico, the plant had a capacity to process twelve hundred tons daily and employed fifteen hundred men.[15]

Major new firms were established in the textile industry. The French-dominated firm, *La Compañía Industrial de Orizaba* (CIDOSA) in 1889 bought out two older Orizaba mills, San Lorenzo and Cerritos, and constructed the Río Blanco mill near Orizaba in 1892. The latter was the largest, most modern in the Republic, operating thirty-five thousand spindles and nine hundred looms, and employing eigh-

15. *Mexican Year Book, 1907–1908*, pp. 514–43.

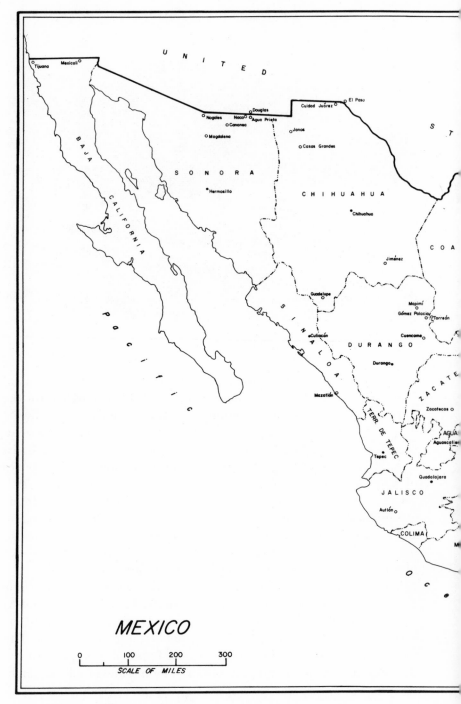

MEXICO

0   100   200   300
SCALE OF MILES

Mexico, 1906
Map by Robert Clay

teen hundred men. One enthusiastic American commercial officer contended that the Río Blanco mill compared favorably with the most modern mills in the world. Another huge mill, the Santa Rosa, was completed in 1899 by the *Compañía Veracruzana* (CIV). It was organized by a group of French dry-goods firms from Mexico City and employed nearly two thousand men.[16]

By the turn of the century, the Mexican industrial census listed over five thousand manufacturing enterprises, not including cottage industry or the smaller artisan shops. Among those factories were three chemical plants, two boot and shoe factories, five carriage works, eight cement works, nine munitions plants, twenty-six furniture manufacturing establishments, thirty-seven breweries, two organ and piano manufacturers, ten glass works, twenty-one iron and steel works, twenty-one metal foundries, four paint and varnish manufacturers, and one nail factory.[17] Mexico was undergoing an industrial revolution in a little less than a decade.

Cotton cloth production increased 5.3 percent annually from 1894 to 1901, compared to a 3.9 percent increase from 1878 to 1894. The sugar industry increased its rate of production 3.6 percent during the same period, as compared to 2.9 percent in the earlier years. Mineral and metallurgical industries did even better; an index of the net value of production that read 30 in 1889 read 90 in 1899. Industry by industry the indices were up. For those with capital to invest, the returns were excellent. In a decade of relatively stable prices, the average annual return on capital invested in the years 1890–1894 was 10 to 15 percent, and from 1895 to 1900, 20 to 25 percent.[18] New machinery, expanded plant and equipment, new factories, greater profits—it was the gay nineties in Mexico, and optimism for the future was everywhere among the nation's businessmen.

The economic developments of the 1880s and 1890s had corollary

16. U.S., Department of Commerce and Labor, *Monthly Consular and Trade Reports*, no. 331 (March 1908), p. 62; *Mexican Year Book, 1909–1910*, pp. 524–25.

17. *Mexican Year Book, 1909–1910*, p. 543.

18. For growth statistics, see El Colegio de México, *Estadísticas económicas*, pp. 105–6, 135. For a description of that decade, see Rosenzweig, "La industria," pp. 311–401, 421–81.

effects on Mexican society; hardly any aspect of Mexican life escaped the relentless consequences of progress. One important characteristic of this period was a dramatic increase in population. By 1895 fully half of Mexico's nearly thirteen million inhabitants had been born in the twenty years that Porfirio Díaz ruled Mexico.[19] As a basic feature of most societies in the early stages of industrial growth, the effect of population growth was initially favorable, providing stimulus to the economy by increasing consumer demand. Its ultimate consequence during the hard times ahead was not yet apparent.

In the countryside, where the great bulk of Mexico's population lived, changes of vast importance were taking place. *Hacendados* in growing numbers throughout the Republic were encouraged by the railroad expansion to renew with vigor the centuries-old encroachment on the lands of the villagers, taking advantage of rising land prices and the growing market for their produce in the cities and the foreign markets. Despite the popular image of the self-contained *hacienda*, modern scholarship now indicates that wherever railroads brought visions of profit and progress, Mexican landholders became less feudal lords and more landed capitalists. As a result, a growing number of *campesinos* lost their land to enterprising large landholders with the proper titles or the right political connections.[20]

The economic effects of the changes in the structure of rural society were initially favorable for the industrial expansion underway in Mexico in the 1890s. Many of those who lost their land became day laborers or wage earners on the large estates or found other jobs which paid them a wage, whereas before they had not often been part of the national money economy. In addition, greater contact with urban areas brought changes in rural tastes that complemented the changes of necessity. Store-bought *manta* became common material

19. El Colegio de México, *Estadísticas económicas*, p. 29.

20. See John Womack, *Zapata and the Mexican Revolution* (New York: Alfred A. Knopf), pp. 43–46; John Coatsworth, "Railroads, Landholding, and Agrarian Protest in the Early Porfiriato," *Hispanic American Historial Review* 54 (February 1974): 48–71; James D. Cockcroft's study of San Luis Potosí in his *Intellectual Precursors of the Mexican Revolution 1900–1913* (Austin: University of Texas Press, 1968), pp. 25–33 and Friedrich Katz's important "Labor Conditions on Haciendas in Porfirian Mexico: Some Trends and Tendencies," *Hispanic American Historical Review* 54 (February 1974): 1–47.

for the traditional garments of the country people, replacing locally- or home-woven cloth, and colored print became popular for the dresses of women. As Rosenzweig notes, the new workers were "precarious consumers" because of their tenuous earning capacity, but they were nonetheless extremely important in the nation's economic development because they provided an expanded market for national industry. Finally, the enforced rural mobility likely helped to keep wages from rising significantly as industry expanded the demand for workers. The increase in the cost of labor declined from a 3.3 percent rate on a yearly average from 1877 to 1892, to a 1.3 percent average from 1893 to 1902. The industrial labor force rose 16 percent, at the very least, in just the half decade from 1895 to 1900.[21]

Meanwhile, the face of the nation had been changing. The northern states, long the backward, isolated part of the nation, had been opened up by the coming of the railroads, attracting capital and men from all parts of the country and from abroad as well. While the population of Mexico increased some 25 percent between 1885 and 1900, states of the north such as Durango and Chihuahua doubled that rate, and Coahuila's population increased 105 percent in the same decade and a half. The opportunities brought by the railroads launched the town of Mapimí, Durango, from barely four thousand in 1877 to thirty thousand in 1910, and its nearby rival Gómez Palacio grew from a small collection of huts to a small city of forty-two thousand in 1910. Torreón grew from less than one thousand in 1877 to a thriving town of twenty-three thousand in 1900 and became one of the most important railroad depots in the north. The population of Monterrey, capital of Nuevo León, estimated at fourteen thousand in 1877 climbed to sixty-two thousand in 1900, well on its way to becoming one of the most important industrial centers in the nation. Population growth and economic expansion in the north took place in conjunction with the expansion of the major export fields of mining, cotton, cattle, and other agricultural products, and in important consumer products such as textiles, tobacco, and beer.[22] The economic

21. Rosenzweig, "La industria," pp. 315–23, 27. El Colegio de México, *Estadísticas económicas*, pp. 25, 39.

22. Moisés González Navarro, ed., *Estadísticas sociales del Porfiriato, 1877–1910* (Mexico: Secretaría de la Economia Nacional, 1956), pp. 7–11; Rosenzweig, "La industria," pp. 398–401.

structure of the north, however, proved to be vulnerable to both fluctuations in the international market and internal consumer purchasing power, as future events revealed.

The year 1899 culminated Porfirian prosperity. Return on capital investment reached 20 to 25 percent in the 1895 to 1900 period.[23] Afterwards it would never be so good. Yet at the time, Mexico's progress did not appear to be.at an end but only beginning. New Year's Eve in 1899 was an exciting one in Mexico. Gala *fiestas* and formal balls were held to celebrate the coming of the last century in this millennium, for it seemed to many people to herald Mexico's coming of age.

The economic problems that tarnished Mexico's prosperity during the first decade of the twentieth century were not long in coming. Mineral production, usually the healthiest sector of the economy, declined in fiscal year 1899–1900. Most other sectors of the economy experienced difficulties from 1900 to 1902, as a major recession foretold of things to come. While most industries recovered slowly from 1903 to 1907 or 1908, the consumer-oriented industries, such as textiles, food and drink, and tobacco, recovered more slowly than most. The textile industry, for example, a leader in the 1890s, was unable to keep up the pace in the new century. Per capita consumption of cotton cloth had increased 2.4 percent from 1894 to 1901 but slowed down to 1.4 percent from 1902 to 1907.[24]

By 1908 most industries were in trouble again. Industrial sales and production generally fell in 1908 and 1909, and although some industries showed an improvement in 1910, the value of manufacturing production never again reached the 1907 level while Porfirio Díaz ruled Mexico. Per capita consumption of cotton cloth fell 3.4 percent from 1907 to 1911; tobacco and alcohol showed similar trends.[25] Everywhere those industries that depended on the purchasing power of large segments of the Mexican people were in deep trouble.

Ironically, the origins of the economic decline in the consumer

23. Rosenzweig, "La industria," p. 328.
24. El Colegio de México, *Estadísticas económicas*, pp. 106–7; Rosenzweig, "La industria," pp. 328–38.
25. El Colegio de México, *Estadísticas económicas*, p. 106; Rosenzweig, "La industria," p. 338.

industries lie partly in the same forces that helped encourage economic development in the previous decade. The first signs of mis-guided progress appeared in the countryside. The expansion of the *haciendas* at the expense of the villages continued unabated in many areas into the twentieth century. It actually increased in some areas, as economic pressures mounted on the large landholders after 1900, encouraging them to expand production cheaply by expropriating village land. This was certainly the case in Morelos where the sugar-cane plantations stepped up their integration of village lands after the turn of the century in order to pay for increased production costs. Entire villages disappeared in that fertile state, "rotted into the earth."[26] San Luis Potosí is another example of stepped-up alienation of village lands, especially after the credit squeeze of 1908, which hit the more business-oriented *hacendados* quite hard.[27]

Of those who lost their land, the lucky ones were able to get work as day laborers on the plantations or as some combination of field hand and sharecropper. Even for those who could find work, and many could not, wages were low in the countryside of the central and south-ern states and actually had declined 17 percent in real purchasing power between 1895 and 1910.[28] Times became very hard indeed for many people of the rural towns and villages of Mexico. Paul Friedrich describes how, in the latter days of the *Porfiriato*, the villagers of Naranja in Michoacán were humiliated by the lack of clothing even to cover themselves, where before they had been well-dressed in colorful garments. By the end of the *Porfiriato*, merchants in some towns rent-ed trousers to villagers on market days, so decrepit were the clothes they normally wore.[29] The *campesinos* and *peones* of Mexico had been marginal consumers in the first place. The deterioration of their economic position effectively removed them from the market economy altogether in many cases.

The government was not entirely blind to the implications of the

26. Womack, *Zapata*, p. 46.

27. Cockcroft, *Intellectual Precursors*, pp. 35–39.

28. Clark W. Reynolds, *The Mexican Economy: Twentieth Century Structure and Growth* (New Haven, Conn.: Yale University Press, 1970), p. 20, n. 4.

29. Paul Friedrich, *Agrarian Revolt in a Mexican Village* (Englewood Cliffs, New Jersey: Prentice-Hall, Inc., 1970). Charles C. Cumberland, *Mexican Revolution: Genesis Under Madero* (Austin: University of Texas Press, 1952; paperback, 1974), p. 14, n. 52.

situation. Both the minister of development, Olegario Molina, and his director of agriculture noted the rise in a rural, landless proletariat as a consequence of what they termed "capitalist agriculture" and saw the inherent economic problems and political dangers in such circumstances.[30] These observations were made in early 1911, however, far too late for the regime of Don Porfirio to salvage its rule through reform.

The purchasing power of the urban prolitariat and perhaps even that of portions of the middle classes as well declined during this decade, as increasing prices ate up what wage and salary increases they obtained. A major factor in rising prices was the actual decline in the production of corn and wheat between 1877 and 1907 and the relative decline of many other consumer foodstuffs as population grew. The reasons for the decline in production relate to the appropriation of food-crop acreage by export crops, especially in the south, and the overall inefficiency of the *hacienda* system in the central states, where high tariffs, cheap labor, and expropriated village lands reduced any incentive for more efficient production. In addition, unemployment increased among urban workers after 1907, decreasing their already ineffective purchasing power.[31]

The international monetary problems of 1907–1908 added to the country's economic problems. The switch to the gold standard in 1905 resulted in higher prices for imported goods, and, as a consequence, the commercial sector of the gross domestic product declined from its 1907 level. An inflexible, monopolistic banking system added to the crisis by pursuing long-term investment loans, necessitating the over-issuing of paper money and hence aggravating the inflation.[32]

In addition, the international nature of Mexican production and financial resources increased the sensitivity of the entire economy to the international business cycle. Due to both external and internal factors, Mexican terms of trade began to decline after 1905, according

30. Quoted in Cockcroft, *Intellectual Precursors*, pp. 31–32.

31. Friedrich Katz, "Labor Conditions on Haciendas in Porfirian Mexico: Some Trends and Tendencies," *Hispanic American Historical Review* 54 (February 1974): 15–18, 24–27, 41.

32. Rosenzweig, "La industria," pp. 318, 330; Albert L. Michaels and Marvin Bernstein, "The Modernization of the Old Order: Organization and Periodization of 20th Century Mexican History," mimeographed (Paper presented to the IV International Congress of Mexican Studies, Santa Monica, California, 1973), pp. 3–4.

to a study by Professor Clark Reynolds, adversely affecting all sectors of the money economy.[33] The leading sectors of the economy were oriented toward the export market and dependent on cheap labor and imported capital and technology, which Professor Reynolds maintains is typical of the export-led development pattern that has occurred in other nations.

These sectors, especially mining and other extractive industries, could not absorb the surplus of workers in other sectors caused by land consolidation, natural increase in population, declining need for artisans, and general unemployment. Hence, many domestic sectors were hurt by the very character of the earlier economic growth, while the net effect was that the "real and financial assets and income" increasingly became concentrated "in the hands of a small group of local and foreign investors."[34] The considerable sensitivity of the Mexican economy to international financial pressures compounded the problem of a declining purchasing power on the part of a broad segment of the Mexican people and presented Mexico with a singularly difficult situation throughout most of the years of the first decade of the twentieth century.

The modernization of the Mexican economy in the nineteenth and early twentieth century exacted a high cost in human misery and social dislocation, in good times or bad. Those who benefited from the changes and those who saw their benefits had to either ignore those costs or rationalize their existence, justifying them as reasonable and necessary for a greater good. Mexican industrial development in the *Porfiriato* was complemented by the predominance of those social ideologies which stressed that the economic and technological progress of man was necessary before social and political progress could take place.

Ideologies of Progress

Each generation tends to redefine its ideologies in the light of its own experience and needs. Many of the men who sought to guide the

33. Reynolds, *The Mexican Economy*, p. 25.
34. Ibid., pp. 23–25.

destiny of post-Imperial Mexico were forced to justify both political dictatorship and the high costs of economic progress borne by the working classes. To do so, certain adjustments were necessary in the predominant ideology of progress, liberalism.

Mexican liberalism in the first half of the nineteenth century theoretically supported political freedom and social equality for all peoples, holding that man by nature had the capacity to govern himself and to improve upon his lot. Yet, as Charles Hale points out in his important work, *Mexican Liberalism in the Age of Mora, 1821–1853*, many Liberals distrusted the leadership of such dark-skinned men of low estate as Vicente Guerrero and Juan Álvarez and doubted the abilities of the lower classes in general to govern themselves. At times, their liberalism had little to differentiate it from conservatism on issues involving the social and economic conditions of the lower classes. After his experience with the abortive Guerrero administration, for example, even the democrat Lorenzo Zavala came to support property qualifications for voting.[35] The Liberals were willing to give the Indian his freedom in theory and to allow talented members of that race, such as Benito Juárez, into the movement, but they were not interested in upsetting the privileged creole-dominated social structure.

Nowhere was this attitude better expressed than in the liberal Constitution of 1857. Article 4 of the constitution provided for freedom of the individual to contract, and Article 5 provided for freedom to withdraw from labor contracts, theoretically guaranteeing the right of workers to strike. Moreover, Article 9 provided for freedom of organization, presumably applying to workers as well as to others.[36] In the debates during the constitutional convention, however, several delegates attacked the premises underlying those articles. Ignacio Ramírez in particular denounced the so-called "freedom" of labor, charging that contracts between employers and workers were "nothing but a means to support slavery." He went on, "If freedom is not to be an abstraction, if it is not to be a metaphysical concept, it is necessary that the fundamental law protect the rights of all citizens. . . . To emancipate the workers from the capitalists is the great,

35. Charles A. Hale, *Mexican Liberalism in the Age of Mora, 1821–1853* (New Haven: Yale University Press, 1968), p. 96, 123–24, 223–24, 240, 246–47.

36. Alfonso López Aparicio, *El movimiento obrero: Antecedentes, desarrollo y tendencias* (Mexico: Fondo de Cultura Económica, 1945), pp. 138–39.

the true social problem."[37] But there were few who spoke this way, insuring that these vague guarantees of men's freedoms would be interpreted by the state in favor of the powerful. The Constitution of 1857 provided no help for Mexican working men and women, as the ensuing decades proved only too well.

During the *Porfiriato* Mexican liberalism underwent certain modifications. Some men retained the core of their earlier liberalism, believing that all men are capable of reason and progress, but these men were forced to rationalize the obvious misery accompanying Porfirian economic progress by considering that it was only temporary, as it had been in England, and that in time ("evolution" was a much used word) education and industrialization would create a better world for all. They also had to rationalize the loss of political freedom for some as an expedient, lasting only until such time as Mexicans acquired the necessary intellectual and moral tools to enable them to appreciate and utilize political democracy.

Yet many men of the governing elites came to doubt entirely the liberal doctrine of the perfectibility of all reasoning people. They accepted in its stead the harsh tenets that not only was misery inherent in this life, as conservatives had always maintained, but that it was *essential* for the progress of mankind. Out of the social struggle for survival and dominance, such men believed, would come an improved race of people, because those better fitted to survive would pass on their abilities while the weak and inferior people would perish. José Y. Limantour, one of the most powerful men of the times, told the National Conference of Science in 1901 that "the weak, the unprepared, those who lack the tools in order to emerge victorious against evolution, must perish and leave the struggle to the more powerful."[38] It was a perverted social application of Charles Darwin's theory of natural selection and a convenient "scientific" justification for the ruthless exercise of power.

37. Quoted in López Rosado, *Historia económico*, pp. 258–59.
38. Quoted in Raat, "Positivism in Díaz Mexico," pp. 213–14. For a source that denies that such essentially racist belief was widespread among Mexican intellectuals, see T. G. Powell, "Mexican Intellectuals and the Indian Question, 1876–1911," *Hispanic American Historical Review* 78 (February 1968): 19–36.

As a complement to social darwinianism, many of those same elites accepted the positivist contention that society should be governed along scientific lines and that there were social as well as natural sciences that governed the order of the world. It was their constant references to science in the congressional debates of the early 1890s that earned certain politicians the sarcastic appellation "los científicos," a name they quickly adopted for their own.[39]

The emergence of the later infamous *científicos* as an important political clique took place in the 1890s. They did not immediately attract favorable attention from Don Porfirio, perhaps because he distrusted both their scientific pretensions and the political reform program which they publicized in the presidential campaign of 1892.[40] With the rise of José Limantour to the post of minister of the treasury, however, the *científicos* had an operating base within the government. As Limantour's obvious talents became a valuable asset to the Díaz regime, his power grew and so did that of the *científicos*.

Científico power was reinforced through major positions at the federal level. One of their most important allies was Romero Rubio, minister of *gobernación* until his death in 1895 and the father-in-law of the president. Rosendo Pineda was another prominent member of the group, having entered the government as undersecretary to Romero. Other important *científicos* were Roberto Nuñez, undersecretary to Limantour; Miguel Macedo, undersecretary of *gobernación* and his brother Pablo, an important economist and banker; Ramón Corral, minister of *gobernación* and vice-president from 1904 to 1911; and Justo Sierra, perhaps the leading intellectual of the era and secretary of the Ministry of Justice and Public Instruction. Many *científicos* and their supporters held seats in Congress, although the actual power of that institution was nominal.

From 1893 to the fall of the regime in 1911, the *científicos* guided

39. Professor Raat maintains that many positivists in Mexico split with the *científicos* over a number of issues; see his "Leopoldo Zea and Mexican Positivism: A Reappraisal," *Hispanic American Historical Review* 78 (February 1968): 1–18.

40. Walter N. Breymann, "The Científicos; Critics of the Díaz Regime, 1892–1903," *Proceedings of the Arkansas Academy of Science VII* (1959), in Ralph Lee Woodward, Jr., ed., *Positivism in Latin America, 1850–1900* (Lexington, Mass: Heath, 1971), pp. 89–91.

the economic policy of the Mexican government, a power that made them a formidable political group, but one which in the process earned them many enemies, even among the elites they served. Because of this power and because of their association with the foreign capitalists, they came to be despised and distrusted by many Mexicans. Rightly or wrongly, they were blamed for many of the problems that beset the nation after 1900.

Despite their various political differences, the ideological assumptions of the various elites tended to merge concerning the economic policies of their government that encouraged private enterprise. Most supported the laissez-faire position of the earlier classical economists, modified by the belief that the federal government should encourage private capital and economic growth by removing obstacles to the "rational growth of industry." In practice, the Díaz regime carried this principle even further, lowering duties on industrial equipment, for example, but increasing duties on imports that would compete with domestic producers.[41]

On the other hand, the federal government throughout the *Porfiriato* until 1906 consistently refused to become involved in labor conflicts, except to maintain the public order. In the early months of the first Díaz administration, an unofficial government spokesman laid down the basic philosophy of the regime's labor policy. Telesforo García, editor of *El Monitor Republicano* and later secretary of *Hacienda*, stated that "private enterprise must have complete independence in labor questions with respect to governmental action."[42] In 1892 the government restated its position. In responding to a request for aid from the *Confederación Obrera de la Fábricas del Valle de México*, the secretary of *Hacienda*, Matias Romero, stated that the law forbade the government from intervening in labor disputes. "Labor," he entoned, "is under the unavoidable natural laws of supply and demand."[43]

41. Charles Hale believes that the origins of the Porfirian modification of classical economic doctrine goes back to the nature of earlier Mexican industrialization, compromising as it did the vestiges of the colonial economic system with the new demands of industrial growth; see his "José María Luis Mora and the Structure of Mexican Liberalism," *Hispanic American Historical Review* 45 (May 1965): 226–27.

42. *El Monitor Republicano*, 12 August 1877.

43. *Diario oficial de los estados unidos de México*, December 1892, quoted in Rosenzweig, "La industria," p. 421.

Later that same decade the arrogant and cantankerous Francisco Bulnes, a major intellectual spokesman for the regime, elaborated on the economic basis for the government's labor policy in a debate in the House of Deputies. Responding to the phrase "just remuneration" used by a fellow deputy, Bulnes pointed out the "absurdity" of the term. "The words 'just remuneration' have no meaning in political economy," he declared. "In political economy nothing is just or unjust as far as remuneration is concerned. Labor is a product like any other, such as corn, wheat, flour, and is subject to the law of supply and demand."[44]

Such natural laws were deeply rooted in the liberal, laissez-faire tradition of classical economics, from Adam Smith to Ricardo. The Mexican Constitution of 1857 had provided for the freedom of labor, but this freedom meant in essence that the workers were free to sell their labor for whatever price they could get, where and whenever they wanted to. A statement of how the regime viewed this freedom appeared in a congressional debate in the fall of 1901. Deputy Antonio Ramos Pedruza, later to be chief of the *Dirección de Trabajo* under Francisco Madero, had just spoken with force and irony against the government's interpretation of freedom of labor, pointing out the exploitation of working men, women, and children that had accompanied its implementation throughout the world. Pablo Macedo rose to the attack. The wealthy banker and well-known *científico* reminded his colleague that "this doctrine of tutelage, of the protection of the weak and unfortunate citizen, these were the doctrines of Spain and of the inquisition. They killed freedom of industry, freedom of labor, and freedom of thought . . . and yet there are those who say that freedom cannot be given to the people because they do not know how to use it."[45]

The debate continued at the following session. Rosendo Pineda, former undersecretary of *Gobernación* and one of the most important politicians in the country, maintained that those who had attacked the concept of freedom of labor wanted to protect the people, while they, "los científicos," sought to enable the human personality to exercise its own political and social rights. The state, Pineda went on, was neither a father nor a mother to the people. Its responsibility was to maintain

44. *Diario de los debates de la Cámara de Diputados, Congreso XVIII*, 3:211.
45. *Diario de los debates de la Cámara de Diputados, Congreso XX*, 3:667, 675.

order and to ensure justice for all men, a justice which would "give to each one that which is his."[46]

While men of power and substance talked of the freedom of labor in the halls of Congress, the progress they were debating had been at work for two decades and more, creating new forces and pressures of which even men closest to the changes were only dimly aware. What follows is an examination of the growth and composition of the industrial labor force in Mexico during the Díaz years and an analysis of the problems which industrial progress entailed.

Mexican Workers: Development and Change, 1876–1911

Who were those workers who were free to come and go; where did they come from, where did they go, in what industries did they work, what patterns of change can be observed over time? These are the kinds of objective questions that need to be answered to provide a basic understanding of working men and women in Porfirian Mexico. Not all these questions can be answered in this study, but the following section will attempt to provide a reasonable picture of working-class Mexicans in the *Porfiriato*. Because the best available data begins with the industrial census of 1895, the treatment will emphasize the years from 1895 to 1910.

The general categories of labor specified by the censuses of 1895, 1900, and 1910 show no dramatic changes between major occupational groupings. Workers engaged in industrial work (defined in this study as those in manufacturing, mining, construction, gas, electric, and petroleum industries, and in transportation) rose from 16.8 percent of the labor force in 1895 to 17.9 percent in 1900, and fell slightly to 16.3 percent in 1910. Workers in manufacturing made up the bulk of the industrial-worker category, representing 12.5 percent of the labor force in 1895 and 12.7 percent in 1900, but falling to 11.6 percent in 1910. Agricultural workers comprised the largest category; from 67 percent in 1895 they declined to 66 percent in 1900, increasing slightly to 68 percent in 1910.[47]

46. *Diario de los debates de la Cámara de Diputados, Congreso XX*, 3:733–34.
47. El Colegio de México, *Estadísticas económicas*, pp. 46–53. The Colegio

There were important variations, however, in the occupational categories. First, a comparison of the years 1900 and 1910 shows that the greatest absolute and relative increase in agricultural workers took place in the northern states, whose economy underwent difficulties earlier than that of other areas (the north was in recession for the most part from 1907 to 1910–1911). Conversely, the increase in agricultural workers in the central states—where enclosure was more widespread—was both absolutely and relatively smaller, even though the central states employed twice as many agricultural workers as the northern states.[48] Moreover, the states of the center that had relatively heavy concentrations of modern industry, the Federal District, Puebla, Veracruz, and Mexico, showed increases in the number of workers engaged in manufacturing, while such states as Jalisco, Hidalgo, and Michoacán, where the figures for manufacturing are likely to include a larger number of artisans, had significant decreases in the manufacturing category. Perhaps, then, the slight decline in the number of industrial workers nationwide between 1900 and 1910 actually indicates a decline in the number of those artisans engaged in the traditional sector of the economy, while the number of workers in the industrial sectory may have increased. Since the data do not distinguish between factory workers and artisans, an overall conclusion is impossible, but various partial sources do break the census figures down into factory workers and craftsmen. These partial sources support the thesis that during this period, the number of artisans was declining, not that of industrial workers. For instance, the number of chemical workers (defined by the census as candle makers, fireworks specialists, and soap and wax makers, all traditional occupations), declined from 10,805 in 1895 to 7,659 in 1910. The same held true for

statistics place both artisans and industrial workers in the manufacturing category. I have added transportation workers to the industrial category and eliminated the "insufficiently specified" from the figure used for total labor force; see Donald B. Keesing, "Structural Change Early in Development: Mexico's Changing Industrial and Occupational Structure from 1895 to 1950," *Journal of Economic History* 29 (December 1969): 724.

48. States placed in the northern zone by El Colegio are Coahuila, Chihuahua, Durango, Nuevo León, San Luis Potosí, Tamaulipas, and Zacatecas. States in the central zone are Aguascalientes, the Federal District, Guanajuato, Hidalgo, Jalisco, México, Michoacán, Morelos, Puebla, Querétaro, and Tlaxcala.

textile workers and tobacco workers, where a decline in the number of small shops took place, but the number of those working in modern factories actually increased during the same period.[49]

It is beyond the scope of this study to follow this transformation of the Mexican economy in great detail. It would be useful, however, to have some rough indication of the portion of the work force that might be identified as modern, either by technological criteria or by the service they provided for the industries of the modern sector. According to my own very rough index for 1895 and Wallace Thompson's estimation of the modern industrial work force in 1910, those workers employed in the modern sector rose from slightly over 2 percent in 1895 to something over 6 percent in 1910. The categories of workers used to compile these figures are those designated by the census of 1895 as factory workers, as well as cotton mill hands, telegraph operators, railroad workers, mechanics, and a portion of the tobacco workers, printing and publishing artisans, and metal product workers. Others should be considered modern, no doubt, but are not included because of the lack of statistics for 1895.[50]

To plot the year-by-year occupational changes would be particularly important for the purposes of this study, especially during the last decade of the Díaz regime. The only industry for which annual employment statistics exist, however, is the textile industry. These figures do give some indication of the trends in employment in the modern sector of the economy, at least. There were, in fiscal year 1899–1900, 144 cotton textile mills in Mexico employing 27,767 mill hands. The number of workers fell off to 24,969 for the fiscal year 1901–1902, as a result of the recession during the first two years of the decade, and then rose steadily to a peak of 35,811 in 1907–1908, falling thereafter to 31,953 in 1909–1910, the worst years of the

49. Keesing, "Structural Change," p. 728; Rosenzweig, "La industria," pp. 402–4.

50. Wallace Thompson, *The People of Mexico: Who They Are and How They Live* (New York: Harper and Brothers, 1921), pp. 337–41. Thompson removed middle and upper class workers from the total labor force, correctly I believe, and I have used his figure for the calculation of percentages. The 1895 figures were gleaned from the statistics provided in Keesing, "Structural Change," pp. 727–31, from Rosenzweig, "La industria," pp. 402–4, and from Thompson, *The People of Mexico*, pp. 337–41.

post-1907 recession. Almost all of the absolute increase in textile workers took place in the central states, largely in the Federal District, Puebla, and Veracruz.[51]

The composition of the industrial labor force by sex and by age varied widely. Overall, women represented about one-third of those employed in the manufacturing category of the three censuses between 1895 and 1910. Regional figures show that in the north, a decline of about 6 percent in industrial workers between 1900 and 1910 was entirely in the number of women employed in manufacturing. In the central states, however, the number of women employed in manufacturing increased from 86,703 to 96,089, while total employment in manufacturing declined from 342,708 in 1900 to 339,953 in 1910.[52] It may well be that this increase was largely in the more traditional occupations rather than in industrial employment.

In several industries, the available data show clearly that the number of women employed declined. The textile industry, unlike its counterparts in the United States and Europe, employed relatively few women, and this number declined between 1890 and 1910. A survey of the industry in 1890 estimated that 75 percent of the textile workers were male, and that figure certainly increased in the following decades. By 1900 Puebla mills, for example, employed few women, some of them none at all. Given the surplus labor force in the states of central Mexico, employers were able to hire men for wages nearly as low as those women received, and they evidently preferred to do so. In the north, however, where wages tended to be higher for men than in the central states, a greater portion of women were employed at wages significantly lower than those for men. Women employed in the cigarette industry declined from 86 percent of the 10,397 workers in 1895 to 78 percent of 6,893 workers in 1910, an apparent result of the increase in the use of labor-saving machinery.[53]

On the other hand, the proportion stayed more or less the same in other industrial occupations, according to Fernando Rosenzweig's study, representing from 55 percent in dressmaking and footware shops to 21 percent in the general category classified as factory work-

51. See chart in Appendix B.1.
52. El Colegio de México, *Estadísticas económicas*, p. 48.
53. Keremitsis, *La industria textil*, pp. 65, 209–10; Thompson, *The People of Mexico*, p. 344.

ers. Other industries with proportions of female employees somewhere between those of these industries were food and drink, pottery,
and glassware. Mining industries employed few women. In 1903, for
instance, of the 86,815 workers, 81,017 were men, 4,942 were boys,
and 856 were women.[54]

Statistics on child labor are scarce. A British consul estimated in
1896 that 12 percent of the textile workers were children of both
sexes, working in the spinning and carding departments and as the
so-called "helpers" in other departments of the mill. Mexican children
under twelve years of age were legally bound to be in school, but few
were, especially after the first several grades. Wallace Thompson
maintained that child labor was not a problem in Mexican industry
under Díaz, and given the availability of low-cost adult labor, he may
have been right.[55]

Whatever the questions that remain unanswered about the composition and development of the Mexican worker in the *Porfiriato*, and
there are many, the statistics do not speak for themselves. Certainly
they do not show the conditions forced upon the men and women
who worked in the fields, the shops, and the factories of Mexico and
on the great bulk of the urban poor, for whom the progress of other
men became a burden for themselves. It was in the cities and industrial towns of Mexico that the full extent of these changes first became
apparent and their cost measured.

The Cities

It can hardly be said that prior to the *Porfiriato* Mexican cities were
healthy, safe, or enjoyable places to live for the bulk of the urban
people. With few studies of urban life prior to that time, we know only
that with the increased rate of urban growth during the Díaz regime,

54. Rosenzweig, "La industria," p. 405. Many of the women employed in
pottery and glassware, and perhaps in food and drink as well, were likely
engaged in the craft sector of the economy; see Thompson, *The People of
Mexico*, p. 233. El Colegio de México, *Estadísticas económicas*, pp. 131–33.

55. Rosenzweig, "La industria," pp. 405, 413. Thompson, *The People of
Mexico*, pp. 342–43.

many aspects of urban living appeared to deteriorate. At the very least, it is obvious that as the cities grew, they became statistically a more important part of the Mexican nation, and their defects, therefore, acquired a greater significance.

The population of the Republic grew 61 percent from 1877 to 1910, and urban areas increased at a faster rate. State capitals nearly doubled in size on the average, while newly industrializing cities such as Orizaba, in the state of Veracruz, and Monterrey, the capital of Nuevo León, grew even faster. The rhythm and rate of this growth varied, of course, but the decade of the 1890s appears to have been the time of the greatest urban growth. Many cities continued to grow after 1900, but some stagnated as the deteriorating economic situation forced people to migrate. Nonetheless, by 1910 the population of Mexico living in towns of 2500 or more had risen to nearly 30 percent. There were twenty-two cities with a population of twenty to fifty thousand, five cities with fifty to one hundred thousand inhabitants, and two cities over that figure—Guadalajara and Mexico City.[56]

It was Mexico City which towered over them all. Combined with the predominantly urban Federal District, this extended metropolitan area accounted for 43 percent of the urban inhabitants in the country living in cities of over twenty thousand population.[57]

The Federal District's population remained stable throughout the 1880s but increased dramatically in the 1890s, just as did that of most towns and cities throughout the Republic. Estimated residents of the Federal District climbed from 324,000 in 1890 to 476,000 by mid-decade and 541,000 by 1900. Moreover, it appears that living conditions were at their worst in the 1890s, reflecting the inability or indifference of city authorities to provide for the increased population.[58]

Unemployed poor and urban workers alike lived in the same crowded conditions, with no plumbing and no water, amid filth and disease. At the turn of the century, the important newspaper *El País*

56. Moisés González Navarro, *El Porfiriato: La vida social,* in Daniel Cosío Villegas, ed., *Historia moderna de México,* 10 vols. (Mexico: Editorial Hermes, 1956–71), 4:20. González Navarro, *Estadísticas sociales* (Mexico, 1957), pp. 9–11, 68–69. El Colegio de México, *Estadísticas económicas,* pp. 28–29.

57. Ibid.

58. González Navarro, *Estadísticas sociales,* p. 7.

called the working-class *barrios* of the city "centers of sickness and death,"[59] and the mortality statistics confirm this judgment. The death rate per 1000 inhabitants for the Federal District as a whole rose from 43.17 in 1895 to 49.51 in 1900, far exceeding the national average of 33.61 and surpassed only by the state of Yucatán with 53.20. Deaths due to respiratory diseases, typhus, and internal disorders such as diarrhea were particularly high in comparison to those in other areas, indicating the lack of decent drinking water and the poor housing available.[60]

A survey of one working-class district in Mexico City at the turn of the century listed 2,550 rooms with 18,523 inhabitants, an average of seven per room. That same year another survey revealed that 16 percent of the city's population had no home at all, many paying a few *centavos* a night to stay in the public lodging houses known as *mesones*. Old and ill-kept, most *mesones* had no toilet facilities and few beds—most patrons slept on soiled, damp mats in crowded rooms. Under these conditions, with polluted drinking water and without sanitation facilities of any kind, respiratory ailments and such diseases as smallpox, meningitis, and typhus were common killers. In one inspection tour, public health officials discovered the presence of typhus in 117 of 486 houses examined.[61]

The problem was widely recognized and deplored at the time. As early as 1883 the daily *La Libertad*, under Justo Sierra, created a stir in the Capital by referring to the Board of Health of the Federal District as the "Useless Club." Special congresses and clinics were held to discuss ways of dealing with the problems of health and sanitation within the city. The enactment of the Health Code of 1902 and increased medical facilities established after 1900 appear to have had some effect. The overall death rate declined from the figure of 49.51 in 1900 to 45.09 in 1905. The average death rate for the District

59. Quoted in González Navarro, *La vida social*, p. 86.

60. González Navarro, *Estadísticas sociales*, pp. 160–61, 171–72. Alberto Pani, *Hygiene in Mexico: A Study of Sanitation and Educational Problems*, trans. Ernest L. de Gogorza (New York: G. P. Putnam and Sons, 1917), pp. 43–44, 71–73.

61. Thompson, *The People of Mexico*, p. 254; Cumberland, *Mexico*, p. 192; González Navarro, *La vida social*, pp. 100, 448–49; Pani, *Hygiene in Mexico*, pp. 192–99.

between 1904 and 1912 declined still further to 42.3 per 1000 inhabitants. Nonetheless, the death rate in 1905 was still higher than in any state in the nation. According to figures used by Alberto J. Pani in his study of the 1904–1912 period, Mexico's death rate for those years was greater than even the rates for Madras, India, (39.5) and Cairo, Egypt, (40.1) and, of course, much higher than the rates for American and European cities of similar densities. Indeed, during that period the death rate for the poorer *barrios* of the District was higher than the 42.3 city average, and in some cases it was nearly double. Although the District's Board of Health boasted of a showpiece laboratory which had the latest thing in up-to-date equipment, there were only twenty-two inspectors to see to the enforcement of the new health code of 1902 in an area of seven hundred thousand people.[62]

In addition, the District was becoming a more dangerous place to live. Not only were deaths by accidents far above the national average in 1900, but crimes of violence such as homicide and robbery had doubled and tripled respectively between 1897 and 1909. Population during the same period increased by barely one-third. Complaints by working-class people about the high crime rates in their areas were common during this decade, often coupled with the protest that the police not only did not protect the poorer classes but extorted money from them and generally harassed them.[63]

Under the prevailing scientific dictums of the day, much of the blame for those conditions was attributed to the people themselves, who were considered to be by nature too ignorant and too indolent to want to improve their living conditions or to be naturally inclined toward crime and violence. Not all those who were forced to live under those conditions agreed. When the unofficial regime spokes-

62. González Navarro, *La vida social*, pp. 89, 96–97, 102–34; Pani, *Hygiene in Mexico*, pp. 34–37, 179, 192–99; González Navarro, *Estadísticas sociales*, pp. 160–61.

63. Thompson, *The People of Mexico*, p. 387; González Navarro, *Estadísticas sociales*, p. 166. On complaints, see letters from workers appearing in *El Paladín* (Mexico City, thrice weekly), 2, 5 January, 29 March, 10 September 1908; 13 February, 10, 17 March 1910; *El Heraldo de Morelos* (Mexico City), 14 February 1909; "various workers" to President Porfirio Díaz, 22 June 1906, Córdoba, Veracruz, General Porfirio Díaz Collection (hereafter GPDC), University of the Americas, Cholula, Puebla, legajo 32:6072; Marcelino G. Presno to Díaz, 1 April 1908, Puebla, GPDC, 34:5021.

man, *El Imparcial,* described the *La Merced* area in Mexico City as a breeding ground for crime, noting parenthetically that it was a place where working-class families lived, the prolabor daily, *México Nuevo,* received a letter from irate citizens of that area demanding not to be insulted.[64] The workers who edited *El México Obrero* denounced the high rents and the poor housing, protesting that the waterclosets of the rich were more hygienic than the homes of the workers in Mexico City. "And who worries about those people who are forced to live this way?" the edtiors asked rhetorically, answering bitterly "No one!"[65]

The Artisans

Among those who crowded into the working-class *barrios* of the cities and towns of Mexico was a growing class of dispossessed artisans, whose talents were less needed in an industrial age. It is difficult to document the fate of the artisans individually, but their history as a class is clearer. Professor Fernando Rosenzweig's economic study of the *Porfiriato* estimates that thirty thousand artisans were added to the roles of industrial workers between 1895 and 1910, with the greatest proportional and absolute changes taking place between 1895 and 1900, the years of the most extensive expansion in modern plants and equipment.

The decline in workers engaged in artisan occupations was much greater than the number of proletarianized artisans, however. A comparison of the industrial census of 1910 with the one taken in 1895 shows significant reductions in numbers of workers in those occupations in which artisans had been particularly numerous in earlier years. Among the workers included in the decline were those in to-

64. *México Nuevo* (Mexico City), 7 November 1909. See particularly Julio Guerrero, *La génesis del crimen en México* (Mexico: Vda. de C. Bouret, 1901).

65. *El México Obrero* (Mexico City), 1 September 1909. For similar complaints about living conditions, see "various workers" from El Carmen (cotton mill near Puebla) to the editor of *La Guacamaya* (Mexico City), 3 September 1903; "Patter Cornonato" of the Santa Rosa mill, Necoxtla, Veracruz, to the editor of *El Paladín,* 27 February 1910. Unless otherwise noted, references to newspapers refer to letters to the editor or articles written anonymously by workers.

bacco, leather goods, silver working, jewelry, and textile industries. The latter suffered the greatest loss, a 26 percent reduction. The number of textile workers in factories, however, as opposed to those in small shops or to home weavers, increased from nineteen thousand in 1895 to thirty-two thousand in 1910. Of the 41,000 artisan weavers in 1895, only 12,000 remained in 1910; the great cotton textile mills such as those on the Río Blanco in Veracruz were displacing men and women whose hand looms had woven the cotton cloth of Mexicans for generations.[66]

A graphic example was the weavers of Guanajuato. In 1876 the state supported 853 cotton textile shops, for the most part small family enterprises of independent artisans. They wove about two hundred thousand pieces of cotton *manta* and fifty-five thousand *rebozos* (shawls, usually woolen), using the pre-Conquest suspended loom in the isolated, rural villages or the Spanish-introduced fixed wooden loom in the small urban shops. By 1910 nearly all the urban weavers and many of the rural weavers were gone. In their place were six cotton mills employing barely one thousand workers and producing two hundred sixty thousand pieces of *manta* and stamped cotton cloth, and 382 tons of yarn. Only the weavers of *rebozos* survived in any numbers, saved by the feminine preference for the traditional styles.[67]

Shoemaking, centered in the state of Guanajuato, was another largely artisan industry until quite late in the *Porfiriato*. The shoemaker obtained his material already cut and worked with his entire family assembling the finished product, selling it to the contractor from whom he had obtained his materials. He often made other leather goods as well, unable to make a living specializing in shoes.[68] Modern shoe factories appeared for the first time in the early 1900s, quickly forcing the shoemakers out of business or considerably reducing their income. In a few cases the shoemaker became a repairer of shoes, working with leather whenever he could find a customer.

Many craftsmen forced out of their trade did not find work in the

66. Rosenzweig, "La industria," pp. 402–3; Reynolds, *Mexican Economy*, p. 25.

67. Rosenzweig, "La industria," p. 340; El Colegio de México, *Estadísticas económicas*, pp. 107–12.

68. Matías Romero, *Mexico and the United States*, p. 538.

factories that replaced them and became unemployed or underemployed rather than proletarianized. Wallace Thompson, for instance, cites the decline in the number of women employed in the weaving handicraft industry from 30,262 in 1895 to 13,990 in 1910. At the same time, women employed in the modern sector of the industry rose from 9,868 to only 12,565 in 1910. The net reduction of all artisan weavers—both men and women—was 29,000, while the number of mill hands of both sexes increased by only 13,000.[69] Throughout Mexico the modernization of the economy uprooted whole families, the artisans adding to the growing numbers of rural people forced off their lands by enclosure.

It is impossible to estimate how many people, including artisans, were forced to migrate to find work. Some no doubt found work close by, in the mines or on the *haciendas* or ranches. Figures do show, however, an increasing rate of interstate migration during the last decade of the *Porfiriato*. The national average of those residents in each state who were born outside of that state increased from 6.45 percent of residents born in the state in 1895 to 7.83 percent in 1910, and many states had higher rates than the national average. In Coahuila, for example, 26.43 percent of the residents in 1895 were born out-of-state and 31.30 percent in 1910. Thirteen percent of the inhabitants of the city of Puebla were born in other states, while in the industrial city of Orizaba, 20 percent were from other states.[70] Intrastate migration was likely higher on the average, but no evidence exists on this point.

Whether such migrants found jobs, and doing what, one can only guess. Some found work in the new factories and mills, certainly; others may have found work in the north, where labor was more scarce than in the central states and where wages were higher. An estimated sixty to one hundred thousand Mexicans crossed the border to the United States to work as *braceros* each year in the early part of this century. Many migrants found no jobs at all, however, swelling

69. Thompson, *The People of Mexico*, p. 344; Rosenzweig, "La industria," p. 403.

70. González Navarro, *Estadísticas sociales*, pp. 73–74. Figures on Puebla and Orizaba are from the *Tercer censo de población de los estados unidos mexicanos* (Mexico: Talleres Gráficos de la Nación, 1918), pp. 122–23, 147–49.

the ranks of the unemployed or just barely surviving as lottery sales-men, shoeshine boys, or beggars in the cities of the Republic.[71]

Certainly not all artisan activities were adversely affected by the industrial developments of the era. Village artisans survived in iso-lated areas, as well as on the *haciendas* and wherever the traditional economic functions were still required. Still basically undisturbed in 1910 were blacksmiths and potters, tortilla makers and mat weavers, among those in the traditional crafts or occupations. In addition, certain urban trades actually grew in size from 1895 to 1910. Those which benefited from the economic expansion, for example, were the building trades such as carpentry and bricklaying, and the newer, modern crafts such as mechanics, plumbing, and metal working. Other artisans came under pressure only late in the *Porfiriato*. Those included workers in the woolen shops, weavers of cotton *rebozos* and *serapes*, shoemakers and leather craftsmen, printers, and candle and soap makers. Even *manta* continued to be woven everywhere, if in declining quantity.[72] Economic change is relentless but slow; the habit of doing what one has always done, despite declining levels of living, was undoubtedly strong among Mexican artisans.

Moreover, to judge objectively the price the artisan paid for indus-trial progress, one must also analyze both the short- and long-term benefits that might have accrued to the individual and/or to his soci-ety. Perhaps individual craftsmen obtained better paying jobs or more steady work. Certainly, there is no evidence to indicate that the arti-san's material rewards for his labor were either substantial or stable before the introduction of factory-produced goods. Conversely a strong argument can be made for the case that the entire handicraft system of production rested on a precarious balance in Mexico, even at the beginning of the *Porfiriato*. One might reasonably argue that such a system offers security to the artisan only in a relatively static society, one sharing a common culture with a common value struc-

71. Victor S. Clark, U.S., Department of Labor and Commerce, *Bulletin of the Bureau of Labor*, no. 71, September 1908, p. 466.
72. Ibid., pp. 338–41; Rosenzweig, "La industria," pp. 320–21, 339–40, 344, 365–68, 403; Keesing, "Structural Change," pp. 727–30; Keremitsis, *La indus-tria textil*, pp. 112–13, 118.

ture. Such a society had not been seen in Mexico since the fall of the Mexica, and although the contemporary economic changes of the *Porfiriato* appeared to undermine the craftsman, in fact many crafts had been under attack from various competitors since the coming of the Europeans and certainly since the eighteenth century.[73] Indeed, one might argue that the artisan's true, long-range interest lay in only one viable alternative—that the artisans join with the growing urban working class to demand their share in the social and material benefits of the new industrial society. It is useless, from this perspective, to lament a way of life that was neither as productive as the one which replaced it nor as materially beneficial for its constituents.

There is another perspective, however. To a displaced artisan, whatever the material realities of his former trade, it had afforded him an accepted place in the community among family and friends, perhaps even one acknowledged by social betters and bosses. It had offered the reasonable security of a known world. Certainly it can hardly be denied that for many artisans and craftsmen, this security had begun to break down long before the *Porfiriato*, but the economic changes of that era had broken the rhythm of this decline, quantitatively worsening the social conditions of their lives. *El Hijo de Trabajo* spoke for many artisans when it noted bitterly that there were shops and factories in which "we are not seen as the free artisan of the nineteenth century but as the miserable slave of Antiquity."[74]

Yet wherever the displaced artisan went, whether to the mill towns of Veracruz, the *barrios* of Mexico City, or the mining towns of the north, his fate was now often bound up with that of other men—a growing, often restless, class of industrial workers.

Working Conditions

The conditions under which Mexican working men and women labored varied greatly, but few were satisfactory from the workers' perspective, and some were wretched by any standards. Safety pre-

73. See Francisco R. Calderón, *La República Restaurada: La vida económica*, in Cosío Villegas, ed., *Historia*, 2:97.

74. Cited in Rosenzweig, "La industria," p. 418.

cautions, for example, were poor in many industries and notorious in others. Among the latter were the coal fields of Coahuila.

In October of 1910 an explosion ripped through the Mina de Palau in Las Esperanzas, Coahuila, killing seventy miners. The Coahuila Coal Company gave the widows twenty-five *pesos* each, providing they would waive any further claims for compensation.[75] Ernest Gruening recalled a conversation in which an official of an American-owned mine stated that before the Revolution of 1910 if a miner were killed on duty the company provided a wooden box in which to bury him. A man crippled at work might receive ten or fifteen *pesos* (two or three weeks' wages) and a job as a night watchman or porter. If no such jobs were available, he was released without further compensation. Despite certain contemporary opinion that the fearlessness or carelessness of the Mexican miner was the cause of the high accident rate in the mines, Gruening's informant noted that since the post-Revolutionary laws required the company to pay three thousand *pesos* to the family of workers killed on duty, the company now spent a great deal of money improving the safety conditions of the mines.[76]

Virtually no accident compensation requirements existed during the Díaz regime. Only two states—México and Nuevo León—had workers' compensation legislation, instituted in 1904 and 1906 respectively. Under the former's provisions, the family of a man killed on duty received fifteen days of salary, as did a worker incapacitated while on the job. An injured worker had a right to receive medical attention and to maintain his company housing for three months. Beyond that the company was not obligated. The Nuevo León law was more generous, obligating the employer of a partially incapacitated worker to pay him 20 to 40 percent of his salary for no more than a year and a half and, if he were totally disabled, full salary for two years. Various existing federal, state, or local laws could have been

75. *La Regeneración* (Los Angeles, U.S.), 15 October 1910. For a description of the conditions in the Coahuilan coal mines, see *La Palanca* (Mexico City weekly), 15 January 1905.

76. Ernest Gruening, *Mexico and Its Heritage* (New York: Appleton-Century-Crofts, 1928), p. 345. For a contemporary opinion, see Allen H. Rogers, "Character and Habits of the Mexican Miner," *The Engineering and Mining Journal*, 4 April 1908, p. 701.

used to force companies to pay accident and death compensation, but they were not enforced.[77]

Illness and diseases common to Mexican working classes reflected the special circumstances of industrial employment. Textile workers developed a high incidence of tuberculosis and other respiratory ailments due to the high degree of humidity in the mills. Workers in the dye rooms of the mills were subjected to special illnesses due to the toxic nature of the chemicals. Miners suffered from a number of occupational ailments, including various kinds of respiratory problems and severe pleurisy caused by the contrasting temperatures encountered when entering and leaving the mines. The miners often worked nearly naked at the lower levels of the mines because of the heat. The tobacco industry was notorious for its poor working conditions and hygienic problems.[78] Specific figures on industrial health problems are difficult to come by at present, but indications are that industrial employment, as in other nations, was not only more dangerous than pre-industrial employment but more unhealthy as well.

Existing state and federal health regulations could have countered some of those conditions but little was done. Medical attention was sometimes provided by the larger factories but paid for by the workers. Both the high cost and the poor quality of this treatment were important issues with the mill hands of the Orizaba area, for example. The few hospitals and the scarcity of physicians combined with social prejudice against the workers to limit the effective treatment of illness. When an Orizaba hospital denied aid to a mill hand suffering from pneumonia, the worker died, and his comrades protested this injustice in the pages of the sympathetic Mexico City paper *El Paladín*, asking bitterly if the workers had any rights.[79]

77. González Navarro, *La vida social*, pp. 290–94. For the Federal District's health and safety code, see *El Estandarte* (San Luis Potosí daily), 15 February 1906. The dependents of a man killed on duty at the Río Blanco cotton mill were given fifteen *pesos*, perhaps two weeks' pay; *El Paladín*, 26 January 1908.

78. Various workers from the San Lorenzo mill (Nogales, Veracruz), *El Paladín*, 13 June 1909; Esteben Baca Calderón, *Juicio sobre la guerra del yaqui y génesis de la huelga de Cananea* (Mexico: n.p., 1956), p. 18; González Navarro, *La vida social*, p. 295.

79. *El Paladín*, 27 December 1908. See also González Navarro, *La vida social*, pp. 115–17; *El Paladín*, 15 February 1906.

Another major source of discontent among industrial workers was the length of the workday and the workweek. Textile workers in the early 1870s in the Valley of Mexico worked thirteen hours a day in the summer and twelve in the winter, a regimen that caused some complaints at the time. In the important Hércules mill in Querétaro, however, the mill hands worked fourteen hours in the winter and fifteen in the summer during this same period. In 1884 workers at El Mayorazgo textile mill were working at one point from early morning until 11:00 or 12:00 P.M. every night of the week. With the advent of electric lighting in the mills in the 1890s, the fourteen-hour day became common, and a sixteen-hour day was not unusual for most industrial workers throughout the nation. Río Blanco weavers in 1896 were working from 6:00 A.M. until midnight two days a week and from 6:00 A.M. until 10:00 P.M. on the other nights of the week.[80] By the beginning of the twentieth century, however, most factory workers received Sunday off but were still working fourteen to sixteen hours a day; many retail employees worked every day of the week well into the first decade of this century. A survey of textile mills in mid-1906 found a seventy-two hour workweek the norm.[81] Not infrequently, factory management increased the workday for specific quotas, forcing the workers to stay past the usual 8:00 or 9:00 P.M. quitting time, for no additional pay and often without prior notice.[82]

Ernest Gruening told the story of a Federal District streetcar operator who began work at 4:00 A.M. and was forced to work until midnight on one particular day because his relief did not arrive at the usual quitting time of 6:00 P.M. The worker tried to get some rest but overslept and did not report until 5:00 A.M. that morning, with barely

80. Workers of the San Idlefonso mill to *El Socialista*, (Mexico City weekly), 23 January 1873, cited in John M. Hart, "Anarchist Thought in 19th Century Mexico" (Ph.D. diss., University of California at Los Angeles, 1970), p. 89; Keremitsis, *La industria textil*, p. 204.

81. Rosenzweig, "La industria," p. 415. González Navarro, *La vida social*, pp. 285–90. Dehesa to Díaz, 2 July 1906, GPDC, 31:8658. Keremitsis, *La industria textil*, pp. 204–5.

82. See Anastacio M. López's article on pre-1900 conditions in Puebla mills in *La Lucha Obrera* (Puebla), 11 July 1909, in GPDC, 34:13735; José Neira, "In the Arena," *Revolución Social* (Río Blanco), 3 June 1906, given in H. Peña Samaniego, "Apuntes históricos de Río Blanco," *El Clarín* (Orizaba), 19 August 1958; *México Nuevo*, 24 July 1909.

three hours sleep. For reporting late to work, he was suspended without pay for a week.[83]

Worker absenteeism was a common complaint by administrators in most industries during the *Porfiriato*, and fines were often levied on workers who did not work the entire week. The prevailing sociological interpretation of such absenteeism is that first generation industrial workers often hold to traditional patterns of behavior, desiring to work only as long as is necessary to meet their customary minimum needs.[84] A minority but growing number of scholars disagree, claiming that sociologists have tended to romanticize the dichotomy between traditional and modern society and that both historical evidence and a more rigorous theoretical analysis reveal that this dichotomy is less important than specific aspects of industrial work itself.[85] If the revisionist position is correct, then the Mexican workers' absenteeism may have been more a reflection of the excessive working hours and other unpleasantness of his work than a product of his traditionalism.

83. Gruening, *Mexico*, pp. 360–61.

84. On miners, see Bernstein, *Mexican Mining*, pp. 88–90. See also Cyril S. Belshaw, "Adaptation of Personnel Policies in Social Context," in *Labor Commitment and Social Change in Developing Areas*, eds. Wilbert E. Moore and Arnold S. Feldman (New York: Social Science Research Council, 1960), pp. 98–100; and Frank W. Young and Ruth C. Young, "Individual Commitment to Industrialization in Rural Mexico," *American Journal of Sociology* 71 (January 1966): 373–83.

85. Morris David Morris, *The Emergence of An Industrial Labor Force in India: A Study of the Bombay Cotton Mills, 1854–1947* (Berkeley: University of California Press, 1965), pp. 84–87; Milton Singer, "Changing Craft Traditions in India," in Moore and Feldman, *Labor Commitment*, pp. 258–76; Wilbert E. Moore, *Industrialization and Labor: Social Aspects of Economic Development* (Ithaca: Cornell University Press, 1951), pp. 308–9; Jean Chesneaux, *The Chinese Labor Movement 1919–1927* (Stanford: Stanford University Press, 1968), p. 86; Richard P. Gale, "Industrial Development and the Blue-Collar Worker in Argentina," pp. 132–36, and David Chaplin, "Blue Collar Workers in Peru," p. 43, both in Norman F. Dufty, ed., *The Sociology of the Blue-Collar Worker*, (Leiden, Netherlands, 1969); Professor Richard Morse is also critical of the concept of traditionalism as a significant factor in rural migrants' integration into urban-industrial society, "Trends and Issues in Latin American Urban Research, 1965–1970 (Part II)," *Latin American Research Review* 6 (Summer 1971): 24–28.

Compensation

One of the most important aspects of industrial employment was the compensation received by the workers. The level of compensation varied, depending on the industry, on the geographic area, on the skill level, and often between factories in the same industry. Unfortunately, there is no trustworthy source of industrial wages by industry or trade and few general guides to wages in the *Porfiriato*. The best available source is the Colegio de México's compilation done by the Seminario de Historia Moderna de México. Given the fact that they provide only "minimum" wages and that these figures are often only projections from a small base of hard data, even the Colegio's statistics must be used cautiously.[86]

The only industry for which detailed figures are available is the cotton textile industry, and even here the information is scattered. From the information provided by mills in the central states, daily wages in 1906 ranged from 50 to 75 *centavos* for "*peones*, boys, and apprentices," to 75 *centavos* to 1.25 *pesos* for full-time employees such as carders and spinners. These wages pertain to the major textile centers of Orizaba and Puebla, with the former generally paying higher wages than the latter. Spinners in Oaxaca made nearly 2.00 *pesos* per day, but Keremitsis believes that they were artisans, not industrial workers.[87]

The weaving departments (*tejidos*) paid their workers by the piece. The average wage for weavers is difficult to ascertain, although there is some evidence to indicate that a daily wage might have approached a *peso* or slightly more by 1909. Piece-work laborers were often subjected to quota increases, thereby decreasing their pay; on several occasions the weaving department of mills struck, while the spinning department continued to work. It was also customary to limit piece work to 2.00 *pesos* maximum daily wage, no matter how ambitious or able the operator was.[88]

86. El Colegio de México, *Estadísticas económics*, pp. 147–54.

87. For wages from specific mills, see the Archivo General de la Nación, Ramo de Gobernación (hereafter AGN-Gob), Mexico City, legajo 817. Keremitsis, *La industria textil*, p. 201.

88. *México Nuevo*, 10 November 1909. *El Paladín*, 2, 23 May 1909, 10 Feb-

Central Mexico, 1906.
Map by Robert Clay

Women and children were paid less, of course, although figures are scarce. Figures for mills in the state of Veracruz in 1900 show that while men received from 56 *centavos* to 2.50 *pesos*, women received from 50 to 80 *centavos*, and children earned from 30 to 60 *centavos*, the variance being between mills. Of the 5,951 workers employed by the eleven mills in the state at that time, only 487 were women and 407 children.[89]

Mining wages appear to have been slightly higher, perhaps because of the scarcity of labor in the areas where most mines were located or because of the higher rate of profit in the industry. In general mining wages ranged from one to three *pesos*, although the latter was exceptional for all but important skilled positions or for foremen. These estimates are for the middle of the first decade of this century, and more likely for mines in the north than those in the older mining areas such as Hidalgo or Guanajuato.[90]

An important source of wage figures for the mid-1890s shows that wages for industrial-related craft occupations often ranged from one to four *pesos* a day. Workers in these occupations included engravers, printers, machinists, mechanics, plumbers, carpenters, etc. Wages for factory workers were noted in this source as generally being under one *peso*. This same study gave the wages for railroad workers as ranging from three to five *pesos* a day, the highest of those in all the major industrial occupations.[91] This particular source, however, shows those wages which prevailed at the peak of the industrial expansion of the 1890s, before the recession of 1900 and the inflation-

ruary 1910; *México Nuevo*, 10 November 1909. Keremitsis, *La industria textil*, p. 200.

89. Moisés González Navarro, *Las huelgas textiles en el Porfiriato* (Puebla, 1970), p. 226.

90. E. A. H. Hays, "Present Labor Conditions in Mexico," *Engineering and Mining Journal* 84 (5 October 1907): 622; T. A. Rickard, *Journeys of Observation* (San Francisco: Dewey Publishing Co. 1907), p. 102. For late nineteenth century comparisons, see Matias Romero, *Mexico and the United States*, p. 547.

91. Matias Romero, *Mexico and the United States*, pp. 515–16. The highest paid were nearly all foreigners, however. Alfredo Navarrete, who worked as a railroadman during the latter years of the *Porfiriato*, began as an engine-washer at 15 *pesos* a month and graduated to substitute (assistant) brakeman at 73 *pesos* a month; see his *Alto a la contrarrevolución* (Mexico: Testimonios de Altacomulco, 1971), pp. 32, 34.

ary prices of the next decade. In addition, they do not show the extent to which the workers' gross wages were often reduced by a number of deductions.

Universally practiced in the textile industry from the 1890s on was the fining of workers for infractions of factory regulations, for misconduct within the factory (known as "dancing without music"), and for defects in the finished product for which a worker was responsible. Infraction of regulations meant anything from failing to clean a machine properly to sleeping on the job. Four pages from the book of fines of the large Santa Rosa cotton mill near Orizaba, Veracruz, show fines ranging from 25 *centavos* to 1.50 *pesos*. The majority were for 50 *centavos* and were for such offenses as poor workmanship, sleeping, shouting, or simply "by the order of" the *jefe* of the department. Such fines were a major catastrophe for a worker who might make scarcely one *peso* per day for fourteen hours of work; these fines became a major issue by 1906. Workers at the Santa Rosa mill charged that they were treated as if they were "slaves from Africa," referring to the hated fines as a prime example. Fines were also used in mining, although how extensively is difficult to say.[92] But wherever and whenever they were used, fines were bitterly resented.

A familiar institution in the factory system, particularly in mining and textiles, was the company store. In remote areas it was usually the only source of dry goods and household supplies or even of food, and wherever it existed, the company store was a source of credit for the workers, who bought this week's groceries on next week's paycheck. Often the workers were paid partly in company script, called *vales*, redeemable only at the store and usually at a discount of from 15 to 25 percent. In some factories the *vales* were also redeemable in local taverns, at the same discount. Not only did the workers resent the discounted *vales*, but they often complained of having to pay higher

92. The fine book, dated 1 June 1906, is found in AGN-Gob, legajo 817. See also José O. Petricioli, *La tragedia del 7 de enero* (Mexico: Casa del Obrero Mundial, 1940); *La Guacamaya*, 1, 13 October 1903; *La Palanca*, 27 November 1904; *El Paladín*, 1 March 1908 and 13 March 1910. See also Morris, *Industrial Labor in India*, pp. 109–12 for a discussion of the system of fines used in the cotton mills of Bombay. Workers of the factory of Santa Rosa to Ramón Corral, 2 October 1906, AGN-Gob, Legajo 817. On fines in the mines, see *El Progreso Latino* (Mexico City weekly), 28 July 1906.

prices at the company store for inferior goods. Most workers in company towns, particularly in textiles and mining, were never free of debt to the company store, and consequently the *tienda del rayo* was universally hated. An American mining engineer admitted that the company store was "very unpopular with the men" but declared that "the sooner you get his money away from the peon, the better for him and the more work he will do."[93]

Until it was officially prohibited in 1907, the textile industry also discounted wages of their workers to pay for the celebration of religious and civil holidays. One source mentions priests collecting money at the factory gates for religious events; in some cases the money was discounted directly from the workers' wages before he received them. Of the twenty-one holidays in 1906 on which the mills closed, sixteen were religious. Another practice was to discount individual wages to pay for wornout or broken parts and equipment under the responsibility of that particular worker, which for mill hands meant bobbins, reels, and spools. Such discounts, or fines as they were sometimes called, ranged from ten *centavos* to five *pesos*.[94] How long such discounts were practiced is not clear, but they had become major grievances by 1906.

Finally, there existed in nearly all factories an unofficial system of petty extortion. Workers in the larger factories in particular complained of being forced to buy raffle tickets and "gifts" from their foremen, of being forced to borrow money at high interest rates, and of being forced to purchase the right to work additional looms or other machinery in the piece-work system. In some cases, workers could bribe their foremen to be kept on when others were being laid off, and, conversely, some were forced to pay to be kept on. Under conditions of surplus labor, with no internal grievance procedure to

93. Allen H. Rogers, "Character and Habits of the Mexican Miner," *The Engineering and Mining Journal* 85 (14 April 1908): 702. See also *El Diablito Rojo* (Mexico City), 29 September 1907; *El Hijo de Azujote* (Mexico City), 5 April 1903; *La Guacamaya*, 8 October 1903; *La Palanca*, 6 November, 18 December 1904; *El Paladín*, 9 July, 22 November 1908, 10 June, 30 September 1909; "Workers of the factory of Santa Rosa to Ramón Corral," 2 October 1906, AGN-Gob, legajo 817; Keremitsis, *La industria textil*, pp. 202–3.

94. *El Hijo de Azujote*, 5 April 1903; *El Paladín*, 26 August 1906; Rosenzweig, "La industria," p. 415; *El Imparcial*, 8 September 1906; Petricioli, *La tragedia*, p. 33; *El Tiempo* (Mexico City), 7 December 1906.

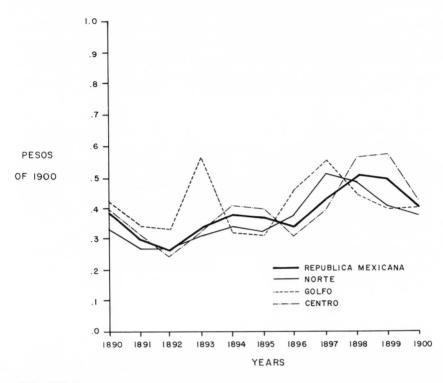

CHART 1

Daily Minimum Industrial Wages, 1890–1900.

Source: El Colegio de México, *Estadísticas económicas del Porfiriato: Fuerza de trabajo y actividad económica por sectores* (Mexico: El Colegio de México, n.d.), pp. 149–50.

protect them, the workers had little choice but to submit to this kind of extortion, even though factory regulations prohibited it as a matter of course. When industrial unrest reached its peak in 1906, this issue was a major grievance.[95]

The critical question in evaluating the remuneration received by Mexican workers is its relative value compared to the cost of living.

95. *El Paladín*, 13 July 1908, 1 August 1909; José Neira to Porfirio Díaz (open letter), May 1907, quoted in Rafael de Zayas Enríquez, *Porfirio Díaz*, trans. T. Quincy Browne (New York: D. Appleton and Co., 1908), pp. 244–46; Fernando Rodarte, *7 de enero de 1907: Puebla, Orizaba* (Mexico: A. del Bosque, 1940), p. 12.

The accompanying chart of "minimum" industrial wages shows clearly that real wages rose slowly and erratically from the mid-1890s to the turn of the century and then declined throughout the next decade as rising prices cut into the workers' purchasing power. Certainly the cost of living became one of the most debated issues in the labor press. Such diverse sources as the radical *El Diablito Rojo* and the moderate, mutualist-oriented *El Heraldo de Morelos* both pointed out the effect of rising prices on the incomes of the workers. *El Heraldo de Morelos* bitterly denounced the rising prices, placing the blame on greedy merchants ("señores agiotistas") and said, in an editorial in

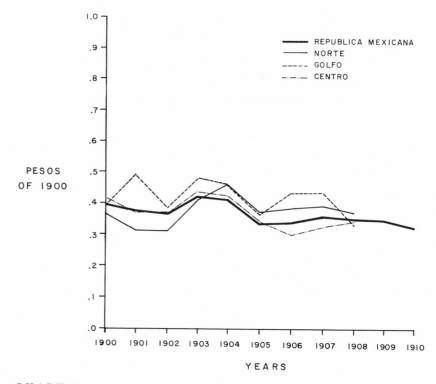

CHART 2

Daily Minimum Industrial Wages, 1900–1910

Source: El Colegio de México, *Estadísticas económicas del Porfiriato: Fuerza de trabajo y actividad económica por sectores* (Mexico: El Colegio de México, n.d.), p. 150.

1909, that it was difficult for a workingman to live in Mexico City because of the rising prices, over the past three years in particular.[96]

The available statistics bear out the fact that prices were indeed increasing. Wholesale prices (Chart A.3), for instance, rose rapidly from 1899 on in most parts of the country. The increase in the price of food, a major item in the budget of working people, was even more spectacular, as Charts A.4–5 point out. In the Federal District the prices of *frijoles* (beans) rose from 2.95 *pesos* a kilo in 1899 to 10.89 *pesos* in 1908. More importantly for the workers' budget, corn rose from 2.19 *pesos* per kilo in 1887 to 6.40 *pesos* in 1908. From 1900 to 1908 the wholesale price of corn rose as follows: Mexico (the state), 30 percent; Puebla, 45 percent; Jalisco, 56 percent; Veracruz, 65 percent.[97] Corn was the most important single expense for most Mexicans, save perhaps rent, and its increasing price was a disaster.

Several examples of working-class budgets from this era will serve to illustrate the problem such families faced when prices began to rise after the turn of the century. Agustín López was a gardener in the public gardens of Mexico City, supporting his wife and mother on his salary of 5.25 *pesos* a week. His weekly expenses were:

corn	$1.04
beans	.48
meat (4.4 lbs.)	.70
wood and charcoal	.60
cotton cloth (*manta*), etc.	.62
rent	.50
pulque	.42
soap	.25
chile	.16
salt	.11
sugar	.11
hair cut (once a month)	.07
	$5.06

96. *El Diablito Rojo*, 11 May 1908; *El Heraldo de Morelos*, 24, 31 May 1908, 27 June 1909.

97. El Colegio de México, *Estadísticas económicas*, pp. 155–59, 172.

Food took up almost 70 percent of López's wages; corn alone consumed 20 percent. One writer to *El Paladín* in 1909 estimated that most workers had to spend a minimum of 77 *centavos* a day (López averaged 72 *centavos* for only three persons) on his family merely to survive. Another estimate of the budget of the "popular class" figured on 30 *pesos* a month, with food taking up a little over 60 percent of the income and rent another 17 percent.[98] Most Mexican workers would have been lucky indeed to take home thirty *pesos* each month.

Furthermore, an unanswered question is how well-fed Mexican workers were on the food they could afford. A classic study of an English working-class diet, done at the turn of the century, concluded that while the workers studied spent 51 percent of their wages on food, a dietary analysis showed them to be "seriously underfed."[99] It is doubtful that Mexican workers were any better off.

While prices were rising, the net earning power of wages declined. In many cases, actual wages increased hardly at all after their peak in the 1890s. Carders in the cotton mills, for example, who earned 1.00 *peso* as a maximum wage in 1896, were receiving the same wage in most cases in 1906, ten years later. Spinners who were paid from .75 to 1.00 *peso* or slightly more a day ($1.12 in Puebla) in 1896, were earning from .75 to 1.25 *pesos* a day maximum in 1906. Weavers made a maximum of 1.00 *peso* a day in 1896 and certainly no more in 1906. Mutsuyo Yamada's research at the Cerritos mill in Orizaba shows that while the average daily wage paid at the mill was 1.71 *pesos* in 1902, it had declined to 1.59 *pesos* by 1907, at the very time that prices were increasing.[100]

Certainly one cannot assume that all workers' wages were being undercut by inflation. Perhaps those with skills which were in demand, such as mechanics and machinists, managed to stay even or even gain net wage increases during these years. Matias Romero's

98. E. D. Trowbridge, *Mexico To-Day and To-Morrow* (New York: The MacMillan Co., 1919), pp. 116–17. *El Paladín*, 31 October 1909. González Navarro, *La vida social*, p. 391.

99. Benjamin Seebohm Rowntree, *Poverty, a Study of Town Life*, 2d ed. (London: The MacMillan Co., 1902), pp. 244, 247–49, 259.

100. Matias Romero, *Mexico and the United States*, pp. 544–47; AGN-Gob, legajo 817; wages were for the years 1906–1907 from several cotton mills in Puebla and Orizaba. Yamada, "The Cotton Textile Industry," p. 81.

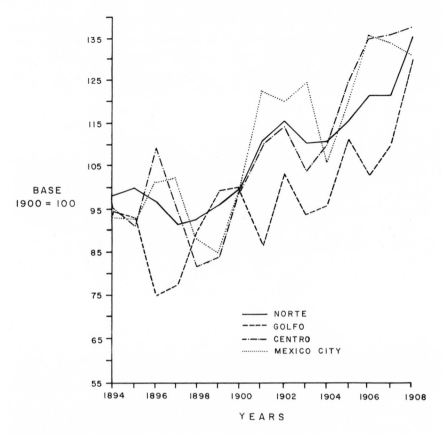

BASE
1900 = 100

NORTE
GOLFO
CENTRO
MEXICO CITY

YEARS

CHART 3
General Wholesale Prices, 1894–1908

Source: El Colegio de México, *Estadísticas económicas de Porfiriato: Fuerza de trabajo y actividad económica por sectores* (Mexico: El Colegio de México, n.d.), pp. 156–57.

statistics are a good base for comparison for the skilled trades, but sources for the later years are lacking. But most workers, probably including many skilled craftsmen, would have found it hard to take home much more than 30 *pesos* a month, as the minimum suggested for survival, and many were forced to take less. Even averaging a *peso* a work day or perhaps $1.25, a worker would have been hard put to make a minimum of 30.00 *pesos* a month. Besides the usual Sundays off, the number of work days a year was 300 or less, depending on

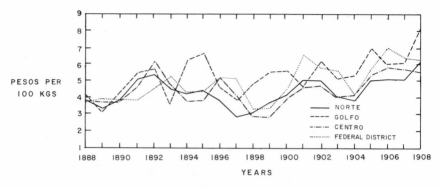

CHART 4
Wholesale Price of Corn, 1888–1908

Source: El Colegio de México, *Estadísticas económicas del Porfiriato: Fuerza de trabajo y actividad económica por sectores* (Mexico: El Colegio de México, n.d.), pp. 158–59.

whether religious holidays were strictly enforced or not. Workers were not customarily paid for holidays.[101]

The overwhelming conclusion is that the wages of most industrial workers in Mexico were barely sufficient to meet their minimum needs. This was especially true after 1900, and perhaps before. In the textile town of Orizaba one writer for a local newspaper noted in 1893 that as the factories were established in the town, misery accompanied them. "There is poverty, great poverty, and the struggle for living is becoming increasingly difficult . . . and today life in Orizaba is painful (but not so for those who have capital). In addition to this, the cost of living increases daily, and labor is compensated disgracefully."[102]

Many white collar workers were paid hardly better than industrial workers. A survey of the monthly wages of the *monte de piedad*, "Vidal-Ruiz," shows that while the top positions such as accountant, chief clerk, and head cashier were paid on the average of 100 *pesos* a month, their assistants and the general line clerks, the guards, and the odd-job personnel were paid on the average of 40.00 *pesos* a month. A

101. Matias Romero, *Mexico and the United States*, pp. 544–47. Keremitsis, *La industria textil*, p. 205.

102. *El Cosmopolita*, 2 July 1893, quoted in Yamada, "The Cotton Textile Industry," p. 77.

clerk on an *hacienda* in Veracruz wrote to president Díaz, complaining that the 40 *pesos* a month he was paid was not enough to cover his expenses.[103]

A major factor affecting the standard of living of the Mexican worker, especially after 1900, was the extent of unemployment. There is no overall statistical summary of the unemployment rate, only impressions of the problem. In a general way, however, it is possible to see the magnitude of the problem. In the first place, the previously described population increases in the 1880s and 1890s had come to represent by the first decade of the twentieth century an increased burden for many people. Although the birth rate declined from 16 percent in the decade of the nineties to 11.5 percent for the decade beginning in 1900, the potential work force actually increased as the children born in the years of rising birth rates attempted to find jobs.

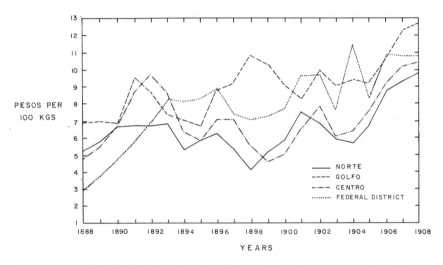

CHART 5
Wholesale Price of Beans, 1888–1908

Source: El Colegio de México, *Estadísticas económicas del Porfiriato: Fuerza de trabajo y actividad económica por sectores* (Mexico: El Colegio de México, n.d.), pp. 162–63.

103. General Mucio Martínez, governor of Puebla, to Díaz, 8 August 1908, GPDC, 33:11406. Francisco de A. Urentia to Díaz, 15 September 1908, GPDC, 33:12636.

Including males only, the number of young people between the ages of eleven and fifteen entering the job market averaged nearly one hundred fifty thousand each year from 1895 to 1910.[104] From 1900 on, however, the number of unskilled or semiskilled jobs available was, at best, stagnant, and most likely declining. When added to the unknown but considerable number of displaced artisans and rural workers and to the increasing number of unemployed urban industrial workers after 1900, the people who could not find work anywhere must have been an increasing burden on those who were working—for in Mexico relatives and friends would have stood by them as best they could.

Not all the hardships faced by Mexican workers can be seen in the material conditions of their lives. One very important issue raised by the workers themselves was the manner in which they were treated by their bosses, by the *patrones* in their lives. Intricately woven into this question of mistreatment was what appeared to many workers to be the lack of respect accorded to the Mexican working classes by the rest of society. This issue came to be one of the most bitterly resented of all the problems confronting the workers of Anáhuac.

Vices and Virtues: Dignity, Respect, and the Mexican Worker

When Joseph A. Kalh conducted his important study of Mexican industrial workers in 1966, he noted that those he interviewed "emphasized quite firmly, the importance to them of being treated with dignity and respect by their bosses."[105] Fully a half century before, Mexico's first generation of industrial workers had raised this same issue, demanding to be treated with respect by their employers and by their fellow Mexicans. The process of industrialization had extracted a harsh price from the Mexican worker. He was forced to confront his

104. El Colegio de México, *Estadísticas económicas*, pp. 25–33.
105. Joseph A. Kahl, "Three Types of Mexican Industrial Workers," in *Workers and Managers in Latin America*, Stanley M. Davis and Louis Wolf Goodman, eds., (Lexington, Mass.: D.C. Heath, 1972), p. 26.

own inferiority—in material well-being, in social standing, and in the respect granted him by the other groups in his nation, even by the foreigners, who were guests in his land.

This lack of respect was evidenced in the common stereotypes of that era. One of the most enduring, and the most bitterly resented by the workers, was that Mexican working men and women were vice-ridden. In 1877 the editor of *El Monitor Republicano* asserted that it was not fatigue that prompted the workers to demand reductions in their working hours but their devotion to vices in their free hours.[106] This simplistic and irrelevant attitude dominated the perspective of many Mexicans toward the workers throughout the *Porfiriato* and colored their understanding of the needs and demands of the workers. The *jefe político* of Orizaba, writing to the officers of a local workers' union, blatantly insulted them with his statement that "the problem between the worker and the industrialist is, in our Republic, arduous, difficult, and complicated more than in any other country since as a general rule the major part of our people are badly educated and dominated by VICES."[107]

Far from being exceptional, this attitude and the emphasis which the *jefe político* chose to give it was extremely common. "Our workers live from day to day," wrote a commission of distinguished representatives of the House of Deputies, "unemployment produces an immediate misery, sickness always finds them without funds, their habits drive them into vice, vice degrades and destroys them."[108] Even the supposedly worker-sponsored paper, *El Obrero Mexicano*, supported this stereotype: "Many of our workers have the habit of leaving their family without food on Saturday, payday, and Sundays, only so that they can get drunk, and are too generous to those they should not be, that is their vice-ridden friends, hurting themselves and society with their immorality."[109]

106. *El Monitor Republicano*, 29 August 1877.

107. *Jefe político* of Orizaba, Miguel Gómez, to José Neira, n.d., quoted in Gómez to Díaz, n.d., GPDC, 34:1588. The capitals are in the original.

108. Comisión del projecto de leyes bancarias, 30 November 1896, *Diario de los debates de la Cámara de Diputados, Congreso XVIII*, 3:659–62.

109. 7 January 1910. *El Obrero Mexicano* was established and controlled by Governor Landa y Escandón of the Federal District. Its editor was not a worker.

An adjunct to the belief that Mexican lower classes were addicted to vices was the belief that Mexican "popular classes" were a violent people, criminally inclined, especially when drunk. The well-known *científico*, Miguel Macedo, described Mexican lower classes as a people armed to the teeth, without order or discipline, with a marked bent for crime. Francisco Bulnes considered that the Mexican people were vicious, ignorant, and melancholy and that alcohol converted the foolishness of melancholy into fierceness and ferocity.[110]

As Bulnes implied, drunkenness was considered to be the vice that underlay all other vices. The Mexican scientists and intellectuals who attended the Mexican Congress of Science in 1895 concluded that Mexicans committed more crimes under the influence of alcohol than the people of nearly any other nation. As with most stereotypes, the belief itself operated as a self-fulfilling prophesy; the police of Mexico City provided the "proof" of the thesis by gaining a considerable reputation for prejudging the guilt or innocence of the person by the amount of alcohol he had consumed.[111]

Mexico's *obreros* were singled out as prime examples of alcoholics, people with no self-discipline or thought of the future. Enough truth to this claim existed to satisfy the amateur sociologists of the day. Certainly drunkenness was common enough on the job to make it forbidden in factory regulations as a matter of course. One recorded practice was for workers to fortify themselves for the workday ahead with a shot or two of *aguardiente*, a habit known as "hacer la mañana" (literally "to make the morning," probably best translated as "to get through the morning").[112] This drink was meant to keep them going from 6:00 A.M. until they could eat breakfast at 8:00 A.M. or so, the hour most factories permitted it. The point is not that there was evidence of alcoholism among Mexican workers but that the evidence was converted into proof in the minds of too many Mexicans that *all* workers were drunkards, or that most workers were drunkards. It became, in other words, a vicious stereotype that provided a convenient rationalization to justify the exploitation of an entire class of people.

110. González Navarro, *La vida social*, pp. 415–16, 419–20.
111. Ibid., pp. 73, 77; Thompson, *The People of Mexico*, p. 386.
112. González Navarro, *La vida social*, pp. 72–73, 77.

For all the supposedly empirical data used to justify such judgments about the morality of the Mexican working people, such opinions actually were linked to long-held, deeply-rooted prejudices. The well-known *científico* and literary critic, Carlos Díaz Dufoo, revealed this, unintentionally perhaps, in a theatrical review written for the popular literary magazine *La Revista Azul.* Critiquing the play *Juan José*, written by the contemporary Spanish playwright Dicenta, Díaz Dufoo charged that Dicenta's social philosophy "menaced the established order with its program of social leveling." He went on to write, with ill-disguised scorn, that the play (which featured a worker as the lead character) was only another romantic cliché. It was oversentimentalized, he added, giving too much credit to the masses of men. People of Díaz Dufoo's stamp tended to regard the Mexican working-class people as intellectually and morally inferior, incapable of progress in their present state.[113] The perceptive Andrés Molina Enríquez, a sociologist and contemporary of Díaz Dufoo, recognized this attitude and its logical effect on labor relations:

> The opinion . . . in our nation is that we are a people that
> know less, are less able, can do less and are worth less
> than . . . the other nations of the earth. Being such a
> widespread opinion, it is clear that the industrialists, almost
> always foreigners and creoles, would feel naturally inclined to
> depreciate the merit of the national worker, and to consider that
> when the wages they pay to them exceeds the average wage, it is
> not only justice but generous.[114]

Not all Mexicans accepted these stereotypes, of course. The moderate Mexico City weekly *La Convención Radical Obrera* denied that workers were generally vice-ridden and protested the unfavorable comparisons made by another newspaper of Mexican to foreign workers. The weekly *El Heraldo de Morelos* praised the working-class family, which it said early developed the habit of work, and suggested that the middle and upper classes could learn something

113. Carlos Díaz Dufoo, "El teatro español contemporáneo—Juan José," *Revista Azul*, 5 (3 May 1896): 26–27.

114. Andrés Molina Enríquez, *Los grandes problemas nacionales* (Mexico, 1908; Ediciones del Instituto Nacional de la Juventud Mexicana, 1964), pp. 232–33.

from the workers on this point. Antonio de P. Escarcega, editor of the weekly, *El Diablito Bromista*, and an old and valiant defender of Mexico's *obreros*, once felt compelled to carry an article entitled "The Mexican Worker *Is* Moral." Even when Escarcega condemned gambling among the workers, he did not patronize them by calling them "our" workers, as did others, and maintained that most workers gambled not because they were addicted to vices but because they made so little money that they had to try their luck at increasing it.[115]

The editor of the weekly *El Renacimiento* of Tuxpan, Veracruz, acknowledged that it was commonly said that all workers were "vice-ridden, drunken, improvident, lazy, cruel, unreliable, etc."[116] but doubted the validity of those generalizations and noted that such judgments, even if true, did not take into account the causes of their conditions. Yet many other self-acknowledged friends of the workers accepted the stereotypes as given and spent as much time moralizing about the deplorable habits of the workers as did less friendly sources. Editorial writers for such important prolabor papers as *El Paladín*, *México Nuevo*, *El Correo de Chihuahua*, and *El Diablito Rojo* constantly preached to the workers to save their money, to stop drinking, to provide for their families, and to stay out of the *cantinas* and other places of sin and iniquity.[117] The workers' response to those attitudes, held by friend and foe, suggests much about the nature of their working experience as it developed and grew, painfully, uncertainly, over the years.

That as workers they should be considered vice-ridden and immoral by mere virtue of their station in life was an affront to many workers' pride and sense of dignity, and among the themes expressed by the workers in what they wrote was a vague but strong desire to be

115. *La Convención Radical Obrera* (Mexico City), 21 September 1902; *El Heraldo de Morelos*, 3 January 1908; *El Diablito Bromista*, 6 January 1907, 25 August 1907, 10 May 1908.

116. Quoted in *La Guacamaya*, 1 September 1902.

117. For the virtues of saving and hard work, see *El Paladín*, 26 December 1909; *México Nuevo*, 26 November 1909; *La Voz de Hidalgo*, 5 February 1910; *El Observador*, 31 March, 26 May 1907; *El Correo de Zacatecas*, 18 November 1906; *El Heraldo de Morelos*, 3 January 1908. On gambling, see *La Guacamaya*, 3 July 1905; *El Paladín*, 17 September 1908. On alcoholism, see *El Observador*, 26 August 1906; *El Diario*, 30 November 1907; *El Diablito Rojo*, 6 December 1909, 24 January 1910.

respected. One Orizaba mill hand expressed this common theme when, at the height of the conflicts of 1906, he appealed to other workers for support, vowing that he and his comrades would continue in their struggle "to acquire dignity for ourselves."[118]

Of the common stereotypes about Mexican workers, they most bitterly resented the image that they were irresponsible drunkards. In a letter to the editor of *El Paladín*, mill hands from the Río Blanco textile factory repeated with bitterness the common adage that "for the rich it is having a good time but for the poor it is drunkenness."[119] José Neira, leader of the Orizaba mill hands in 1906, noted that some of their fellow citizens attributed the workers' problems to alcohol. "No señor! It is not because of drunkenness that we have become such miserable workers or unhappy slaves. If we feed ourselves on tortillas and sleep on a straw mat, and do not have more ways of amusing ourselves than the tavern, it is because, notwithstanding that we work fifteen and seventeen hours a day . . . we receive a wage so miserable that others would be ashamed to accept it in exchange for such work."[120]

Some workers saw in their organizations the means by which they might gain respect. T. E. Paniagua, president of the *Gran Liga de Electricistas Mexicanas de Chihuahua*, spoke for many industrial workers when he gave as the objectives of his union: "We want to be strong, powerful and respected by society in general."[121] Copper miners from the huge mining complex at Cananea, Sonora, proud of their hard-won reputation of standing up for their rights, asserted that they belonged to a union respected throughout the Republic, adding bitterly, "not withstanding the ignorance that is attributed to us."[122]

One group of workers suggested that the *científicos* were responsible for the negative image of the worker and the popular classes in general. During the political campaigning in 1909, the *Gran Partido Nacional Obrero*, made up largely of artisans and retail employees from Mexico City, proclaimed that they were supporting General Bernardo

118. *El Paladín*, 26 August 1906.
119. Ibid., 8 May 1910.
120. Quoted in Peña, "Apuntes históricos," 19 August 1958. See also *La Convención Radical Obrera*, 23 November 1902.
121. *El Correo de Chihuahua* (Chihuahua City), 22 April 1909.
122. *El Paladín*, 7 April 1910.

Reyes for the vice-presidency because he considered the worker worthy of attention, "while the 'científicos' call the people inept, disgusting and miserable."[123]

Perhaps the most eloquent statement of all was a petition from a group of Tlaxcalan workers who were requesting the governor's aid in their struggle with the mill owners. Asking rhetorically why they, the workers, did not have the rights that all citizens were supposed to have, they answered sarcastically, "That is the way it has to be. The poor man is . . . a lowly beast of burden, he does not have the qualities that deserve this name [citizen]. All of them are vice-ridden, evil and violent people."[124]

A few other men recognized and understood their desires for respect and dignity. The *jefe político* of Ciudad Juárez in Chihuahua noted in a letter to President Díaz that he treated the workers under his jurisdiction with respect and that this enabled him to maintain good relations with them.[125] A report commissioned by the governor of Veracruz shortly after the bloody Río Blanco strike of January 1907 stated simply that "the workers wish to be considered human beings . . . and that therefore their ideas are sound and progressive."[126]

But such understanding was either exceptional or little practiced. It seems fairly clear that many Mexicans of the middle and upper classes throughout most of the years of the *Porfiriato* were not convinced that the ideas of the working peoples of the nation were either sound or progressive. Rather all too many assumed that the workers were, in fact, morally and intellectually inferior and that their misery simply reflected their lack of abilities and their proclivity for vice or was a direct result of their laziness. If the realities of their conditions were to be changed, therefore, the Mexican workers would have to force the changes themselves. They would have to organize and demand respect for their rights and their existence.

123. *México Obrero*, 1 September 1909.
124. *Comisión de obreros industriales de "El Dique"* to Col. Próspero Cahuantzi, governor of Tlaxcala, 31 May 1906, GPDC, 31:5887.
125. *Jefe político* to Díaz, 18 September 1907, GPDC, 32:10364.
126. María Elena Sodi de Pallares, *Teodoro A. Dehesa: una época y un hombre*, (Mexico: Editorial Citlaltepetl, 1959), p. 155.

Paternalism and Technological Change

One unanswered question is the extent to which the good will of the *patrón* might have mitigated the abuses of the industrial system; that is, the extent to which the reputed traditional paternalism of the *hacienda* carried over into the factories and industrial employment. I would suggest that, although precapitalistic paternalism existed throughout the *Porfiriato*, it was never a significant characteristic of the Mexican industrial system and that after the 1870s it became less and less a meaningful buffer between the worker and the harshness and insecurity of the developing capitalist structure.

The worst aspects of the factory system as it developed in Mexico appeared first in the Federal District, perhaps because the size of the market there stimulated competition and encouraged the profit motive. Workers in pre-Porfirian factories of the Federal District were often forced to doff their hats in the presence of the *patrón* and take a position of subservience. This was a common practice on the landed estates of the Republic, certainly, but the paternalistic relationship which shored up such rituals on the *hacienda* was less common in the factories. Acknowledging their dissatisfaction, the mill hands at the Tlalpan textile mill proclaimed that "we know that . . . slavery does not legally exist in our country,"[127] but then went on to say that at many factories the workers were treated as if they were slaves. The workers blamed the government for its lack of concern for their fate and the capitalists for their greed and inhumanity.

In the provinces beyond Mexico City, paternalism may have survived for a longer time as a system mitigating the worse aspects of industrial work. The key factor is not the policies of the owners per se but the workers' feelings about those policies. Here, however, evidence is lacking. The impression that I have is that in such areas as the Puebla textile centers, industrial work may have been accepted with as much enthusiasm as farm work. Perhaps those small Puebla mills, with their patios, their fountains and benches, their little chapels, and their generally paternalistic policies, offered sufficient security and

127. Luis González y González, Emma Cosío Villegas y Guadalupe Monry, in Daniel Cosío Villegas, ed., *Historia moderna de México*, vol. 3, *La República Restaurada: La vida social*, pp. 424–25.

benefits for the workers so that conflicts did not arise in the pre-Porfirian years.[128]

Yet paternalism has many sides. While Rafael Escandón, the manager of the Cocolapán mill in Orizaba, was well-loved by the workers and few conflicts took place until the mill was absorbed into the French-owned CIDOSA system in 1899, Cayetano Rubio had a reputation for ruthlessness as the equally "paternalistic" owner of the Hércules mill in Querétaro. Workers who violated the rules at Hércules were sent to an underground dungeon as punishment.[129] The power to impose benefits is also the power to inflict harm, and the further away one gets from a socially rigid, self-contained social system, the more likely it is that impersonal market and institutional forces will dominate individual benevolence.

If benevolence was ever a significant factor in Mexican industrial relations, its decline became a matter of public record in most industries during the 1880s. It was during this decade that ill-treatment—which the workers equated with the lack of personal respect—first appeared as an important reason given by striking workers as the cause of their discontent.[130] A related issue appeared in the next decade, that of changing factory regulations. In response to increased competition within the textile industry and to the potential profits held out during the economic growth of the 1890s, many firms attempted to institute more efficient work policies. From the workers' perspective, these changes were a definite kind of ill-treatment—uncalled-for, greed-motivated regulations that caused additional misery in their lives.

It was during the first decade of this century, however, when both boom and reversal encouraged even greater efficiency in production methods and personnel practices, that working-class protest of ill-treatment reached its height. By mid-decade all the working-class weeklies and several of the more sympathetic dailies regularly carried charges against factory supervisors and foremen for mistreating the workers under them. The type of insult or ill-treatment varied widely. Workers complained of being treated "as if we were irrational beings"

128. Keremitsis, *La industria textil*, pp. 118–19, 197.
129. Yamada, "The Cotton Textile Industry," pp. 86–88, 93, 130.
130. See Appendix A.7 for the table of grievances.

or of being insulted by disparagingly-used labels such as "indios," "greasers," or "Mexican dogs." Grievances were registered about physical abuse as well, where workers were kicked, beaten, or slapped around by their bosses. Workers also frequently accused foremen of forcing them to pay extortion money or to buy raffles and of taking advantage of female workers.[131]

Foreigners were particularly singled out as offenders, although it is difficult to say whether this was because many of the foremen of the larger plants were foreigners (brought in, generally, to supervise the use of the new equipment), or because Mexican workers were especially sensitive to such treatment from non-Mexicans. After one particularly brutal incident, the proworker editor of *El Paladín* charged: "Three centuries have passed since the Conquest and still there are foreigners who come to our country, treating our countrymen as things and not as men." [132]

Occasionally, workers went out of their way to single out a particular foreigner for praise, saying that they were not against all foreigners, only those who mistreated them. Among the few so honored was the English manager of the CIDOSA mills in Orizaba. He knew how to treat the mill hands "as human beings" wrote one of his workers anonymously.[133] Yet even this was not sufficient; the CIDOSA mill hands were among the most militant in the Republic. One man's good intentions, even when practiced, could not change the system.

131. La Comisión de la fábrica de Río Blanco to Governor Dehesa, 24 May 1907, GPDC, 32:5216; *La Palanca*, 27 November 1904; *El Tiempo*, 10 January 1907; *El País*, 13 January 1907; José Neira to Díaz, 10 May 1907, GPDC, 32:6337; Yamada, "The Cotton Textile Industry," p. 83; *La Guacamaya*, 18 August 1902; *El Paladín*, 6 September 1908, 12 August 1909; *El Diablito Rojo*, 23 March 1908; *México Nuevo*, 22 June 1909, 1 January 1910. There were many more complaints of ill-treatment, especially in 1908 and 1909. Charges against foremen for taking advantage of women workers were particularly bitter: see *La Guacamaya*, 18 August 1902; *La Palanca*, 27 November 1904; *El Paladín*, 4 March 1906. See also article 4 of the worker *reglamento*, Appendix C.

132. *El Paladín*, 2 January 1908. Of the nineteen foremen in the four CIDOSA mills, fifteen were foreigners: Yamada, "The Cotton Textile Industry," p. 84.

133. *El Paladín*, 13 February, 29 March 1908. On occasion, offending foremen were disciplined; see *El Paladín*, 26 January, 9 February, 23 April 1908; *México Nuevo*, 9 June 1909.

Here and there, the documents divulge images of an earlier age, romantic "flashbacks" in which workers paid homage to paternalistic *patrones* of the past, casualties of the industrial age. Disgruntled mill hands at the small cotton factory La Tlaxcalteca lamented the passing of the father of the present and very unpopular owner, pointedly remembering that the father had never permitted his workers to be mistreated while he was alive. He had always been fair and just in his dealing with them, they declared, noting that "even after his death the workers still say his name with respect."[134] An anonymous working-class poet also expressed this longing for older times when the *patrón* had been a friend and a father to his workers: "Today in Mexico the *patrón* is not the father / that yesterday he was. / He is the terrible predator / without feelings / who increases our work / in exchange for a trifle."[135]

Many workers undoubtedly believed that in the past, life had been better for themselves or for workers such as themselves. They believed that they had once been respected and had had a place of stature in their society. Whether this picture was true and not their romanticized view of the past is a question that deserves to be studied for its own sake. But if it was a myth, it was a convenient illusion, because in a time when Mexican workers perceived that their life was growing harder, they needed to believe that it did not have to be that way, that somehow things could be different, that life and work could be better because it once had been so.

Among these people, artisans and industrial workers, the struggle to create a place for themselves was carried on over many years. What follows is a description and analysis of this struggle, from its beginnings in mid-nineteenth century through to 1906—the year of their greatest trial.

Labor Organization and Industrial Conflict, 1850–1905

The early development of workers' organizations is not well known. Gastón García Cantú gives 1850 as the date of the first workers'

134. From a flyer entitled "Digna Actitud de los Obreros de la Tlaxcalteca," signed by Guadalupe M. Zavala, *Secretario General*, n.d. but circa July 1909, GPDC, 34:11247.

135. *El Pinche* (Mexico City), 7 July 1904.

mutualist society, founded in Guadalajara. John Hart, however, maintains that the first modern mutualist organization was *La Sociedad Particular de Socorros Mutuos*, founded in October 1864 by Mexican followers of Proudhon and the Russian anarchist Bakunin. In any case, by the early 1870s mutualist and cooperative societies had been formed among such Mexico City artisans as the shoemakers, tailors, and carpenters and among the mill hands at various Federal District cotton textile factories.[136]

Among those various groups, the goals differed as to both the ends and the means for protecting and enlarging Mexican workingmen's rights. Most numerous were those artisan mutualist societies whose goals were to protect the economic and social positions of their members by such cooperative efforts as the establishment of savings funds for medical expenses, unemployment compensation, and pensions for their old age. In addition, they often sponsored night classes, established libraries, and generally concerned themselves with the moral and intellectual development of their members.[137]

An active minority, however, influenced by European anarchism or the early socialist movements, supported mutualism as an organizational tactic but encouraged both artisans and industrial workers to view their long range objectives as a struggle against capitalism and the state. Leadership among this group was furnished in part by artisans under the ideological influence of an anarchism brought to Mexico by a Greek immigrant, Plotino C. Rhodakanaty, and spread by his followers in the 1860s and 1870s. John Hart's study of Mexican anarchists in the nineteenth century holds that the first industrial strikes took place in Mexico under the guidance of artisans influenced by Rhodakanaty. These strikes took place in June 1865, during the rule of Maximilian, at the textile mills San Ildefonso and La Colmena, near Mexico City. Both failed, but they were a beginning.[138]

136. Gastón García Cantú, *El socialismo en México siglo XIX* (Mexico: Ediciones Era, 1969), p. 93; John M. Hart, *Los anarquistas mexicanos, 1860–1900*, trans. María Elena Hope (Mexico: Secretaría de Educación Pública, 1974), pp. 35, 50–51. Hart notes that the mutual society had been first formed in 1853 among the sombrero makers of Mexico City but that it was given a different ideological orientation when it was revived in 1864.

137. López Aparicio, *El movimiento obrero*, p. 106. For a discussion of mutual societies from 1867 to 1911, see Luis González, *La vida social*, pp. 434–41 and González Navarro, *La vida social*, pp. 344–53.

138. Luis González, *La vida social*, pp. 428–34; John Hart, "Nineteenth

The Maximilian empire collapsed in 1867, bringing the Liberals under Benito Juárez back to head the government. Within a year two textile conflicts took place, the first in the Restored Republic (1867–1876). Workers at La Fama Montaneasa in the Federal District, organized by the anarchist Santiago Villanueva, carried out a successful strike in July 1868, obtaining better working conditions from their employers. Encouraged, mill hands at six textile factories in the Federal District refused to accept a reduction in wages (to the 1862 level), and in an effort to force their compliance, the owners locked out nearly nine hundred workers.[139]

Refusing to give in, representatives of the workers appealed to President Juárez for aid. They were honorable workers, they told the president, and would neither rob nor create a disturbance, but they needed to work to feed their families. And they kept their word throughout the nearly five months that the dispute dragged on. *El Siglo XIX* noted that not one case of robbery had been recorded in the entire district where the workers lived since the lockout began. The workers lived on aid from friends and relatives, on public charity when it was available, and by begging. A few had found work on farms nearby, but most had not. Although they wrote the president again, he never replied to their pleas. Subsequently, the laws protecting the workers that had been enacted by the government of Maximilian were abrogated by the Juárez administration.[140]

The 1870s were the most fruitful years for labor organizing in the nineteenth century. In the fall of 1870, under the leadership of Santiago Villanueva, a number of mutualist organizations in the Valley of Mexico founded the *Gran Círculo de Obreros de México* with the objective of forming the growing mutualist groups into a national labor central. In 1875 the *Círculo* had twenty-eight branches in twelve states and the Federal District, including the more important cotton mills as well as

Century Urban Labor Precursors of the Mexican Revolution: The Development of an Ideology," *The Americas* 31 (April 1974): 298–318. Still unresolved is the extent of artisan influence in the industrial conflicts of the early *Porfiriato*. See García Cantú's discussion of this controversy in *Socialismo en México*, pp. 442–43, n. 3.

139. Hart, *Los anarquistas*, p. 75.

140. García Cantu, *Socialismo en México*, pp. 27–28; Luis González, *La vida social*, pp. 96, 411.

the artisans. Total membership was about two thousand workers. By 1878 the *Círculo* had forty-three associated groups.[141]

Until the death of Santiago Villanueva in 1872, the proanarchist group dominated the leadership positions of the *Círculo*, even though the *Círculo* membership itself was divided on the proper activities and goals of working people in Mexico. The radicals, particularly those influenced by the anarchist group *La Social*, felt that the new organization should "fight for the total emancipation of the working class . . . through social revolution," accepting no alliance with any political party but accomplishing their objectives through militant working-class action.[142]

A moderate faction of the *Círculo* advocated reform through legislative action. Their organ, *La Unión de los Obreros*, supported a mild, noncombative position: "We are looking for the aggrandizement of our country through the protection of labor by wise laws, adapted to our necessities. We do not want one class to dominate the others."[143] This moderate-liberal faction, lead by Epifanio Romero and Juan Cano, came to control the *Círculo* after the death of Villanueva, bringing it into closer relationship with the government. The labor weekly *El Socialista*, official spokesman for the *Círculo* and once loosely allied with the Villanueva group, evidenced this development. In the years after 1872, *La Socialista* rarely supported the use of the strike as a proper action for the working class and often disassociated itself from all but the mildest form of working-class protest. Meanwhile, in the period from 1872 to 1875, the anarchists temporarily dissolved *La Social* in favor of regrouping within the Mexico City mutualist central, *La Sociedad Artística Industrial*. Their spokesman was the weekly *El Obrero Internacional*.[144]

Despite the sentiment against the use of the strike, a position common to artisan mutualist societies, a number of strikes did in fact take place in Mexico during those years. Between 1865 and 1880, workers struck at least twenty-seven times, seventeen of which were in the

141. Hart, *Los anarquistas*, p. 76.

142. Ibid., pp. 76–78.

143. Quoted in Victor Alba, *Las ideas sociales contemporáneas en México* (Mexico: Fondo de Cultura Económica, 1960), p. 103.

144. Hart, *Los anarquistas*, pp. 79–82. Niblo, "Political Economy," pp. 102–5, 109–11.

textile industry, and five in mining. Most took place at the larger mills such as La Colmena, Hércules, Magdalena, or San Ildefonso or at the larger mining complexes in Hidalgo, Guanajuato, and Zacatecas. The issues were overwhelmingly concerned with wages, which in the case of the miners were hardly greater than those paid the *peones* on *haciendas*. Miners in the Zacatecan mines had formed a mutual society as early as 1869, vowing to strike if necessary to promote the intellectual and material betterment of their members and to do whatever was necessary to gain respect for "the destitute class of our country."[145]

Over half the strikes took place between 1873 and 1877. Miners at Real del Monte in Hidalgo struck from August 1872 to January 1873, returning to work with a moderately favorable settlement. Later on, however, the government deported a number of miners to work camps in Campeche and the Yucatán for their labor activity. Sombrero makers struck over wages in a number of Federal District shops in the summer of 1875. As the strike dragged on, they received the support of such important figures as the economist Guillermo Prieto and the well-known intellectual Ignacio Manuel Altamirano. Even the Cuban patriot and exile, José Martí, gave publicity to their cause. The *Gran Círculo* supported the *sombreristas*, both financially and in their press.[146]

It was in March 1876, in the midst of growing labor unrest, that the *Círculo* issued an invitation to its associated groups and to all other worker and artisan groups in Mexico to attend the *Primer Congreso Obrero Permanente* for the purpose of developing a united front for the Mexican worker. On 5 March 1876 thirty-five delegates met in the solon of the *Sociedad Artística* to elect officers, organize committees, and determine the business of the Congress. Among the delegates were representatives of both the moderate and the radical factions of the mutualist movement. Out of this Congress came a statement of objectives, including support for increased adult and child education,

145. Luis González, *La vida social*, pp. 416–23. See Appendix A.1 for statistics on strikes.

146. Hart, *Los anarquistas*, p. 81. This ancient silver mine had a long history of labor conflicts; see Robert W. Randall, *Real del Monte: A British Mining Venture in Mexico* (Austin: University of Texas Press, 1972), pp. 23–27, 126–52. García Cantú, *Socialismo en México*, pp. 105–8.

the founding of artisan-run shops and outlets for their work ("fostering the spirit of initiative and enterprise among the artisans"), and the right of the Congress to operate as the agent for all the workers of the Republic, including the right to establish wages by industry and by region. Such goals were reminiscent of the long-dead *gremios*. Significantly, the Congress hinted that the use of the strike was legitimate to achieve these ends, a stronger stand than the *Círculo* itself had ever taken. Its manifesto also demanded various social guarantees in order to "emancipate the worker from the yoke of capitalism," strong words indicating the influence of Rhodakanaty, Villanueva, and their anarchist followers.[147]

Although the Congress took no official stand on the then raging political struggle between General Porfirio Díaz, popular hero of the Reform movement, and the current president, Miguel Lerdo de Tejada, who had succeeded Benito Juárez on the latter's death in 1872, the political situation effectively destroyed the initial semblance of working-class unity. Many members of the Congress were clearly pro-Lerdo, reflecting the relationship Lerdo had already established with Romero and the moderates. *El Socialista* supported Lerdo, and its position as the official organ of the *Círculo* (and therefore, indirectly, of the Congress) gave its opinion some importance. The more radical of the anarchists refused to support any candidate, warning of the dangers of political involvement.[148]

At least a strong minority of the Congress supported Porfirio Díaz, however, initially including many of the members of the anarchist-dominated *Sociedad Artística Industrial*, as well as the society's spokesman, the weekly *El Hijo de Trabajo*. Professor Stephen Niblo contends that many of the workers and artisans supported Díaz because they believed or hoped that Díaz would better their situation when he got into office. Díaz's Plan de Tuxtepec had promised social reforms. It may well be also that many workers and their spokesmen saw him as a man of the people and a patriot because of his humble origins and his struggles against the conservatives and the French. General Díaz defeated Lerdo after a long and difficult military campaign and marched into Mexico City on 23 November 1876. Unfortunately, Díaz

147. Hart, *Los anarquistas*, pp. 88–89.
148. Niblo, "Political Economy," p. 116.

did not prove to be as friendly to the workers as some had hoped, and *El Hijo de Trabajo*, as spokesman for this group, retreated from its earlier support of him.[149]

The labor unrest which preceded the Congress continued on into 1877; four textile mills were struck, including three in the Federal District. An alarmed capital city daily accused the editors of *El Hijo de Trabajo* of instigating the unrest, referring to them as "thieves, communists, rabble rousers and rebels."[150] Living up to their reputation, an editor of *El Hijo de Trabajo*, José María González, warned Mexico's entrepreneurs:

> If some day instead of factories you behold ruins; instead of shops you see ashes; instead of riches, you have misery; instead of walking on carpets, you walk on blood, do not ask why. Your workers are today still sheep. Tomorrow perhaps they will be lions. . . . Then those who are so humble, so resigned, so degraded will cry out on the day of justice: 'Off your knees, *miserables*.'[151]

Alarmed by González's rhetoric, the editor of *El Monitor Republicano* attempted a rebuttal in a series of editorials. He admitted that there was a latent conflict between the rich and the poor in industrial nations but asserted that such conflicts were less hateful in Mexico because of her "customs." The situation of the worker was hard, he further admitted, but the difficulty was the result of the general malaise of the times. Furthermore, the conflicts generally were not the product of honest workmen but were due to the influence of the foreign ideas and unprincipled agitators that the editor believed abounded in the Federal District.[152]

With working-class agitation increasing, the Workers' Congress called its second conference at the end of 1879 in Mexico City. Workers and artisans marched in a spirited parade, bands playing and

149. Ibid., pp. 125, 133–34, 140–46.
150. Quoted in Hart, "Anarchist Thought," p. 120, n. 1.
151. Quoted in González Navarro, *La vida social*, p. 301.
152. González Navarro, *La vida social*, pp. 301–2. See also *El Monitor Republicano*, 29 August 1877.

banners waving in the crisp December air. In the session, the delegates to the Second Workers' Congress made brave resolutions, promising to provide financial support for strikes, to fight for wage increases for all workers, and to better the conditions of the rural workers as well.

Yet it was, as García Cantú noted, the end of an epoch. The 1870s were the highwater mark for the mutualist and the cooperative movement in Mexico. Despite the initial show of unity by the Second Congress, the presidential election of 1880 brought discord. While the hard-core anarchists of *La Social* maintained their traditional attack on all organized establishment politics, a significant number of the labor groups supported General Trinidad García de la Cadena, a progressive candidate from Zacatecas who was opposing the hand-picked Díaz candidate, General Manuel González. Unable to resolve the differences, the Congress broke up in the spring of 1880. Although various labor groups, particularly the anarchists, remained active through 1882, the new González government soon initiated a repressive campaign against moderates and anarchists alike. The overt provocation was an armed agrarian uprising by one wing of the movement, led by Zalacosta. The rebellion was crushed in 1880 and its adherents jailed or executed. Other arrests of labor leaders followed and in 1883 the *Gran Círculo de México* was closed by the federal government. Various attempts were made in the 1880s to reorganize the mutualist movement, but all failed.[153]

Mutual societies eventually became less an alternative to working-class organization than a supplement. Upon the failure of the anarchists to radicalize the mutualist movement, the surviving labor societies were reduced to scattered local organizations with limited goals. In good times they served as a source for low interest loans, collected funds to provide their members with a decent funeral, held poetry readings and literary discussions, and served as centers of good fellowship. But when times were hard and they were faced with the necessity of dealing with hostile or indifferent interests in order to preserve basic living standards, the mutualist societies often folded, unable to defend their members against the power of the indus-

153. García Cantú, *Socialismo en México*, p. 118. Hart, *Los anarquistas*, pp. 96–98, 110–11, 120–30.

trialists or the uncertainties of the business cycle. Mutual societies survived among artisans in urban crafts and among *empleados* such as public employees and various white-collar workers, but generally for reasons of professional status rather than as a leverage against their employers. When a more militant working-class movement developed in 1906, it sprang from independent origins, in the main, and was not the product of the mutualist experience.[154]

The 1880s were hard years for the Mexican worker. In addition to official hostility, the economy stagnated throughout most of the decade, bringing hard times to the workers of Mexico. Estimated minimum daily wages for urban workers and artisans declined in that decade and did not again reach the peak 1877 level until 1893. The mutualist movement had stagnated, and even a number of the former anarchist leaders had moved to more moderate positions by the end of the decade, some taking a pro-Díaz, promutualist stance in their organ *La Convención Radical*. The economic problems of the 1880s led employers to reduce wages or to raise the workers' production quotas in order to maintain their profit margins; the majority of the fifty strikes from 1881 through 1889 were concerned with these issues. Nine of the strikes were in the tobacco industry.[155]

The tobacco industry was in trouble throughout the 1880s and ran into further problems in 1887 when cigarette taxes were introduced. Despite earlier agreements to the contrary with the *Congreso Obrero*, the owners of the tobacco shops often raised workers' production quotas without increasing their technical capacity to do so, effectively lowering wages. A majority of the tobacco workers were women, who lacked any better employment alternatives. Wages were so low that by the end of the century a *maestro* earned only seventy-five *centavos*, while regular workers made from twelve to fifty *centavos* daily. Only women employed as seamstresses made less in industrial jobs.[156]

Of the twenty-two conflicts in the textile industry from 1881 to

154. For similar conclusions on other labor movements, see James L. Payne, *Labor and Politics in Peru: the System of Political Bargaining* (New Haven: Yale University Press, 1965), pp. 37–41 and Alan Angell, *Politics and the Labour Movement in Chile* (London: Oxford University Press, 1972), p. 15.

155. González Navarro, *La vida social*, pp. 345–54. Hart, *Los anarquistas*, p. 147. See Appendix A.1 for statistics on grievances.

156. González Navarro, *La vida social*, pp. 294–97, 310–12.

1889, only seven were in the Federal District; Puebla, Tlaxcala, and especially the state of Veracruz began to experience industrial unrest. One of the few successful strikes occurred in 1884. Mill hands at the important Puebla mill El Mayorazgo struck in the fall of that year in opposition to a reduced pay scale and increased working hours. They were supported financially by various groups of Puebla workers, and by sombrero makers and tobacco workers of the Federal District as well. An agreement was reached that decreased the work day (they had been frequently working to midnight), abolished script, provided the freedom to buy in noncompany stores, and instituted other reforms. Encouraged by their success, Puebla textile hands formed *La Confederación Obrera en Puebla*. Although the union failed to survive the decade, it was the first textile workers' organization in that important industrial center.[157]

The most widely publicized labor conflict of the decade took place in January 1883 at a British-owned mine in Pinos Altos, in the state of Chihuahua. The owner paid half the workers' wages in script redeemable only at his company store, continuing the practice despite the protests of the miners. A disturbance broke out among the workers, and in attempting to calm it, the owner was badly hurt and later died. Troops were called in, and five workers—Blas Venegas, Cruz Baca, Ramón Mena, Juan Valenzuela, and Francisco Campos—were given a summary court-martial and executed.[158]

Other strikes were called by the construction workers on the railroad lines, by miners in San Luis Potosí, by bakers in Veracruz and the Federal District, and even by public employees of the federal judiciary. Nearly all the strikes failed, broken by strike breakers (*esquiroles* or "squirrels"), by the intervention of the political authorities against the workers, or simply because the workers' reserves were too small to permit them to hold out for more than a few days.[159]

The Constitution of 1857 had not forbidden strikes and had appeared to guarantee the right of workers to organize. The *Codigo Civil*, enacted in 1870 and amended in 1884, defined the right of association still further, but seemed in no way to deny the right for workingmen to organize. In the absence of federal laws specifically

157. González Navarro, "Las huelgas textiles," pp. 208–9.
158. García Cantú, *Socialismo en México*, pp. 110–11.
159. González Navarro, *La vida social*, p. 298.

defining labor's constitutional rights, however, most states passed their own labor legislation. Usually those laws were patterned after Article 925 of the Federal District's Penal Code (1871), which imposed fines and jail sentences for anyone who attempted to "impede the free exercise of industry or labor." This article provided a convenient legal pretext for governmental intervention in labor conflicts against the workers and was used on various occasions.[160]

More often than not, however, the state or federal government's lack of interest in resolving labor conflicts was sufficient to decide it in favor of the owners. Without active government aid, the position of the workers was too weak to enable them to confront their employers.[161] Poorly organized, with scant financial reserves, and faced with a large surplus labor supply, strikes in the 1880s were often acts of desperation and failed because of these conditions alone.

Despite the prosperity of the 1890s, strike activity remained at about the same level as in the previous decade. The issues underlying the conflicts shifted, however, from a predominance of the wage issue, which characterized the conflicts of the 1880s, to an increasing discontent with the nature of industrial work itself—the longer hours that electric lighting permitted, the introduction of new and stringent factory regulations, and the increasing instances of mistreatment. Of the forty-four strikes recorded from 1890 through 1899, nineteen were in the textile industry, eleven on the railroads, five in mining, and three in the tobacco shops of the Federal District. While the textile strikes had remained proportionally the same, strikes on the railroad lines went up, and those in tobacco shops went down.

There were several strikes in the tobacco shops at mid-decade, and then there were no reports of any for an entire decade, until 1905. The reason for this cessation appears to be that although sales and production increased dramatically after 1892, the number of workers engaged in the industry manufacturing cigarettes actually fell from

160. López Aparicio, *El movimiento obrero*, pp. 138–39. González Navarro, *La vida social*, pp. 298, 303.

161. For examples of the authorities' refusal to become involved in labor disputes see González Navarro, *La vida social*, pp. 282–83, 285, 288, 303; Matt S. Meier, "Industrial Unrest in Mexico 1887–1910" (Master's thesis, Mexico City College—now the University of the Americas, 1949), p. 64.

10,397 in 1895 to 6,893 in 1910. The introduction of more efficient methods and labor-saving machinery, particularly the Decoufle crimping process, had forced out of business those shops depending predominately on artisan hand labor. From 743 tobacco shops in Mexico in 1898—undoubtedly a decline from earlier in the decade—the number fell to 351 by 1910, throwing out of work a great number of workers and thereby weakening the bargaining position of those that remained.[162] The fact that three-quarters of the cigarette workers were women even further reduced their bargaining position.

Nonetheless, after the turn of the century, the tobacco workers again began to organize, and a number of strikes occurred. Professor González Navarro mentions five strikes in 1905 and early 1906 and indicates that there may have been more. In October 1905 workers at the important Veracruz factory El Valle Nacional founded the *Gran Liga de Torcedores de Tabacos*. A successful strike followed in which the *Liga* won the important right to serve as the official agent representing the workers before the owners. By the summer of 1906 the *Liga* was strong enough to call a National Congress of Tobacco Workers, attended by eighteen delegates from the major factories in the country.[163]

While the number of strikes by tobacco workers declined in the nineties, railroad strikes increased. Besides the fact of the natural growth of the railroads in that decade, the strikes reflected the increased organization among the workers by the turn of the century. The lines were almost all United States-owned, and North Americans held down nearly all the executive positions. North American workers, along with a few Canadians and Europeans, also dominated the better paying working-class positions. As late as 1909, 68 percent of the engineers on the major lines and 86 percent of the conductors were foreigners, while Mexicans made up the majority only in the lesser-paying skilled jobs of fireman, brakeman, mechanic, and

162. Rosenzweig, "La industria," pp. 362–63; Thompson, *The People of Mexico*, p. 344; González Navarro, *La vida social*, 310–13; *The Mexican Year Book, 1909–1910*, pp. 531–35; El Colegio de México, *Estadísticas económicas*, p. 113.

163. González Navarro, *La vida social*, p. 312; Luis Araiza, *Historia del movimiento obrero mexicano*, (Mexico: n.p., 1964–1965), 2:39–41, 95–98. Their weekly organ was *La Palanca del Obrero*, Mexico City.

boilermaker, as well as the various unskilled jobs such as those of section hand and crew chief. Of those holding the skilled jobs (except engineers and conductors), most were paid hardly better than unskilled workers, and Mexicans were paid less than foreigners doing the same job. Trade unionism was first introduced by the American-based Brotherhood of Locomotive Engineers in 1884, followed by the conductors' Order of Railway Conductors in 1885, the firemen in 1886, the carmen in 1891, and the telegraphers in 1902 and the clerks in 1903. Few Mexicans were "invited" to be members, an unusual procedure of obvious origins, as the American brotherhoods came increasingly dedicated to retaining their monopoly on jobs and promotions.[164]

Unable to break the North American monopoly on jobs, the Mexican employees banded together to form their own brotherhoods. In 1887 *La Sociedad de Ferrocarril Mexicano* was formed in Nuevo Laredo. In San Luis Potosí in August 1890 the *Orden Suprema de Empleados* was founded, its name later being changed to *La Sociedad de Empleados de Ferrocarriles en la República*, a mutualist-oriented brotherhood. Most Mexican railroad unions in the *Porfiriato* were craft unions, however, patterned after the North American brotherhoods, with branches on the various lines throughout the country. They were usually apolitical, fighting for better pay and working conditions. The more ideologically-oriented industrial railroad unions were introduced only later, under President Larzaro Cárdenas (1934–40).[165] Despite their organizational similarities, the Mexican and American unions were separated by fundamental differences in interest, or so it seemed to them; instances of cooperation between their competing unions were rare.

Among the most important Mexican unions was the *Unión de Mecánicos Mexicana*, founded by Teodoro Larrey in Puebla in August of 1900. Later that year, Silvino Rodríguez, returning from a job as a

164. Richard U. Miller, "American Railroad Unions and the National Railways of Mexico: An Exercise in Nineteenth-Century Proletarian Manifest Destiny," *Labor History* 15 (Spring 1974) 243–49.

165. Marcelo N. Rodea, *Historia del movimiento obrero ferrocarrilero en México (1890–1943)* (Mexico: n.p., 1944), pp. 80–82; Miller, "American Railroad Unions and Mexico," pp. 259–60. For a viewpoint which asserts that the Porfirian railroad unions were syndicalist, see Cockcroft, *Intellectual Precursors*, p. 140.

mechanic on the Southern Pacific line in Texas, organized in Chihuahua what later became the major branch of the Mexican mechanics' brotherhood. The following year, the able and dynamic Rodríguez took over the leadership of the entire Mexican mechanics' union, relocating its head offices from Puebla to Chihuahua.[166]

At the turn of the century *La Unión de Caldereros* (boilermakers or steamfitters) was organized by Mexican railroadmen in the shops of the Mexican Central Railroad in Aguascalientes. Several years later, in August of 1903, the steamfitters founded the *Sociedad de Hermanos Caldereros Mexicanos*, and with Blas López as president, enrolled their colleagues throughout the Republic. The *Unión de Fogoneros del Ferrocarril Nacional de México* (firemen) was formed in October 1902. Another major railroad brotherhood, *La Gran Liga Mexicana de Empleados de Ferrocarril*, was founded in January 1904 by Ernesto Hernández Espejel, chief of the Banderilla Station on the *Ferrocarril Interoceánico* and included Mexican telegraph operators, despatchers, station managers, and their assistants. It was officially reconstituted in March 1905, and Felix C. Vera, former editor of a railroad workers' periodical, *El Ferrocarrilero*, was elected president. Eventually the *Liga* came to represent *empleados* (generally, white-collar workers) on the major lines, as well as various groups of brakemen, carpenters, firemen, and even mechanics.[167]

Although a number of short, localized strikes took place in the 1890s on the nation's railway lines, including an important mechanics' strike on the Mexican Central in May 1894 (coinciding with the great U.S. Pullman strike), it was not until the organizational achievements of the early 1900s that major conflicts took place. A strike of American engineers on the Monterrey to Nuevo Laredo line in July 1901 received considerable publicity in the newspapers of the country because Mexican workers agreed to take the place of the strikers, raising the question of why Mexican workers were not employed in such positions on normal runs. Other important conflicts were a strike in March 1902 in the Orizaba shops of the Mexican Railroad; a strike in October 1902 by the Mexican firemen and the American and Mexican

166. Rodea, *Obrero ferrocarrilero*, pp. 99–100. Alfredo Navarrete maintains that Larrey received aid in forming his union from a socialist, Francisco Salinas: Navarrete, *Alto*, pp. 89–92.

167. Rodea, *Obrero ferrocarrilero*, pp. 99–112; Navarrete, *Alto*, pp. 93–103.

engineers (there were several) on the Mexican National lines throughout the north; a strike of brakemen on the *Ferrocarril Interoceánico* in early 1903; and one of the firemen on the Mexican Central between Monterrey and Tampico in October 1905.[168] The major issues motivating the strikes were immediately practical matters such as wages and working conditions, although preference and favoritism for non-Mexicans became more and more a major concern for Mexican railroad workers as the first decade of the twentieth century wore on.

By 1907 the major Mexican railroad brotherhoods and their membership were: *La Gran Liga Mexicana de Empleados del Ferrocarril*, 5,000; *La Unión de Mecánicos Mexicanos*, 3,000; *La Unión de Hermanos Caldereros Mexicanos*, 2,000; *La Unión de Forjadores Mexicanos* (shop iron and metal workers), 1,500. The total unionized railroad men constituted nearly one-half of the railroad workers in the Republic, the greatest percentage of workers organized in any industry before the fall of the Díaz regime in 1911.[169]

The textile workers were not as well-organized as the railroadmen, but from the mid-1890s on into the next decade a growing climate of discontent spread throughout the mills of central Mexico, from Querétaro in the west to the industrial city of Orizaba in the east. The key to understanding this discontent lies in the technological changes in the industry which brought new competitive arrangements and in turn a more rigidly-enforced industrial discipline.

The most critical technological innovation was the introduction into Mexico in the 1890s of high-velocity, electrically-powered machinery, particularly the electric spindle. The new equipment forced basic structural changes in the mills themselves, necessitating greater capital investment in plants as well as equipment, a condition which favored the larger companies with greater resources, usually those backed by foreign capital. The CIDOSA textile firm had originally located near Orizaba because of the abundant water resources in the area, but it was not until 1897 that the Río Blanco mill was run entirely on hydro-electric power. In the United States, textile mills first introduced electric-powered machinery only in 1893. CIDOSA acquired

168. Rodea, *Obrero ferrocarrilero*, pp. 289–92, 300–305; González Navarro, *La vida social*, p. 307; Navarrete, *Alto*, pp. 93–96.
169. González Navarro, *La vida social*, p. 356.

The carding department in La Hormiga cotton textile mill at Tizapán, the Federal District, c. 1906.

the oldest cotton mill in the area, Cocolapán, primarily because of its excellent water resources. The older Hércules mill in Querétaro had converted to electrical power in 1895, and a number of mills in Puebla installed new electrical equipment by the end of the century. Many Puebla mills still operated with equipment installed before 1845, however, and the mills of the Federal District and Coahuila maintained coal-burning or steam-generating facilities for a while longer, unable or unwilling to make the changes.[170]

There were eight strikes in the textile industry from 1890 to 1894, but at least sixteen from 1895 to 1900. The single major issue was wages, but the majority of the grievances related to the workday, the mistreatment, and, in general, the efforts of the owners to change work regulations or factory discipline in order to improve the effi-

170. Keremitsis, *La industria textil*, pp. 99–110; Rosenzweig, "La industria," pp. 333, 341; Yamada, "The Cotton Textile Industry," pp. 19–20, 38–39.

ciency (and profitability) of their operation. The important mill San Antonio de Abad in the Federal District was struck because the administration refused to allow the workers to continue the long-standing practice of bringing *pulque* to the mill for their lunch. The mill hands at San Miguel in Tlaxcala struck when the owner refused to permit them to take off a traditional holiday. In addition, complaints were common wherever new machinery was installed, because workers found that the high-velocity machinery was more difficult to operate than the older types, more fatiguing and exacting.[171] In other words, the older mills, especially in the Federal District where older machinery meant a competitive disadvantage, were rationalizing their production methods both to take advantage of the promise of increased profits held out by the expanding markets of the 1890s and in response to the competition now offered by goods from the newer, more efficient factories.

The times were changing, and still the workers' protests did not move their bosses. Almost all the strikes failed. The only major victory took place in 1898 when seven hundred workers struck the La Colmena mill, located on the outskirts of the Federal District. Significantly, the local and state authorities (of the state of Mexico) forced the factory to take back the strikers and to agree not to decrease wages as they had originally intended to do.[172]

The Mexican economy suffered a sharp reversal at the turn of the century, and its impact on the working men and women of Mexico set the stage for the explosive conflicts that were to take place at mid-decade, especially in the textile industry. During the late 1890s the markets for cotton textiles were expanding fast enough to provide a demand for the production of the new, low cost *manta* and cloth print of the large plants and that of the smaller, less efficient plants as well. Despite the modernization going on, in 1898 old spindles still outnumbered new ones in the mills of Mexico by nearly two to one, and old weaving machinery outnumbered new by a nine-to-five ratio. The recession changed all that. Thirty-one mills closed their doors between 1899 and 1901, forced into bankruptcy by the hard times. Of

171. González Navarro, "Las huelgas textiles," pp. 211–14; Keremitsis, *La industria textil*, pp. 109–10. Of the nineteen strikes between 1890 and 1899, fourteen were in the Federal District.

172. González Navarro, "Las huelgas textiles," pp. 213–14.

those that survived, most invested in the new equipment used by their competitors to keep from going under. By 1907 new spindles outnumbered old by a six to one ratio, and new weaving machinery had almost totally displaced the older, slower machines. Almost all the mills were now operating on hydro-electric power, obtained either from their own generating plant or from public power—which was far from meeting the demand—or by buying power from other mills with a surplus generating capacity.[173]

The technological innovations were accompanied in most mills by stricter industrial regimes for the workers and harsher personnel practices, accelerating a trend noted in the previous decade. The investments had to be paid for, and the workers were forced to assume a major portion of the cost, both in a relative decrease in the "ease" of their work and, often, in absolute declines in their levels of living. However, except for a widespread strike of Puebla mill hands and several conflicts early in 1900, few grievances reached the strike stage during the first half-decade of the twentieth century. The workers' weakness was dramatically underscored during a strike in November of 1900. Wages at Puebla's largest mill, El Mayorazgo, were lowered, and the mill hands quit work *en masse* in protest. The strike spread to nearly all the mills of that city, involving three thousand workers. The governor of the state ignored the workers' appeal for state intervention, and after nearly two weeks the workers returned to their machines with no satisfaction.[174]

The Puebla strike was the last important conflict in the textile industry for nearly five years; only six small strikes took place in five years from 1901 through 1905. On the railroad lines, there were six strikes in 1901, declining to three the following year and falling off to only three from 1903 through mid-1906. There were none in the tobacco industry until 1905, and only two were recorded in mining from 1896 through 1905. Although there were six industrial strikes in 1905, most were short and inconsequential.

Despite the dearth of industrial conflicts during those years, one

173. Keremitsis, *La industria textil*, pp. 105, 110–15; Rosenzweig, "La industria," p. 338.

174. González Navarro, "Las huelgas textiles," pp. 214–15; *El Imparcial*, 14, 23 November 1900.

can detect an undertone of bitterness in the evidence that is available. From the new and important Metepec cotton mill, near Atlixco, Puebla, came a letter written by various workers to the sympathetic director of the Mexico City weekly *La Guacamaya*. "Is it reasonable," the workers asked, "that we, who are slaves to our work, and who provide the impetus for industry . . . after receiving such a small compensation for our work, must also be deprived of the Public Instruction that all civilized nations bestow upon their children?"[175] Unable to change their own fate, some workers were concerned that their children might also have no other opportunity but to work in the mills.

Workers at the El Carmen textile mill in San Martín Texmelucán, Puebla, wrote a bitter letter to the director of *La Guacamaya*, charging that they, the workers, who had the misfortune to be poor, were constantly humiliated by men "who only see in us a vein of ore to be exploited," without any kind of human consideration. The letter went on to request aid from their state government in order to end the "outrages of which we are the victim."[176] The letter made many other charges, including those of harsh treatment, low wages, and inattention of the political authorities to their plight.

One incident which aroused popular indignation during those years was the murder of a poor worker by a man who, because of his wealth and connections, was not punished for his crime. A *corrido* was written and sung about the incident, and its theme fit the mood of many workers: "Only he who has money enjoys the guarantees [of the law]," sang the balladeer, "only the rich get the advantages of the peace."[177]

Yet in the middle of the first decade of the twentieth century, most middle- and upper-class Mexicans were unaware that a labor problem existed. Strikes were regarded as the work of agitators, and the workers' grievances were tucked away in obscure weeklies, unnoticed by the authorities or the general public. Many nonworking-class Mexicans would probably have agreed with one supposedly well-informed

175. *La Guacamaya*, 19 November 1903.
176. Ibid., 23 August 1903.
177. Merle E. Simmons, *The Mexican Corrido as a Source for Interpretive Study of Modern Mexico (1870–1950)* (Bloomington: Indiana University Press, 1957), p. 72.

foreigner who wrote that Mexican workers were a "tractable and easily managed people, seldom rebelling against recognized authority."[178] If the important newspapers carried reports on the "labor question," as it was called in the press of the day, they concerned the United States or Europe, not Mexico. But beneath placid appearances, deep problems lay unresolved, and major questions of social policy went unattended. The dam finally broke in 1906, shattering forever the vaunted *Pax Porfiriana*. "The year of the strikes" was about to begin.[179]

178. Percy F. Martin, *Mexico's Treasure-House (Guanajuato): An Illustrated and Descriptive Account of the Mines and Their Operations in 1906* (New York: The Cheltenham Press, 1906), p. 66.

179. González Navarro, *La vida social*, p. 322.

Chapter 3
The Year of the Strikes

*"The twentieth century worker . . . is not going
to bend his knees before the tyrants."*
—Flier from the *Segundo Círculo de Obreros Libres,*
Puebla, 11 November 1906.

The year of 1906 became the most decisive for Mexican workers of the thirty years of Porfirian rule. Although the first few months were uneventful, Mexican industrial peace was shattered by a surge of strikes beginning in May, as the Mexican worker dramatically claimed his due and demanded to participate in the progress of his nation.

The conflicts caught most nonworking-class Mexicans offguard. The common opinion had been that the indolent, careless *obrero* was too apathetic and ill-adapted by nature to organize for the advancement of his class. In January 1906 the editor of the daily *El Universal* wrote that the Mexican worker did not organize because of his "distinctive character" and commented that, until the workers awoke from their indifference, "the social question" would not arise.[1] Yet even as he was writing, the organization of industrial workers was taking place at a greater rate than at any time since the early years of the *Porfiriato.*

Confrontations took place in the cotton mills of Orizaba, Puebla, and Tlaxcala, in the copper mines of Cananea and Sonora, and among the mechanics of the major railway lines; workers protested low and eroding wages, hazardous working conditions, ill-treatment by foremen, and favoritism shown to foreign employees over Mexican workers. Hidden among these issues were political questions of governmental policy toward the workers and their unions and of the possible relationship between the workers and the revolutionary oppositionist group called the *Partido Liberal Mexicano* (PLM). Amidst rumors of a worker uprising against the foreigners in the land and perhaps even against the regime itself, concern and apprehension

1. (Chihuahua daily), 7 January 1906.

began to grow within the Díaz administration regarding the political implications of the labor conflicts.

Responding to what was perceived as a threat to the political stability of the regime, the national administration began, for the first time in its three decades of rule, to consider the problems of the workers and to search for the means to defuse the accumulating tension and dissatisfaction among several groups of industrial *obreros*. Of those who received such attention, the cotton textile workers of the important mills of Puebla and Orizaba were the most notable.

With the exception of mining, cotton textile manufacturing at mid-decade was the largest industry in Mexico, accounting for almost one-quarter of the total value of manufactured goods produced in the Republic. Thirty-one thousand workers operated the looms and spindles of 150 cotton mills throughout the country. The major centers of cotton textile manufacturing were located in the states of Puebla, Tlaxcala, Veracruz, México, Querétaro, Coahuila, and the Federal District.

At the beginning of the century the most important textile center in Mexico in terms of sales was the city of Puebla, but it was being challenged by the young, aggressive industrial city of Orizaba, Veracruz. By 1906 Puebla had only a slight lead in total production and sales over her nearby rival, and the technical quality of her mills could not compare with the latter's modern plants and equipment. It was in Orizaba and the nearby mill towns that Mexican industrial workers first made their collective protests in the year of the strikes.

Orizaba lies east of Puebla, approximately half-way along the *Camino Real* towards the port of Veracruz. Situated in one of the numerous upland valleys between the coastal lowlands and the central plateau, it is surrounded on two sides by steep, wooded hills, scarred by centuries of charcoal gathering. The nearby Río Blanco provided the source of power for the factories in the area during the early years of this century. The region's natural humidity also served as an important competitive advantage for the Orizaba textile mills, the technical processes often requiring high levels of humidity in the mills.[2]

2. *Mexican Yearbook, 1909–1910*, pp. 524–29; Rosenzweig, "La industria," p. 399. In addition to the humidity, temperatures exceeding ninety degrees were often required. During that same era, for example, Bombay mills kept

Cotton textiles, mainly *manta* and threads for local consumption, were being produced in the area even before the Conquest and continued on through the colonial era. The conservative statesman, Lucas Alamán, in cooperation with the Legrand brothers, saw the natural competitive advantages of the area because of its high humidity and nearness to the cotton plantations of the coast, and in 1838 they initiated the construction of the Cocolapán mill. Completed in 1838, the mill was powered by a thirty-foot high waterwheel and employed 575 spinners and 500 weavers. Hard times hit the cotton textile production from the 1840s for the next several decades, but the construction of the Veracruz-Mexico City railroad in 1873 revived the industry. From 75,000 pieces of *manta* produced in the area in 1876, Orizaba mills increased production to 1,206,040 pieces of *manta* by 1895.[3] Orizaba was fast becoming one of the great industrial centers of the Republic.

By the turn of the century, Orizaba had close to three hundred retail stores, four banks, five breweries—including the important Moctezuma firm—five flour mills, ten tobacco shops, a dressmaking shop, and four iron works. The metropolitan Orizaba area grew from fifty-three thousand people in 1887 to a burgeoning ninety-seven thousand by 1906, one of the fastest growing cities in Mexico.[4]

Yet it was the cotton mills which dominated the economy of Orizaba, accounting for 80 percent of the area's industrial production, according to one estimate. Six cotton mills and a major jute mill were established within the canton, employing approximately seven thousand hands in 1906. The industry produced satin, flannel, calicos, colored shirtings, crepes, serges, and handkerchiefs, as well as yarn and plain *manta*. The jute mill Santa Gertrudis was the largest of its kind in the Republic and made bags, rope, and other fiber products.[5]

One firm, the *Compañía Industrial de Orizaba*, known as CIDOSA, owned four of the mills—Río Blanco, San Lorenzo, Cerritos de San Juan, and Cocolapán. The Río Blanco plant alone contained 15 per-

---

the temperature between 90 and 100 degrees: Morris, *Industrial Labor Force in India*, p. 114.

3. Yamada, "The Cotton Textile Industry," pp. 10–18, 27–28.
4. Ibid., pp. 63–76.
5. Ibid., pp. 48, 68.

cent of the total spindles and looms in the country when constructed in 1892. By the turn of the century, CIDOSA's four mills were capitalized at one-quarter of the invested capital of the entire cotton textile industry and its common stock brought more on the Mexico City exchange than nearly any other enterprise operating in the Republic. Its stockholders could hardly be disappointed in its performance; CIDOSA paid 15 to 25 percent dividends from 1893 to 1900, 12 to 14 percent from 1902 to 1907, and 8 percent from 1908 to 1911. Its products sold well throughout central Mexico and won a grand prize in expositions at Paris and St. Louis.[6]

The other major cotton mill in the area was Santa Rosa, founded by the *Compañía Industrial Veracruzana* (CIV) in 1898. The mill was second to Río Blanco in the value of its production, and its stock sold only slightly lower than CIDOSA on the Mexico City exchange. The firm paid its stockholders 12 to 14 percent dividends from 1902 through to 1911, one of the best records of any of the nation's cotton firms.[7]

Both companies were controlled by French capitalists in residence in Mexico and were financed through domestic and European sources. French entrepreneurs had immigrated to Mexico as early as the 1840s, although most had not established Mexican citizenship. By the 1890s various groups had founded such giant retail-wholesale stores as the Puerto de Veracruz, Puerto de Liverpool, and El Palacio de Hierro, displacing the Germans who had earlier controlled the clothing retail operations. In 1889 Lambert Reynaud founded CIDOSA, aided by major French capitalists Leon Signoret Honnorat, Joseph Tron, Eugenie Roux, and, perhaps the best known industrialist of the era, Thomas Braniff, a North American from Staten Island. CIV was established by those same men and their business partners and was linked administratively to CIDOSA in the person of Antonio Reynaud, director and secretary of CIDOSA and president and treasurer of CIV. In addition, those men also served as members of the board of directors, managers, and investors in other important and powerful firms. Leon Signoret Honnorat, for example, was an investor and a member of the boards of the *Banco de Londres, Cer-*

6. Ibid., pp. 17–20; Rosenzweig, "La industria," pp. 332, 455–57; *El Florecimiento de México* (Mexico: n.p., 1906), pp. 122, 129–30.

7. D'Olwer, "Las inversiones extranjeras," 2:1116–17; *El Florecimiento*, pp. 122, 129–30.

vecería Moctezuma, and the *Compañía Metalúrgica de Monterrey*, among others. Thomas Braniff was president of the *Banco de Londres y México*, manager and director of San Rafael, the most modern paper mill in Mexico, and one of the founders of the *Compañía Fundidora de Fierro y Acero de Monterrey*.[8] Using their considerable economic power and political influences, the men behind CIDOSA and CIV played a major role in the labor crisis of 1906. The mill hands of Orizaba were forced to confront some of the most wealthy and powerful of the nation's industrial elite.

The *Gran Círculo de Obreros Libres*

At the beginning of 1906 the only Orizaba textile workers' organizations were two mutualist societies, the *Sociedad de Socorros Mutuos*, founded in 1873, and the *Círculo Liberal Mutualista*. Neither group was concerned with improving the workers' situation through confrontation with the mills. Either sometime in 1905 or early in 1906 a group of workers from the Río Blanco mill began to meet regularly at the house of Andres Mota to discuss their situation, particularly the necessity of forming a more militant workers' organization than currently existed. Meeting under the auspices of a Protestant missionary, José Rumbia, ostensibly for religious purposes, the group grew to a size of nearly two hundred workers, as workers talked and argued every Sunday about what the goals and tactics of such an organization should be. In April the group agreed upon a name for their union— the *Gran Círculo de Obreros Libres* (GCOL). Some among them must have remembered the early attempts to form a meaningful working-class organization, because the *Gran Círculo* had been the name of the major labor federation in the 1870s. In any case, the GCOL was destined to become the most important labor group in the nation that year. Although sentiment had existed among the founders to limit the organization to mutualist activities, the majority held out for a more combative organization. Members finally decided to form a secret association with the *Partido Liberal Mexicano* (PLM), a revolutionary

8. See Auguste Genin, *Les français au mexique du xvi siècle á nos jours* (Paris: Nouvelles editions Argo, 1931), pp. 430–34; Yamada, "The Cotton Textile Industry," pp. 53–56; Keremitsis, *La industria textil*, pp. 133–38.

movement whose leadership was largely in exile in the United States. While the GCOL's public charter was moderate, a secret charter was drawn up which called for maintaining relations with the PLM and pledged the GCOL to fight against the "abuses of capitalism and the dictatorship of Porfirio Díaz."[9]

Manuel Ávila, an active labor leader in the past, was elected president of the union. José Neira (also spelled Neyra) was chosen as vice-president. Neira was a sympathizer of the PLM and the leading advocate of the more radical position in the debates on union tactics. José Rumbia became an informal advisor to the group.[10]

In May the GCOL established branches at the nearby mill of San Lorenzo and at El Dique in Jalapa, the state capital. By early June a branch had also been established at the Santa Rosa mill. Only one hundred workers at Santa Rosa joined initially, but as time went on, more were recruited. Sometime in May, Manuel Ávila committed suicide over a broken love affair, and Neira assumed the presidency.[11] The consequences of the leadership change were not long in coming.

On 27 May Neira called a meeting to present his program. Only one paragraph of the program has survived. It read: "In case of difficulties with the firms we will strike; if the strike does not accomplish anything we will resort to dynamite or revolution."[12] As might be expected, opinion was divided on the wisdom of either dynamite or revolution as a means of achieving their goals. The workers finally agreed to establish a newspaper entitled *Revolución Social*, indicating that the bolder voices won the day. Neira was elected to run the paper, assisted by Porfirio Meneses and Juan A. Olivares. All were supporters of a politically active stance for the GCOL.

9. González Navarro, *La vida social*, pp. 201–16; Germán y Armando List Arzubide, *La huelga de Río Blanco* (Mexico: Dept. de Biblioteca de la Secretaría de Educación Pública, 1935), pp. 5–8; Petricioli, *La tragedia*, pp. 7–11; Peña, "Apuntes históricos," 29 July, 5 August 1958. The only copy of the secret charter I have seen is in List Arzubide, pp. 14–16, and it contains several inconsistencies; see my "Mexican Textile Labor Movement, 1906–1907: An Analysis of a Labor Crisis" (Ph.D. diss., The American University, 1968), p. 80.

10. Peña, "Apuntes históricos," 5 August 1958.

11. Ibid. 5, 12, and 26 August, 14 October 1958; a flier to "Whoever It May Concern" from *La Comisión de Obreros Industriales de "El Dique,"* Jalapa, Veracruz, GPDC, 31:5889; Petricioli, *La tragedia*, pp. 13–14, 26.

12. Quoted in Peña, "Apuntes históricos," 12 August 1958.

Within the month of May the GCOL had won its first victory. At the insistence of the GCOL and supported by Carlos Herrera, the *jefe político* of Orizaba, an unpopular supervisor was reprimanded by the administrator of the Río Blanco mill for intentionally injuring a worker. Even more important, CIDOSA agreed to abolish the hated system of fines at all their mills in the area.[13] Herrera's aid would prove important in the months ahead.

Encouraged, the GCOL opened a full-scale propaganda campaign to attract more workers. They attacked "the oppressive hand of capital," demanding better working conditions and fair treatment. As citizens of the Republic, they insisted that they deserved to be treated with justice and respect.[14] The governor of the state began to send reports of pending strikes and copies of the workers' fliers and broadsides to President Díaz. In one long, eloquent flier the workers of El Dique asked, "Why do we, who have no more fault than to be born of poor parents, not have even our most just demands met?"[15] They went on to demand justice and even raised the specter of the rising of the masses in the French Revolution as a thinly veiled threat to the authorities.

Then in early June the first issue of *Revolución Social* appeared in the mills of Orizaba and the nearby states of Puebla and Tlaxcala. Its message was militant and tough, arousing the fears of both the administration of the mills and the government. In the lead article, an open letter to all the workers of the Republic, Porfirio Meneses Córdova condemned the industrialists and called for violence, if necessary, "in order to obtain our golden dream."[16] The second article was written by José Neira and was entitled "In the Arena." An eloquent, sometimes moving denunciation of the conditions under which Mexican textile workers labored, the article placed the blame not only on the capitalists but on "the despotic regime of A CRIMINAL AND CORRUPT GOVERNMENT." He called for a struggle to the death

13. Ibid., 12, 18 August 1958. Fines continued to be levied, however, and were a constant source of discontent; see *El Paladín*, 16 July, 23 August 1906.

14. Carlos Herrera to Teodoro A. Dehesa, governor of Veracruz, 28 May 1906, *Seminario Histórico de la Universidad Veracruzana* (hereafter cited as SHUV), Jalapa, Veracruz.

15. GPDC, 31:5889.

16. Peña, "Apuntes históricos," 26 August 1958; see also GPDC, 31:6373.

against tyranny, saying that "the cowards will pound the rostrum while the valiant will launch the fight in search of our freedom."[17]

The first issue contained other articles and poems, all in the same vein. Atanasia Guerrero declared that "if the great firms, if the greedy capitalists refuse to grant us that which in justice belongs to us, we will assert ourselves by force; we will wash our land with blood, avenging past and present injustices."[18] The paper appeared publicly only once or twice after its first issue, and perhaps several times clandestinely, before it was suppressed.[19]

The day after the appearance of *Revolución Social*, the GCOL won another confrontation with CIDOSA, but this phase of the history of the union was fast drawing to a close. On Sunday, 14 June, Carlos Herrera led a squad of *rurales* to arrest the leaders of the GCOL, then meeting in secret session. News of the impending arrests reached the meeting, and most of the officers managed to escape. A few were caught and consigned to the military on the charge of sedition. Among those who escaped were Neira, Juan Olivares, and Porfirio Meneses—all three of whom were destined to play a larger role in the conflicts in the years ahead.[20]

The future of the *Gran Círculo* looked grim. Few of the original leaders survived the purge, and official hostility toward the union seemed assured. Yet the issues and the discontent were real and could hardly be expected to disappear with the repression of the union's officers. In times of trouble and need, men have always been found to assume the burden of leadership. And even defeat may be instructive.

17. Peña, "Apuntes históricos," 26 August 1958. Capitals are in the original.

18. Ibid.

19. Ibid., 19 August 1958. Peña mentions one other edition around 10 June 1906 but concedes that some accounts tell of another, secret issue. Petricioli (*La tragedia*, p. 15) states that there were three public editions and others published secretly. Sources in the Díaz papers refer to two clandestine issues, one on 17 June in Río Blanco and another on 24 June at the Cerritos mill: name illegible to Díaz, 29 June 1906, Veracruz, GPDC, 31.

20. Herrera to Dehesa, 4 June 1906, SHUV, 1906, 22-L; Peña, "Apuntes históricos," 2 September, 14 October 1958; Petricioli, *La tragedia*, pp. 21–26, 31–32. For an official version of these events, see a report by Lic. Ramón Rocha, judge of the *primera instancia* in Orizaba, to Gen. Rosalino Martínez, 9 January 1907, GPDC, 32:933.

The early, radical phase had given the workers an opportunity to articulate their grievances, and it had provided initial victories to show that with organization they might have a chance to change things. It had also shown that the government would not tolerate threats of violence or attacks on the authorities. All of these lessons proved valuable for the hard times ahead.

Hardly a week after the flight of José Neira and his fellow officers, a group of workers representing the major mills of the area offered the presidency of the union to José Morales, one of the few Mexican foremen at the Río Blanco mill. Accepting the charge, Morales resigned his job and immediately informed the political chief of Orizaba, Carlos Herrera, that the new GCOL would request recognition from the government. Morales admitted past mistakes of the GCOL and promised to obey the law and support the government. Eventually, on Herrera's recommendation, both the governor of the state, Teodoro A. Dehesa, and Díaz formally recognized the union. The president grumpily informed Dehesa, however, that he would be responsible if the new group did not obey the laws.[21]

The Orizaba authorities, notably Herrera and Lic. Ramón Rocha, a federal judge of the area, went to considerable efforts to gain the confidence of the officers of the reconstituted GCOL. Both showed willingness to aid the workers because, as Rocha explained to Dehesa, this was the best way to keep the workers peaceful and law-abiding. Díaz went out of his way to compliment Rocha on his approach and expressed the hope that his good work would be successful.[22]

By July Morales had brought all the textile mills of the area into the GCOL and had begun a period of rapid growth which by the end of the year had added branches in mills in Tlaxcala, Puebla, México, and the Federal District. In addition, contacts had been established with mill hands of a number of other states. The most important addition

21. Peña, "Apuntes históricos," 23, 30 September 1958; José Morales to Carlos Herrera, 23 June 1906 in Peña, "Apuntes históricos," 30 September, 7 October 1958; *El Periódico Oficial del Estado de Veracruz*, 22 September 1906, p. 2.

22. Ramón E. Rocha to Dehesa, 13 October 1906, in covering letter from Dehesa to Díaz, 20 October 1906, GPDC, 31:13171; Díaz to Dehesa, 23 October 1906, GPDC, 31:13175.

was made early in October when Pascual Mendoza, president of the Puebla textile workers' *Liga Obrera Esteban de Antuñano*, sent word to Morales that his union would be willing to join the GCOL as an independent affiliate, changing its name to the *Segundo Gran Círculo de Obreros Libres del Estado de Puebla*. Lic. Rocha estimated that by December the total membership of the union was between nine and ten thousand workers.[23]

Meanwhile, Morales had begun a campaign to force CIDOSA to change a number of its regulations and policies. In late June he presented to the administration of the Río Blanco mill a list of grievances, including an unannounced extension of the workday, the practice of discounting wages to pay for worn-out tools, the levying of fines for faults in the finished products, and the hated system of script to be used at the company store. A 5 percent wage increase was also requested. The company sent a terse reply, saying that the petition would be given to the proper person.[24]

Perhaps wishing to make a point, in mid-July the GCOL struck at the Río Blanco mill over the regulation that forced workers leaving the mill for lunch to register in the time book, often standing in line most of the lunch hour.[25] The outcome is not known, but the owners and managers for the most part resisted any changes in factory regulations that would appear as concessions to the union.

Confronted with complete owner intransigence, the main thrust of the *Gran Círculo*'s drive turned toward forcing the government to intervene. Following a practice that had become an important means by which the workers throughout the Republic publicized their grievances, in July the Santa Rosa branch of the GCOL sent an open letter to the Mexico City newspaper *El Paladín* outlining their grievances. The letter noted particularly the fines and other financial penalties that reduced their already meager earnings. In addition, it requested

23. González Navarro, *La vida social*, p. 331; Peña, "Apuntes históricos," 2 September, 7, 21 October, 4, 11 November 1958; Rocha to Gen. Martínez, 9 January 1907, GPDC, 32:933. (Note: references to multi-page documents in the GPDC will be to the first page of that document.) I suspect that the membership figure is too high if it is supposed to reflect dues-paying members.

24. Peña, "Apuntes históricos," 30 September 1958.

25. Petricioli, *La tragedia*, p. 33.

that compulsory schooling be provided and complained about the poor treatment the workers received from the *rurales* who guarded the mills, and the lack of treatment they received from the company doctor. The workers accused the Necoxtla officials of favoring the mill owners in labor disputes and specifically requested government intervention to force the owners to resolve their problems. Several days later *El Paladín* carried a letter from the GCOL announcing that they were sending a delegation to deliver a petition to Governor Dehesa outlining their grievances. Mexico was a democratic country, the workers wrote, and therefore they had the right "to be treated as citizens." *El Paladín* later carried a notice that the Governor had received the petition and that, according to the paper, he intended to remedy the situation.[26]

Significantly, one issue received immediate attention. Morales had collected complaints about the local police and the federal *rurales* and had presented them to Herrera. The *jefe político* passed them on to Dehesa, and sometime in July the local head of the *rurales* was replaced with a more amenable officer, despite the protest of the rank and file *rurales*. The new chief met with the officials of the GCOL and told them to report any future abuse directly to him. On the other hand, Morales received no cooperation at all when he requested that the local authorities of the textile village of Río Blanco investigate charges of police brutality, excessive fines, and general harassment of his workers by the local police. The mayor of Río Blanco de Tenango was an official of the CIDOSA mill.[27]

Throughout the summer months, the *Gran Círculo* tried to force official intervention into their conflicts with the mills or publicly to shame the firms into action on their petitions. Neither effort was successful, beyond the replacement of the head of the *rurales*. Yet while the textile workers attempted to resolve their grievances without striking, other workers were less patient. Of the ten industrial strikes

26. *El Paladín*, 16, 22 July, 5 August 1906. The mayor of Necoxtla was also the company doctor at the Santa Rosa mill, a position paid for by deductions from the workers' wages; *El Paladín*, 26 August 1906.

27. Peña, "Apuntes históricos," 21, 28 October 1958; *El Paladín*, 2 August 1906; workers at Santa Rosa to Ramón Corral, 29 October 1906, AGN-Gob, leg. 817. The *rurales* were administered by the *Secretaría de Gobernación*, headed by Corral.

between June and the end of August, several were of major importance.

Cananea Copper Workers' Strike

Colonel William C. Greene was a hard-headed, wily American entrepreneur, and when he was given the chance to purchase the rights to the huge copper deposit in the isolated northwestern town of Cananea, Sonora, he seized the opportunity. Through shrewd deals and a rising market, Greene built his investment into a multimillion dollar operation. His firm, the Cananea Consolidated Copper Company, employed about thirty-five hundred men, approximately one-third of them Americans. Greene paid Mexicans a standard wage of three *pesos* a day for common laborers, good wages for workers at that time. Nonetheless, his workers were discontented over the high prices of the company store and, what was particularly galling to the Mexican workers, the fact that American miners received double the pay that their Mexican comrades collected for the same work.[28]

Rumors were circulating in early 1906 of an impending workers "revolt" and of revolutionary forces at work among the workers. The company feared trouble, and its armed guards were on the alert. As an added precaution, Col. Greene was assigned a special code for messages to Col. E. Kosterlitsky, head of the federal *rurales* for the state of Sonora; the code was to be used in case of hostilities by the miners.[29] The trouble was not long in coming.

In the evening of 31 May the night shift of the Oversight mine received word that beginning in the morning the company was planning a work contract change that would result in miners being laid off

28. Bernstein, *Mexican Mining Industry*, pp. 58–59; Lyle C. Brown, "The Mexican Liberals and Their Struggle Against the Díaz Dictatorship: 1900–1906," *Anthology Mexico City College, 1956* (Mexico: Mexico City College Press, 1956), p. 329; Greene was roundly criticized after the trouble there by one American who blamed the disturbance on the fact that Greene paid too high wages to Mexicans, who did not have "the spirit of advancement and self betterment" of their American counterparts; Tays, "Present Labor Conditions in Mexico," p. 624.

29. A. G. Dwight to Col. Kosterlitsky, 31 May 1906, GPDC, 31:6183.

and an increased work load for those remaining. As their shift was leaving the mine just before dawn, they began shouting "Five *pesos* and eight hours of work; *Viva México!*"[30] The miners on the day shift refused to enter the mine, and other sections of the copper complex were struck as soon as the word was received of the new contract. Miners' representatives were unable to reach an agreement with the administration during negotiations held throughout the morning, and the growing crowds of restless strikers eventually began to march through the streets of Cananea, recruiting workers from the various company installations and workshops. Met with water hoses and then rifle fire from the two American supervisors of the company lumber yard, the enraged workers killed the supervisors and set fire to the structure. Throughout that day and the next, confrontations between the workers and the armed American guards of the mines, as well as the town police, resulted in at least eighteen Mexicans dead and a number wounded.[31] The workers were, for the most part, unarmed.

The number killed may be higher; one official account listed twelve dead on the first day, and armed clashes occurred throughout the next day. Another report confirmed the figure for the first day but indicated that many of the wounded would die because the Americans had used "dum-dum" bullets.[32]

On the second day of the unrest, three hundred American volun-

30. The most complete account of the strike is Brown, "The Mexican Liberals," pp. 328–43. For the personal account of Esteban Baca Calderón, one of the leaders of the workers, see his *Juicio sobre la guerra del yaqui y génesis de la huelga de Cananea*. For documents, see Gonzalo Mota and Ignacio Morales, *El General Esteban Baca Calderón* (Mexico: n.p., 1917), pp. 7–17; Manuel González Ramírez, ed., *La huelga de Cananea* (Mexico: Fondo de Cultura Económica, 1956); Francisco Medina Hoyos, *Cananea, Cuna de la Revolución Mexicana: En el cincuentenario de la primera gran huelga proletaria de México* (Mexico: CTM, 1956); Cesár Tapia Quijada, *Apuntes sobre la huelga de Cananea* (Hermosillo, Sonora: University of Sonora, 1956); Manuel J. Aguirre, *Cananea: garras del imperialísmo en la entrañas de Mexico* (Mexico: Libro-Mex, 1958).

31. Calderón, *Juicio sobre Cananea*, pp. 31–32; Brown, "The Mexican Liberals," p. 335. That the violence was initiated by the Americans at the lumber yard is confirmed by two sources: Kosterlitzky to Díaz, 6 June 1906, GPDC, 31, and Thomas H. Rynning, *Gun Notches, the Life Story of a Cowboy-Soldier* (New York: Frederick A. Stokes Co., 1931), p. 306.

32. González Ramírez, *La huelga*, pp. 37, 123.

teers from Naco, Arizona, arrived to help restore order. They had accompanied the Governor of Sonora, Rafael Izábal, who had accepted their services, fearing that the crack *Cordada rural* outfit under Col. Kosterlitsky would not arrive at the remote Sonoran town in time to prevent further violence. Captain Thomas Rynning of the Arizona Rangers had volunteered unofficially to lead the group, after telephone calls by Greene gave an exaggerated picture of the threat to American lives posed by the Mexican strikers.[33]

The American volunteers found everything under control and were sent back across the border when Kosterlitsky arrived on the afternoon of 2 June. But when word filtered back to Mexico of the volunteers, all hell broke loose. The great bulk of the Mexican press, and presumably most of the Mexican people, viewed the expedition as nothing less than an invasion of Mexican territory, violating Mexico's national sovereignty. The presence of Rynning and several fellow rangers made matters worse by giving the appearance of official U.S. involvement.[34] The fact that Mexicans had been killed by American guards at the mines further incensed most Mexicans, who saw no difference between the guards and the volunteers.

The outrage crossed political lines. The important conservative, procleric daily *El Estandarte* of San Luis Potosí condemned Izábal, asking: "In fifty years have we so little advanced that the same crimes [U.S. invasion of Mexico in 1846–1848] can happen again?"[35] The business and commercial weekly, *El Progreso Latino*, was markedly

33. Brown, "The Mexican Liberals," pp. 337–38. Rynning's autobiography is factually inaccurate in places, but as an example of Western American views of Mexico and Mexicans at the turn of the century, it is undoubtedly, if unfortunately, accurate..

34. The territorial governor of Arizona refused Rynning's request to head the expedition, but the telegram arrived too late: Brown, "The Mexican Liberals," p. 336. The United States officially offered to intervene, but Díaz declined: Root to Thompson, 2 June 1906 in cover letter Thompson to Sec. of State, 4 June 1906, U.S., Department of State, National Archives, Washington, D.C. (hereafter abbreviated as USNA). The Mexican Vice-Consul in Douglas was instructed "under no circumstances" to allow the volunteers cross the border. His instructions also arrived too late: Ignacio Mariscal (secretary of Foreign Relations) to Antonio Maza, 2 June 1906, AGN-Gob, unnumbered, entitled "Asuntos Federales, 1905–06: Penitenciaria," leg. 4.

35. *El Estandarte*, 7 June 1906.

sympathetic to the Cananea miners, picturing them as Mexicans fighting for their rights against foreigners, as did such dailies as the anticleric *El Diario del Hogar* and the procleric *El Tiempo* and regional papers such as *El Obrero de Tepic, El Observador,* and *El Universal*; all expressed indignation and outrage at the incident, often praising the miners for their devotion to their country. One group of citizens even filed a legal suit against the government of Sonora under a section of Article 1077 of the penal Code, which provided punishment for those aiding or allowing a violation of national territory by foreign elements.[36] (Governor Izábal defended his enlistment of the American volunteers on the technical grounds that they had entered Mexico legally as individuals and then had volunteered to go to Cananea under his command.)

The government initially suggested to the Governor of Sonora that those responsible for the disorder be severely punished but thought better of it as the public outrage mounted. Ramón Corral, vice president and secretary of *gobernación*, refused the Governor's suggestion that the major agitators (according to the government's investigation, Manuel Diéguez, Esteban Calderón, and José María Ibarra) be executed, saying that such an example would have a bad effect on an already agitated public.[37] Díaz acknowledged that the intervention of the Americans forced him to deal with public opinion, "making foolish people happy."[38]

Yet the old *Caudillo* made no effort to reprimand the governor, much less prosecute him. Instead, the federal government furnished Izábal with a detailed report of the affair and then had it published under the governor's name, asserting that the volunteers were not

36. See *El Progreso Latino*, 28 August, 7 September 1906; *El Universal*, 10 June 1906; *El Observador*, 10 June 1906; *El Obrero de Tepec*, 30 June 1906; *El País*, 1 August 1906. See González Ramírez, *La huelga*, pp. 88–105, for other examples.

37. Corral to Izábal, 2 June 1906, Izábal to Corral, 6 June 1906, and Corral to Izábel, 8 June 1906, in González Ramírez, *La huelga*, pp. 47, 78–79, 83. This opinion was supported by the important Catholic daily, *El Tiempo*; in its 6 June 1906 edition it warned that the execution of any of the strikers would cause bitter criticism against those who ordered it..

38. Quoted in Ronald Chambers, "Cananea, 1906: A Harbinger of Warning," mimeographed (Paper, Department of History, University of the Americas, 1972), p. 28.

U.S. military personnel but merely American citizens who desired to go to Cananea for personal reasons, as was their right under Mexican law. The report also maintained that the workers had no just cause for striking or for causing any disturbance.[39] With no apologies and no regrets, Díaz must have appeared in the minds of many Mexicans to place himself on the side of the foreigners, condoning an affront to national dignity and pride. Whatever Izábal's rationalization, many Mexicans must have believed that what happened at Cananea was an obvious infringement of national sovereignty. And the image was etched in blood—Mexican blood shed by Americans. "National territory may or may not have been violated," wrote the editor of *El Cosmopolita*, "what no one denies is that . . . Mexicans were villainously assassinated by Yankees during the strike at Cananea."[40] It is hard to see how the regime of Porfirio Díaz could have avoided that indictment.

A major problem of historical interpretation remains to be explored. Historians have generally interpreted the Cananea strike to have been politically motivated, instigated by the Revolutionary Junta of the *Partido Liberal Mexicano* as part of its program to overthrow the dictatorship of Porfirio Díaz.[41] The evidence seems convincing enough. The two major workers' representatives were admitted Liberal sympathizers, influenced to support the PLM through reading the party's organ, *Regeneración*. These two, Manuel M. Diéguez and Esteban B. Calderón, helped establish an anti-Díaz political group called the *Unión Liberal Humanidad* early in 1906. Calderón worked in various jobs at the mine, while Diéguez was an assistant cashier at Oversight Mine. The *Unión Liberal Humanidad* was small. Its members included some miners, but it was generally composed of skilled artisans, shopkeepers from the town, and white-collar employees of the

39. The report was published in *El Diario Oficial de los Estados Unidos Mexicanos* 84 (28 June 1906): 806–8.

40. 24 June 1906 (an Orizaba weekly).

41. See David M. Pletcher, *Rails, Mines, and Progress: Seven American Promoters in Mexico, 1867–1911* (Ithaca: Cornell University Press, 1958) and Lowell L. Blaisdell, *The Desert Revolution: Baja California, 1911* (Madison: University of Wisconsin Press, 1962), p. 8. The major exceptions are Brown, "The Mexican Liberals," pp. 342–43, and Aguirre, *Cananea*, pp. 76–86.

mine. The group was in contact with members of the *Partido Liberal Mexicano* (PLM) and in particular with the PLM's Revolutionary Junta located in St. Louis, Missouri. A secret organization, the *Club Liberal de Cananea*, was formed in April to organize workers both in the mines and in the town as the first step in extending the influence of the PLM throughout Mexico under the guise of a miners' league. Word of their plans leaked out, however, and Díaz received a warning through Col. Kosterlitsky.[42] Nevertheless, before counteraction could be taken, the workers struck.

As with so many historical events, the strike at Cananea might have been expected, but it probably was not planned. The Junta in St. Louis denied having anything to do with it, asserting that they had only published the truth about conditions at Cananea. Given the illegality of using American soil for revolutionary acts against friendly governments, such a position was to be expected. Writing years later, however, Calderón denied having instigated the strike. He claimed that it had been spontaneous and that Liberal leadership had simply tried to regain control over the strikers.[43] This is important evidence, because Calderón had no motive to deny his leadership at the time of his writing. Also important is that Ricardo Flores Magón, the leader of the Junta, wrote to a follower in Cananea on the eve of the strike and failed to mention either the strike or any Liberal effort to organize the miners. Indeed, Ricardo, his brother Enrique, and Juan Sarabia, another important member of the Junta, had fled to Canada to avoid persecution by both hostile American authorities and Mexican agents and may have been out of touch with the Cananea situation altogether. Of the leaders, only Antonio Villarrael, Librado Rivera, and Manuel Sarabia remained behind in St. Louis.[44]

On the other hand, a clandestine circular made the rounds the day of the strike, calling for an open revolt against Díaz. In his later recollections, however, Calderón insisted that the circular was not the

42. Calderón, *Juicio sobre Cananea*, p. 21; Brown, "The Mexican Liberals," pp. 328–32; Ramírez, *La huelga*, pp. 106–11; M. Dweight to Col. E. Kosterlitzky, 31 May 1906 in cover letter Kosterlitzky to Díaz, 1 June 1906, GPDC, 31:6183.

43. Brown, "The Mexican Liberals," p. 342–43.

44. R. F. Magón to Gabriel Rúbica, 27 May 1906, Dept. of Justice, RG 60, exp. 30, Appel. Case 21153, USNA. Brown, "The Mexican Liberals," p. 342.

work of the Liberals, pointing out that it was simply written and crudely printed, indicating that the author was not a man of "intellectual resources."[45] All in all, the evidence seems to indicate that the strike was spontaneous and not a conspiracy of the PLM to begin the revolution against the regime. However, the government had its own motives for stressing conspiracy.

In the months that followed Cananea, the federal government, in its efforts to have Liberals extradited from the United States to stand trial in Mexico, accused them of fomenting the Cananea strike. Anxious to crush the PLM, Mexican authorities even kidnapped Manuel Sarabia from Douglas, Arizona, and spirited him across the border to stand trial. One of the crimes with which he was charged was the incitement of sedition and riot at Cananea. Forced to take action by the publicity given to the kidnapping by the American press, U.S. officials reluctantly ordered an investigation of the affair. In order to justify this unusual manner of extradition, the Mexican government presented two witnesses to testify against Sarabia. First, a representative from the Furlong Detective Agency, which had been hired by the Mexican government, testified that one of their agents had gained the friendship of Sarabia and that the latter had admitted that he was aware of the conspiracy to instigate a strike at Cananea. Buttressing the government's position was the second witness, Col. Greene himself. Greene testified that Sarabia had been in Cananea the day of the strike and published "incendiary handbills at Cananea, made inflammatory speeches, and took a very prominent part in organizing the mob."[46]

45. For a copy of the circular, see González Ramírez, *La huelga*, pp. 19–20. Calderón, *Juicia sobre Cananea*, p. 40.

46. Thomas Furlong to Enrique C. Creel, 2 January 1908, Los Angeles, U.S., *Archivo Central de la Ministería de Relaciones Exteriores* (hereafter cited as Rel), *Ramo de Ricardo Flores Magón* et al. (hereafter cited as Rel-RFM), L-E-931; W. C. Greene to Asst. Sec. of State (Robert E. Bacon), 5 July 1907, Justice, RG 60, no. 90755, USNA. Greene had some difficulty deciding exactly who was to blame. He was quoted as saying that his business enemies fomented the strike to drive his company's stock down on the New York Stock Exchange (*El Correo*, Chihuahua daily, 1 September 1906). Charges were also made by Greene and others that certain Americans were among those who instigated the strike, but no evidence was given; Fenochio to Díaz, 6 June 1906, Magdalena, Sonora, GPDC, 31:1128; Gen. Luis Torres to Díaz, 8 June 1906, GPDC, 31:8294.

No other evidence supported these charges, however. Sarabia was declared ineligible for extradition by the American court reviewing the matter, and Mexican authorities were asked to return him forthwith. Reluctantly they complied. The workers and Liberals arrested at Cananea were not so lucky. Twenty-five prisoners were remitted to the state capital to stand trial. Eventually, a number of them were sentenced to hard labor at the federal prison at Veracruz, San Juan de Ulúa, where they remained until their release after the fall of Díaz.[47]

Whoever shares the blame or the glory of Cananea, the obscure should not take precedence over the obvious. First, whatever their role in the strike itself, Liberal organization and propaganda prior to the strike helped prepare an environment favorable to the rebellion that eventually took place.[48] Second, the effect of what transpired at Cananea is by far the most critical question in this analysis. It is clear that the regime suffered from the adverse reaction of many Mexicans to Cananea, and if its apparent strength in June of 1906 seemed to belie this, appearances turned out to be deceiving. Cananea may well have been the watershed of the Old Regime. Almost five years later, the once unassailable regime of Don Porfirio crumbled under the assault of small bands of determined men. Cananea was the beginning.

Railroad Mechanics' Strike

Another important strike that summer was one called by the mechanics on the Mexican Central Railroad. Led by Silvino Rodríguez, the well-organized, Chihuahua-based Union of Mexican Mechanics struck the line in late July, shutting down repair shops all the way to Mexico City. By mid-August the original fifteen hundred mechanics had been joined by nearly three thousand other employees of the Mexican Central, creating one of the most economically critical work stoppages to date in the Republic.[49]

47. Ward S. Albro, "El secuestro de Manuel Sarabia," *Historia Mexicana* 18 (January–March 1969): 400–407. Fenochio to Díaz, 26 June 1906, GPDC, 31:1352; Brown, "The Mexican Liberals," p. 338.

48. Brown, "The Mexican Liberals," p. 343.

49. Gov. of Chihuahua (Enrique C. Creel), 25 July 1906, GPDC, 31:1733; Bernardo Reyes (gov. of Nuevo León) to Díaz, 29 July 1906, *Archivo de General Bernardo Reyes* (hereafter AGBR), Mexico City, Correspondencia del Pres-

The major issues were the right of the union to bargain collectively for the mechanics, overtime pay, apprenticeship regulations, length of workday, dismissal without cause (referring particularly to the firing of union officers), seniority rights, and equal pay for equal work. The latter grievance centered on the bitterly disputed practice of paying higher wages to Americans than to Mexicans doing the same work.[50]

The governor of Chihuahua, Enrique Creel, kept in touch with the developments, privately suggesting to the president that if the railroads had been willing to pay wages as high as other lines and pay them equally without regard to nationality, the trouble would not have arisen. Díaz, however, considered the workers' demands unacceptable to the company. At the suggestion of Creel, and at the request of the mechanics' union, Díaz agreed to arbitrate the conflict.[51]

In an historic hearing—a Mexican president serving as the arbitrator of a major labor dispute—the president received Silvino Rodríguez and his commission in the National Palace. After the amenities were concluded, Díaz proceeded to deliver his statement without interruption or comment. His remarks would be, he began, the position of the government on this and similar matters. Expressing his personal sympathy for the workers and noting that they undoubtedly deserved the support of the government, the president nonetheless called their demands "notorious and unjust and unacceptable," because, he asserted, they violated the prerogatives of the company and they violated the Constitution of 1857—which articles he did not specify.

---

idente, 1903–1909. The strike was sympathetically covered by the conservative San Luis Potosí daily *El Estandarte*; see 2, 4, 14 August 1906.

50. The copy of grievances in C. R. Hudson (vice-pres. Mexican Central) to Lic. Justino Fernández, 8 August 1906, GPDC, 31:9031, contains the company's comments such as "very objectional," "ridiculous," "absurd" for most of the seventeen articles.

51. Creel to Díaz, 28 July 1906, GPDC, 31:9832; Díaz to Creel, 1 August 1906, appendage to Creel to Díaz, 28 July 1906, GPDC, 31:9832; Creel to Díaz, 3 August 1906, GPDC, 31:9889; Díaz to Creel, no date, appendage to Creel to Díaz, 3 August 1906, GPDC, 31:9889: Lic. Diodoro Batalla (workers' lawyer) to Díaz, 6 August 1906, GPDC, 31:9931. Marcelo N. Rodea gives a slightly different version of events leading to the arbitration; Rodea, *Historia del movimiento obrero ferrocarrilero en México: (1890–1943)* (Mexico: n.p., 1944), pp. 308–11.

Further, Díaz maintained that the national progress depended upon guaranteeing the profits of domestic and foreign investors, as did ultimately the welfare of the workers themselves. "So it is," Díaz continued, "that the government is resolved, when it is within its power, to give these guarantees to capital."[52] *El Diario del Hogar's* reporter also noted that the president spoke in a benevolent and paternal tone, but with the firmness which characterized the manner in which he always treated "the sacred national interests."

Rodríguez and his men listened to the president in uneasy silence. When Díaz finished, Rodríguez rose and, speaking for the commission, noted that they too were interested in the welfare of their nation. He asked Díaz to see that the company take back all the strikers and, where justified, convince the company to improve their conditions. Díaz replied that he was truly interested in their welfare and that as proof he would do what he could to obtain whatever was just and legitimate for the workers. Afterwards, the representatives were promised by Ramón Corral that he would always be willing to listen to their just grievances.[53] Beaten, offered only vague promises, the railroadmen went back to work.

Rumors of Revolt

The railroad conflict had taken place in the midst of increasing rumors that Mexican workers were involved in a vast, underground conspiracy to overthrow the government and drive all foreigners out of Mexico.[54] The date of the uprising was supposedly 16 September, the anniversary of Padre Hidalgo's revolt against Spanish rule. The U.S. State Department was not a little concerned, despite assurances from Díaz that such rumors were completely unfounded. Reports from American consuls throughout the country generally played down the possibility of a worker revolt, although several commented

52. *El Diario del Hogar*, 14 August 1906.

53. *El País*, 14 August 1906.

54. In fact Díaz directly related his desire to arbitrate the conflict to his concern over increasing signs of a rumored worker-PLM uprising; F. Mallen to Díaz, 11 August 1906, GPDC, 34:1868 (letter encountered in a 1909 legajo).

that there were certainly concrete reasons for the workers to be discontented with their lot.[55]

Privately, the regime was not completely confident and indeed believed that such an uprising was quite possible. Authorities were well aware that the PLM was planning a revolution against the government and had reason to believe that the labor movements at Cananea and Orizaba had strong links with the Liberals. This belief was underscored in late July by warnings from the governors of the states of Chihuahua and Nuevo León of a possible PLM-led workers' revolt in the north. At the same time, Díaz had received certain documents intercepted by the postal service that were to have been delivered to Americans, demanding that they leave the country by 16 September. From the government's perspective, therefore, the threat was real, not rhetorical, and even though leaders from the textile and railroad unions had protested their peaceful intentions, the regime was preparing for the worst. Federal troops were assigned to stations in Orizaba and Cananea to take care of any problems that might develop in these already troubled towns.[56]

The traditional independence celebrations in mid-September passed without incident, but on the night of 26 September a small group of Liberals attacked the town of Jiménez, Coahuila. Within the next few days, other PLM organizations had risen elsewhere in Coahuila and in the states of Tamaulipas and Veracruz as well. All were put down, and the rebels were either killed, captured, or dispersed. A major move against Ciudad Juárez in Chihuahua and another against

55. Acting secretary of state (Robert Bacon) to Ambassador Thompson, U.S., Dept. of State, *Papers Relating to the Foreign Relations of the United States, Part II, 1906* (Washington, D.C.: Government Printing Office, 1862–), p. 1125. The American press avidly circulated these rumors; see major articles in *Harper's Weekly*, 25 August 1906 and *The New York Herald*, 10 August 1906. See the reports of the consuls in Thompson to Asst. Sec. of State, 20 July 1906, State, RG 59, despatch 40, USNA.

56. Creel to Díaz, 24 July 1906, GPDC, 31:8128; Reyes to Díaz, 24 July 1906, GPDC, 31:8974; Fenochio to Díaz, 26 July 1906, GPDC, 31:8574, 8619; Simón Machuca to Díaz, 22 July 1906, Eagle Pass, Texas, GPDC, 31:7775; José Morales to Díaz, 10 September 1906, GPDC, 31:11375; Morales to Díaz, 8 October 1906, GPDC, 31:12749; Reyes to Díaz, 24 July 1906, GPDC, 31:8974 contains a letter from railroad workers protesting their peaceful intentions; see also Rodea, *Historia obrero ferrocarrilero*, p. 316.

Agua Prieta, Sonora, were betrayed by informers and many of the Liberals arrested.[57] The time would come when armed men rising from the countryside would not be turned back, but that time had not yet arrived.

In the industrial towns of Veracruz and Puebla, in the railroad depots of Monterrey, San Luis Potosí, and Aguascalientes, and in the mines of Sonora and Hidalgo, this critical period passed almost without incident. José Neira, ex-president of the Orizaba *Gran Círculo de Obreros Libres,* had written to a former comrade in Orizaba just prior to the abortive Liberal attack on Ciudad Júarez saying that "it is worth much more to give one's life fighting for our improvement than to worship stupidly a peace that offers us only miseries and slavery."[58] Yet the workers had not offered their life fighting for their own betterment. Why? Certainly their grievances were real, and a solution to them was long overdue from their perspective. James Cockcroft's important study of intellectual precursors to the Mexican Revolution maintains that "thousands of industrial workers" were recruited to the PLM ranks after Cananea.[59] The PLM had made a major effort to attract working-class support through their famous Program of July, issued that very year, in which they called for major labor reforms, including an eight hour day, a minimum wage, equal pay for equal work, accident compensation, and other reforms being sought by the workers themselves.[60]

No clearcut answer emerges from the available historical evidence.

57. Cockcroft, *Intellectual Precursors,* pp. 144–49.
58. José Neira to Gilberto Torres, 8 October 1906, El Paso, AGN-Gob, "Asuntos diversos magonistas y revolucionarios, 1907–1908," leg. 12.
59. Cockcroft, *Intellectual Precursors,* p. 138. For similar conclusions, see: Blaisdell, *The Desert Revolution,* p. 8; Ezequiel Montes Rodríguez, *La huelga de Río Blanco* (Río Blanco, Veracruz: Sindicato de Trabajadores en General de la CIDOSA, 1965), pp. 68, 89; Rosendo Salazar and José G. Escobedo, *Las pugnas de la gleba 1907–1922* (Mexico: Editorial Avante, 1923), p. 26; Howard F. Cline, *The United States and Mexico,* rev. ed. (Cambridge, Mass.: Harvard University Press, 1965), p. 117.
60. Cockcroft, *Intellectual Precursors,* pp. 81–82, 108–14. For a translated copy of the 1906 PLM program, see Cockcroft, pp. 239–45. The labor section was written by Juan Sarabia, with recommendations from the Cananea labor leaders and textile worker José Neira; Cockcroft, p. 129 and Enrique Flores Magòn, "El Partido Liberal," *El Nacional* (Mexico City), 15 January 1904.

First, Cockcroft's assertion that thousands of workers joined the PLM cause is, at best, conjecture. No evidence supports this position. Although a number of Mexican industrial workers were undoubtedly aware of the PLM's prolabor attitudes, few showed any willingness to support the PLM's call for revolution. Perhaps they were afraid of the repressive hand of the government, remembering Cananea and the fate of the GCOL officials who earlier had supported the PLM. Yet during the *maderista* rebellion of 1910–1911, workers would risk their lives to fight against the government. Why not in 1906?

The answer to the question, if it can be answered at all, lies in the workers' experiences between 1906 and 1910. The only answer provided by the evidence available to the historian is that in September 1906 the majority of those Mexican workers who were actively involved in conflicts with their employers believed that and acted as if the best means of remedying their grievances were through governmental intervention. Juan Olivares, former GCOL officer and a PLM activist at the time of the revolts, acknowledged this situation when, in September 1906, he wrote to a friend, criticizing the GCOL leadership for "continuing to resort to the authorities in order to better the situation of our comrades."[61]

The Response—Porfirian Labor Policy, 1906

The men who guided the destiny of Mexico in those days were not unaware of the political implications of the disgruntled rumblings from below. The rise of the militant textile workers' union in the spring, the events at Cananea, and the general labor unrest undoubtedly emphasized the obvious threat to the stability of the entire Porfirian structure if such die-hard political opponents as the Liberal Party were allowed to unite their cause with that of the workers.

The regime had initiated its counterattack at the first signs of the political dangers accompanying the unrest. Within days after the militant *Revolución Social* appeared in the mills, Díaz ordered state

61. Juan A. Olivares to Rafael Rosete, 2 September 1906, El Paso, Texas, AGN-Gob, "Asuntos diversos magonistas y revolucionarios, 1907–1908," leg. 12.

governors to apprehend and punish any newspaper writers agitating the workers. It was most likely these instructions that forced Neira, Olivares, and the others to flee Orizaba. In addition, the publishers of *Revolución Social*, Jesús Martínez Carreón and Federico Pérez Fernández, were jailed in Belem Prison in the Federal District. Martínez Carreón died in prison from an illness contracted in the infamous, pestilence-ridden cells of that prison.[62]

As an alternative to militant unionism, the administration sponsored a Worker and Mutualist Congress in an attempt to revive the defunct *Congreso Obrero* of the previous century as a more acceptable working-class organization. Meeting in Mexico City on 7 July 1906, the Congress represented sixty-four societies with an official membership of more than eleven thousand workers throughout the country.[63] Mutualism did not prove to be any more a solution to the workers' problems in 1906 than it had been in early years, having practically no impact on the industrial workers' movements.

Díaz then began a covert campaign to obtain information on the nature of the newly emerging labor movement and the extent of its grievances. Ramón Corral was evidently a major figure in the administration's handling of the labor problem. His office, for example, requested the state governors to send him copies of all telegrams bearing on the labor movement.[64]

Not depending on his official sources, Díaz asked Rafael de Zayas Enríquez, former Mexican Consular General in San Francisco and a native journalist-scholar from Veracruz, to make a study of the labor problem, considering particularly the influence of radical doctrines on the workers in the textile mills of Veracruz. Over a period of four months, Zayas made trips to the mills in Orizaba, Jalapa, and Veracruz, talking with workers and writing articles on the labor question for

62. Sodi de Pallares, *Teodoro A. Dehesa*, p. 132; *El Diario del Hogar*, 12 July 1906; Peña, "Apuntes históricos," 14 October 1958. The paper had been printed on the press of the satirical weekly *El Colmillo Público* (Mexico City).

63. *El Imparcial*, 7 July 1906.

64. Sodi de Pallares, *Teodoro A. Dehesa*, p. 125. Corral kept tabs on the workers, at least under certain circumstances, before 1906: see Bernardo Reyes to Corral, 13 October 1905, AGBR, Correspondencia del Sr. Presidente, 1903–1909.

the press. During this period he wrote Díaz numerous letters, had several audiences with him, and submitted two major reports.[65]

In his first report, submitted sometime in June, Zayas criticized traditional liberal economic theory, declaring that unless the state took some action to remedy working-class grievances, the power of the socialists would only increase.[66] His second report, dated 3 August, dealt with broader issues.

Zayas bluntly asserted that if Díaz wished to avoid revolution, he would have to take action against official corruption and the lack of justice at all levels of society. If these things were not done, Zayas prophetically warned, "the accumulated experience of history teaches us that when no one looks out for the public, the public looks out for itself; and when the public looks out for itself, it ceases to be a river running in its natural channel and becomes a flood, an inundation."[67] On several other occasions he warned Díaz to make a public investigation of the Cananea affair, since it was giving the opposition press an issue on which the public had strong feelings.[68] Díaz did not heed the advice of Zayas Enríquez to speak out publicly about Cananea. He continued to work surreptitiously through intermediaries on the labor problem; Porfirio Díaz was master of Mexico and would act as he wished, allowing the public to think what it damn well pleased.

In addition to Zayas's efforts, Díaz had requested the governor of the state, Teodoro A. Dehesa, to obtain reports from each mill in the

65. Rafael de Zayas Enríquez, *Porfirio Díaz: The Evolution of His Life* (New York: D. Appleton and Co., 1908), p. 222. His correspondence with Díaz is contained in the GPDC, 31:8659–8664, as well as throughout the months of July through September.

66. Zayas Enríquez to Díaz, 2 July 1906, GPDC, 31:7646.

67. Zayas Enríquez, *Porfirio Díaz*, pp. 224–43; quote on p. 234.

68. Ibid., p. 241, and Zayas Enríquez to Díaz, 6 August 1906, GPDC, 31:9194. He resigned his commission in November and left for the United States. Continuing to write for Mexican newspapers, Zayas's articles often appeared in the more oppositionist press such as *El Paladín* and *México Nuevo*. Eventually he was dropped from the good graces of the old *Caudillo* because Díaz discovered that Zayas was writing an unfriendly biography of him; see Díaz to Bernardo Reyes, 5 September 1908, AGBR, Correspondencia presidencial, 1903–1909. For an unflattering evaluation of Zayas, see Cosío Villegas, *Vida política interior*, 2:731–33.

state on production and average working hours, strongly intimating that the mills might consider reducing the work load to twelve hours a day. The prevailing working hours for mill hands varied, but for the weavers and spinners, who made up the majority of the textile workers, the average work day began at 6:00 A.M. and ran through to 7:30 or 8:00 P.M. The standard work week was seventy-two hours. Not infrequently, the management increased the workday for specific production quotas, forcing the *obreros* to work at night or on Sunday with little or no advance notice and at the same rate of pay.[69]

Most of the owners and managers of the mills rejected the government's subtle overture that perhaps the workers would produce as much or more working twelve as fourteen hours a day. One did not. The English manager of CIDOSA's Orizaba mills, George Hartington, agreed on the need to reduce working hours and later wrote his boss in Mexico City, suggesting the need for reforms in factory regulations and procedures. Hartington believed that production would actually rise if the standard seventy-two hour workweek were reduced to sixty hours. He envisioned a day when the workers would accept their jobs as a challenge and dedicate themselves to their work. Of all those who appeared on the industrialists' side of the conflicts, Hartington emerges as the most reasonable. The workers appeared to believe so too and specifically exempted Hartington from the charges of mistreatment they made against many foreign supervisors.[70] When he retired in 1909 and left Mexico to return to his native England, there were workers who were sorry to see him go.

Continuing to gather information, the administration also initiated a newspaper campaign through the so-called subsidized press designed to encourage peaceful solutions to worker problems. Leading the effort was *El Imparcial*. The most important of the government's

69. Levino (illegible) to Díaz, 25 June 1906, GPDC, 31:6696; Dehesa to Díaz, 2, 9 July 1906, GPDC, 31:8658, 8685; see "In the arena," by José Neira, *Revolución Social*, GPDC, 6373 and his letter to the editor, *México Nuevo*, 24 July 1909.

70. Dehesa to Díaz, 2, 9 July 1906, GPDC, 3:8658, 8685; Herrera to Dehesa in Dehesa to Díaz, 9 July 1906, GPDC, 31:8685 and Hartington to Reynaud, 17 November 1906, in Sodi de Pallares, *Teodoro A. Dehesa*, pp. 130–32; and *El Paladín*, 29 March 1908, 25 April 1909.

semiofficial spokesmen, this *científico* paper carried over forty editorials and articles on the labor question from July through November of that year.[71]

Reflecting their "scientific" emphasis, *El Imparcial's* lead-off editorial held that the problem of the working class was a sociological, not a political, problem; hence it would only be solved through peaceful and harmonious evolution. No specific remedies were proposed, because the labor problem was, after all, one that "only the eminent thinkers are able to treat . . . with any proficiency."[72] This theme is repeated throughout the following months, usually coupled with the position that there was no basic conflict in Mexico between capital and labor; hence, the writer would point out, the unrest among the workers was obviously artificial, created by agitators for their own ends.

El Imparcial did not go unchallenged. The strongly Catholic but politically independent daily *El Tiempo* maintained a running feud with *El Imparcial* over the basis of the labor unrest, asserting that the basic problem was the rising cost of living. The workers could hardly survive on the wages they were making, the paper asserted. *El Imparcial* countered by declaring that wages were rising as well as prices and that Mexican workers made more than they had ever made before. Of all of the major Mexico City dailies, *El Tiempo* and its respected director, Victoriano Agüeros, maintained the most consistently sympathetic editorial policy toward the workers throughout the mounting labor crisis of 1906, with the possible exception of *El Diario* under Juan Sánchez Azcona.[73]

Despite its down-play of the labor problem, *El Imparcial* reinterpreted the government's traditional noninvolvement policy, suggesting that the federal government ought to give to the workers the

71. The American Consul General informed Washington of this program: U.S. Con. Gen. to Sec. of State, 20 July 1906, State, RG 59, USNA. *El Imparcial* was founded in 1897 by Rafael Reyes Spíndola. By 1907 its circulation was approximately one hundred thousand copies daily throughout the Republic, by far the largest circulation of any paper of the era. It cost one *centavo*, a very competitive price made possible by official subsidy.

72. 5 July 1906. See also 7, 10 July, 11, 13 August, 21, 26 September 1906.

73. *El Imparcial*, 25 August, 23 September 1906. *El Diario del Hogar*, 9 November 1906, published the arguments of both papers. *El País*, the other popular, strongly Catholic daily, also often rebuked and attacked *El Imparcial's* editorials on the labor question.

"freedom to organize, . . . and to attempt to guide them as to the means they should use, and to see to the general welfare, for peace, order, justice and equality."[74]

Lest a worried business community mistake the regime's intentions, the administration also made clear that it would maintain order in the mills and mines of Mexico at all costs. Speaking for the regime, Justo Sierra warned the National Congress of Tobacco Workers in August that sedition would not be tolerated and, furthermore, that in the event of a strike, the government would put "all its resources, all its political organization, all its army, all its authority, on the side of even a single worker who wants to work."[75]

Years later, a tobacco worker who was present at the speech remembered that the president of the Congress, Julio M. Platas, rose to his feet after the conclusion of Sierra's remarks and commented with grave sarcasm, "Please excuse me, comrades, for having made a very serious error. Instead of inviting the respected Minister of Public Instruction and Fine Arts to this gathering, I must have invited the Minister of War; only a high military commander would talk of bayonets."[76]

Yet the regime was careful to affirm both publicly and privately the workers' right to strike. When an overzealous state governor wished to move against a peaceful strike, Díaz demurred, suggesting the punishment only of those who broke the law.[77] Even though local officials at times disregarded this right, federal policy in 1906 clearly permitted peaceful strikes to be held without official repression.

What is also clear, however, is that the legal right to strike was not of critical importance to Mexican workers because of their economic disadvantage when confronting their bosses. Even the strongest un-

74. *El Imparcial,* 12 August 1906.
75. Ibid., 8 August 1906.
76. Pedro E. Martínez, *Apuntes para la historia del movimiento obrero nacional* in Teodoro Hernández, "Un congreso obrero: Incidente con el Ministro Justo Sierra," *La Prensa* (Mexico City), 4 January 1952.
77. Sierra confirmed the right to strike in his speech, as did Díaz in his address to Congress the following month. See also Díaz to Dehesa, 2 June 1906, GPDC, 31:1061; Díaz to Reyes, 30 July 1906, AGBR, "Correspondencia del presidente, 1903–1909"; gov. of Puebla (Muncio P. Martínez) to Díaz, 4 December 1906, GPDC, 65:4072; appendage dated 1 November 1906 of Martínez to Díaz, 30 October 1906, GPDC, 31:14577.

ions in these years—those of the cotton textile workers and the railroad employees—did not have the resources to carry their members through a prolonged strike. It was far more important for the workers to obtain governmental support for their grievances. This fact of life forced most Mexican workers to hinge their hopes for change in the industrial system on the government of Porfirio Díaz.[78]

Moreover, the Díaz regime was not adverse to such a relationship, within reason. Díaz cautioned various state governors to be careful in the use of force against the workers and to consider establishing a working relationship with them. When the GCOL opened in Puebla under Pascual Mendoza, Governor Martínez wrote Díaz that he was going to consign Mendoza to the army. The president replied by writing one of his rare two-page letters, suggesting that if the workers kept the peace it was better to establish contact with them and, indeed, that it would be counterproductive to arrest Mendoza. Martínez evidently was uncertain about what Díaz wanted, because the following month he again indicated that, fearing future conflicts, he had decided to move against the workers. What did Díaz think? The reply came back, short and curt—punish only those who break the law.[79] For the time being at least, Mendoza and his officers remained free to organize.

In the neighboring state of Tlaxcala, the governor, Col. Próspero Cahuantzi, was known for his lack of sympathy toward the textile workers of his state. In the summer of 1906 José Morales was forced to cut short a recruiting trip to the Tlaxcalan mills because he received word that Cahuantzi had ordered his arrest. The governor immediately issued a circular to all the mills, stating that any worker who

78. For similar conclusions, see Payne, *Labor and Politics in Peru*, p. 17, and Miguel Urrutia, *The Development of the Colombian Labor Movement* (New Haven: Yale University Press, 1969), pp. v, 113–98. See David Chaplin, *The Peruvian Industrial Labor Force* (Princeton: Princeton University Press, 1967), pp. 80–82 for a critical evaluation of Payne's thesis. For a Marxist perspective, see Chesneaux, *Chinese Labor Movement*, pp. 386–93.

79. Martínez to Díaz, 22 September 1906, GPDC, 31:11383; Díaz to Martínez, 27 September 1906, GPDC, 31:11385; Díaz to Martínez, 1 November 1906, addendum to Martínez to Díaz, 30 October 1906, GPDC, 31:14577. In fact, the *jefe político* of Puebla, likely under instructions from the governor, served as a mediator for three strikes in October; Martínez to Díaz, 27 October 1906, GPDC, 65:3364.

joined the GCOL would be sent to the army. Díaz likely requested him to moderate his stand, because in October, shortly after Morales complained to Díaz about Tlaxcala, Governor Cahuantzi initiated a series of meetings with the mill owners, asking them to consider a wage increase. He later explained his change of heart by declaring that a government must discharge its responsibilities toward "such an important evolution" as the industrial workers' movement.[80]

On the other hand, in the state of Jalisco, where Governor Miguel Ahumada had established a workable relationship with the workers' mutualist groups, and where signs of militant labor activity had yet to surface, the president had no need to intervene and did not do so.[81] Where no political problem existed, the regime had no reason to exercise control or even to advise, and the Porfirian system functioned without the *Caudillo*'s interference.

The writing of history is almost by definition a demythologizing process, a role in which the historian may be particularly uneasy if he has a natural sympathy for the myth itself. The Mexican Revolution, in overthrowing the regime of Porfirio Díaz and his *científico* advisors, fashioned many hostile images of the Old Regime that have survived to the present day. This process is a natural one, for one must hate what one has destroyed. Of the images that emerged in the years after the fall of the regime, one of the most honored is that when confronted with the labor problem, the regime responded with force alone, testifying to its absolute inability to understand, much less deal effectively with, the social problems of a modernizing society. Marjorie Clark, for example, in her major work on the Mexican labor movement, maintained that the Díaz government "was quite satisfied to arrest or exile the leaders of the workers' groups, establish martial law when a strike actually occurred, break up the incipient labor organizations, and impose its will by force."[82]

80. *El Diario Oficial de Tlaxcala*, no. 59, 6 April 1907. Compare with his comments at the opening of the last session of the Twentieth Legislature in *El Diario Oficial de Tlaxcala*, no. 33, 6 October 1906; Morales to Díaz, 8 October 1906, GPDC, 31:12749.

81. See *Jalisco Libre* (Guadalajara), 4, 7 March, 3 June 1906.

82. Clark, *Organized Labor*, p. 4. See also Jorge Fernando Iturribarría, *Porfirio Díaz ante la historia* (Mexico: Carlos Villejas García Condor 100, 1967), pp. 238–40. The major exceptions to this interpretation are González

This is a myth, not because it is false but because it has been raised to the stature of complete truth by the image-makers of the Revolution of 1910 and after. Beneath the surface of the myth run counter-currents of reality both more complex in their makeup and more uncertain in their design. What appears to be true is that when labor agitation started to threaten the stability of the regime, Díaz began a search for a political solution to the problem. He sought to pacify the most politically dangerous workers' movements, without endangering his basic plans for the economic modernization of the nation. The methods the regime used were not systematic or institutional and therefore were hardly effective even for the limited goals the president had in mind. In any case, time and events took the initiative away from him; having abandoned the workers to their fate for so many years, he could not easily placate their grievances. Soon he was able only to react to an increasingly worsening situation.

The Developing Crisis—The Fall of 1906

While the regime was exploring the nature of the labor problem, the tempo of labor strife began to accelerate, especially in the mill towns of the central states. By a curious irony of history, although the Independence Day celebrations in September did not mark the revolt against the Díaz regime, they did mark the beginning of a series of labor conflicts that ultimately shook the regime to its very foundations.

The beginnings were innocuous enough—a short strike at San Lorenzo, a textile mill owned by the powerful CIDOSA. The day that work resumed at San Lorenzo, the workers at Santa Gertrudis, an important English-owned jute mill in Orizaba, walked out for higher pay and the elimination of fines. That same week, two Puebla mills were struck over the issues of mistreatment by foremen and the responsibility of the workers to replace at their own expense broken and worn-out parts and tools. The *jefe político* of Puebla intervened, result-

Navarro, *La vida social*, pp. 326–29 and Daniel Cosío Villegas, *Vida política interior*, 2:706–7.

ing in settlements favorable to the workers.[83] It was to be in Puebla that the final stage of the crisis took shape.

The month of October began with rumors circulating that the Orizaba workers were arming themselves. In view of the PLM revolts in the state of Veracruz at that time—particularly at Acayucán, southeast of Orizaba—authorities immediately checked local arms distributors, only to find that the rumors were unfounded.[84]

But the conflicts continued. The workers struck again at Santa Gertrudis, staying out nearly all the month of October in response to a wage cut. Those who could not find work were supported by the GCOL strike fund. The day they returned, 26 October, mill hands walked out in various departments of the huge Santa Rosa plant, forcing the entire mill to shut down. The major economic issues leading to the strike were the hated practices of fining workers for defects in finished materials, for violations of company regulations, and for "dancing without music"—misconduct.[85]

Underlying the economic issues, however, was a strong current of growing bitterness against the foreigners who seemed to dominate their lives. At the Santa Rosa mill, or "Santa Rusia" as one flier facetiously called it, most of the foremen and supervisors were foreign, a common characteristic of the newer, more modern factories throughout Mexico.[86] In a long, rambling, often bitter letter written by various workers from the mill and sent to Ramón Corral to request his intervention in their dispute, the writers protested:

We believe that our government opens the doors to foreign

83. Herrera to Dehesa, 18, 19, 28 September 1906, SHUV-Gob, 1906, H-2; *El Imparcial*, 8, 22 September 1906; Pascual Mendoza to Francisco Santibañez (owner of mill San Juan B. Amatlán), 9 September 1906, in cover letter Gov. Martínez to Díaz, 22 September 1906, GPDC, 31:11384. For other Puebla strikes, see Martínez to Díaz, 27 October 1906, GPDC, 65:3364.

84. Ramón E. Rocha to Dehesa, 13 October 1906, in cover letter Dehesa to Díaz, 23 October 1906, GPDC, 31:13170.

85. Herrera to Dehesa, 26 October 1906, SHUV-Gob, 1906, H-14; Rocha to Dehesa, 13 October 1906, in cover letter Dehesa to Díaz, 23 October 1906, GPDC, 31:13170; Herrera to Dehesa, 26 October 1906, SHUV-Gob, 1906, H-14.

86. Flier "Los obreros de la República al público en general," AGN-Gob, leg. 817.

capital . . . for their usefulness, and to protect the Mexican people more, and not that they should come to violate our reform laws, laws which cost much bloodshed by our heroes who defended them with justice and loyalty for the good of a free people; but here in this factory everything is contrary to this. These foreigners violate the laws of our Magna Carta and these fines, which are shameful for us in a democratic country, as our Mexican Republic is called, are erasing our rights and our guarantees. . . .[87]

These feelings were not confined to Santa Rosa workers. Writing in support of the striking Santa Rosa workers, the Puebla GCOL lashed out against the foreigner who "with his so-called 'peaceful conquest' has enthroned himself in Mexico, believing that the citizens who are descendants of the indomitable race of Cuauhtémoc, Hidalgo, and Morelos are destined to humiliate themselves in order to receive a crumb of bread in exchange for kicks and humiliations." The broadside went on to declare that such a belief was mistaken. "If they believe that the workers of today are those of yesterday, listen clearly! The twentieth century worker has awakened from his apathy; he is not going to bend his knees before the tyrants."[88]

The economic issues were real and sufficient to motivate the conflicts, but the environment of discontent was heavily laced with a growing feeling of injured national pride. As time went on, the question of the foreign domination of Mexico became inextricably linked with the labor question, both from the workers' perspective and from that of their fellow citizens as well.

The Santa Rosa strike increased the regime's apprehension about the possibility that the textile labor movement was being infiltrated by radical, socialist elements. *El Imparcial* blamed the strike on socialist propaganda, a viewpoint probably close to the official one.[89] Certainly, the harshness of the letters and fliers sent to Corral were worrisome. One handwritten poster which found its way to Corral's desk

87. (Workers of the) fábrica de Santa Rosa to Ramón Corral, 29 October 1906, AGN-Gob, leg. 817.

88. Flier "A los proletarios del Segundo Círculo de Obreros Libres en el Estado de Puebla y los dignos ciudadanos de la República Mexicana," 11 November 1906, AGN-Gob, leg. 817.

89. 30 October 1906.

ended with: "Long live the Great Circle of Free Workers, long live our president, José Morales, and death to the bourgeoisie."[90] Another anonymous letter to Corral threatened to burn down the Santa Rosa factory if the complaints of the workers were not acted upon. These were tough words, and although Morales had disclaimed responsibility for such threats, an administrator in the Río Blanco mill wrote Corral that Morales's peaceful intentions were often resisted by others. He enclosed a list of five men he named as the agitators, advising that if they were jailed, peace would return to the Orizaba mills. The writer also noted apprehensively that the workers sometimes shouted "death to foreigners." Three additional units of federal infantry moved into the Orizaba area as a precautionary measure.[91]

Unable to reach an agreement, the GCOL reluctantly ordered its men back to work on 10 November. Angry and frustrated, the Santa Rosa workers turned against Morales. He was accused of not supporting their strike and of selling out to the industrialists and the authorities. The charge was unfounded, but Morales had been cautious in his tactics against the firms, not wishing to force a showdown until the GCOL was stronger. He had been especially careful to keep on the good side of Herrera and Rocha; both men had shown some sympathy for the workers' problems. Underlying the charges of the Santa Rosa workers, however, was an earlier rift in the leadership ranks.

When Morales had accepted the presidency, he imposed one condition, that the union would remain committed to the resolution of their grievances within the present political system. In other words, the secret alliance with the PLM was to be abandoned. Not all the officers had agreed. Both Rafael Váldez and Samuel A. Ramírez, presidents of the GCOL branches at the Cerritos and Santa Rosa mills respectively, had been arrested because of their correspondence with the PLM's Revolutionary Junta in St. Louis. Váldez was sentenced to San Juan de Ulúa, but Ramírez was freed through the efforts of legal

90. See handwritten flier headed "Abiso," AGN-Gob, leg. 817.
91. "Varios obreros" to Ramón Corral, n.d., AGN-Gob, leg. 817; Anonymous to Sr. Antonio Reynaud, 4 November 1906, AGN-Gob, leg. 817 (the letter contains a fairly detailed discussion of the owners' side of the strike, including their justification of fines, a practice they contend was common in modern textile mills); *El Imparcial*, 5 November 1906.

counsel hired by the GCOL. Morales forced Ramírez, however, to resign his union position.[92]

Nonetheless, Ramírez retained his influence among his comrades at Santa Rosa, and the discontent over the strike gave him the opening to attack Morales directly. At a dramatic meeting of the rank and file, Ramírez accused Morales not only of weak and indecisive leadership but of betraying his comrades to the government for personal gain. After a rancorous debate, a resolution was introduced by the Santa Rosa delegation calling for Morales to resign. It was voted down, but the Santa Rosa delegates threatened to walk out of the GCOL, and many workers, undoubtedly fearing that the loss of such an important mill would destroy the union, changed their votes. A second ballot was held, and Morales was voted out of office. Ramírez was then elected in his place.[93]

The new president immediately ran into difficulties. Hostility at the pro-Morales Río Blanco mill forced him to move the union headquarters to Nogales. More importantly, Herrera refused to officially recognize the change, obviously fearing its political implications. Meanwhile, Morales contacted Pascual Mendoza, head of the *Segundo Círculo* in Puebla, and requested his support to regain the presidency. Mendoza responded by requesting a general membership meeting of the Orizaba GCOL, ostensibly to appeal for their support in what was developing into a major confrontation with the Puebla mills. Meeting in early December, Mendoza used the forum to praise Morales and to ask for his presence on a commission to seek the intervention of President Díaz in the Puebla conflict. Pro-Morales forces capitalized on the moment, introducing a successful motion to return the presidency to their ousted chief.[94]

92. Peña, "Apuntes históricos," 4, 11 November 1958.
93. According to the account of Lic. Ramón Rocha, several of Morales's own officers were pro-Ramírez, as was José Rumbia, the influential Protestant minister; Rocha to Gen. Rosalino Martínez, 9 January 1907, GPDC, 32:933. Peña, "Apuntes históricos," 4, 11 November, 2, 9 December 1958; Araiza, *El movimiento obrero*, p. 103; Samuel A. Ramírez, Mariano Castillo, Raphael Moreno, Miguel Ponce, and others to Díaz, 23 November 1906, GPDC, 31:14182. By one account, the meeting was of branch presidents only; Rocha to Gen. Martínez, 9 January 1907, GPDC, 32:933.
94. Peña, "Apuntes históricos," 9 December 1958. See also Ramírez to Hart-

The split within the *Gran Círculo de Obreros Libres* never really healed. Later that same month, several hundred pro-Ramírez workers gathered outside the office of the Orizaba *jefe político*, Carlos Herrera, in a futile attempt to force official approval of a new election.[95] Motivated by personal and local rivalries, and aggravated by ideological differences, this conflict within the GCOL later proved decisive in the crisis, and with tragic consequences.

Two other major textile strikes took place that fall outside the Orizaba-Puebla area. In late October, workers affiliated with the GCOL struck at the large La Hormiga mill in the San Angel area of the Federal District. They were demanding an increase in wages or a decrease in the hours worked, but they agreed to return to work on 7 November pending negotiations. Hardly had the La Hormiga mill begun working again when the important San Antonio Abad mill, also in the Federal District, was shut down over a change in work schedules. The union, an affiliate of the GCOL, asked for higher wages and a decrease in the work day. The administrator of the mill revealed privately that he would be willing to decrease the work day by half an hour but that the dignity of the company would not allow such a concession at that time. The manager also believed that the Mexican worker was naturally docile and only struck when incited by outside agitators.[96] The management yielded nothing; the workers, resources exhausted, returned to their machines.

In the summer and fall of 1906 many Mexican industrial workers appeared restless and discontented. Some struck and others did not, but all must have felt the bitter uneasiness of the times. Strikes, martyrs, rumors of revolution, visions of reform, general employer intransigence—all were elements of the labor question in the fall of 1906. Every indication pointed to the Orizaba mill hands, the Cananea miners, or the well-organized railroadmen as the probable source of crisis, but the volatile situation erupted instead in the mills of Puebla.

ington, n.d. circa November 1906), GPDC, 31:1060; Araiza, *El movimiento obrero*, p. 103; *El Cosmopolita*, 2 December 1906.

95. Herrera to Dehesa, 12, 13 December 1906, SHUV-Gob, 1906, C-65.

96. *El País*, 1, 20 November 1906.

Chapter 4
La Huelga de Río Blanco

And we are not anarchists,
nor do we want revolution,
but less working hours
and a better distribution.

From "Río Blanco," a *corrido* written and sung by Francisco Zavala and Guillermo Torres, textile workers.

The industrial unrest in the "year of the strikes" culminated in the great Puebla textile strike in December and reached its climax on 7 January 1907 in the tragic events known to Mexican history as *la huelga de Río Blanco*. These two industrial conflicts are benchmarks in Mexican labor history, but in a subtle but very real way they are benchmarks for the *Porfiriato* as well.

The city of Puebla had been founded by the Spaniards only a few years after the fall of Tenochtitlán. It soon became, and still is, a clerical, conservative city. During three centuries of colonial rule it grew into one of the major commercial centers of New Spain, rivaled only by Guadalajara and surpassed only by Mexico City itself. At the beginning of the *Porfiriato* the state of Puebla was the fourth most populous state in the union; by 1910 it was second only to Jalisco. Yet the truth is that by 1910 Puebla's economic position had deteriorated relative to such traditional rivals as Veracruz and Mexico City, as well as in comparison to such northern cities as Monterrey or Torreón. Nowhere was this better illustrated than in the cotton textile industry.

Puebla had been the colonial center of the spinning and weaving trades and had converted its *obrajes* into the most mechanized industry in the Republic in the 1840s. By 1906, however, the thirty-odd mills in and around the city could hardly compare, with few exceptions, to the larger and more modern mills of Orizaba. In the critical area of power, for instance, Puebla facilities after 1900 were insufficient to meet the increasing demand for power, while Orizaba mills had excess generating capacity. The owners of the mills were, for the most part, local families like the Quijanos and the Velascos, who perhaps held on to their businesses out of affection for family tradition or for what status the mills afforded.[1]

The depression of the textile market in 1900 and 1901 and its halting, slow recovery through to 1906 had forced the Puebla mills to modernize their plants and production methods, cutting costs wherever they could. Of those that survived, most still operated on a slim margin, and the labor unrest of 1906 found several firms on the edge of bankruptcy. Sales for the fiscal year 1905–1906 declined slightly from those of the previous year for the Puebla mills, although total production increased, forcing most mills to expand their inventory and hope for better days.

Among the problems faced by the mills in 1905 had been a 50 percent increase in the price of cotton. As a result, wages throughout the area were reduced in early 1906. The workers had not accepted this cut gracefully, and only by agreeing to restore the wage cuts when cotton prices declined did the owners avoid strikes that they could ill-afford.[2] It was, therefore, with some apprehension that Puebla mill owners saw the spread of trade unionism in their mills, as disgruntled workers turned to Pascual Mendoza's *Liga Obrera Esteban de Antuñano.* The merger with the Orizaba-based *Gran Círculo* in October had strengthened Mendoza's hand still further. When Díaz forbade Governor Mucio Martínez to consign Mendoza to the military, the industrialists knew they could no longer count on political influence to take care of their labor problems.

Sometime in the fall of 1906 the Puebla industrialists formed their own association, the *Centro Industrial Mexicana* (CIM).[3] During the good times in the 1890s they thought that they could live with the foreign-dominated giants and still prosper. The harsh reality of their economic inferiority must have been a bitter pill to swallow. Harassed even by their once-docile workers, the beleaguered mill owners may

1. Jan Bazant, "Evolución de la industria textil," pp. 473–516; Rosenzweig, "La industria," pp. 323, 394, 434, and 456; *The Mexican Yearbook, 1909–1910,* pp. 516, 524–29. For a history of several of Puebla's older mills, see González Navarro, *Las huelgas textiles,* pp. 274–87.

2. *El Imparcial,* 13 December 1906; Rosenzweig, "La industria," p. 76.

3. Araiza, *El movimiento obrero,* p. 103.

have turned to formal union to reassert control over their lives as well as to meet the growing militancy of labor. Now at least they had acted.

The *Centro* wasted little time in bringing about a confrontation. In mid-November the owners issued a new, unified set of factory regulations affecting all aspects of the workers' lives, inside and outside the mill. *Article 1* of the *Reglamento Interior,* as it was called, set the working hours at 6:00 A.M. to 8:00 P.M., with forty-five minutes set aside for breakfast and the same for lunch. On Saturday work would stop at 6:00 P.M. *Article 2* forbade workers to enter work under the influence of alcohol. *Article 3* stipulated that workers were to be paid after work on Saturday afternoon. This meant that, in the larger mills, some workers would have to stay several hours waiting to be paid. *Article 4* forbade roughhousing, including the striking of workers by their superiors, and vice versa. *Article 5* prohibited foremen from taking money in exchange for allowing a worker to operate additional machinery, under the piece-work system. This abuse was a common practice. *Articles 6* and *7* required the workers to maintain their machines in good working condition, while requiring them to replace, at their own expense, bobbins, shuttles, and other such equipment, whether broken through negligence or simply worn out through use. *Article 8* prohibited gambling in the mill or such "entertainments" as magazines, newspapers, letters, firearms, matches, etc. *Article 9* gave the administration the right to fire any worker who caused "prejudice" to the firm or created a disorder, meaning union leaders. *Article 10* provided for the registration of each worker as he entered the mill. *Article 11* declared that fines would be imposed for defective material produced by any worker. *Article 12* prohibited the workers from having guests in their company housing without permission and stipulated that a worker separated from work for any reason was obligated to vacate his house the same day. The *reglamento* also reduced the number of holidays the workers were entitled to.[4]

Hardly an article was acceptable to the *Segundo Círculo.* Many were issues of long standing, and the new regulations simply represented an escalation of the conflict. Old issues included fines for defective material and payment to replace worn-out bobbins and shuttles, requirements which the mills around Puebla had been attempting to

4. For a copy of the *reglamento,* see AGN-Gob, leg. 817.

introduce in recent years.[5] Others, such as the regulations governing
the reading of newspapers on the job and the necessity of obtaining
prior permission for guests in their homes, were new and represented
efforts to control areas of their lives which workers felt belonged
outside the prerogative of the mill.

The owners defended the new regulations as being in the best
interests of the workers. One representative of the CIM stated that
the increase in the time the workers were obliged to spend in the mill
and the reduction of the days off for holidays were instituted in order
to get the workers out of the taverns. He explained that the administration's concern for the welfare of its workers was the motivation
behind restricting entrance to the workers' housing, since robbers and
other such undesirable people sometimes frequented the company
housing areas. Indeed, even the prohibition of reading materials had
its rationale in the betterment of the workers' moral conditions, "inasmuch as the books are indecent and the magazines are those which
have caused the demoralization into which the class has fallen, while
before they were a model of discipline, hardworking, sober, and
well-conducted in their homes."[6] In the milieu of the times such blatant paternalism was an acceptable argument. Indeed, although sympathizers from other classes undoubtedly questioned the motivation
of the owners, most honored the basic value assumptions on which the
argument rested—that the workers were morally inferior as a class.

The Puebla Strike

The Puebla GCOL struck on Thursday, 4 December, after nearly
two weeks of futile negotiations, shutting down thirty mills throughout the state and involving nearly six thousand workers. By Friday
the strike had spread to the neighboring state of Tlaxcala, closing
ten more mills. It rivaled the mechanics' strike of the previous
August as the most extensive industrial labor conflict in the history of
the Republic. The key issues were fines, replacement of broken or
worn-out tools, and the two articles of the *reglamento* that particularly

5. For example, see Pascual Mendoza to Francisco Santibañez, 9 September
1906, GPDC, 31:11384.
6. *El País*, 7 December 1906.

incensed the workers—the prohibition against reading newspapers and the requirement to obtain permission for visitors in their homes. One worker caught the irony of the latter, commenting, "How good it would be to apply to certain *burgueses* the clause for being themselves guests in our nation."[7]

That Sunday one of the great events in Mexican industrial labor history took place in the Guerrero theater in Puebla. The *Segundo Círculo* of the GCOL of Puebla held an open session with over two thousand workers attending. A carnival mood prevailed, with band music, laughter, and general excitement. Perhaps never before had so many people gathered together in Mexico to contest the prevailing power structure without guns in their hands. Letters were read from other workers' groups supporting them; a delegation was there from Cananea to lend the moral support of the copper miners to their brothers of the mills. From Orizaba came a large group of fellow mill hands to let their Puebla comrades know that this was not only their fight; they would not stand alone.[8]

When the meeting was called to order, various men rose from the floor to speak, one after the other, calling for unity and order, and condemning the industrialists' *reglamento*. Flavio R. Arroyo spoke of the peaceful intentions of the GCOL and underlined the ideological assumptions of the workers when he declared that the "Constitution of Benito Juárez" was the hard rock of their goal. Abraham Trujillo entered the pages of Mexican labor history with this often-quoted remark: "Mexico has had only two revolutions: Independence and the Reform; today we begin the third revolution, the conflict between Capital and Labor."[9]

The presiding officers finally brought the meeting around to a discussion of a list of counterproposals to be submitted to the industrialists. The workers' *reglamento* presented at the meeting and hammered out during the next several days by the GCOL leadership dealt with nearly every grievance that had been raised by the cotton textile

7. *La Lucha Obrera*, 16 December 1906. On the beginnings of the strike, see *El Tiempo*, 7 December 1906; *El Imparcial*, 13 December 1906; telegram from Martínez to Díaz, 4 December 1906, GPDC, 65:4072; Cahuantzi to Díaz, 7 December 1906, GPDC, 31:17200.

8. Rodarte, *7 de enero*, p. 8; *La Lucha Obrera*, 16 December 1906.

9. Rodarte, *7 de enero*, p. 8. A reporter for *El Tiempo* considered the general tone of the speeches to have been conciliatory (9 December 1906).

workers during the previous months, going far beyond the *Centro*'s initial *reglamento*. The final copy, signed by Pascual Mendoza, Adolfo Ramírez, and Antonio Espinosa, representatives of the Puebla, Tlaxcala, and Atlixco workers respectively, also contained a detailed schedule of wages. After further discussion from the floor, the meeting closed with a round of *vivas* for President Díaz, for Governor Martínez, and for Joaquín Pita, the *jefe político* of the city of Puebla.[10]

The major points of the workers' regulations were: (1) Workers would not be responsible for replacement of tools and equipment broken by accident or worn out through use. (2) Neither reading materials nor personal correspondence would be confiscated; reading in the factory would be prohibited only when it interfered with the job. (3) Fines or deductions from wages would not be permitted, except for the value of the cloth in the case of poor workmanship. (4) Company stores were not to be permitted. (5) Workers were not to be fired because of their union activity. (6) Workers disabled while on the job should be pensioned at half salary for as long as they remained in the mill town. (7) Wage scales in various departments would be based on skill and job difficulty. These were the major issues, although many others were mentioned, including child labor restrictions, job seniority, a 25 percent pay increase for the night crew, and even a request to have paper provided in the rest room in order to avoid the use of cotton or cloth scraps (for which they were fined). The *reglamento* agreed that no worker should enter work drunk and accepted the working hours of 6:00 A.M. to 8:00 P.M. daily, except Saturday.

Although there were many points of disagreement, it was not a militant list of demands. Even the semiofficial *El Imparcial* declared that it was "quite reasonable on all points."[11] As the major government spokesman, its opinion is interesting and important.

However reasonable their position, the union's financial resources were slim. The strike fund that had sustained strikes at individual mills was no longer being replenished. Paying the cost of transportation, the GCOL encouraged workers to find temporary work elsewhere. By

10. *El Tiempo*, 9 December 1906. For a copy of the counter-*reglamento*, see Appendix C.

11. *El Imparcial*, 8 December 1906.

January, from two to three thousand mill employees had left the Puebla area in search of work, including over four hundred workers and their families who had been offered jobs on the lands of Francisco I. Madero and his family. Those who remained in Puebla received aid from various sources. The Orizaba GCOL increased its dues from fifteen to twenty-five *centavos* in order to raise funds for the strikers. Local merchants contributed 640 bushels of corn. An *hacendado* donated 64 bushels of miscellaneous foodstuffs, while certain rich *hacendados* from Morelos had offered 3200 bushels of corn if the strike should continue more than eight days. Various "respectable" persons in Orizaba published a circular asking for contributions to help the Puebla striker.[12] Other Mexicans must have seen in the cause of the workers a significance broader than its working-class origins.

The *Gran Círculo* had no intentions of forcing the owners' hands by themselves. They early sent an open letter to President Díaz and to the governors of Puebla and Tlaxcala, requesting their intervention. When that appeal brought no results, they sent a telegram to the president, formally requesting him to arbitrate the conflict. Díaz replied immediately, agreeing to serve as arbitrator but requesting more information. Earlier, the GCOL had refused the offer of Puebla's bishop, Dr. Ramón Ibarra y González, to arbitrate the conflict, preferring to seek the president's good offices instead.[13]

Sometime the following week, perhaps on Monday, 17 December, Mendoza and his commissioners arrived in Mexico City seeking an audience with Díaz. There is no record of a meeting with the president, but on Friday, 21 December, they met with representatives of the Puebla owners' association in order to hear a special message from the president. In a letter read aloud to the group, the president requested each party to the dispute to submit to him a copy of its suggested *reglamento* and to provide him with written authorization to

12. *El Tiempo*, 20 December 1906 and 6 January 1907; *The Mexican Herald*, 9 December 1906; *El Diario del Hogar*, 10 January 1907; Petricioli, *La tragedia*, p. 25; Peña, "Apuntes históricos," 12 August 1958 and 17 February 1959; *El Imparcial*, 14, 19, 20, 22, 30 December 1906; Rodarte, 7 *de enero*, p. 9; flier "Triunfo de las huelguistas," GPDC, 31: (number misplaced).

13. *El Imparcial*, 13, 14 December 1906. Pascual Mendoza and José Morales to Díaz, 14 December 1906, GPDC, 65:4236; Díaz to Mendoza, 15 December 1906, GPDC, 31:4237.

arbitrate the disagreements. The public, he warned, wanted an end to the conflict.[14]

The strike appeared about to end, and none too soon for the preservation of the public order, according to General Martínez, governor of Puebla. He warned Díaz that the workers were approaching disorder and enclosed in his letter a newspaper article that called on the workers to rise and "prove that you are Mexicans worthy of the blood of Cuauhtémoc and Juárez. . . . Enslaved people, break your chains! Arise!"[15]

On Saturday the owners squelched public optimism by announcing they had informed the president that they did not desire his services as arbitrator. It was, as *El Tiempo* put it, "an unexpected reply."[16] The old *Caudillo* had been publicly rebuffed.

The Lockout

The following Monday, 24 December, the conflict escalated into a national crisis. When workers reported for work at the CIDOSA and CIV mills in Orizaba, at Hércules and Purísima in Querétaro, and at a number of mills in the state of México as well as in the Federal District, they found the doors locked; a nationwide lock-out (*paro*) was underway by the nation's leading mill owners. Before it was over, 93 of the nation's 150 mills had closed down, putting nearly thirty thousand workers out of jobs in twenty states. Of those that remained open, most were small mills employing few workers. Virtually the entire textile industry had stopped operations.[17]

Meeting in secret session on Saturday, 22 December, the industry's major owners or their representatives had unanimously adopted a

14. Mendoza to Díaz, 20 December 1906, GPDC, 31; *El Tiempo*, 23 December 1906. How the workers and the owners got together is not known. However, in AGN-Gob., leg. 817, is an undated letter from "Puebla workers' representatives" to Díaz, requesting his intervention in the strike in the name of both the owner's organization, CIM, and the GCOL.

15. Martínez to Díaz, 21 December 1906, GPDC, 31:16370.

16. *El Tiempo*, 27 December 1906.

17. *El País*, 24 December 1906.

resolution ordering the closing of the mills. The reason for the lock-out was clear. "The Puebla strikers do not yield," the resolution de-clared, "and have no reason to as long as the workers of other fac-tories sustain them; our situation is difficult but we are forced to make the regrettable decision to suspend work in all our mills."[18] Textile workers from a number of mills, particularly those in Orizaba, had been making regular contributions to the *Segundo Círculo*'s strike fund.[19] A few days later, an unidentified industrialist stated in a news-paper interview that all the owners and major stockholders in the industry agreed with the action taken. He offered the opinion that if the lockout succeeded "the strike is dead in Mexico," and noted grimly that "now is the opportune time to throttle these movements—at their beginning."[20]

In fact, the French-dominated inner circle of the industry had left the owners of the Puebla mills no choice but to join them. Even as early as the previous October, the French mills had considered seriously the use of a lockout to crush the Orizaba GCOL. Action had been deferred, however, until the current crisis. Then on Wednesday, 19 De-cember, these firms signed an agreement to lock out their own work-ers until the Puebla strike was broken, obviously intending to destroy the entire Gran Círculo as much as to rescue the Puebla mill owners. Only the date of the lockout was left open, as the document noted, pending agreement by the Puebla and Tlaxcala owners.[21] The latter were still negotiating with the GCOL and perhaps were not aware of the meeting of their industrial comrades until after the lockout deci-

18. *El Imparcial*, 25 December 1906.

19. Ibid., 27 December 1906. The tobacco workers' *Liga* offered aid as well; González Navarro, *Las huelgas textiles*, p. 515.

20. *El Imparcial*, 30 December 1906. See also ibid., 28 December 1906, and *El País*, 28 December 1906.

21. *Jefe político* to Dehesa, 2 November 1906, Orizaba, in Dehesa to Díaz, 6 November 1906, GPDC, 31:15456. The agreement was part of a document entitled "Bases para el reglamento de la asociación 'Centro de México,'" found in AGN-Gob, leg. 817. The firms who initially signed the *reglamento* produced well over 40 percent of the total sales for the industry and included the largest mills. The relative importance of every mill in the country can be seen by comparing the 5 percent sales tax levied against each mill; see the list of mills in *La Semana Mercantil*, 25 June 1906, pp. 301–3.

sion was made. Whether this was the case or not, the crisis that had appeared to the general public to be resolved on Friday had been significantly escalated on Monday morning.

It is difficult to imagine anything which could have garnered more sympathy for the workers' cause from a wider range of interests than the lockout. At the practical level, contributions of food and cash increased. A local charitable organization in Atlixco raised a substantial sum of money and collected a variety of goods for the workers of that industrial town and for those of the nearby mills of León and Metepec. In Orizaba several merchants provided credit and made outright gifts of corn and other goods. Carlos Herrera, the *jefe político,* gave 96 bushels of beans, 128 bushels of corn, and 50 *pesos* to the *Gran Círculo* for distribution to its members.[22]

Meanwhile, the reactions of the press to the lockout had ranged from disbelief to anger. The important dailies *El País* and *El Tiempo* had covered the Puebla strike thoroughly and were obviously chagrined by the turn of events. The editor of *El País,* Trinidad Sánchez Santos, demanded that this "terrible crisis" be brought to an immediate end, citing the sufferings of not only the workers but their families as well. *El Tiempo* accused the owners of being apathetic toward solving the crisis and complemented the workers on their dignified, peaceful attitude, even in the face of such provocation. *El Tiempo* did commend, however, the restraint of the owners in allowing the workers to remain in company housing during the lockout.[23]

Interestingly enough, the strongest initial reaction against the lockout came from *El Imparcial.* Its fullpage headline on Tuesday, 25 December—Christmas Day—read accusingly: "Close to 100,000 Persons Are Without Support," and the reporter covering the story noted that "the situation of the workers could not be worse—the strikers and their families lack even bread." He concluded his sympathetic story with the subtle moral judgment that "the industrialists will lose large sums of money. . . . But they do not fight for that which is indispensable to maintain life."[24] In the same vein, one of the editors wrote: "Almost all the mills are controlled by corporations whose

22. *El Tiempo,* 5 January 1907; Petricioli, *La tragedia,* p. 40.

23. *El País,* 24 December 1906; *El Tiempo,* 27 December 1906, 9 January 1907.

24. *El Imparcial,* 25 December 1906.

stockholders are rich and will not suffer seriously because of the sus-
pension of operations. The strikers, on the other hand, are going to
be deprived of the only source of income they have."[25] He then called
on the owners to improve working conditions, not only for humanitarian reasons but because a better treated worker, laboring under good
working conditions, would produce more. In the opinion of the editorial writer such violent methods as the lockout were not necessary to
solve the labor problem.

The question is: Given the close ties of *El Imparcial* with the regime,
did its opinions represent the official position of the federal government? Shortly after the regime fell in 1911, the governor of Veracruz
at the time of the lockout, Teodoro A. Dehesa, charged that José
Limantour had been responsible for the industrialists' decision to lock
out the workers and that the federal government itself had issued
instructions to the owners to close their mills. Limantour denied the
charge but offered no evidence to refute it.[26] At present, the known
facts support the thesis that the government was attempting to
negotiate the conflict but was unable to convince the powerful French
industrialists that negotiation was necessary. Perhaps the regime saw
only too well the possible adverse political results the lockout was
likely to bring, as well as the potential danger to the public order.
Indeed, perhaps even the *científicos* closest to the regime, such as *El
Imparcial*'s owner, Rafael Reyes Spíndola, may have felt some distaste
for the heavy-handed, unimaginative, and politically naïve show of
force by their partners and friends, the foreign industrialists. Whatever the truth, *El Imparcial* did not repeat its criticism of the lockout
and on several occasions was critical of the workers' demands.[27]

Meanwhile, in the textile villages near Puebla and Tlaxcala, some
workers were beginning to despair of a favorable settlement. The
strike was entering its fourth week with barely enough left in the

25. Ibid.
26. See correspondence between Dehesa and Limantour on the matter in
Sodi de Pallares, *Teodoro A. Dehesa*, pp. 199–202. See also Araiza, *Historia del
movimiento*, p. 105. Díaz had previously indicated that he was not opposed to a
lockout (Díaz to Dehesa, no date, but circa 8 or 9 November 1906, GPDC,
31:15457). According to *El Imparcial*, 25 December 1906, the government had
prior notice of the owners' intentions.
27. See 26 December 1906 and 5 January 1907.

strike fund to last to the coming weekend. The numbers of workers appearing at the gates of the mills asking to return to work was increasing daily, some of them grumbling that the strike had been the work of a few agitators led by Mendoza.[28] Yet the majority of the mill hands still supported Mendoza. If they were no longer optimistic or enthusiastic, most were still grimly determined to hold out.

In Orizaba workers began migrating to find work soon after the lockout was imposed on them. They had been unprepared for it, and with the depletion of the strike fund for earlier strikes and now for the Puebla workers, little was left for the emergency in which they found themselves. Some left for the small villages and *ranchos* of their parents; others went to Mexico City or wherever they thought work might be found. Some went north, looking for work on the railroads or in the mines or in the small textile mills still operating.[29] Yet most stayed home, supporting their families as best they could from odd jobs or small gifts from friends and relatives, by credit from friendly merchants, and from the meager support the union could offer.

As bitterness and frustration grew among the jobless workers, local officials nervously reviewed their plans and procedures for the repression of any violence that might erupt. The federal government added to the uneasiness by moving two thousand additional troops into the major textile areas, a clear sign that they were expecting trouble. Yet surprisingly little violence took place. The few incidents worth recording were easily controlled by the *rurales* who normally were stationed at the mills. Anonymous threats were made against various mill owners and their managers, but none were carried out.[30]

The day the lockout began, the GCOL commission asked to see Díaz and was granted a presidential audience for Wednesday, 26 December. The commission included José Morales, representing the Orizaba GCOL, Pascual Mendoza, representing the Puebla workers and the chief delegate, Antonio Hidalgo, Adolfo Ramírez, and San-

28. *El Imparcial*, 26 December 1906; *El País*, 27, 28, 29 December 1906.

29. *El País*, 4 January 1907; *El Imparcial*, 29 December 1906.

30. *El Dictamen* (Veracruz), 27 December 1906; *El Imparcial*, 25, 29 December 1906; *El Cosmopolita*, 3 January 1907; *El Tiempo*, 5 January 1907.

tiago Cortés from the Tlaxcalan mills, and Antonio Espinosa of the Atlixco mills. What took place during that interview was never published, but afterwards the commissioners held a brief press conference at which they outlined their major demands. First, they desired a differentiated wage scale based on job difficulty and skill, in place of the present system that recognized neither and paid poorly at that. In addition, they were determined to eliminate fines and to abolish the common practice of discounting wages to pay for public festivities on civil or religious holidays in the company towns. Also, they believed that it should not be necessary to obtain company approval to have visitors in mill housing. Finally, they were adamant that workers should not have to pay for bobbins, shuttles, and other parts and equipment broken only through usage, not negligence. The Tlaxcalan representative, Adolfo Ramírez, told the reporters that they would accept whatever the president should decide about wages but that the questions of housing, discounts, and the replacement of parts and equipment must be resolved. In the course of the meeting with the press, someone on the commission noted that prices were rising but not wages, commenting bitterly that everyone was making money but the workers.[31]

In fact, the industrialists were divided on whether to give concessions to the workers. Representatives of mill owners from the state of Mexico, the Federal District, and some of the Puebla mills were willing to compromise, but others, principally from the large, French-owned mills, opposed any concession. An urgent telegram was sent to Puebla by the group opposing concessions in order to enlist the support of those owners who had not been represented at the meetings at which the concessions had been discussed. A special train was promptly dispatched from Puebla carrying owner representatives with special authorization to veto any attempt to bring about a compromise solution to the conflict. Officially representing the Puebla owners were Manuel Rivero Collado, Ignacio Morales y Bember, and Adrian Reynaud; the latter as an officer in CIDOSA and CIV represented a

31. Mendoza to Díaz, 23 December 1906, GPDC, 65:4389. *El Imparcial*, 26, 27 December 1906; *El Diario del Hogar*, 28 December 1906. See names of commissioners penciled on the back of the workers' *reglamento*, AGN-Gob, leg. 817.

hard-line position. Accompanying the industrialists was General Mucio Martínez, the governor of the state.[32]

Throughout the weekend, owners, major stockholders, and company lawyers met in extended session, arguing over whether to extend the lockout or to offer concessions to the workers. Finally, on Monday, 31 December, they voted to accept an arbitration award by Díaz. The administration may have applied pressure on the hardliners, perhaps indicating that such an award might have certain benefits for them. *El Imparcial,* the consistent government spokesman throughout the crisis, had said in its Saturday edition that if the "small advantages" conceded to the workers in the earlier meeting were allowed to stand, the mills could open by Wednesday.[33] It may well be that this position was strongly seconded by the smaller mills, who stood to lose the most by a prolonged lockout.

Both Pascual Mendoza and Manuel Rivero Collada, president of the *Centro Industrial Mexicano,* returned to Puebla to hold last-minute discussions with their respective constituents. Meeting again at the Guerrero theater after nearly four weeks on strike, the Puebla GCOL voted to accept unconditionally an arbitration award by the president. The Puebla industrialists, meeting in secret session, also agreed to accept presidential arbitration.[34]

On Thursday, 3 January 1907, Díaz called both groups to his office in order to hear their final presentations. The president, as always, listened silently.[35] Later that day the GCOL commission received word at their headquarters in the Hotel Central that the president would receive them the next morning at eleven o'clock to announce the arbitration *laudo* (award). The long fight was over.

Arriving at the office of the vice-president promptly at ten o'clock the next morning, the commission members received a few words from Corral in preparation for their meeting with the president. At eleven o'clock, the workers were ushered before the president. After a

32. *El Imparcial,* 29 December 1906. See Araiza, *El movimiento obrero,* pp. 106–7, for a copy of the authorization signed by the Puebla owners.

33. *El País,* 29 December 1906, 1 January 1907; *El Imparcial,* 29, 30 December 1906.

34. *El Tiempo,* 4 January 1907; *El Imparcial,* 3 January 1907.

35. *El País,* 4 January 1907.

brief, formal ceremony, Díaz read the nine-article arbitration *laudo* personally to the assembled group of workers and industrialists. When he finished, Mendoza, Morales, and the other commission members could not conceal their joy and emotion, according to the *El Tiempo* reporter, giving repeated thanks and demonstrations of their gratitude to the president and vice-president.[36]

The *laudo* is obscure enough to have been generally overlooked by historians or overshadowed by the events that followed. Those few writers who dealt with it have dismissed it as meaningless or condemned it as an example of the regime's alliance with foreign and domestic business interests.[37] But it is neither a meaningless gesture nor a blatant defense of Mexican moneyed interests. Rather it is a clear example of the regime's willingness to break with its past laissez-faire labor policies in order to impose a settlement sufficiently attractive to the workers, but one which did not wreak any harm on the basic economic interests of the industrialists.

Article 1 of the *laudo* stipulated that the mills would open the following Monday, 7 January. *Article 2* provided for uniform wage rates for weavers, using the average wage paid these workers in the same geographic area. It was specifically designed to meet workers' complaints that wages varied widely from mill to mill in the state of Puebla.[38] A system of bonuses was also suggested as an incentive for increased worker productivity. *Article 3* required workers to carry notebooks on their person in which their "conduct, industry, and efficiency" could be noted by their supervisors. Such a notebook would be required

36. *El Tiempo*, 5, 6 January 1907; *The Mexican Herald*, 4 January 1907. The representatives of the owners were Henrique Tron, Luis Barroso Arias, José Signoret, and the leading figures from Puebla's CIM.

37. For example, see Florencio Barrera Fuentes, *Historia de la Revolución Mexicana: la etapa precursora* (Mexico: Talleres Gráficos de la Nación, 1955), p. 218, and Montes Rodríquez, *La huelga de Río Blanco*, p. 77. The author of the *laudo* appears to have been Corral. Of the four drafts of the settlement located in the Archivo General de la Nación, the original is handwritten on Corral's personal stationery (AGN-Gob, leg. 817). For comments on Corral's role in the settlement, see *El País*, 1, 6 January 1907. For comments on the historical significance of the *laudo*, see Daniel Cosío Villegas's introduction to Moisés González Navarro, *La vida social*, pp. xxiii–xxiv.

38. See *El Diario del Hogar*, 28 December 1906.

before a worker could transfer mills and was a common blacklisting device. It was to become the most resented provision of the *laudo*.[39] *Article 4* contained five clauses. Clause 1 provided that all fines go into a fund for widows and orphans of the workers, a reform obviously intended to placate the workers on one of their most frequent complaints. Clauses 2, 3, and 4 eliminated discounts on wages for any reason, made the workers responsible only for tools or equipment broken through negligence, and gave them the right to have anyone in their homes subject only to civil law. Each had been a major grievance. Mills were also required to hire a company medic. Clause 5 gave workers leaving a mill six days to vacate their homes, starting from the day they received their pay. Standard procedure was that the workers leaving their jobs had to vacate their homes the same day on which they were paid.

Article 5 provided for a fifteen day cooling-off period after a grievance had been presented in writing to the manager of the mill. If satisfaction were not obtained, the article specifically gave the workers the right to strike. *Article 6* required the mill owner to improve the schools within company towns and to establish new ones where needed. *Article 7* forbade the hiring of children under seven years of age and ordered that older children working in the mills be allowed time to attend school; state governors were to see that these instructions were complied with. The GCOL had demanded that children under fourteen not be allowed to work in the mills. *Article 8* authorized the local *jefe político* to supervise the publication of the workers' newspapers in order to prevent what the award termed "objectionable doctrines" from being spread among the workers. *Article 9* stipulated that the workers agree not to strike outside the provisions of Article 5, eliminating wildcat strikes and walkouts.

On one level of analysis, the *laudo* is a remarkable success because it so clearly represented what the federal authorities had been seeking since early summer. Focusing entirely on the problem of law and order within his domain, Díaz and his advisors had been working to keep this troubled group of Mexicans from supporting any revolutionary group or socialist doctrine. In order for this end to be achieved, however, powerful industrial interests had to be persuaded

39. This was suggested by the industrialists. See their document "Para el reglamento de la asociación 'Centro de México'," AGN-Gob, leg. 817.

to accept the legitimacy of governmental intervention in labor conflicts, for reasons other than merely to preserve public order. The initial efforts of Díaz and Dehesa to suggest to the mill owners even such minimum changes as the reduction of working hours had met with resistance, as had Díaz's initial efforts to arbitrate the Puebla strike. The major opponents to arbitration were the large French-dominated firms, supposedly the regime's closest allies. Yet, in the end, even they acquiesced to arbitration, perhaps because they came to believe, or were persuaded, that the *laudo* would not hurt their vital interests. It is likely that the financial burden of any wage increase would fall mainly on the smaller, family-owned mills, which generally paid below the average regional wages, rather than on the French mills. Nonetheless, it seems clear that the larger firms, having failed to crush the strike and the labor movement, must have been uneasy over the entrance of the government into an arena they once could call their own.

From the perspective of the Puebla-Tlaxcala workers, the *laudo* was a mixed victory, but at least there was something to show for the long struggle. They had obtained governmental intervention, as they had requested, and the results provided concrete benefits in a compromise on fines and in the elimination of restrictions on visitors to their homes, of discounts on wages, and of deductions to pay for broken equipment. The housing and education stipulations were reforms in favor of the workers. The *laudo* also eliminated wage differential within the industry on a regional basis and would therefore result in wage increases for many Puebla workers.

On the other hand, the award ignored the question of establishing a wage differential scale within each mill. In addition, the award ignored many of the lesser articles in the workers' *reglamento,* and in particular it failed to deal with the abuses of the company store, an issue that would receive wide publicity in the days ahead. And perhaps most important, the *laudo* did not establish job protection for union members or their leaders. Indeed, the notebook requirement provided a convenient means for blacklisting such "agitators" throughout the industry.

Yet there is no reason to believe that the initial emotions of the *Gran Círculo*'s commissioners were not genuine. If nothing else, the long ordeal was over, and they had their organization intact and a few concessions to take home to the rank and file. Even more, they had defied rich and powerful men, and in the end it was the industrialists who broke ranks, not the workers. At that moment, in the benevolent shadow of the president, they had every reason to consider the award a victory.

La Huelga de Río Blanco

The tragic events which took place in the textile towns near Orizaba on Monday, 7 January, do not constitute a strike in the usual sense, yet they are most often referred to as the Río Blanco strike—*la huelga de Río Blanco*—and so they are here, too.[40]

When Pascual Mendoza and his commissioners read the *laudo* to their men in Puebla and Tlaxcala, it was accepted with relatively little open dissatisfaction.[41] They later reconsidered, but for the moment the mill hands of the area were relieved that the strike was over and proud that they had won concessions from their *patrones*. Now they wanted to go back to work.

In Orizaba it was a different story. When José Morales presented the *laudo* to a meeting of the rank and file on the morning of Sunday, 6 January, strong opposition developed over several provisions, the most bitterly resented being Article 3 on notebooks. As the opposition grew, someone shouted "better martyrs than slaves."[42] It was to be the course they followed.

Unable to reach an agreement, Morales finally adjourned the meeting. Leaving the Gorostiza Theater where the meeting was held,

40. In defense of the legitimacy of the term, some sources claim that the Orizaba GCOL officially struck when their members were locked out on the twentieth of December; see Turner, *Barbarous Mexico*, pp. 170–71; Petricioli, *La tragedia*, p. 47. The best published accounts are: Moisés González Navarro, "La huelga de Río Blanco," *Historia Mexicana* 6 (April–June 1957): 510–33; Petricioli, *La tragedia*; Montes Rodríquez, *La huelga de Río Blanco*; Cosío Villegas, *Vida política interior*, 2:730–37 and Peña "Apuntes históricos."

41. *El Tiempo*, 6 January 1907. Metepec workers were not satisfied with the *laudo* and requested the *jefe político*, Ignacio Macharro, not to implement it; Escobedo and Salazar, *Pugnas de la gleba*, pp. 23–25.

42. *El Diario del Hogar*, 11, 12 January 1907; Morales's own account of the strike is given here in an interview.

Morales and several deputies hurried off to take the word to the various mill towns. In Nogales he found his people tranquil, due mainly to the distribution of grain there by Carlos Herrera, but in the more heavily populated villages where the Río Blanco and Santa Rosa mills were located, the mood was tense and hostile. Many families in both towns had been forced to pawn nearly everything they owned in order to buy food. The Río Blanco company store, run by a Frenchman, had refused them credit, as had most other company stores in the area. By Sunday, there were families with no food in their homes and no means to buy any. Even though they would begin work on Monday, they would not be paid until Saturday.[43] In a flier that circulated the following day, the workers pleaded with the townspeople of Orizaba to aid them, explaining that "we have exhausted all our financial resources with which to give BREAD TO OUR BELOVED CHILDREN," and asked for contributions "in order to sustain our families who have suffered the terrible consequences of the whims of the industrialists."[44]

Meanwhile, a group of dissidents spent Sunday afternoon trying to convince their comrades in the mills not to return to work. Although their identity is not known, it is likely that workers from the Santa Rosa mill, still convinced that Morales had sold them out, played a prominent role. Later that evening, a group of workers confronted Morales in his home, but he refused to talk with them, saying that it was not a proper hour to discuss business and telling them to return before work in the morning. They never came back.[45]

Exactly what happened the following morning is not clear even now, nearly seventy years later. As with so many great events, we must pick and choose from the various and often contradictory accounts that have survived the years. We do know this, however: when the company whistle broke the stillness of the morning for the first time in over two weeks, there were men in the textile village of Río Blanco who were determined not to return to work.

43. Ibid.; *El Cosmopolita*, 3 January 1907.

44. See the flier "Señores Comerciantes, Propietarios y Compatriotas en General," in Luis Barroso Arias to Corral, 7 January 1907, AGN-Gob, leg. 817. Capitals in the original.

45. Peña, "Apuntes históricos," 18 June 1959. *El Diario del Hogar*, 11, 12 January 1907.

The most popular image of how the strike began is that as the hour to enter work approached, a group of mill hands gathered near the Río Blanco factory and started toward it in a hostile manner, a Mexican flag held high, throwing stones and shouting "down with the dictatorship, death to Díaz!"[46] An adjunct to this image is the common belief that the *Partido Liberal Mexicano* (PLM) instigated the strike through its working-class contacts or that the PLM was the main political force behind the strike, as Professor James Cockcroft asserts.[47] It is appealing to imagine Mexican workers shouting defiance, attempting to bring down a dictatorship with stones, precursors to the great Revolution barely three years away. Most likely it is incorrect. There simply is no substantial evidence that *la huelga de Río Blanco* was politically motivated.[48] Precursors they were, but not as self-conscious rebels against the regime. Their enemies were much closer at hand.

A more plausible account is that a group of workers opposed to the *laudo* blocked the two major entrances of the mill. Unable to enter the plant, several thousand workers gathered around outside, growing restless and disgruntled. At that point a *panadero* carrying a large basket of *bolillos* (the popular hard Mexican breadrolls) from the nearby company store attempted to enter the factory and was knocked to the ground. In the ensuing scuffle, someone threw a rock at the mill; the rock was followed by a barrage of stones.[49]

Exactly what happened next is not clear and may never be fully

46. Escobedo and Salazar, *Pugnas de la gleba*, p. 13, and *El Tiempo*, 9 January 1907.

47. Cockcroft, *Intellectual Precursors*, pp. 48, 134, 140. See also Montes Rodríguez, *La huelga de Río Blanco*, pp. 68, 89; Blaisdell, *The Desert Revolution*, p. 8. Teodoro Hernández, "La huelga de Río Blanco," *El Popular*, 7 January 1948.

48. José Neira, the PLM activist most often associated with the strike, was charged by the regime with "intellectual" contribution to the events at Río Blanco, not with actual participation. The charges likely stemmed from his letter in October to a former comrade in Orizaba, calling on the workers to join the PLM revolts of that fall. In a letter intercepted by the Mexican authorities, the PLM claimed no responsibility for, or previous knowledge of, the strike (R. M. Caule, pseudonym for Ricardo Flores Magón, to an unknown recipient, 17 January 1907, in the *Archivo Central de la Secretaría de Relaciones Exteriores, Ramo de Ricardo Flores Magón* (hereafter Rel-RFM), L-E-924, 7:23–24).

49. Peña, "Apuntes históricos," 25 June 1959; Petricioli, *La tragedia*, pp. 50–52; *El Diario*, 11, 12 January 1907.

known. From the many partial and conflicting accounts, it appears that a group of workers broke off from the main body and headed for the company store, barely a block away on the opposite side of the street. It was not yet seven o'clock, but the store was opening up for business, as was usual in the mill towns. Several accounts maintain that the store employees, seeing the crowd descending on the store, panicked and fired into the workers, killing several and turning the hostile crowd into a raging mob. Both Carlos Herrera and Ramón Rocha, the federal judge for the area, believed this account to be true, judging by their own accounts of the events,[50] although both were also vulnerable because of their past sympathies and connections with the workers. When Díaz read Herrera's judgment of how the blame should be allocated, he wrote to Governor Dehesa with hardly veiled sarcasm (having chosen to believe another account), "He informs me that they burned and robbed the store and that it seems to him that the employees were imprudent in having defended themselves by firing [on the workers]."[51]

A more compelling variation of the above events, and one often alluded to by contemporary accounts, is that several women, among them Margarita Martínez and Isabel Díaz de Pensamiento, were denied credit and perhaps insulted that morning by the clerks at Garcin's company store. Angry and humiliated, they harangued the workers milling around the area, calling them cowards and demanding that they take some action against the store. Even though the store was a block from the mill, with several thousand workers in the area, undoubtedly there would have been many workers quite nearby. At that moment, as a large group of workers perhaps showed some hostile intent against the store, the shots from the interior rang out, adding rage to anger and frustration.[52]

50. Rocha to Dehesa, 7 January 1907, in cover letter Dehesa to Díaz, 8 January 1907, GPDC, 32:201; Carlos Herrera to Dehesa in *El Periódico Oficial del Estado de Veracruz-Llave* 25 (12 January 1907): 1–2. See also *El Imparcial*, 11 January 1907; *El Diario*, 11, 12 January 1907; *El Diario del Hogar*, 12 January 1907; Petricioli, *La tragedia*, p. 52.

51. Díaz to Dehesa, 7 January 1907, GPDC, 66:130. All pieces of correspondence in legajo 66 are telegrams.

52. On the role of the women, see José B. Escasan, "El Trágico 7 de enero de 1907," *Excelsior*, 9 April 1931; *El Tiempo*, 12 January 1907; Peña, "Apuntes

The Río Blanco company store in flames. The picture was taken from the mill on 7 January 1907. Mounted figures in the left center of the picture are presumably rurales.

In any event, the workers stormed into the store as a clerk desperately tried to hold the main door shut. The men ripped the store apart and carried off food, dry goods, and two small safes or cash registers. In the melee, several employees of the store were seriously wounded, most likely in retaliation for the shooting. Among the things taken from the store were a number of bottles of liquor, undoubtedly adding to the dynamics of the events that followed. As the store was being looted, a fire broke out; several photographs taken from the roof of the mill show the flames, accompanied by black smoke, reaching skyward.[53]

The assault on the store is a key to understanding the story of Río Blanco. With one important exception, the only buildings deliberately burned that day were the company stores of the textile mills in the area. Forced to buy at the company stores because of their location or because wages were paid partly in discounted script, the workers were often in debt to them and universally believed that they paid high prices for inferior goods.[54] Because they confronted the workers day in and day out, the company stores at the larger foreign-owned mills became the most hated symbol of capitalist exploitation and foreign domination, perhaps even more hated than the industrialists themselves.

Meanwhile, Carlos Herrera had been alerted and set out for the mill on horseback, accompanied by six mounted policemen. His arrival calmed the crowd still milling around the burning store, for the workers knew him as a friend and an ally in their conflicts with the mills. By 9:00 A.M. two companies of the 13th Battalion of federal infantry stationed in Orizaba had arrived at the mill. The workers were peaceful, so Herrera made no arrests but posted the troops around the mill.[55]

---

históricos," 25 June 1959; *La Voz de México* (Mexico City), 11 January 1907; Montes Rodríguez, *Río Blanco*, p. 79.

53. *Mejicanos que sufren* to Díaz, 12 January 1907, GPDC, 32:101. This is a two-page letter that Díaz received from a worker or workers ("suffering Mexicans") at Río Blanco; hereafter referred to as "Mejicanos." See also *El Cosmopolita*, 13 January 1907. For photographs, see Montes Rodríguez, *Río Blanco*, p. 64, overleaf.

54. Peña, "Apuntes históricos," 30 September 1958; workers of the *fábrica de Santa Rosa* to Corral, 29 October 1906, AGN-Gob, leg. 817.

55. Carlos Herrera to Dehesa in *El Periódico Oficial del Estado de Veracruz-*

The calm was broken at one point in the late morning or early afternoon. Word of the violence had spread through the mill towns around Orizaba; workers were in the streets, and the mills were closed and locked. The *rurales*' commander at Río Blanco reported that a large number of Río Blanco workers started for Nogales at around one in the afternoon. Garcín operated two more stores in Nogales; sometime that day they were looted, and at least one was burned to the ground. Several other stores were looted as well. Troops of the 13th Battalion under their commander Col. José María Villarreal encountered a group of workers in the vicinity of one of Garcín's stores in that town and opened fire, killing and wounding a number of workers. More than fifty workers were taken prisoner.[56]

Intimidated, the remaining workers fled along the road toward the Santa Rosa mill; the company store of that huge mill had already been burned down earlier that day. After confining their prisoners, the soldiers set out after the workers. Arriving at the Santa Rosa mill, they came upon a group of workers. Whether barraged by stones, as one report maintained, or without cause, the soldiers opened fire again, and more workers fell.[57] Nearly thirty workers were killed and

---

Llave 25 (12 January 1907): 1–2; Lt. Gabriel Arroyo to Inspector General de la Policía Rural (General Francisco M. Ramírez), January 1906 [*sic*] AGN-Gob, leg. 895:5196–5203.

56. Sources differ as to when the Nogales stores were burned and whether the soldiers fired first or were assaulted with rocks or even shot at. See Petricioli, *La tragedia*, pp. 53–54; Rodarte, *7 de enero*, pp. 24–25; *El Diario del Hogar*, 11, 12 January 1907; *El Imparcial*, 11, 12 January 1907; *El Tiempo*, 9, 10, 13 January 1907; Montes Rodríguez, *Río Blanco*, pp. 83–84. Lic. Rocha declared that the prisoners taken at Nogales were caught in the act; according to his report, they appear to have been the only ones so designated; Rocha to Dehesa, 10 January 1907, GPDC, 32:931.

57. Petricioli, *La tragedia*, pp. 54–55; *El Diario*, 10 January 1907; *El Tiempo*, 10 January 1907, "Xochitl" (pseudonym for unknown author), "Anselma Sierra, la verdadera heroína de la tragedia del 7 de enero de 1907 en Río Blanco, Veracruz," *El Universal*, 7 January 1954; *El Tiempo*, 9 January 1907. One participant in the event reported that a few of the workers were armed; Daniel Castillo, "Apuntes de un obrero" in Peña, "Apuntes históricos," 7 June 1959. So did Herrera in his report to Dehesa in cover letter Dehesa to Díaz, 7 January 1907, GPDC, 66:124. Several soldiers received wounds during the encounter at Santa Rosa, though whether from rocks or bullets was not specified; *El Diario del Hogar*, 11 January 1907.

wounded as a result of these encounters. In an official report of the strike never made public, eleven workers were listed as dead and thirteen wounded during the first day's violence. Other official sources give similar figures. The author of "Mejicanos que sufren," presumably with no motive to underestimate the casualties, told of seventeen killed at Nogales, perhaps meaning at Santa Rosa too. The most accurate independent source appears to be the Mexico City daily *El Diario del Hogar,* edited by the well-known oppositionist journalist, Filomeno Mata. It listed eighteen dead and eleven wounded from the first day's violence and furnished names for most of the victims.[58]

In a related incident that day, a group of workers from the jute factory Santa Gertrudis attempted to sack a local loan office, also the object of much hatred, but were surprised by the police and a number of prisoners were taken. In another case, reported by Professor González Navarro, a number of workers from the Cerritos mill obtained arms and used them to take over two railroad stations between Orizaba and Maltrata. The most serious incident, however, took place in the evening, when the home of José Morales was set on fire. Evidently those responsible intended to include Morales as well, but forewarned, he escaped. The evidence indicates that Morales's enemies from the Santa Rosa mill set the fire, which quickly consumed seventy-eight of the small wooden homes in the workers' company housing.[59] Of all the elements which led to the tragedy of Río Blanco, one must consider the hostility between the Morales and the Ramírez factions as one of the more important.

Many prisoners were taken that day, crowded into small prison cells, without food or water. Fearful of official wrath, other workers fled into the hills that flank the Orizaba valley. The American consul from

58. Subsecretary of War (General Rosalino Martínez) to Díaz, 11 January 1907, GPDC, 66:227. Rocha reported thirteen dead and thirteen wounded in his report to Dehesa in cover letter Dehesa to Díaz, 12 January 1907, GPDC, 66:285. Rural Corps officer, Lt. Arroyo, noted "20 victims" in his initial report to the Inspector General. "Mejicanos," GPDC, 32:101. *El Diario del Hogar,* 11 January 1907.

59. Herrera to Dehesa in cover letter Dehesa to Díaz, 7 January 1907, GPDC, 66:124; González Navarro, "La huelga de Río Blanco," p. 522; Rocha to Dehesa, 8 January 1907 in cover letter Dehesa to Díaz, GPDC, 66:201; Dehesa to Díaz, 9 January 1907, GPDC, 66:208.

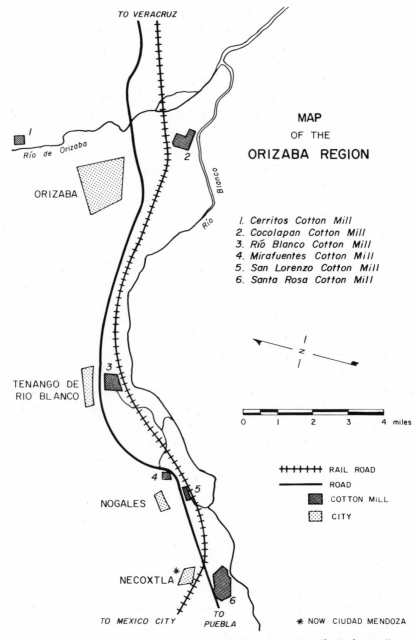

MAP

OF THE

ORIZABA REGION

1. *Cerritos Cotton Mill*
2. *Cocolapan Cotton Mill*
3. *Río Blanco Cotton Mill*
4. *Mirafuentes Cotton Mill*
5. *San Lorenzo Cotton Mill*
6. *Santa Rosa Cotton Mill*

┼┼┼┼┼┼┼ RAIL ROAD

───── ROAD

▨ COTTON MILL

▨ CITY

✳ NOW CIUDAD MENDOZA

Orizaba Region. Adapted from Yamada, "The Cotton Textile Industry," p. 1.

Veracruz reported that the workers who fled to the hills were pursued by soldiers; he intimated that many were summarily executed. No official source lists such casualties, but one worker told of buzzards circling those hills, feeding on the bodies of people "who did no more wrong than to be poor but honorable workers, assasinated by the troops of our own country."[60]

Early in the morning of 8 January federal troops under the command of General Rosalino Martínez, the subsecretary of war, arrived by train from Mexico City. Col. Francisco Ruiz, former chief of police of the Federal District and one-time *jefe político* of Celaya, accompanied General Martínez with orders to replace Carlos Herrera, accused by various textile company officials of encouraging the workers' violence by his friendliness to their cause. In an exchange of coded telegrams with Dehesa, Díaz ordered the governor to suspend Herrera, noting ominously that the *jefe político*'s "benevolent character is not suitable for the energetic measures that will be necessary to repress the commotion in such a way that it will not be repeated."[61] Dehesa defended Herrera, but Díaz would not be moved, saying that the rioting would continue until Dehesa agreed to replace Herrera with Col. Ruiz. Reluctantly, Dehesa complied.

In compliance with specific orders from the president, General Martínez spent all that day, Tuesday, 8 January, questioning witnesses to ascertain who were the principal instigators of the violence. By evening the list was complete.[62]

Early Wednesday morning, as thousands of workers gathered to enter the mills for the first time since Monday, six prisoners were taken by military escorts to the burned-out ruins of several company stores in the area and executed in full view of their comrades. Among the dead were Manuel Juárez, vice-president of the Santa Rosa branch of the GCOL, and a comrade, Rafael Troncoso, shot to death by a firing squad on the ruins of *El Modelo*, Garcín's store near Santa Rosa. Rafael Moreno, president of the same branch, was executed near another looted store in Santa Rosa. Three unidentified workers were killed on the ruins of *El Centro Comercial* in Nogales and Garcín's

60. "Mejicanos," GPDC, 32:101. Official records list 117 prisoners, including 5 women; Martínez to Díaz, 11 January 1907, GPDC, 66:255.
61. Díaz to Dehesa, 7 January 1907, GPDC, 66:133, 135.
62. Díaz to Martínez, 7 January 1907, GPDC, 66:114.

store in Río Blanco. A seventh worker was shot and killed at Río Blanco as he defiantly cursed the soldiers, unable to contain his rage at what he had seen.[63]

The burden of guilt for the executions must be laid upon Díaz himself; the evidence is clear if not conclusive. Díaz had earlier hinted at the executions when he ordered that Herrera be replaced by Ruiz, citing the necessity of taking "energetic measures" to prevent a reoccurrence of the disorder. It was an obvious warning of his intentions. Then, in a preliminary report to Díaz on Tuesday, after his investigations, General Martínez mentioned that certain individuals then in custody were the "principal authors and instigators of yesterday's crimes and . . . unquestionably deserve to be punished in such a way as to set an example."[64] The phrase "ejemplar castigo" is a euphemism for "to execute conspicuously" and was so used, for example, in the headline for *El Diario*'s story of the executions. In that same telegram Martínez carefully noted that he was sending the prisoners to Orizaba where they could be better guarded. He was implying, as it turned out, that the *ley fuga* would be applied. The prisoners would be shot while trying to escape. The president replied to General Martínez's message, writing several instructions on the bottom of the original telegram, but made no mention of the prisoners. There would be no mercy.

And so it was that on the following morning, Wednesday, Díaz received from General Martínez a telegram stating that five prisoners had been shot while trying to escape. Soon, however, the cover-up story became confused. Early in the afternoon Díaz received a telegram from Governor Dehesa stating that Ramón Rocha had informed him that five individuals had been shot while attacking a guardhouse. One of the victims was Manuel Juárez, named in General Martínez's morning report. Díaz then telegraphed Martínez, simply repeating Dehesa's version of the story, adding that reports of executions had

63. Only two Mexico City dailies dared print the details of the executions, *El Diario* on 12 January and *El Tiempo* the following day. It was also carried on the front page of the *New York Times*, 13 January 1907.

64. Martínez to Díaz, 8 January 1907, GPDC, 66:159. The Spanish is ". . . como principales instigadores y autores de los crimenes cometidos ayer y quienes incuestionablemente merecen ejemplar castigo."

been published in Capital newspapers, "something that is not believable." He asked for a report on this matter.[65] Although he did not point out the discrepancy between the two versions of the executions, he undoubtedly counted on Martínez's being astute enough to perceive that two different official explanations would hardly strengthen the government's credibility.

Martínez's final report was received in the Capital on Friday. He summarized the entire operation of his troops since arriving and repeated his earlier story that five "guilty" individuals had been shot when they attempted to escape from their guards while being transferred to the authorities in Orizaba. He gave Col. Ruiz as the source of his information.[66] The federal government never published either a denial of the executions or the government's story of the events at Río Blanco, as it did in the case of Cananea. It simply remained silent.

There the matter rested until 1935. That year Ramón Prida, a young politician and intellectual in the Díaz regime, published an article on the Río Blanco strike in the journal of the Mexican Geographic and Statistical Society. He related a discussion to which he had been a party in which General Martínez claimed that before he had left the Capital for Orizaba, he refused Díaz's verbal orders to execute the leaders of the violence. Díaz had relented, according to Martínez, and agreed to send Col. Francisco Ruiz with that responsibility as temporary political authority for the area.[67]

The story is consistent not only with the events that followed but with the politics of the repression as well. Díaz, determined to teach the workers a lesson, no doubt picked General Martínez because he was a political enemy of Governor Dehesa, dating back to Martínez's stint as chief of the military zone of Veracruz, and hence would not likely cooperate with the governor in any way that would block Díaz's intentions. The general, on the other hand, had definite political ambitions toward the governorship of Veracruz and could not hope to

65. Díaz to Martínez, 10 January 1907, GPDC, 66:226; Martínez to Díaz, 9 January 1907, GPDC, 66:197; Dehesa to Díaz, 9 January 1907, GPDC, 66:206. Official correspondence always referred to five prisoners, whereas six were reported executed in the newspaper accounts.

66. Martínez to Díaz, 11 January 1907, GPDC, 66:227.

67. Ramón Prida, "Los sucesos de Río Blanco en enero de 1907," *Suplemento al boletín de la Sociedad Mexicana de Geografía y Estadística* (1935), pp. 94–97.

realize these ambitions if he were obviously and directly responsible for a bloody massacre. Martínez requested written instructions from Díaz, and the president sidestepped this maneuver by sending a personal hatchetman along with the general to carry out the dirty work. Dehesa, of course, realized the purpose of replacing Herrera with Ruiz, and he resisted the president as strongly as he dared. It failed to deter Díaz, and after several impatient, sharply worded telegrams from him, Dehesa gave his permission for the change.[68]

Although rumors circulated in Veracruz later on that month that General Martínez would replace Dehesa as governor, the latter held on to his position until the fall of the regime in 1911. Martínez, however, died not long after Río Blanco, generally identified as the man responsible for the death of the hundreds of workers rumored to have been killed by his soldiers. Ironically, as a young Lt. Colonel, Martínez had commanded the execution squad of suspected rebels in the port of Veracruz in 1879, the infamous "matalos en caliente" incident that caused such a scandal in the first Díaz administration.[69]

In conjunction with the execution of the workers, there is a minor story that needs to be reexamined. Carlos Herrera publicly accused the *rurales* who were assigned to the Río Blanco mill of neglect of duty in their failure to prevent the workers from assaulting the company store. The *rurales* were present when the store was looted and burned but did not attempt to interfere, according to Herrera. Lt. Gabriel Arroyo, in charge of the squad, maintained that Herrera had issued a standing order that the *rurales* were not to fire on the workers, adding that his squad had performed their duty as they saw it, at one point preventing the workers from setting fire to the mill. Several contemporary newspaper accounts reported that the *rurales* had been executed for cowardice. This charge was denied by *El Imparcial*, whose reporter had interviewed Arroyo after he and his men were supposed to have been executed. Nonetheless, the story often found its way into

68. Prida, "Los sucesos de Río Blanco," pp. 94–95; for the Dehesa-Díaz exchange, see GPDC, 66:109, 111, 133–36, 182.

69. *El Tiempo*, 15 January 1907; Sodi de Pallares, *Teodoro A. Dehesa*, p. 153; Alberto María Carreno, ed., *Archivo del General Porfirio Díaz*, 30 vols. (Mexico: Universidad Nacional Autónoma de México, 1947–1958), 25:7. See Prida, "El 25 de junio de 1879," in the *Suplemento al boletín*, pp. 32–33, for a defense of Martínez in this incident.

accounts of the strike in later years.[70] Given the *rurales*' general image in later years, their place of honor alongside of the martyred workers is no small irony.

In truth, their fate was not so severe. After an investigation of the charges, Díaz ordered all the members of the squad to be released except Lt. Arroyo, whom he ordered to be turned over to the military authorities of the state of Veracruz for "processing." His ultimate fate is not known, but since he was alive as late as February, it is unlikely that he was executed.[71]

Exactly how many workers died in the encounters with the soldiers on the road or in the hills or how many were taken out and murdered by the authorities, as some accounts contend, will never be known. Although a conservative figure of the number who died is close to thirty, including those shot down in the initial clashes on 7 January and those executed on 9 January, without a doubt there were more.

The common belief is that hundreds of workers were shot down by federal troops at Río Blanco. Even the most recent revisionist study of the *Porfiriato* by Jorge Fernando Iturribarría records the figure of 140 dead. In his article "La huelga de Río Blanco," Professor González Navarro accepted a contemporary estimate of 150 workers and 25 soldiers dead. Ironically, a powerful source for the belief that hundreds were killed was the government's own censorship of the press, which only encouraged rumors that a great number of workers had been shot down. Moreover, those brave souls among the Mexican press that dared to print what was happening carried rumors of scores of casualties. *El País* initially stated that nearly

70. Herrera, *El Periódico*, pp. 1–2; *El País*, 12 January 1907, and *El Diario del Hogar*, 15 January 1907; *El Imparcial*, 13, 16 January 1907; Petricioli, *La tragedia*, p. 59; González Navarro, "La huelga," pp. 523–24; Arroyo to I.G., 28 January 1907, AGN-Gob, leg. 718.

71. Martínez to Díaz, 8, 11 January 1907, GPDC, 66:159, 165, 255; see the Rural Corps commander's record of correspondence with Arroyo in "Correspondencia de enero 2 a junio 30, 1907," AGN-Gob, no *legajo* number. Efforts to locate Arroyo's service record in the *Cuerpo Rural* archives have been unsuccessful. He was not listed as one of the seventeen officers assigned to the 9th *Cuerpo Rural* in October 1911, when they were reorganized under President Francisco Madero (AGN-Gob, leg. 1017).

two hundred workers had been summarily executed but later retracted the statement.[72]

El Diario reported that thirty had died and passed on the rumor that up to eighty had been killed by the soldiers, perhaps even executed. Its correspondent described a macabre scene in which an open railroad car full of bodies arrived at the Orizaba station, presumably bound for Veracruz for disposal in the sea. Carlo de Fornaro was on the staff of *El Diario* during the strike and evidently drew on this report in writing a polemic entitled *Díaz, Czar of Mexico* (1909). In it, he told of hundreds of victims and of railroad cars, now plural, full of bodies. Later on, such widely circulated indictments of the regime as de Lara and Pinchon's *The Mexican People: Their Struggle for Freedom* and John Kenneth Turner's *Barbarous Mexico* repeated the story. Turner described two flat cars piled high with bodies, the information provided by an informant who rode with a group of *rurales* searching for workers in the hills. In addition, he told of extensive murder of workers after Río Blanco, the victims of a secret official killer organization called *La Acordada*. This time his informant was an official of the company, whom Turner describes as sickened by the bloodshed.[73]

Peña Samaniego's series of newspaper articles contains a document, purporting to be a communication between General Martínez and the president, which stated that over three hundred "agitators" had been killed.[74] This document could not be located in either *El Imparcial* or *El Diario Oficial*, the two sources given by Peña. Moreover, it hardly makes sense for the regime to publish so damaging a report. Three

72. One of the most commonly used sources citing hundreds of casualties is Germán y Armando List Arzubide's *La huelga de Río Blanco*, pp. 26–30. Iturriabarría, *Porfirio Díaz*, p. 316, González Navarro, "Río Blanco," p. 523. U.S. Consul General to Asst. Sec. State, 8 January 1907, State, 36:3916, USNA; *El País*, 11, 13 January 1907; *La Voz de México*, 19 January 1907.

73. *El Diario*, 7–9 January 1907; on 10 January *El Diario* gave reduced figures of the dead without repudiating the earlier figures. Carlo de Fornaro, *Díaz, Czar of Mexico* (New York, 1909), pp. 51–55; Lázaro Gutiérrez de Lara and Edgcomb Pinchon, *The Mexican People: Their Struggle for Freedom* (Garden City: Doubleday, Page, and Co., 1914), p. 329; Turner, *Barbarous Mexico*, pp. 126, 136–37, 172–73. The original *Barbarous Mexico* appeared in *American Magazine*, October–December 1909, while his book came out in late 1910. Petricioli mentioned five boxcars full of bodies in *La tragedia*, p. 56.

74. Peña, "Apuntes históricos," 7 June 1959.

hundred dead workers would not have been accepted by the public as anything but mass murder, and given the reaction to Cananea, Díaz would have known this.

From the documents that I have seen and from what historical sense I have developed from the study of the events, I suspect that fifty to seventy workers died as a result of the events at Río Blanco. Whatever the figure, it was too many. Yet no matter what the historical truth, the historical reality is that, at the time, it was widely believed that government troops had massacred hundreds of workers at Río Blanco, and it is this belief that became, in many different ways, the most significant effect of those tragic events. What men choose to believe, rather than what is, has always been the more powerful mover of events.

Charges were initiated against 255 people for engaging in violence or the looting of stores. The actual number convicted is not known, but most likely the fever-ridden work camps of Quintana Roo added to the victims of those tragic days.[75]

Consciously or not, the historian creates the past in his own mind, for his own purposes, and in behalf of his own times. But the events themselves belong to those who lived them. *La huelga de Río Blanco* was to the textile villages around Orizaba a time of suffering and fear. In the common custom of the day, *El Cosmopolita*, an Orizaba weekly, carried an anguished poem on Río Blanco by someone from the town. It ended, "God justify it! / Why, good God, why?"[76]

From the workers themselves came an angry *corrido*, written and sung at the time of the strike.

Río Blanco, with what pain I saw
your children lawlessly shot down,
after suffering without food so long.
The damned troops come at the command
   of the industrialists
to kill the worker, the poor freedomless worker.
And we are not anarchists,
nor do we want revolution
but less hours of work
and a better distribution.

75. Dehesa to Díaz, 4 June 1907, GPDC, 66:2107.
76. 3 February 1907. The poem is "The Strike," by Ruperto J. Aldana.

We do not want *las tarjetas*,
we protest with valor,
because they only profit
the woman without honor

"Río Blanco," by Francisco Zavala
and Guillermo Torres[77]

The bitter memories of Río Blanco were not forgotten. A visiting journalist the following year found the workers still grieving over that "horrible spectacle." In 1910, on the anniversary of the tragedy, a worker wrote *El Paladín*, reminding its readers that "today is the sad anniversary on which three years ago many of our brothers were sacrificed." He paid tribute to those who died and hoped for "better days of liberty."[78]

Soon after those words were written, the regime that caused the anguish fell to new men, but the workers' struggle had only begun. In the years that followed, the name of Río Blanco was invoked over many causes and on many occasions when times were as hard and bitter as they had been under the old regime. As the decades passed, the strike came to be regarded as a "symbol of proletarian unity," and the *mártires de Río Blanco* are today honored on the seventh of January by ceremonies in union halls throughout the nation.[79] *La huelga de Río Blanco*, along with the Cananea strike, has come to have a broader meaning for the Mexican people. It is now a nationalist symbol representing the long historical struggles for social justice and for the economic independence of the Mexican nation.

But for those who lived through it or who felt its impact, *la huelga de Río Blanco* had a different effect. An illusion of an age died in the

77. Both authors were arrested for singing their *corrido* in public, and Guillermo Torres spent two years of forced labor in the infamous Valle Nacional. The reference to "women without honor" undoubtedly is a *doble sentido*, perhaps suggesting either that by accepting the *tarjeta* system, the workers would be selling themselves ("women without honor" referring to prostitutes) to another man's advantage, or, more likely, simply that the industrialists were the lowest order of humans. The source is a newspaper account discovered through a reference given in Stanley R. Ross, ed., *Fuentes de la historia contemporánea de México: Periódicos y revistas*, 2 vols. (Mexico: Colegio de México, 1965–67) 1:3–232, but was inadvertently, and embarrassingly, misplaced.

78. 9 January 1910; *El Paladín*, 31 May, 17 September 1908.

79. Quote is from a story on Río Blanco in *CETEME*, 4 January 1969.

shock of Río Blanco, and recognition of this change can be seen in how Mexicans of all classes and loyalties prepared for the future after those days. From their different perspectives, they were no less determined to hold on to what they had or to gain what they did not. But few men any longer talked of a progress unencumbered by the cost industrialism had exacted from other societies—deep social divisions and the bitter discontent of the men from the factories and the mines.

Chapter 5
Mexican Society in the Aftermath of Río Blanco

"The excessive harshness of the remedy [the
executions and bloodshed at Río Blanco]
constituted an injustice that profoundly affected
the entire nation."
Antonio Manero, *El antiguo régimen y*
  la Revolución, 1911

The *huelga de Río Blanco* had effects transcending itself, like the ripples of a stone thrown into the water. We can never know exactly what those effects were, for they were impressions on men's minds, engendering emotions of outrage and hate, of shock and relief, of fear and disbelief. What we can know is what men did and said in the aftermath of Río Blanco, and we can suggest how the tragedy at Río Blanco and the growing labor discontent that preceded it affected the nature and direction of those events. In particular, we can ask whether any large or important groups of Mexicans reoriented their view of Mexican workers and their needs in the wake of Río Blanco. And did the regime's use of force at Río Blanco constitute a shift in policy toward a harder line than before? What of the workers themselves; would fear of similar repression silence them once again, destroying what little advances they had made so far?

The immediate effect of Río Blanco varied widely. For a small but influential group of Mexicans and foreign businessmen, order had been upheld. Various officials of the textile firms wrote Díaz to give their appreciation for his personal intervention in preserving order. From Mérida came a letter by a Yucatán railroad official congratulating the president on his "firm and vigorous hand" in reprimanding the criminal acts of the Orizaba strikers. *El Economista Mexicano*, an important commercial journal, regretted that the "Government has seen itself obligated to employ such energetic repressive measures in this case, but it would not have fulfilled its principal duty if it had not acted as it did to defend individual property attacked and to pacify an aroused population."[1]

Various groups of Mexican workers reacted to the news of the massacre at Río Blanco with consternation and outrage. Workers at La Hormiga mill in the Federal District and at various Tlaxcalan mills declared sympathy strikes when word of the bloodshed began to circulate. Still others talked of stronger action, and several arrests were made by Tlaxcalan authorities out of fear of violence by workers at the mills. Puebla workers were upset and shaken by the reports of the deaths and the executions of their comrades in Orizaba, who had supported their strike in December. Pascual Mendoza worked long and hard to prevent sympathy strikes from taking place in his mills.[2]

The reactions of other Mexicans to Río Blanco are more difficult to assess, however. The press, which might have reflected public opinion as it did in the case of the Cananea strike, carefully avoided any discussion of the government's role in the bloodshed at Río Blanco. Even the more outspoken dailies such as *El Diario*, *El Diario del Hogar*, *El País*, and *El Tiempo* were silent on this point. If they needed an example, it was the arrest of Paulino Martínez, valiant editor of *La Voz de Juárez*. Martínez had allowed the *Gran Círculo*'s organ, *La Unión Obrera*, to be printed on his press and was jailed shortly after Río Blanco on the charge of "intellectual contribution" to the disturbance.[3]

For the most part, in their discussion of the events at Río Blanco, the Mexican dailies took the position that the worker was peaceful and hardworking and that there was no basic conflict between capital and labor in Mexico. Instead, the press generally blamed the workers' violence at Río Blanco on two scapegoats. One was the so-called "agitator," instigating contented workers to riot. To support this argument, *El Imparcial* pointed out that since Puebla workers, who were

1. CIDOSA officials and others to Díaz, 11 January 1907, GPDC, 32:586; Rudolfo Cantón to Díaz, 15 January 1907, GPDC, 32:1020; *El Economista Mexicano*, 12 January 1907, p. 310.

2. Cahuantzi to Díaz, 9 January 1907, GPDC, 32; Pascual Mendoza to Díaz, 11 January 1907, GPDC, 32:236; Cruz Guerrero to Inspector General (*Cuerpo Rural*), 18 January 1907, AGN-Gob, leg. 718.

3. *El Paladín*, 26 March 1908. *El Paladín* was closed down from early fall 1906 through April 1907 because its editorial staff was in jail, serving out the six-month term reserved for newspapermen who violated the regime's loosely interpreted limit on freedom of expression.

worse off than the better paid Orizaba workers, did not rebel, the Río Blanco mill hands must obviously have been duped into revolting by agitators. The conservative San Luis Potosí daily *El Estandarte* continued to maintain its previous position that there was no labor problem in Mexico and that strikes were the work of agitators and anarchists.[4]

Nearly all the major dailies agreed upon the other cause of the violence. It was Garcín, the French owner of the company stores that lay in blackened ruins in three textile towns. Some editors suggested curbing the abuses of the company store as an institution, but most did not carry the issue beyond Garcín himself. They were probably relieved to have found such an obvious scapegoat.[5]

Only one major daily tried to see beyond the immediate events to evaluate the industrial system as a whole. *El Tiempo*'s distinguished editor, Victoriano Agüeros, took the position that the industrialists should be more concerned for the welfare of the workers and that if voluntary reforms were not instituted, then government action should require those changes. Agüeros even asserted that "material progress ought to come after social progress."[6] It was not a position commonly found in the press of the *Porfiriato*.

If the major dailies were circumspect in their discussion of Río Blanco, several of the Mexico City weeklies were not. In one of the few direct and immediate protests by the press, Alvaro Prueda, director of the weekly satire magazine *Tilín-Tilín*, drew a scathing cartoon featuring Díaz as the Roman governor Pontius Pilate and a worker as Christ. The crowd, gathered around the worker as he faces Díaz on his throne, were recognizable as well-known industrialists and politicians.[7]

Antonio de P. Escarcega, editor of *El Diablito Bromista*, would not let his readers forget the massacre. "We knock at the doors of your conscience," he wrote in September 1907, "evoking the memory of

4. *El Imparcial*, 12, 15 January 1907; *La Semana Mercantil*, 14 January 1907; *El País*, 8 January 1907; *El Estandarte*, 28 July, 22 August 1906, and 11, 19 January 1907.

5. *La Semana Mercantil*, 21 January 1907; *El Imparcial*, 16 January 1907; *El Estandarte*, 19 January 1907; *El País*, 16 January 1907.

6. *El Tiempo*, 12, 16 January 1907.

7. Cited in Salvador Pruneda, *La caricatura como arma política* (Mexico: Talleres Gráficos de la Nación, 1958), p. 332.

the victims of Río Blanco. Those corpses rise from their tombs and ask for justice in heaven, since on earth it was denied them." On the 1904 anniversary of Díaz's 1867 triumph at Puebla against Emperor Maximilian's forces, the prolabor weekly, *La Guacamaya*, had praised Díaz as a hero of the Reform; however, on the 1908 anniversary of his Puebla victory, the paper carried a Posada cartoon which showed a group of workers presenting Díaz with a huge floral arrangement of bones and skulls labeled "the workers of Río Blanco."[8]

Undoubtedly, there were some who accepted the rumored executions as just reprisal for riot and looting. Writing a few years later, Francisco Bulnes maintained that government repression was not a proven fact and that even if it were, it was hardly unusual for a government to react strongly to what he called a "Bolshevik outbreak."[9] Yet what evidence there is indicates that other Mexicans were more horrified and repulsed by the bloodshed.

Barely a year after Río Blanco, Díaz's former labor advisor, Rafael de Zayas Enríquez, declared that the widespread rumor that workers had been executed at Río Blanco caused an unfavorable public reaction against the regime of Porfirio Díaz. His impression was seconded by Antonio Manero in his description of the Díaz era written shortly after the regime fell in 1911. Manero stated categorically that the "excessive harshness of the remedy [the executions at Río Blanco] constituted an injustice that profoundly affected the entire nation." Alberto Pani, cabinet minister under Carranza, wrote in his autobiography that he had been receptive to the Anti-Reelectionist movement because of the "bloody, arbitrary solutions of Velardena, Río Blanco. . . ." Francisco Madero himself was shocked by the brutality of the government's repression and expressed his feelings to Francisco de P. Sentíes when he wrote of the workers who died at Río Blanco saying, "May their beloved blood water the tree of liberty." Madero blamed both the government and the industrialists for the violence at Río Blanco.[10]

8. *El Diablito Bromista*, 29 September 1907; see similar condemnations in *El Diablito Rojo*, 7 July 1907, 31 March, 9 April 1908; *La Guacamaya*, 31 March 1904, 9 April 1908.

9. Francisco Bulnes, *El verdadero Díaz y la Revolución* (Mexico: 1920; reprint ed., Editora Nacional, 1952), p. 61.

10. Zayas Enríquez, *Porfirio Díaz, The Evolution of His Life*, p. 256; Antonio

Another question that remains to be answered is what effect Río Blanco and the general labor agitation had on public awareness of the problems of Mexican workers and on their attitudes toward the workers themselves. There are, for instance, several important examples of Mexicans who came to view the workers with more sympathy and respect than they had previously shown. One such was Silvestre Terrazas, editor of the daily *El Correo de Chihuahua*. Terrazas had earlier worked as the private secretary to the first Catholic bishop of Chihuahua, establishing *El Correo* in 1899 as a secular organ with a procleric orientation.[11] Nonetheless, Terrazas acquired a national reputation for honest, hard-hitting journalism and was elected president of the Associated Press Association of Mexico. He was a man whose opinions on the labor question must be considered significant in understanding the general nonworking classes' views of the worker and his protests.

In the years prior to 1906, Terrazas had taken a moderate, paternalistic view of the worker, considering crime, vice, illiteracy, and alcoholism as the major obstacles to the progress of the Mexican worker and favoring mutualism as the best means for raising his moral and material level. Terrazas's attitude toward Mexican workers changed abruptly with the Cananea strike in June 1906. He strongly criticized the official version of the strike, carrying the first photo in the history of *El Correo* showing American "troops" (the Arizona volunteers) in that mining town. In the months after the strike, Terrazas more often praised the Mexican workers, calling their desires legitimate and supporting the more militant position of the trade unionists rather than that of the mutualists. Robert Sandels's study of Terrazas concludes that Cananea and the other strikes forced him away from

Manero, *El antiguo régimen y la revolución* (Mexico: Tipografía y Litografía "La Europea," 1911), p. 194; Alberto J. Pani, *Apuntes autobiográficos* (Mexico: M. Porrúa, 1951), pp. 69–70; Stanley R. Ross, *Francisco I. Madero: Apostle of Mexican Democracy* (New York: Columbia University Press, 1955), pp. 43–44; Madero to Francisco de P. Senties, in Alfonso Taracena, *La verdadera revolución mexicana, primera etapa (1909 a 1911)*, 2d ed. (Mexico: Editorial Jus. 1965), p. 138.

11. Robert L. Sandels, "Silvestre Terrazas, the Press, and the Origins of the Mexican Revolution in Chihuahua" (Ph.D. diss., University of Oregon, 1967), p. 39.

his paternalistic view of the labor question to an open acceptance of militant unionism and the use of the strike as regrettable but unavoidable.[12]

In addition, the labor problem may have evoked a sense of outraged nationalism from Terrazas, as it likely did with others. Toward the end of the mechanics' strike in August 1906, *El Correo* reprinted an editorial from *Renacimiento* of Monterrey entitled "Mexico for the Mexicans" and then defended itself with vigor when it came under heavy attack for its antiforeign content. The editorial had read "from now on we propose to open an energetic campaign, constant and without apology, without limits, against the foreigners who dominate this country, because the campaign is necessary, it is urgent."[13] The Mexican worker, because his conflicts were often with foreign enterprises, stood in the vanguard of that campaign, and indeed, his struggles were important symbols and catalysts to other Mexicans who were becoming alarmed over the extent of foreign penetration of their nation.

Another important example is Juan Sánchez Azcona, editor and director of *El Diario*. Founded in October 1906, *El Diario* covered the labor conflicts of December thoroughly. It was *El Diario*, along with *El País*, who reported the bloodshed with growing alarm and then, with shock, the executions of the workers. Throughout 1907 this paper took up the cause of the Mexican worker, providing him for the first time with a major spokesman among the Mexican dailies. Río Blanco appears to have been the catalyst for this support.[14]

At thirty-one years of age, from a well established family with connections in the administration, a former deputy in Congress, Juan Sánchez Azcona had a promising future. Yet within a year he was forced out of his job; he had set a too independent course, steering the paper into many stormy battles against the established powers and interests. His last fight was with *El Imparcial* over the causes of the many fatal accidents on the city's foreign-owned trolley lines. *El Imparcial* defended the firm, while *El Diario* defended the operators of

12. Ibid., pp. 77–78, 82–83, 105–9.
13. Ibid., p. 107.
14. See *El Diario*, 21 March, 1, 18 June 1907. *El Diario* had a daily circulation of about fourteen thousand.

the cars, contending that if they were paid decent wages and worked shorter hours, fewer accidents would result.[15]

With Sánchez Azcona gone, *El Diario* took a decidedly more conservative approach to the labor problem. During a strike at La Camelia mine, the paper carried these lines: "Well known is the character of the workers of the mines, . . . people with bad habits, vicious and dissolute, who value their lives very little and even less the money they squander with great extravagance in the taverns and bars."[16]

Ironically, however, the same month that Sánchez Azcona was fired, another defender of working-class interests appeared. *El Diablito Rojo*, edited by Ramón Álvarez Soto, was first published in February 1908 and promised to "defend the humble people, to call attention to the arbitrary acts committed against the poor people of all the Republic, by bosses as well as *caciques*, by the policemen as well as the chief of police or the municipal judge. This is our proposal."[17] Álvarez Soto was also director of *El Paladín* during those years. *El Diablito Rojo* became a strong supporter of trade unionism for the workers instead of the traditional mutualism. Mainly a source of political satire and an outlet for grievances of all kinds, including those of the workers, the paper also became a regular outlet for the cartoons of José Guadalupe Posada.

Even the industrialists themselves were divided in their opinions as to how to handle the workers' demands. The major industrialists perceived the events of the previous year as a threat to their interests and moved to protect themselves through the establishment of a permanent organization. In February 1907 *La Semana Mercantil* announced the formation of the *Centro Industrial de México*. The avowed purpose of the *Centro* would be to "defend the rights and interests of the manufacturing industry of the Republic, and principally those of the cotton industry."[18] The charter members were the large French cot-

---

15. See Díaz to Gen. Bernardo Reyes, 6 June 1905, AGBR, "Correspondencia del Sr. Presidente, 1903–1909"; Sánchez Azcona to Díaz, 30 January 1909, GPDC, 34:2; *El Diario*, 8 January 1908, 7 March 1908.

16. *El Diario*, 28 April 1908.

17. 5 February 1908. See 8 June 1908, and August 1909.

18. *La Semana Mercantil*, 11 February 1907, p. 72. The Constitution was signed on 5 February 1907 by the following firms: CIDOSA, CIV, Industrial

ton textile firms, who, through a complicated voting procedure based on the number of looms per factory, clearly intended to dominate the new organization. In deference to what they must have perceived as public opinion, if not out of any major change of heart, the authors of the constitution of the new organization provided that the *Centro* "will give constant study to the moral and material necessities of the workers and come to an agreement on the general measures that should be taken to better the social and economic conditions of the workers and their families so that they will identify their own progress and welfare with the manufacturing industry that utilizes their services." [19] If the *Centro* ever came to any agreement as to how to accomplish this objective, the general labor policies of its membership did not clearly reflect it.

The two leading spokesmen for the major Mexican business interests showed a slightly greater willingness to accept certain changes in industrial labor relations. One was *La Semana Mercantil*, a weekly commercial and business journal edited by Everardo Hegewisch. The journal was the official organ of the Chamber of Commerce of Mexico City, primarily representing foreign capitalists residing in Mexico and their Mexican partners. Its board of directors consisted of the following: Alfonso Michel, Agustín Garcín, León Signoret, Federico Albert, Enrique Tron, Mauricio Honnorat, Julio Beraud, Valentín Elcoro, Quintin Gutiérrez, and Antonio Barrios. *La Semana Mercantil* blamed the Río Blanco strike on agitators but admitted that its position on the labor problem had changed over the years, as indeed it had. In 1895 the journal had recommended governmental intervention in case of a strike, "not to regulate it but to repress it." By 1906 the editor agreed that peaceful strikes were legal but demanded that disturbances of the public order be severely punished. In the months after Río Blanco the editor reluctantly agreed that there should be a limited amount of

---

Manufacturera, Industrial de Atlixco, Industrial de San Antonio Abad y La Hormiga, Señores Donnadieu Vexan and Company, and Francisco Martínez Arauna. The representatives signing were, by order of firm noted above: A. Reynaud, manager; A. Reynaud and Company, managers; B. D. Salceda, manager; H. Gerard, manager; Juan N. Nieto, manager; Emilio Meyran, vice president; Antonio Donnadieu, Francisco Martínez Arauna. See documents in GPDC, 32:3152.

19. *La Semana Mercantil*, 18 March 1907, p. 141.

governmental intervention to protect the worker, suggesting a labor code along the lines of the law in effect in Belgium.[20]

The second spokesman for Mexican business was *El Economista Mexicana*, edited by the *científico* economist Carlos Díaz Dufoo. Díaz Dufoo had close connections with the administration; the journal itself was even printed on the federal government Office of Revenue press, located in the National Palace. After Río Blanco, the journal also agreed that the workers' situation should be governed by at least a minimum of governmental regulation. It warned, however, against too much of what it termed "state socialism."[21] Furthermore, neither journal would accept any adjustment of the workers' wages, agreeing that wages were always in harmony with the laws of supply and demand. Everardo Hegewisch, editor of *La Semana Mercantil*, commented further on his personal attitude toward wage increases for workers:

> The needs of our working class are almost non-existent. . . . They do not need fire to counteract the rigors of the low temperatures, they do not need special clothes for this or that position. . . . The raising of wages . . . has led, not as one might expect, to the raising of the moral or social level, but to the increasing of vices, most particularly drunkeness. . . . No one would think of raising wages despite the labor shortage because . . . the needs of the worker impose a positive limit on such a raise.[22]

Another segment of the Mexican business community, however, held opinions on the labor question which were different from those of their foreign counterparts, if more obscure. Although the evidence is far from complete, medium and small domestic capitalists and commercial establishments likely felt little sympathy for their foreign

20. Ibid., 1 January 1907; 20 May 1895, cited in Matt S. Meier, "Industrial Unrest in Mexico 1887–1910," (Master's thesis, Mexico City College—now University of the Americas, Cholula, Puebla, Mexico, 1949); *La Semana Mercantil*, 11 June 1907, p. 279; 8 July 1907, p. 370; 25 February 1907, pp. 115–17; 13 March 1907, p. 252; 8 July 1907, pp. 369–70.

21. *El Economista Mexicano*, 22 August 1908, pp. 425–27. For its various positions on the labor question, see 11 August 1906, p. 398; 5 January 1907, pp. 287–88; 3 August 1907, pp. 376–78.

22. 19 August 1907, cited in Meier, "Industrial Unrest in Mexico."

comrades and competitors on the labor issue. For one thing, the labor conflicts thus far had been mainly confined to foreign-owned enterprises or public utilities and not directed against domestic capitalists. In the areas where foreign interests had conflicted with domestic concerns, the interests of the workers might not have appeared to domestic businessmen to be so far from their own. One spokesman for the domestic entrepreneur, *El Progreso Latino,* made this feeling quite clear.

Subtly antiforeign and anti-*científico,* this weekly commercial journal carried fourteen editorials on the labor question from June through December 1906, all expressing a markedly sympathetic attitude toward the Mexican industrial worker in his struggles against such foreign enterprises as Col. Greene's Cananea company and the French textile mills. What the journal's position was after Río Blanco was not available for this study, but clearly, certain Mexican businessmen considered their interests separate from, and perhaps counter to, the larger foreign firms.[23]

There is other evidence that the conflicts of 1906 and the Río Blanco strike raised the public awareness of the industrial workers and their problems. Professor Moisés González Navarro demonstrates that social themes, particularly those dealing with the labor question, became common in the Mexican theater during the last few years of the *Porfiriato.* To be sure, the best received by the established critics were such conservative plays as *La huelga* by Juan A. Mateos and *La huelga de los herreros* by Francisco Coppe, both stressing the harm that strikes do to the workers themselves and to their families. However, Dicenta's *Juan José* was brought back again, although it received no better reception from the drama critics of the major Mexico City dailies in 1909 than it had from Carlos Díaz Dufoo when it was performed in 1896. The *catalán* playwright Santiago Rusinol's *La fea* was condemned as anarchistic by both the progovernment press and the Catholic-oriented papers.[24] Even if the establishment elite was as conservative as before, such popular theaters as the Arbeu and the Teresa Mariani and such popular troupes as the Virginia Fábregas

23. See, for example, "Cuestiones sociales—las huelgas," 21 August 1906. For antiforeign sentiment among business interests in the state of San Luis Potosí, see James D. Cockcroft, *Intellectual Precursors,* pp. 19–24, 40–43.
24. González Navarro, *La vida social,* pp. 351, 807–11.

players often confronted their audiences with social themes, forcing them to consider the issues that the workers' protests were raising. They could no longer assume that Mexico would be spared the working-class unrest that had accompanied other nations' industrial expansion, and the presence of social themes in the Mexican theatre in the late *Porfiriato* is only one evidence that Mexicans of position and means were at last acknowledging that there was, indeed, a labor problem in their nation. What they would do about it, if anything, remained to be seen.

And so Río Blanco and preceding worker protests had made their mark on Mexican society. Many members of the emerging middle groups and certain elements from the upper class elites, dissatisfied with the national administration under the *científicos,* were coming to view the Mexican worker from an altered perspective. Perceiving no direct threat to their own economic interests and outraged for many different reasons by the seemingly inordinate amount of influence exercised in Mexico by foreigners, these men saw the martyred Río Blanco workers as nationalists as well as workers. If this is true and the workers' protests were seen by others as the legitimate aspirations of patriotic and loyal Mexican citizens, then the effect of Río Blanco on nonworking-class Mexicans was significant indeed.

The Mexican Church and the Labor Problem

Led by a few high churchmen and a number of allied laymen, a small group within the Mexican Catholic Church made a sincere and at times determined effort to bring the moral power and prestige of the Church to bear on the social problems of their emerging industrial society. They were often frustrated by Church conservatives and lacked a clear understanding of what were the proper goals and tactics to pursue, but these men and women nonetheless stood almost alone in their early efforts to extend succor to the Mexican worker.

The Catholic social action movement, as the efforts were called, originated in the last years of the nineteenth century. Responding to the obvious miseries that industrialization forced on so many of the working-class faithful and fearful of the potential danger that the secular religions of the Left represented, the Roman Catholic Church in the last quarter of the nineteenth century began to study the social issues bound up in the labor conflicts of the day. Out of this ferment came Pope Leo XIII's papal encyclical *Rerum Novarum* of 1891, calling for Catholic social action to fight the evils of capitalism and socialism.

For many years the Mexican Church had officially supported the position that the workingman's reward would be in heaven. The editor of *El Pueblo Católico* spoke for this position when, in 1891, he wrote that public laws should protect the owners of businesses from the workers' "obscure" pretext of equality and should limit strikes in the public interest.[25]

Some members of the Church disagreed. In 1890 the editor of the pro-Catholic daily, *El Tiempo,* had called for governmental action to insure social justice for the worker, maintaining that charity was no longer sufficient.[26] Its editor, Victoriano Agüeros, remained for the next two decades a staunch, persistent defender of this position. From Rome, Pope Leo XIII set the goals for Catholic social action, writing in his now-famous *Rerum Novarum* that the Church should go to the workers to organize them into Christian unions and that it should support governmental legislation protecting workers.

The Mexican liberal press attacked the papal encyclical, calling it "white socialism," while the Catholic press defended it, either out of choice or out of obligation. Stimulated by the debate within the Church on the labor question, a series of social congresses was held at which major Church and lay figures discussed social issues and made resolutions on what actions and attitudes should be taken by Catholics to resolve these problems. One of the most important proponents of the congresses was Dr. Ramón Ibarra y González, bishop of Puebla, and it was at his initiative and encouragement that the first social congress met in Puebla in February 1903. One of the eight committees of the Congress dealt specifically with workers' problems. The general recommendations were that the Church should encourage the establishment of night schools, lectures, libraries, and mutual funds. One interesting discussion took place when Juan N. Quintana

25. 6 September 1891, located in the *Museo Nacional de Antropología*, Mexico City, series "León," microfilm roll 43.

26. 26 April 1890, cited in Ciro Hernández, "Some Aspects of the Mexican Catholic Social Congresses, 1903–1909," (Master's thesis, Mexico City College, 1959), p. 26.

"The hooked ones." A José Guadalupe Posada cartoon criticizing the enganche *system. With permission of the* Fondo Editorial de la Plástica Mexicana.

of Sonora attacked the phrase "the more humble classes," maintaining that it debased the laboring classes. Although some delegates asserted that the phrase was a compliment, the Congress voted to substitute the term "working classes."[27]

The second congress was held in Morelia in October of 1904. Recommendations included the forming of Catholic workers' clubs, the encouragement of legal action against the *enganche* system of labor contracts, and the establishment of trade schools and savings cooperatives. The *enganche* system (literally, "to be hooked") was particularly notorious as a source of labor abuse. Under this system the *contratista* recruited workers from rural areas or wherever there was surplus labor by promising certain wages and often room, board, and transportation for the labor of the worker for a specified length of time. Once on the job, workers often found themselves in a particularly dangerous or unhealthy situation, but they were unable to leave be-

27. González Navarro, *La vida social*, pp. 360–68 Hernández, "Catholic Social Congresses," pp. 27, 35–36, 54, 71.

cause they had signed a contract for a specified period of time or because they had run up debts at the company store and were forced to pay them off before they could leave. To force a worker for any reason to remain on the job when he did not want to was absolutely illegal but was nonetheless common in certain areas and in certain industries.[28]

Some delegates resisted what they considered to be a too liberal approach, insisting, as one put it, that the owners had to be protected from the "rapacity, laziness, and infidelity of the workers." The Catholic press was asked to devote space to articles aimed at bettering the moral welfare of the working classes, and an amendment was agreed upon limiting the membership in the Catholic workers clubs to a "sincere Catholic, one not professing questionable beliefs," presumably meaning socialism.[29]

Two years later the third social congress met in the charged atmosphere of the labor conflicts of the fall of 1906. Bishop Ignacio Montes de Oca y Obregón, a leader of the conservative wing of the Church, opened the congress in Guadalajara in October with an address stressing that religious matters should come before material questions in the priority of business before the congress. Nonetheless, the conflict within the Church was revealed quite dramatically when Francisco Elguero, in the inaugural address to the congress, declared that the Church knew well "the necessities of the times" and would support the legitimate aspirations of the poor and the working classes. The Church, Elguero maintained, would be the conscience of the age.[30]

28. Hernández, "Catholic Social Congresses," pp. 77–80. On the *enganche* system, see "Jefatura política, Districto de León, a jefes y jueces auxiliares," *Museo Nacional de Antropología*, Mexico City, series "León." Bernstein, *The Mexican Mining Industry*, p. 89; *El Papagoya* (Mexico City weekly, 21 August 1904; *La Guacamaya*, 10 September 1903, 11 August 1904; *El Sufragio Libre* (Guadalajara weekly), 5 October 1910. For material on the business side of the arrangement, see request for permission to recruit workers under the *enganche* system sent to Alejandro Vázquez del Mercado, governor of Aguascalientes, 9 September 1908, GPDC, 33:11550. The firm, an oil company working a site on the Gulf of Mexico, specifically stated that the workers would be well treated and that their contract would be honored.

29. Hernández, "Catholic Social Congresses," pp. 77, 80.

30. *El Estandarte*, 24, 25 October 1906. It was the best attended Congress of any held, with 60 lay members and 100 clergy, including 3 archbishops and 12 bishops.

In keeping with the emphasis of the congress, the best-attended session was the meeting of the committee on labor problems. Working against subtle pressures from important members of the Church hierarchy, liberal prelates and laymen pushed for strong measures in support of justice for the working classes. By the end of the congress, the committee had passed resolutions recommending that capitalists should provide pensions for the workers in their old age, that workers should not be dismissed from their jobs without proper reason, and that they should be paid just wages, reflecting not simply supply and demand but also their abilities and the material requirements necessary for a minimum level of living. A specific proposal calling for the establishment of a joint employer-worker commission to work out wage disputes was passed, despite the objections of some who thought that it went against Díaz's decision in the Cananea strike. As an afterthought, a resolution was added condemning communism and socialism.[31] It was a surprising document, one which, if supported by the Church hierarchy, would have put the Church in the vanguard of the fight for social justice in Mexico.

The recommendations were not without opposition. Primo F. Velázquez, director of the important procleric daily *El Estandarte* of San Luis Potosí, gave a major address to the full congress toward the end of its session in which he cautioned against taking a strong stand on the labor question. Undoubtedly reflecting the conservative viewpoint, Velázquez admitted that wages were often not in line with the necessities of life, but, he asserted, misery was an evil that could only be remedied by persistent work, sober habits, and thrift. The maintenance of relations between classes, he went on, was not a question of politics but one of morality. He concluded his remarks with a pointed rejection of the idea that the Catholic Church should "accommodate all eras and all social transformations."[32] Alarmed by the political implications of the labor resolutions and perhaps too beholding to the regime to contest its leadership on the labor question—especially after the bloody intervention at Río Blanco—the Church failed to hold another congress until early in 1909.

The fourth social congress, held in Oaxaca in January 1909, reflected an approach quite different from that of the previous one.

31. Hernández, "Catholic Social Congresses," pp. 98–99, 102–3, 106.
32. *El Estandarte*, 30 October 1906.

The tone of the congress was set in a pastoral letter issued by the archbishops and bishops of the Church to the delegates upon their arrival in Oaxaca. The letter reminded them that the congress was not a legislative session and that the only objectives were to open lines of communication between clergy and laymen and to study the social problems of their society from a Christian, religious perspective.[33]

The congress focused on the problems of accident insurance, industrial hygiene, conditions of work on the *haciendas* and in the mines and factories, and especially on the vices of the workers. The recommendations made on these issues were conservative, and their implementation was left entirely up to the Christian good will of the industrialists. Resolution number nine specified that the ambition of the Church was to instruct employees and their employers regarding obligations toward each other in order to avoid strikes, which often end in violence. Various members of the congress were disappointed by the Church's stand on social issues. Victoriano Agüeros urged the congress not to be content with the good intentions of the industrialists but to take practical action to relieve the workers' problems, as well as to teach them their responsibilities. He suggested the kind of labor legislation that such Catholic countries as Belgium and Germany had already adopted to protect their workers.[34]

The congress ignored the appeals of Agüeros and other reformers within the Church. On nearly every point it was more conservative than the one that met in Guadalajara in October 1906, although the reasons for this shift are not readily apparent from the available evidence. Whatever the reason, those who favored a conservative approach to the labor issue seem generally to have come to dominate the Church's social action program by 1909. This was true certainly of the lay groups founded to implement the resolutions of the congresses. Most followed the same conservative, generally mutualistic approach of the 1909 Oaxaca congress.

One of the most important lay organizations was the *Operarios Guadalupanos*, founded by José Refugio Galindo in 1905 in the town of Tulancingo, Hidalgo. Among their projects were the establishment of recreation centers for the workers, night schools, Reiffeisen Funds,

33. González Navarro, *La vida social*, pp. 366–68.
34. Hernández, "Catholic Social Congresses," pp. 110–13; *El Tiempo*, 27 January, 14, 15 May 1909.

and *Montes de Piedad*. *Operarios Guadalupanos* were installed in other parts of the country among Catholic workers.[35]

In 1908 the *Unión Católica Obrera* was founded by Father José María Troncoso, Father Superior of the Josephine Fathers. It was composed of the mutualist workers' circles he had organized in the Federal District, and its purpose was to raise the moral and material well-being of the workers through such mutualist projects as night schools, savings institutions, and the like. The *Unión* absorbed most of the OG members already organized in the District, while the latter organization continued to remain active in the various states. Perhaps because the *Unión* was dominated by priests, it retained its very mutualist approach. According to one source, the organization spread to other states, and by the end of 1911 it had forty-six circles and 12,320 members.[36]

Under the guidance of Dr. Galindo, the OGs organized the *Semana Católico-Social*—reunions of laymen and workers from the various OGs to study social issues pertaining to workers. In the first session of the *Semana Católico-Social*, held in León in 1908, the goals of Catholic social action were defined as respect for private property, justice for the workers, eradication of poverty, and social peace founded on charity and justice. It discouraged the use of the strike and warned the workers against agitators and socialism.[37]

Yet when the second *Semana Católico-Social* met in October 1910, amid rumors of rebellion, the means for achieving social justice had become more advanced. At the meeting, attended by many of the most active lay members in the Church on social questions and by worker representatives from the OGs of Puebla, Tulancingo, Aguascalientes, Zamora, and Guadalajara, a number of suggestions were made calling for governmental action, particularly in the area of wages, food prices, and maximum working hours.[38] The reason for

35. López Aparicio, *El movimiento obrero*, p. 138; González Navarro, *La vida social*, pp. 358–59; José Castillo y Pina, *Cuestiones sociales* (Mexico: Impresores, S.A., 1934), pp. 58, 253. Reiffeisen Funds were credit organizations based on the ideas of F. W. Reiffeisen (1818–1888), a German scholar; *Montes de Piedad* were nonprofit pawnshops (Meier, "Industrial Unrest in Mexico," p. 20).

36. López Aparicio, *El movimiento obrero*, p. 138; Castillo, *Cuestiones*, pp. 253–56.

37. González Navarro, *La vida social*, p. 366.

38. *Restauración Social*, 15 November 1910, the bulletin of the *Semana*

the more progressive stand on the labor question compared to that of the previous meeting is obscure. It may well be that the political campaigns of 1909–1910 clarified the labor issue for socially concerned laymen, as it did for others. Whatever the reason, with the *maderista* rebellion just weeks away, the stronger stand was too late to influence either Church or worker opinion. The Revolution eventually forced the Church to the political right, leaving little room within the Church for reformers and social activists.

Mexican Workers in the Aftermath of Río Blanco

Whatever the attitudes of other social groups, Mexican workers would have to fight their own battles. What effect did Río Blanco have on their ability and determination to do this? After the harsh use of force at Río Blanco, did Mexican workers still look to the government as their only hope for overcoming the disadvantage they faced in their struggles with their employers? Did they now fear rather than want the regime's intervention in labor conflicts? And did they at last turn to the revolutionary PLM or European socialist doctrines because Río Blanco destroyed their belief in reform from within the system? Few of these questions can be answered with any degree of certainty, and in no case does Río Blanco stand as the only factor in the equation of influence and effect. Looking backward, historians pick out benchmarks to impose order on their material and provide meaning for their work. For those who live in history, events that happen to other men, even to one's comrades-in-arms, may not as clearly mark the boundaries of their lives. Nonetheless, Río Blanco was a major event in the labor movement of the day and one of its clearest effects is what happened to the formal labor organizations and leadership in the textile industry.

The *Gran Círculo de Obreros Libres* was ordered disbanded by the regime; its leadership for the most part was dead or in jail or had withdrawn from the movement, at least for the time being. José Morales was cleared of any responsibility for the events at Río Blanco,

---

Católico-Social and organ of the *Operarios Guadalupanos*, in the *Museo Nacional de Anthropología*, microfilm series "Conferencias religiones," roll 1.

but he left the Orizaba area and, it appears, active participation in the labor movement. Adolfo Ramírez and Antonio Hidalgo, leaders of the Tlaxcalan workers, were arrested shortly after Río Blanco on charges of sedition. Ramírez was sent to a work camp in Quintana Roo and died in March 1908 from the effects of his treatment there. Hidalgo became involved in the Anti-Reelectionist movement after his release from jail. He led rebels during the Revolution against the Díaz regime in 1910 and served as governor of Tlaxcala from 1911 to 1913 before being ousted in the coup by General Victoriano Huerta in February 1913. As governor, Hidalgo hired José Rumbia as his private secretary. Rumbia had served time in jail as an intellectual accomplice to the Río Blanco strike. Although Hidalgo escaped the Huerta forces, Rumbia was captured and executed on 22 February 1913.[39]

José Neira, radical leader from the early GCOL phase, served a year and a half of a sentence for being an "intellectual author" of the crimes of rebellion, robbery, and arson—presumably for his letter to a friend in Orizaba just prior to the PLM revolts in October 1906 urging the workers to rise up against the regime. He was released in 1908 and returned to Orizaba, where he edited a working-class newspaper for a while. In 1908 or 1909 he again became active in the reorganized textile workers' union. Neira later joined the *maderista* revolt against the regime in 1911.[40]

Of all the men who led the GCOL in its brief and turbulent struggle, however, only Pascual Mendoza stayed firmly in his leadership position. When the word of violence in Orizaba reached Mendoza, he immediately wrote to Díaz, disassociating his organization from such acts. He assured Díaz that his people were loyal, peaceful workers, adding that Díaz was a "true father" to them. His energetic actions at

39. Various references to a José Morales were found from time to time, but none definitely identified him as the former GCOL leader (see *El Paladín*, 10, 24 April 1910). Cahuantzi to Díaz, 16 January 1907, GPDC, 66:346; *El Paladín*, 19 March 1908; René Cuéllar Bernal, *Tlaxcala a través de los siglos* (Mexico: B. Costa-Amic, 1968), pp. 245–48, 256; Gen. Maass to Díaz, 18 January 1907, GPDC, 66:378.

40. Neira to Díaz, 10 May 1907, GPDC, 32:6332; *jefe político* to Díaz, n.d. (circa 1908–1909), GPDC, 34:1588; Cockcroft, *Intellectual Precursors*, pp. 188–89.

that time kept the Tlaxcalan-Pueblan workers at work and peaceful, as even his antagonists among the factory administrations grudgingly admitted. To emphasize his position, Mendoza disbanded the "Segundo Círculo" of the GCOL in favor of his old organizational title, the *Gran Confederación Nacional de Obreros "Esteban Antuñano."* [41] In the years that followed, Mendoza became a noted and controversial labor leader.

Mendoza was born in Puebla in 1879, following his father to the mills when he was eleven years old. In his early twenties, he quit his job to write for a small newspaper, eventually establishing his own in 1904. His popularity among the workers of the area enabled him to organize the *Gran Confederación* in 1906. [42]

By mid–1908 Mendoza had expanded his organization to include workers in sixteen mills, always making it clear to his subordinates that the union must be loyal, peaceful, and "prudent." Strikes were forbidden under the Confederation's by-laws, except in accordance with the fifteen-day waiting period stipulated by the presidential *laudo*, and then only after authorization from the union's executive board. In two instances, Mendoza actually turned over to the authorities several of his own men whom he described as agitators. Nonetheless, Mendoza appears to have energetically represented the interests of the workers, occasionally calling a strike if everything else failed. [43]

Even though his enemies within the labor movement called him a lackey of the government, he was still considered an agitator by the

41. Mendoza to Díaz, n.d. (*circa* January 1907), AGN-Gob, leg. 817; Mendoza to Corral, 10 January 1907, AGN-Gog, leg. 817; Rivero C. to Corral, 9 January 1907, AGN-Gob, leg. 817; Mendoza to Díaz, 10 January 1907, GPDC, 66:236; flyer dated 12 January 1907, AGN-Gob, leg. 817.

42. Biographical data from Mendoza's autobiography, written when he was 29; *El Paladín*, 5 January 1908.

43. Mendoza to Díaz, 30 June 1908, GPDC, 33:8881; flyer dated 12 January 1907, AGN-Gob, leg. 718; Mendoza to Antanacio Guerrero, 4 June 1907, AGN-Gob, leg. 817; see instructions to factory representatives in GPDC, 33:14446; Mendoza to Díaz, 26 July 1907, GPDC, 32:7406; Mendoza to Díaz, 17 November 1907, GPDC, 32:13020; *El Paladín*, 30 January, 24 May 1908; GPDC, 32:10352; Mendoza to Díaz, 30 June 1908, GPDC, 33:8880; Mendoza to Díaz, 2 October 1908, GPDC, 33:14445; Mendoza to Díaz, 21 July 1909, GPDC, 34:11246.

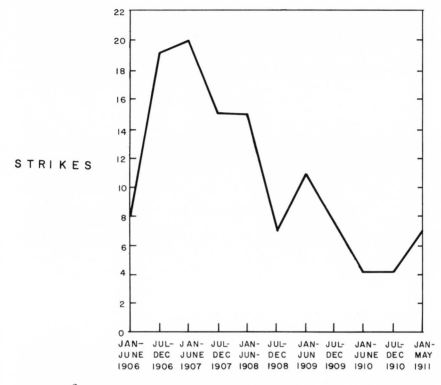

CHART 6
Strikes In Mexico, 1906–1911

governor of Tlaxcala, Col. Próspero Cahuantzi. Díaz knew better. His long years in politics enabled him to spot an ambitious, useful man. Not only was Mendoza loyal to his regime, but he provided the president with direct, inside information on the labor movement. The cost to Díaz was minimal, the right to use his name in union propaganda, his picture taken with Mendoza and the Confederation's officers, looking the stern but benevolent father that he undoubtedly believed he was.[44]

44. *El Paladín*, 23 April, 7 May 1908; *El Diablito Bromista*, 2 November 1909; Cahuantzi to Díaz, 28 July 1909, GPDC, 34:11681; see reference to Díaz in flyer, 12 January 1907, AGN-Gob, leg. 718 and various issues of *La Lucha Obrera*, Mendoza's weekly.

Despite the disbandment of the GCOL, the proscription of many of its original leaders, and the awesome warning contained in the government's actions at Río Blanco, industrial peace did not return to Mexico in the aftermath of Río Blanco. At least twenty separate strikes took place in the first six months of 1907, fifteen in the last half of the year, and fifteen in the first half of 1908. Textile workers struck fourteen more times from January to June, even with the memory of Río Blanco fresh on their minds; five of these strikes were in Orizaba. Boilermakers struck on the Mexican Central railroad in June 1907, and the *Gran Liga de Empleados Ferrocarrileros de México* struck early the following year, both shutting down most of the lines between Mexico City and the border. Bakers struck in Mexico City in July 1907, trolley car drivers and conductors struck several times in Guadalajara as well as in the Federal District in 1907 and 1908, foundry workers struck in Aguascalientes, and the militant miners of Monte de Real in Hidalgo struck several times in the same period. And there were more. A Río Blanco weaver may have assessed the effect of those tragic events that began at his very mill when he proudly warned strikebreakers during a strike in May 1907 that they would not be allowed to enter the mill "because here there are *men*."[45] Mexican workers were inspired by the sacrifices of their comrades at Cananea and Río Blanco, not intimidated.

In conjunction with the continued conflicts, there was a rising consciousness among various groups of workers, an awareness of their potential strength, yet a growing understanding of their inferior position in the emerging industrial society. During an editorial debate between *El Diario* and the conservative *El Heraldo* over the right to strike, one tobacco worker wrote to *El Diario* expressing his combativeness and confidence: "The worker is not now the ignoramous that *El Heraldo* believes. He knows his rights and duties, and that it is his right to progress as civilization advances."[46] To celebrate the reestablishment in early 1908 of a union at the Metepec mill, one worker sent *El Diablito Rojo* a poem describing his feelings of pride and awareness

45. *El Diario*, 31 May 1907. For details on the strikes, see: *El Paladín*, 2 January 1908 and other issues; *El Diario*, 7 March, 8 July 1907 and other issues; AGN-Gob, leg. 718 and 817; GPDC, 32:3611, 7406, 8780, 10352, 11151, 13019, 14397; 66:1508, 1650, 1835.
46. *El Diario*, 18 June 1907.

of his rights, directing his enmity at the foreigner owners and supervisors:

> Do the foreigners think
>   that the Mexican workers,
>   working so proudly,
> are still unaware of their rights?
> The beggars are deceived.
> Whether they like it or not,
>   the new Union grows
>   from the disappointments
>   of yesteryear. . . .
> We do not long for power
>   from he who rules;
>   the workers in the cotton industry
>   already have dignity and a true
>   [feeling of] brotherhood,
>   that is the foundation of the Union;
>   we have justice and the Law as our standard;
>   we have our breast as our bastion;
>   and our heart for our hero.
>
>   By a member of the *Círculo Fraternal*, "Cantos
>   de un obrero"[47]

Above all else in the months after Río Blanco was the indignation, the bitterness at the abuse the worker was subjected to in the factories and at the lack of respect not only for his rights as a citizen but for his dignity as a human being. A commission of Río Blanco workers demanded that their manager "turn his humanitarian attention to the workers and put an end to the poor treatment given them by the foremen, the *celadores* and the employees [of the administration] because many times treating us as if we were irrational beings leads to outbursts of rage, and stupid acts are committed which with a little more judgment [by the administration] would not be committed."[48] Charges and demands of this type show a decided increase in the period after Río Blanco, reaching their peak in 1908 and 1909. A

47. *El Diablito Rojo*, 5 February 1908.
48. Río Blanco Commission to Gov. Dehesa, GPDC, 32:5216. See Chapter 2, above, pp. 72–78.

woman tobacco worker from the Federal District wrote a letter, re-served yet bitterly eloquent, to *El Diario*. "I am not a polished writer," wrote María Fenelón y García, "for the first time in my life I am writing a long letter, and I am afraid of not being able to express all the indignation that I would want to communicate to you." She talked of the conditions under which she and her fellow tobacco workers labored and how, as working women, they were treated like scum. She told of "the misery, . . . the cold, hungry nights and, in addition, the wounded pride, the self esteem battered by the harsh treatment of the boss."[49]

Anger and indignation over ill-treatment did not originate in the labor conflicts of 1906 or the Río Blanco strike, but the public expression of dissatisfaction was particularly evident among textile workers and railroad workers and among workers in various occupations in the Federal District.[50] One example of rising consciousness among workers was a growing demand for more educational opportunities for themselves and their children.

As early as 1902 various workers from the Metepec mill in Puebla complained that there were no public schools in their company town. But it was during the conflicts of 1906 and in the months that followed that education appeared as a major issue among industrial workers. In 1908 a Metepec mill hand again complained of the lack of public education and complained that the church schools were poor and no substitute. Workers from the Río Blanco mill charged that the school *maestros* in his textile town did not teach the children anything. Copper workers of Cananea and textile workers of the Santa Rosa mill near Orizaba made similar complaints.[51] The demand for educational opportunities for their children is a clear indication that Mexican workers in various industries were becoming aware of the inherent inequities in their situation.

49. *El Diario*, 21 March 1907.

50. See particularly letters to the editors of *El Paladín*, *El Diario*, *El Diablito Bromista*, and *La Guacamaya*.

51. *La Guacamaya*, 19 November 1902; *El Paladín*, 26 January 1908. See complaints from Tlaxcalan and Puebla workers in *El Paladín*, 27 May 1906, 12 May 1907, and complaints from railroad workers in 1908, Ramón Corral to Reyes, 29 January 1908, 7 February 1908, AGBR, "Correspondencia Ministeria, 1903–1909"; *El Paladín*, 20 December 1909, 3 March, 24 April, 9 June 1910.

A José Guadalupe Posada cartoon showing a worker complaining to Díaz about the abuses of the foremen in the factories. In the drawing the foreman is clearly a foreigner. With the permission of the Fondo Editorial de la Plástica Mexicana.

Not only were the workers interested in schools for their children, but they made efforts to establish night schools for themselves. In May 1907 Río Blanco workers offered to work all religious holidays if the government would establish a night school for them and requested that the mill permit them to leave work at 6:30 P.M. to attend. Without government help, the *Sociedad Mutualista de Ahorros "Ignacio de la Llave"* of Orizaba was founded by the textile workers in 1909 for the purpose of providing a chance for the workers to attend night classes. Metepec workers collected funds for a teacher in a night school for workers and requested that work stop at 7:00 P.M. to allow attendance at the school. In Monterrey a school for railroad workers was founded by the *Ferrocarril Nacional* after many such requests.[52]

Just how much education did the workers acquire for themselves?

52. Río Blanco Commission to Dehesa, 24 May 1907, GPDC, 32:5216; *El Paladín*, 7 January 1909; *México Nuevo*, 9 June 1909, 22 February 1910.

The official figure for literacy in Mexico in 1910 was 20 percent. The popular assumption that most workers were illiterate is probably incorrect. Working-class literacy among the artisans and skilled workers, for example, was undoubtedly much higher. Although no figures exist that isolate workers as a group, an estimate of 30 to 35 percent literacy might not be too high for workers in many industrial occupations, considering the number of letters to the editors written by workers, the circulation of newspapers among the workers, and the use of flyers, broadsides, etc. by workers' organizations. By way of inference, the census of 1895 gave the male literacy figure for the Federal District as 44 percent; in 1900 it was 44 percent, and in 1910 it was 55 percent.[53]

Although the demand for education is an important part of a rising consciousness, illiteracy itself does not automatically make a man ignorant, incapable of being aware of his working conditions or unconcerned with his fate. I suspect that literate or not, few industrial workers in urban areas, or wherever conflict was common, were ignorant. On the contrary, many were aware of their conditions, disgusted over their predicament, and indignant about mistreatment by their employers.

Whatever the literacy rate among Mexican industrial and urban workers, many of them wanted more for themselves and for their children. This fact alone indicates clearly that Mexican workers had every intention by the first decade of the twentieth century of demanding admittance to the progress of their nation, a progress which they were fully aware they had been denied.

Industrial conflicts fell off dramatically in the last half of 1908. There had been fifteen strikes during the first six months of that year; there were only six from July through December. In the textile industry, strikes had fallen off a year earlier. From fourteen during the first six months of 1907, the number of strikes fell to three in the second half of that year, rose slightly to five in the first half of 1908, and fell to four in the last half of that year. Railroad strikes fell from six in 1907 to only three for the entire three years from 1908 through 1910.

53. Thompson, *The People of Mexico*, 199; González Navarro, *Estadísticas sociales*, pp. 122–23.

The only strike to attract national attention in 1908—except for the *Gran Liga* railroad strike in April to be discussed elsewhere—took place at the small cotton textile mill of San Bruno in Jalapa, Veracruz. The Spanish administrator of the mill refused to give permission to the workers to celebrate the birthday of Padre Hidalgo. They disregarded the order and stayed home for the day. For this breach of industrial discipline eight workers were fired, and the rest refused to work until the eight were rehired. The strike lasted six months, making all the papers in the Capital because of the issue—a slight to a patriotic hero. The workers themselves requested Governor Dehesa to intervene, but they received only advice from him. *El Paladín* carried the story as part of its subtle but consistent attack against foreigners.[54]

As the strike dragged on, comrades from Río Blanco, Santa Rosa, and Metepec collected money for the strikers. One worker boasted about this show of solidarity, "God is great and labor unity is a fact."[55] Nonetheless, administration disinterest and the owners' intransigence finally forced the San Bruno mill hands back to work early the following year. To many Mexicans it must have again seemed that Mexican workers were being penalized for upholding the honor of their fatherland.

The reasons for the decline in the number of conflicts after mid-1908 appear to be both that the regime had withdrawn from active arbitration of disputes after mid-1907 and, particularly, that hard times had come to the Mexican economy by 1908. Interest rates were up, investments were down, and more than a few workers were out of jobs. During the fall of 1908 twenty-eight hundred Cananea copper workers were laid off because of market reversals. By the end of the decade barely three thousand miners worked the Cananea mines, compared to 7560 in 1906. The new year was hardly three weeks old when Puebla textile mills laid off nearly one-third of their work force in a dramatic move to cut production costs. By fiscal year 1909–1910, the

54. Workers of San Bruno to Gov. of Veracruz, 7 August 1908, SHUV, Gob, 1908, R–34; Sec. of Gob. to *jefe político* of Jalapa, 27 August 1908, SHUV, Gob, 1908, R–34; *El Paladín*, 6, 16, 23, 30 August 1908; flyer "Los obreros en huelga," *El Paladín*, 7 January 1909.

55. *El Paladín*, 17 September 1908.

number of workers employed in Mexican textile mills had declined to 31,963 from the peak of 35,811 in the fiscal year 1907–1908. For nearly all workers, real wages were falling due to the rise in prices of the basic essentials such as food and rent. In September and October of 1908 severe frosts ruined corn and bean crops throughout the nation, promising an even harder year to come.[56]

As with hard times in most nations, fewer workers were willing to risk losing their jobs when substitute employment was hard to find. A strike scheduled for the Orizaba textile mills on the January 1908 anniversary of the Río Blanco strike was cancelled because the company threatened to fire all strikers. At the volatile Metepec mill there were no work stoppages at all in 1908; beginning in the middle of August the owners suspended work on Friday and Saturday.[57]

Yet despite the declining strikes on the railroads and in the textile mills, workers' organizations were on the rise again. Meeting only days after the Río Blanco tragedy, twenty-two carpenters from Mexico City, principally from the railroad yards, formed the *Unión de Carpinteros y Similares* with Espiridión Arroyo as their president. They met under the auspices of the president of the tobacco workers of the city, José Fuentes, who invited them to use the tobacco workers' hall. Later that June, Mexican clerks in a previously American-dominated Brotherhood of Railway Clerks formed their own organization, the *Alianza de Ferrocarrileros Mexicanos*.[58] In the textile industry, workers began to regroup in early 1908.

Back in the hopeful days before Río Blanco, Metepec mill hands had affiliated with the *Gran Círculo de Obreros Libres*. After the repression, the *jefe político* of Atlixco banned the GCOL from the mills in the area. At the beginning of 1908, however, the workers at Metepec organized a *Círculo Fraternal de Obreros* in its stead. Their leader was

56. Samuel T. Lee, Consul, to Huntington Wilson, Nogales, Mexico, 28 October 1907, State, n.f.:9723, USNA; El Colegio de México, *Estadísticas económicas*, pp. 46–47, 106; *El Paladín*, 16 January 1908; State, n.f.:8057, USNA. Many workers wrote to Díaz asking for help in finding work; see GPDC, 32:4372, 4739, 10316 and 33:16121 and 34:268. They were never answered.

57. *El Paladín*, 12 January, 19 July 1908; Antonio Gómez, 2nd Lt., *Cuerpo Rural*, to Gen. Francisco M. Ramírez (General Inspector or I.G.), 19 August 1908, AGN-Gob, leg. 852.

58. Navarrete, *Alto*, pp. 103–4, 116–17.

Samuel A. Ramírez, the Santa Rosa worker who had contested Morales's control of the Orizaba GCOL. He was not implemented in the Río Blanco riots and stayed in the Orizaba area until mid-1907 before he left for Metepec. Ramírez had once worked at Metepec and evidently reestablished his connections rather easily. The organization drew up a formal complaint on various grievances and sent it to the administration of the mill and to the *jefe político*. The petition went unanswered, and the frustration of unresolved grievances built up. One evening in the early fall of 1908 a group of disgruntled workers began throwing rocks at the mill. Plant employees responded with pistol fire, wounding one worker. He was sent to Atlixco to recover and stand trial.[59]

In Orizaba textile workers began formally to organize again sometime in the first part of 1908 when Santa Rosa mill hands formed *La Sociedad Mutualista "Cuauhtémoc,"* but the organization was ordered dissolved by Miguel Gómez, *jefe político* of the area. In the fall, workers at the Río Blanco mill organized a workers' group called the *Alianza Obrera*. This time, although Gómez had strong reservations about it, both he and Díaz wrote letters to the officers wishing them well and reminding them of their responsibilities to maintain the peace and to respect the legally constituted authorities. Privately, Díaz ordered Gómez to watch the new society very carefully.[60] From the government's perspective, this order was not simply a precaution. The PLM had risen again only a few months before.

The *Partido Liberal Mexicano* and Mexican Industrial Workers

Beginning with the Cananea strike, the government had viewed with alarm the possibility of disgruntled workers linking up with the PLM revolutionaries in a conspiracy to overthrow the regime. Despite the

59. Mendoza to Díaz, 30 May 1908, GPDC, 33:7163; Aurelio to Dehesa, n.d. (circa May or June 1907), cited in Sodi de Pallares, *Teodoro A. Dehesa*, p. 159; *El Paladín*, 1 March, 2 April 1908; A. Gómez to I.G., 2 September 1908, AGN-Gob, leg. 852.

60. Gómez to Díaz, 10 October 1908, GPDC, 33:13512; Díaz to Gómez, 21 October 1908, GPDC, 33:13514; *El Paladín*, 11, 22, 25 October 1908.

lack of worker-participation in the PLM uprisings in the fall of 1906, the regime closely monitored all contacts between the exiled PLM leadership and labor groups. The events at Río Blanco, from the government's perspective, had only underlined this danger, for in the violence they saw the sinister hand of the PLM.[61]

The PLM did have sympathizers among the workers of Mexico, although not as many as the government feared. In the months after Río Blanco several workers in the Orizaba area were arrested and jailed because they had received correspondence from the exiled PLM. In order to take advantage of the discontent with the regime over Río Blanco, the PLM attempted to step up its recruitment campaign among Mexican industrial workers, particularly at Cananea and Orizaba. In June 1907 Ricardo Flores Magón sent to his colleague Tomás Sarabia a list of thirty-two persons in the Orizaba area whom he thought would at least circulate their propaganda among the workers. In particular, their weekly *Revolución* was aimed at the Mexican workers, calling on them to arm themselves in anticipation of the revolution against the regime, because, as one issue reminded them, "peaceful strikes achieve nothing more than a Cananea or a Río Blanco."[62]

The government made every effort to prevent such propaganda from reaching the hands of the workers. When *Revolución* first appeared in mid-1907, the Cananea postal service immediately notified the president himself and seized all copies that were sent through the mails. When the PLM paper, *Reforma, Libertad y Justicia* appeared in May 1908, the authorities in at least three states took immediate steps to take all copies out of circulation and prevent future ones from being sent through the mail. And as a matter of course postal authorities intercepted and opened thousands of letters to and from suspected PLM sympathizers in Mexico.[63]

61. See government charges against the PLM for "fomenting the strike at Río Blanco," Rel-RFM, L-E-931.

62. Quote from *Revolución* (Los Angeles, U.S.), 28 December 1907, in Rel-RFM, L-E-931, 14:3; *jefe político* of Orizaba to Díaz, 4 July 1907, GPDC, 32:2469; Ricardo Flores Magón to Sarabia, 12 June 1907, Rel-RFM, L-E-925, 8:190.

63. Name illegible to Díaz, 18 June 1907, GPDC, 32:7255; J. Fenochio to Díaz, 15 August 1906, Magadelena, GPDC, 31:1908; José M. Sánchez to Díaz, 4 June 1908, Chihuahua, GPDC, 33:7630, gov. of Puebla to Díaz, 27 June

Yet despite these efforts, throughout 1907 persistent rumors made the rounds in Orizaba that the workers there were arming secretly. In each case local officials following up the rumors could find no evidence of conspiracy on the part of the workers, and no arms stored for some future uprising. If the workers were planning to revolt it was a well-kept secret. Miguel Gómez tended to discount the rumors but he promised the president that he would maintain vigilance.[64]

Meanwhile the PLM leadership in the United States began to plan their second uprising. Although three important leaders, Ricardo Flores Magón, Librado Rivera, and Antonio I. Villarreal, had been in jail in Los Angeles since August 1907 charged with violation of the U.S. neutrality laws, they managed to slip plans for the revolt to confederates on the outside. June 1908 was set as the date of the uprising. The party had already made plans for the Cananea copper miners. They were to use dynamite to seize the town and obtain arms, as were the Orizaba mill hands. To encourage the participation of the latter, Juan Olivares, PLM activist and former officer of the GCOL, was sent to recruit his old comrades to the cause. Along with his PLM credentials, Olivares carried a list with the names of five trusted contacts among the textile workers of Orizaba, Nogales, Puebla, and Atlixco.[65] In the last days before the revolt was to take place, *Reforma, Libertad y Justicia* called on the workers to join the rebels. "Destroy the factory, cave in the mine, burn the estates, and with arms in hand resist the attack of the Cossacks," the paper exhorted the workers of Mexico.[66] Whether they would or not would soon be known.

1908, GPDC, 33:7263; L. A. Guajardo to Díaz, 10 June 1908, Muzquiz, Coahuila, GPDC, 33:7796.

64. Enrique Tron to Dehesa, 28 May 1907, GPDC, 32:5218; Díaz to Gen. Maass, 30 May 1907, GPDC, 32:2010, 2048, 2074; Yñigo Noriega to Díaz, 3 February 1907, GPDC, 32:2127; *jefe político* to Díaz, 14 October 1907, GPDC, 32:11749.

65. Ricardo Flores Magón to Tomás Espinosa, n.d., (circa June to October 1906), Toronto, Rel-RFM, L-E-922, 5:142; Ricardo Flores Magón to Enrique Flores Magón, 8 June 1908, Los Angeles, Rel-RFM, L-E-940, 23:34–44, 112; Mexican Consul to Sec. Relaciones Exteriores, 23 November 1908, Tucson, Arizona, Rel-RFM, L-E-944, 27:108–10; Ethel Duffy Turner, *Ricardo Flores Magón y El Partido Liberal Mexicano* (Morelia, Michoacán: Editorial "Erandi," 1960), pp. 158–59, 167.

66. 15 June 1908 in Thompson to Sec. of State, State, n.f. 8183: encl. 100–4, USNA.

In late June 1908 the uprising took place. PLM rebels attacked local garrisons and government offices in Viesca and Las Vacas, Coahuila, in Palomas, Chihuahua, and in a number of other small engagements in the northern states. They fought well but without success. Within a few days most of the rebels had been killed or captured. Only a few managed to escape to the mountains, where they made their way back across the border or went into hiding. But in the industrial towns of the Republic, in the mining centers and mills, June passed without incident as the workers made no move to join the PLM in revolt. For reasons that will be explored later, Mexican industrial workers had not taken up arms against the regime.[67]

Yet in the days that followed the violence at Río Blanco, no one knew what the future held. The regime only knew that working-class agitation was a threat to the stability of its government and that earlier policies had failed to contain the violence in the mills. What its policy would be in the aftermath of Río Blanco was a matter of major concern to the regime of Porfirio Díaz.

Federal Government Labor Policy in the Aftermath of Río Blanco

In the early days of January 1907, the government of Porfirio Díaz stood at the crossroads where all industrializing societies stand, sooner or later. How would the regime deal with the emerging industrial working class? Would the momentum of the bloody repression at Río Blanco dominate the government's labor policy, or would the initial efforts at conciliation made in 1906 be restored and strengthened, and if so, would they prove adequate to resolve the conflicts? Would Mexico be spared the violence and unrest that were then common headlines in the press of Europe and the United States, conflicts which a few months earlier had seemed so unlikely to disturb the iron peace imposed by Porfirio Díaz? In those days of early January, when

67. For coverage of the revolts, see Cockcroft, *Intellectual Precursors*, pp. 150–54 and State, n.f. 594, USNA. Cockcroft suggests that the workers *would* have revolted except for heavy governmental surveillance and repression.

the shock and pall of the violence of Río Blanco still hung in the air, few men could guess the answers, and no man knew for sure, not even the old *Caudillo* himself.

Even before the events at Río Blanco, Díaz had informed the industrialists that any wage increase due because of the *laudo* should become effective within fifteen days. By the middle of the month the new wage scale had been implemented, bringing an increase in wages for many workers in the Puebla-Tlaxcala mills. Meanwhile, the temporary *jefe político* of Orizaba, Col. Francisco Ruiz, made energetic attempts to remedy some of what he perceived to have been the causes of the violence by the workers; he abolished company store script and reduced the rent paid by workers on their company-owned housing.[68] The intent of the government with regard to other provisions of the *laudo* remained to be seen.

Whatever the president's intentions, however, the effectiveness of the *laudo* as a long term settlement of the textile workers' grievances was doubtful from the start. What was lacking was a way of thinking and acting on this kind of social problem. In attempting to resolve what the regime viewed primarily as a political problem, the regime failed to establish a governmental system for the implementation of policy, and the available bureaucratic equipment simply could not do the job. The paperwork on the *laudo* had been done in Corral's office, because nothing more appropriate could be found than the agency that handled internal security. Although the Mexican government was not attempting to resolve the labor question through the *laudo* but to defuse it, even this limited objective would be unobtainable unless the regime broadened and institutionalized its labor policy. Under the current regime, the willingness to carry out such reforms had yet to be proven.

Certainly the regime's public pronouncements did not indicate such flexibility. In his congressional address in September 1906, Díaz had called for the good sense and willingness to compromise of all concerned. His address to Congress in April 1907 stressed the point that

68. Luis Barroso Arias to Corral, 9 January 1907, AGN-Gob, leg. 817; *El Tiempo*, 13 January 1907; *El País*, 12 January 1907; Ruiz to Díaz, 15 January 1907, GPDC, 32:419. Having served his purpose, Ruiz was replaced at the end of the month.

the government stood ready to maintain the public order.[69] It sounded very much like a threat.

Although the regime still supported the right to strike, those who instigated strikes or even planned a strike were rounded up by the police. In one case in May 1907, the acting governor of Veracruz suggested to Díaz that two leaders of a recent peacefully-settled strike at the textile mill San Bruno be confined to the army. Díaz agreed and added the advice that they be shipped to the military work camps in Quintana Roo, a much harsher punishment than assignment to military units for regular duty. When a minor disturbance broke out in an otherwise peaceful strike at the Río Blanco mill, the new *jefe político* of Orizaba, Miguel Gómez, consigned twenty-two workers to Quintana Roo, after having received authorization from the president. *El Diario* covered the strike and pointed out the illegality of the deportations, but the workers were shipped off to Quintana Roo anyway.[70] Obviously, the government was determined to carry out a hard-line policy on labor disturbances, one quite consistent with its actions at Río Blanco.

Another major characteristic of Porfirian activism on the labor question was the gathering of information to keep the government informed of any dangers to the public order. In Orizaba the military chief of the zone, the *jefe político*, and the head of the *rurales* all watched the workers and reported regularly to Díaz. General Joaquín Maass, as head of the military zone for the area, made it his special responsibility to keep secret watch over the sale of arms and ammunition.[71] These sources of information were augmented by special re-

69. *El Diario de los Debates del Congreso de los E.U.M.*, 1 April to 31 May 1907, p. 12.

70. Eliezer Espinosa to Díaz, 26 May 1907, GPDC, 66:1964; Díaz to Maass, appended to GPDC, 66:1964; *jefe político* of Orizaba to Díaz, 30 July 1907, GPDC, 32:7558; *jefe político* of Orizaba to Gov. of Veracruz, n.d., SHUV, Gob, 1907, H-9. See correspondence between Gómez and Díaz in GPDC, 32:15823, 15854; GPDC, 66:1508, 1650, 1835, 1984, 2004, 2010, 2048, 2051–52, 2074. *El Diario*, 2, 23 June 1907. For reasons not clear, Díaz later ordered two workers freed who had been sent to Quintana Roo because of the May disturbance at Río Blanco; *jefe político* to Díaz, 4 January 1908, GPDC, 33:366, 1620, 14569.

71. See correspondence with Maass, GPDC, 32:15854, 8780–82, 12562.

ports from Mendoza, the industrialists, and the governors of Puebla and Tlaxcala.

Inevitably, such a system led to occasional conflicts in lines of authority and uncertainty as to presidential policy by all concerned. What appears to be inefficiency, however, was most likely designed by Díaz for maximum centralization of powers in his own hands. It was institutionalized *caudillismo*, and in times of peace it worked remarkably well. He was rarely dependent on only one source of information, he kept lines of communication open to various groups and individuals, and he maintained maximum flexibility by revealing a minimum of his intentions. His correspondence is a marvel in noncommittal directiveness. Yet the system was designed for another age; local abuse had already eaten away much of its foundation. Under the impact of determined foes, its effectiveness would later prove only too inadequate.

Nonetheless, in mid–1907 the system appeared to be operating well enough when the government again involved itself in the settlement of a labor dispute among the Orizaba textile workers. The workers at the Río Blanco mill had struck in May 1907 because the management, disregarding the presidential *laudo*, implemented a new *reglamento*. Miguel Gómez supported their demands and asked Díaz to use his influence to obtain a document more acceptable to the workers. The president responded by ordering Teodoro Dehesa, as governor, to draw up a set of new regulations for use in all the mills of his state. The governor worked out the substitute regulations in close cooperation with the president and then submitted them to CIDOSA for comments. The directors of the firm were not happy with the government initiative, but they did not reject it.[72]

The new government *reglamento* was considerably expanded and more generous to labor than either the mill's regulations or the earlier *laudo*. Among the reforms of the new regulations, child labor

72. Gómez to Díaz, 29 May 1907, GPDC, 32:16836; Gov. of Veracruz to E. Tron, 13 June 1907, GPDC, 32:16060. For the correspondence between Dehesa and Díaz, along with copies of the old and new *reglamentos* and related documents, see GPDC, 32:16062–65, 16575, 16077–78. Incomplete copies of their correspondence are found in Sodi de Pallares, *Teodoro A. Dehesa*, pp. 137–48.

minimum age was raised to ten, three years above the minimum expressed in the presidential *laudo*, and maximum working hours for all
employees were reduced to twelve from the usual fourteen or more.
Sundays, national holidays, and five religious celebrations were to be
days off, although not, of course, with pay; current factory regulations required the worker to work on holidays if requested. An arbitration committee would be established, at the worker's request, to
judge cases of defective material. The arbitrator would be selected by
joint agreement of the company and the worker. Current factory
regulations simply gave that responsibility to the company, without
recourse by the worker. Díaz had suggested the change.

The presidential *laudo* had originally given workers six days to vacate company housing when no longer working at the mill, but Díaz
mentioned to Dehesa that this time limit might be raised to ten days.
Complaints submitted by workers to company management under the
Dehesa-Díaz *reglamento* required a reply within eight days, as compared to the fifteen days in the *laudo*. The Dehesa-Díaz regulations
prohibited a foreman from taking money from a worker on any pretext. This was a widespread abuse. The company's regulation provided for the expulsion of both the guilty supervisory personnel and
the worker(s) involved, whereas the Díaz-Dehesa plan called for the
expulsion only of the foreman.

The Díaz-Dehesa *reglamento* also specifically stipulated that the
workers were to be treated with moderation, something that the Puebla workers' *reglamento* in December 1906 had demanded but which
was not mentioned in either the presidential *laudo* or in the current
factory regulations. In compliance with state health regulations, the
factory would have to employ a physician if over one hundred workers were employed, a requirement in the *laudo* that had been neg-
lected by the mills. Finally, the factory was to give an eight-day notice
of any change in the current pay scale. The industrialists' regulations
simply stated that "prior notice" would be given—usually a period of
one day. Unmentioned and evidently discarded were the hated
notebooks.

Unquestionably, Díaz hoped to placate the Orizaba mill hands with
the reforms, as he called the new *reglamento*, and defuse the hostility
still very much in evidence in the area. Several times in his correspondence with Dehesa he mentioned the necessity of avoiding

strikes. At mid–1907 he was still very much concerned with the potential for violence within the labor movement and with the danger that this posed for his regime. Cananea and Río Blanco had had their effect.

The regime's labor policy was not strictly centered within the federal governmental structure, although Díaz chose to keep careful watch over the major centers of labor unrest. Certain of the state governors acquired a reputation on their own of involvement with the labor problem. One of these was Díaz's partner in drawing up the new *reglamento* for the textile workers, Teodoro A. Dehesa.

Cosío Villegas writes that of all the Porfirian governors in 1910, none was popular or well-liked in his state, with the possible exception of Teodoro Dehesa. Dehesa was born into a moderately well-off family, with important social connections on his mother's side. He became an early partisan of Díaz and later a close political ally. During the nineteen years he served as governor of the state (1892–1911), he developed a genuine concern for the welfare of the state's industrial workers. When the industrialists accused the textile workers of breaking the law during the labor conflicts of 1906, Dehesa defended the workers, suggesting that the real cause of the trouble was the greed of the owners. After the Cananea strike he quietly sent one hundred *pesos* to Sonora for the families of those workers killed in the violence. *El Dictamen*, the major daily in the state and a political supporter of the governor, often ran editorials friendly to the labor movement and encouraged their aspirations.[73]

In his political philosophy, Dehesa viewed the role of government as a mediator between capital and labor. During the crisis of 1906 he urged Carlos Herrera, *jefe político* of Orizaba, to perform this function. He himself was only moderately active in the labor conflicts prior to Río Blanco, perhaps because the president himself was involved in the area, and he did not wish to conflict with his chief's plans. Although he publicly defended the industrialists after Río Blanco, saying that capital is the blessed and sacred fruit of labor, privately he

73. Cosío Villegas, *La vida política interior*, 2:493; Ramón Prida, "Los sucesos," p. 88; SHUV, Gob. 1906, S-32; *El Dictamen*, 1, 2, 6 March 1906; Sodi de Pallares, *Teodoro A. Dehesa*, pp. 7–10. Juan Malpica Silva, owner of *El Dictamen*, was a close friend of Dehesa; interview with Sr. Gabriel Cházaro, former newspaperman for *El Dictamen* during this era, 17 February 1966.

ordered a thorough investigation of the workers' needs. Dehesa used this investigation as the basis for his suggestions in the substitute *reglamento* he worked out with the president. Yet in the short time that remained before the Revolution of 1910, Dehesa was unable to resolve the continuing Orizaba labor problem. One reason may be that he lost control of the *jefe político* of Orizaba, Miguel Gómez, whose orders on labor issues of any significance came directly from Díaz. Dehesa disagreed with Gómez on several occasions.[74] Another reason may have been his own political ambitions. Given his friendship with Díaz, he might have hoped to go further than the governorship, perhaps even the vice-presidency, should Díaz turn against Corral. In sum, Dehesa was an enlightened and progressive governor, but a man encumbered by ambition and working within a system unconducive to easy change.[75]

Two other state governors had shown some willingness to at least explore the workers' needs and to attempt to resolve some of the more obvious problems, even before the events at Río Blanco. Enrique Creel, governor of Chihuahua, had been sympathetic to the demands of Silvino Rodríguez's mechanics' union in the strike of August 1906. In the fall of 1907 the Chihuahua state legislature passed a workers' housing law, presumably at Creel's suggestion.[76]

The other governor was General Bernardo Reyes, governor of Nuevo León. The historical reputation of Bernardo Reyes has not survived the years untarnished. His repression of the Liberals in Monterrey in 1903, his unwillingness to face up to Díaz in the vice-presidential movement of 1909, and his later intrigues against the Madero administration have seen to that. Nonetheless, with Dehesa,

---

74. Dehesa to Herrera, 28 November 1906, GPDC, 31:16061; GPDC, 32:5222; Sodi de Pallares, *Teodoro A. Dehesa*, pp. 155–57; *jefe político* to Sec. Gob., Veracruz, 13 March 1908, SHUV, Gob, 1908, 11-R. Two sources report that Dehesa commissioned the noted jurist and educator Silvestre Moreno Cora to draw up a state labor law; Sodi de Pallares, *Teodoro A. Dehesa*, pp. 72, 132, and Agustín Aragón, *Porfirio Díaz*, 2 vols. (Mexico: Editora Intercontinental, 1962), 2:30.

75. In the last few months before the 1910 election, a movement developed in support of Dehesa as the vice-presidential candidate in place of Ramón Corral, but Díaz refused, saying only that it was not always possible to do what you wanted in politics; Taracena, *La verdadera Revolución Mexicana*, p. 287.

76. *El Economista Mexicano*, 10 November 1907, p. 132.

General Reyes was the most sensitive to the problems of the workers in his state. Reyes had sponsored the most advanced labor accident compensation insurance then in effect in Mexico, in November 1906. In addition, he supported the Monterrey railroad workers in 1906 in their efforts to gain approval from Díaz for their branch of the *Gran Liga Mexicana de Empleados de Ferrocarril.* At the same time, however, he kept a close watch on the organization, forcing the leadership to remove certain "socialist" and combative articles from their constitution.[77] Toward the end of 1907, Reyes proposed to Ramón Corral that at the upcoming convention of the *Gran Liga*, a resolution calling for mandatory arbitration of all labor disputes be placed before that body. A commission composed of representatives from the workers, the firm, and the government would be established for this purpose, thereby avoiding strikes. Corral expressed serious reservations about one part of the project which would have made the union the legal negotiating representative. In addition, he criticized the suggestion to have workers on such a commission, maintaining that they would have difficulty being impartial and dispassionate. Reyes replied with ill-concealed sarcasm, acknowledging receipt of Corral's letter, which did not give "any importance to the personal morality of the workers' associations."[78] Reyes afforded the workers the dignity of a "moral" position equal to that of their bosses. Reyes had his proposal introduced to the convention anyway, but it died in committee; the railroadmen themselves were divided as to its effect on their position.[79]

Reyes was popular among Mexican workers, as the political campaigns of 1909 would demonstrate. Certainly his labor policy needs to be evaluated in the context of his entire administration, but whatever

77. Feyes to Díaz, 28 March 1906, AGBR, "Correspondencia del Sr. Presidente, 1903–1909"; Díaz to Reyes (coded telegram), 4 April 1906, and Reyes to Díaz, 12, 26 April, 21 May 1906 in AGBR, "Correspondencia del Sr. Presidente, 1903–1909."

78. Reyes to Corral, 8 January 1908, AGBR, Correspondencia Ministeria, 1908; Reyes to Corral, 13 December 1907, Corral to Reyes, 2 January 1908, AGBR, Correspondencia Ministeria, 1908. The formula of representation from the union, management, and government to settle labor disputes was eventually adopted in Article 123 of the Constitution of 1917 and implemented on a national scale by the Labor Code of 1931.

79. Reyes to Corral, 23 January 1908, 7 February 1908, AGBR, Correspondencia Ministeria, 1908.

that verdict, General Bernardo Reyes must be considered one of the few Porfirian politicians who saw the working-class people as worthy of his attention.

While Dehesa and Díaz were working out the textile workers' *reglamento* in June 1907, another major conflict broke out on the nation's railroad lines. The boilermakers (*caldereros*) of the Mexican Central in Monterrey walked off the job, having waited a month for resolution of a maltreatment complaint against the American head of their department. They were soon joined by comrades in Hipólito, Victoria, Jimulco, and Torreón, effectively curbing operations all along the line. Overriding the initial issue, the main concern of the striking workers was what they believed to be the preference shown to foreign employees of the railroad over Mexican workers. Initially, Díaz asked General Reyes, as the governor of the state, to use his prestige with the strikers to end the dispute, but he eventually agreed to arbitrate himself after both the railroad management and the workers separately requested his good offices.[80]

In order to obtain a first-hand account of the problem, the president sent a private commission to visit the workshops of the Mexican Central, as well as those of the National Railroad and the *Fundición de Fierro y Acero*, all in Monterrey. The commissioner reported that the situation had reached an intolerable point for the workers with regard to the foreign supervisors' ill-treatment of Mexicans. Apparently as a result of this report, the American supervisor was released, and other reforms were promised by the president.[81]

At the beginning of the summer of 1907, after a year in which more strikes took place than in the previous ten years combined, the regime of Porfirio Díaz appeared heading toward a decided effort to resolve the labor question, an effort involving direct and open governmental intervention to enforce a compromise settlement of labor grievances. Yet for reasons still obscure, by the end of the year the regime had reversed its policy of direct intervention, except to maintain order.

80. See GPDC, 66:2148, 2174, 2189, 2194; Díaz to Reyes, 11 June 1907, and Reyes to Díaz, 13 June 1907, Correspondencia del Presidente, 1903–1909.

81. Illegible to Díaz, GPDC, 32:7307; González Navarro, *La vida social*, p. 339.

The first public hint of this retrenchment came in the president's semiannual message to Congress in September 1907. At that time, Díaz observed that labor conflicts had declined somewhat in frequency and importance and that those that had occurred were short and limited, "without, in general, [it] having been necessary for the authorities to intervene to break them up before they became a threat to the public order."[82]

Further indications of the government's change of policy are the continued complaints of the textile workers about the issues that the *laudo* and then the Díaz-Dehesa *reglamento* were supposed to resolve. Although Puebla mill hands had reacted favorably to the initial wage increase in 1907, for example, discontent surfaced over other issues. In particular, the notebooks were universally resented, as was the fact that in Puebla neither fines nor the hated company store script were eliminated. In the years that followed, many of the same issues remained alive throughout the textile industry, especially those involving fines, the company store, and the notebooks.[83] Over a year after the Río Blanco strike, a commercial agent who had business in many of the mills noted that the "*reglamento* that ended the strike of January 1907 is a dead letter."[84] Whatever the government's intentions, its efforts to resolve these particular grievances failed because it did not, or could not, enforce its own settlement.

Other proof of governmental disengagement was provided by the regime's unwillingness to become involved in the labor disputes that continued to take place. Informed by the governor of Querétaro in early 1908 that striking workers at the Hércules textile mill were beginning to migrate elsewhere and that local merchants were upset because of the resulting decline in business, Díaz replied that the situation was "truly regrettable" but suggested no other action than for the governor to preserve the public order. In addition, Díaz had discouraged Pascual Mendoza from acting as a negotiating agent for the Hércules workers.[85]

82. Cited in *El Economista Mexicano*, 21 September 1907.
83. Rivero C. to Barroso, 26 January 1907, Puebla, AGN-Gob, leg. 817; Gov. of Puebla to Díaz, 15 January 1907, GPDC, 66:332. On various issues, see *El Paladín*, 1 March, 19 April 1908, 18 April, 22 November 1909, 27 February 1910.
84. *El Paladín*, 12 March 1908.
85. See correspondence in GPDC, 32:1610, 1612, 1645, 1646; *rurales'* re-

In a similar case late in 1908, Pascual Mendoza was requested by the San Bruno workers' association to negotiate with the owners on their behalf. Mendoza wrote Díaz, asking his permission to take on that responsibility. The president suggested that Mendoza come to the Capital to discuss the matter with his personal secretary, Don Rafael Chousal. There is no evidence to indicate that Mendoza ever took on the task, perhaps because the president discouraged it.[86]

In October 1908, when the *jefe político* of Orizaba recognized the new workers' organization at the Río Blanco mill, *La Alianza Obrera*, he specifically stated that they could not count on any help from the authorities. He admitted to the workers that they had a right to associate under Article 9 of the Constitution of 1857, but he said that Article 3, the right of the community to tranquility and peace, was equally important and gratuitously reminded them that to violate the public order would bring upon them a punishment both firm and severe. The *jefe político* of Puebla rejected a request by striking Puebla tobacco workers for his intervention in their dispute with the owners of La Basa factory.[87] But the most dramatic example of the regime's unwillingness to intervene actively in labor conflicts came during the great railroad strike of April 1908.

Since the defeat in 1906 of Silvino Rodríguez's mechanics union, the most active of the railroad organizations was the *Gran Liga Mexicana de Empleados de Ferrocarril*. Founded in 1904, the *Liga* was principally, although not exclusively, concerned with organizing Mexican white collar workers on the national lines. In June 1907, for example, the *Liga* had represented the Mexican station agents and telegraph operators of the Mexican Central Railway and won certain concessions on wages, firing practices, and the use of Spanish on the lines. By 1908 the *Liga* had branches in Monterrey, Chihuahua, Tampico, Jimulco, Jiménez, San Luis Potosí, Aguascalientes, Silao, Acam-

port in AGN-Gob, leg. 718; *comandante* 3rd *Cuerpo Rural* to I.G., 3 January 1908, AGN-Gob, leg. 582:416; Mendoza to Díaz, 28 December 1907, GPDC, 32:14397.

86. Mendoza to Díaz, 7 November 1908, GPDC, 33:15699; Díaz to Mendoza, 10 November 1908, GPDC, 33:15700.

87. Gómez to Díaz, 10 October 1908, GPDC, 33:13512; Gómez to Joaquín J. Sánchez, Pablo Corona, and others, 10 October 1908, GPDC, 33:13513; Díaz to Gómez, 21 October 1908, GPDC, 33:13514; *El Paladín*, 27 December 1908.

baro, Hipólito, and Apizaco. Felix Vera, president of the *Liga*, had been baptized under fire, spending seventeen months in jail in 1906 and 1907 because of the supposed socialist nature of the league's organ, *El Ferrocarrilero*. Released in November 1907, Vera organized the third *Gran Convención* of the league, meeting in Monterrey from 19 January to 6 February 1908. At that time Vera had written to assure Díaz that his organization was mutualist only and concerned primarily with the moral and intellectual advancement of its members.[88]

The trouble began in March 1908, when V. M. Holland, the chief of the line's office in San Luis Potosí, fired a worker who had been with the company for fourteen years, giving no reason for the dismissal. The league charged that he had been fired because of his union activities, which was likely the case. Petitions to the company went unanswered, as did a letter to Díaz asking to see him about the matter. Finally Vera called his men out; three thousand Mexican telegraph operators, dispatchers and other white collar workers, as well as brakemen, mechanics, carpenters, and firemen struck. The entire line was shut down.[89]

During the week that the strike lasted, other issues were raised, the most important being the favoritism shown to foreigners and the difficulties placed in the way of Mexicans who desired to hold better jobs such as those of conductor or engineer. Vera appealed first to the governor of San Luis Potosí and then again to Díaz. Neither would intervene, and Vera was forced to call off the strike. According to some reports, the governor showed Vera a telegram from Díaz that hinted of a Río Blanco type solution to the problem, and the *Liga*'s executive committee voted to end the strike before that could happen. Whatever the case, the strike was broken, and the workers returned to work unsatisfied, defeated again. As a result, Vera resigned his post in May. The following year he was jailed without trial because of his

88. See information on Vera and the *Liga* during these years in GPDC, 31:5617; GPDC, 32:2574; GPDC, 33:1263; AGBR, Correspondencia del Sr. Presidente, 1903–1909, March through May 1906; *El Diario*, 4 September 1907; *El Heraldo de México*, 19 January 1908; Ramón Corral to Reyes, 23 January 1908, AGBR, Correspondencia Ministeria, 1903–1909; Navarrete, *Alto*, pp. 100–103, 114–15.

89. Vera to Díaz, 13 April 1908, GPDC, 33:4387; *El Diario*, 22, 30 April 1908.

political activities in support of Bernardo Reyes for vice-president. The defeat of the *Liga* meant that the reforms that Díaz had promised to striking boilermakers in June 1907 were still largely unrealized.[90]

Given what appears to have been a major reversal of policy, what were its origins? Perhaps the answer was provided by Díaz himself. In both September 1907 and April 1908, the president pointed out the declining frequency of strikes in his biannual message to Congress. In September 1908 he did not even mention labor, its first absence from the congressional addresses since April 1906.[91] In other words, Díaz may have been satisfied that the political danger inherent in the labor problem had diminished, along with the strikes. On the other hand, the number of strikes did not drop off dramatically until after June 1908, but the regime had abandoned its policy of intervening to arbitrate major disputes at least six months previously.

Perhaps the answer lies in the problems that began to plague the Mexican economy after mid-1907. Just as the president was winding up his efforts to force a new factory *reglamento* on the textile owners and was promising reforms to the railroad workers, the National Bank of Mexico suspended all loans for three months, and other banks started recalling their outstanding debts. Although the American consul general blamed the problems on depressed *henequén* prices, the situation proved to be more serious and complex. When secretary of the treasury, José I. Limantour, presented his yearly report to Congress in December 1907, he noted that the Mexican economy had been developing too rapidly in the past few years and needed what he termed a "rest." He cautioned that the necessarily higher rates of interest should be expected to retard investment somewhat. The president himself insinuated that Mexico's economic problems could largely be blamed on the United States' financial crisis of the previous year. The problems continued, however, and Limantour was forced to admit to Congress in September 1909 that the previous fiscal year had been one of "unmixed business depression." Nonetheless, he was encouraged, he said, by recent signs of returning

90. For union documents, see *El Estandarte*, 24–26 April 1908. Gov. of San Luis Potosí to Díaz, 24 April 1908, GPDC, 68:939. See reports of the threat in Turner, *Barbarous Mexico*, p. 177. GPDC, 31:5617.

91. *El Economista Mexicano*, 4 April, 19 September 1908.

health.[92] The president may not have wished to discourage business any further by forcing changes in labor relations.

Whatever the effect of the economic problems on the president's labor policy, existing evidence indicates that during the period when the regime had withdrawn from active involvement of individual labor problems, it was attempting to develop broader instruments to handle labor problems than random arbitration.

One piece of evidence comes from the American ambassador to Mexico, who alerted Washington in September 1907 that he had confidential information that a law was being considered that would make all strikes severely punishable. The original *laudo* which settled the textile strike-lockout permitted strikes if no action was taken on a grievance submitted at least fifteen days before. It also appears that such a law would include mandatory arbitration of all labor disputes. During the exchange of letters between Corral and Reyes in the winter of 1907–1908, the vice-president mentioned that his office was working on a draft of a law that would be submitted to the Congress making the arbitration of labor disputes mandatory. Such a law would resolve, according to Corral, "a problem which daily becomes more serious." The details of such a law were never released, but one source indicates that it would have provided for jail sentences of from three to five years for those who instigated strikes that resulted in disorder, injury, or death. In addition, those workers who participated in three strikes were to be fired by their employers.[93]

The proposed legislation seems not to have been submitted to Congress and was never made into law. Perhaps the administration concluded that to implement such a law would require greater involvement in the labor problem than it was prepared for, given the limited bureaucratic capabilities of existing governmental structures and the potential opposition from both workers and industrialists. To know the story of the fate of the law would go a long way toward unraveling the process of decision-making and influence within the administra-

92. Consul-General to Asst. Sec. of State, 6 August 1907, State, n.f.:8057, USNA; *Mexican Herald*, 15 December 1907, cited in n.f.:8057; *El Economista Mexicano*, 4 April 1908.

93. Thompson to Sec. of State, 18 September 1907, State, n.f.:1203, USNA; Corral to Reyes, 17 December 1907, AGBR, Correspondencia Ministeria, 1907; Sodi de Pallares, *Teodoro A. Dehesa*, p. 161.

tion. In any case, while the regime was pulling back from involvement in individual labor conflicts, it was clearly considering an institutionalized procedure to take its place. Whether or not such a law would have been effective in either repressing or resolving the labor problems is another story, interesting but speculative. It should be pointed out, however, that mandatory arbitration eventually became the norm for the settlement of labor conflicts within the post-Porfirian political system.

An interesting and curious case is the accident compensation law. In April 1908, during a period when the regime was withdrawing from direct intervention in labor troubles, Lic. Luis Méndez, president of the *Academia Central Mexicana de Jurisprudencia*, addressed that body on the labor question. He suggested that there was a need for a national labor law, particularly in the area of accident insurance. As long as the law did not require the companies to provide such compensation, Lic. Méndez declared, they would not do so, because the owners were "completely indifferent" to the life and health of the workers.[94] Whether Lic. Méndez was acting as an administration spokesman is not known, but in fact such a law was indeed being considered for the mining industry in conjunction with major revisions of the federal mining codes.

Revision of the mining codes had long been in the process, and in early 1908 Díaz received the government's draft of the law prior to submission to Congress for debate and approval. At this point, foreign interests became alarmed at what they considered the antiforeign nature of many of the proposed revisions, among them being restrictions on the ownership of mining property in border states and a strong section on the owner's responsibility for mining accidents. As the outcry mounted, the regime made various efforts in the commercial press both in the United States and in Mexico to assure businessmen that the law was not antiforeign and that its provisions were even less restrictive than such legislation in other industrialized nations.[95]

94. *El Diario*, 26 April 1908.

95. See "There Is No Anti-foreign Sentiment in Mexico," *El Economista Mexicano*, 4 July 1908, pp. 272–74; Marvin D. Bernstein, *The Mexican Mining Industry*, pp. 78–80.

Certain foreign investors were not satisfied: at the end of July, Díaz received a long letter from no less than Daniel Guggenheim himself, president of the American Smelting and Refining Co. and, as he himself admitted, a representative of "enormous interests" in Mexican mining and related industries. After protesting recent freight rate increases on fuel, ores, and smelter products and the new currency laws that converted Mexico from a silver to a gold standard, Guggenheim proceeded to attack the proposed revisions of the mining law as "a most concrete example of the apparent desire on the part of the Government of Mexico to place an undue burden upon the capital which has already been invested by the citizens of this and other countries in Mexico, and which will make it absolutely impossible in the future for such capital to be invested in Mexico."[96]

Although there were many aspects of the law that he disliked or considered harmful to his interests, Mr. Guggenheim had a special antipathy for the accident compensation regulations in the revisions of the mining law. The accident regulations would place "a very serious burden upon the employer," he charged, who would then be responsible for accidents which resulted from the carelessness, ignorance, and even malice of the miners. "It has been found by us absolutely impossible to secure labor of sufficient intelligence to warrant the belief that they can be expected to always save themselves from injury even where every reasonable precaution has been taken by the employer."[97]

In a long, detailed, and at times caustic reply, the minister of development, Olegario Molina, answered each charge in turn. He denied that the accident compensation provisions of the mining revisions would harm mining interests, except for those that disregarded mining safety standards and procedures already existing. Besides, the minister went on, surely such laws in England and the United States had not forced the ruin of foreign concerns in those societies. In any case, "the responsibility for accidents is not only a social convenience but a humanitarian necessity."[98]

96. Daniel Guggenheim to Díaz, 24 July 1908, GPDC, 33:10813.
97. Ibid.
98. "Memorandum relativo a la carta del Señor Daniel Guggenheim dirigida al Señor Presidente de la República," from O. Molina, 11 August 1908, GPDC, 33:10792.

Evidently the necessity was not as urgent as the minister suggested, because when the new mining law went into effect on 1 January 1910, after two years of public and legislative debate, the provision for accident responsibility was gone. It had been stricken from the proposed law by the Congress after submission by the government.[99] Perhaps the government acquiesced to the deletion of the accident protection regulations from the mining law to make it more palatable to foreign investors. All that is known is that the federal government continued to work on separate legislation regulating accidents after the mining bill became law. In October 1910 an explosion destroyed Mina de Palau, a coal mine in Las Esperanzas, Coahuila, killing seventy miners. As a result of this accident, the governor of Coahuila wrote the president to suggest the urgent necessity of a federal mining accident law. On the top of the governor's letter, Díaz wrote in his tortuous handwriting one sentence: "A complete regulation is now being concluded which anticipates everything [you suggested.]"[100] By then the administration of Porfirio Díaz was only days away from the beginning of a rebellion that threatened to topple the regime, and precious little time was available for labor legislation.

In the search for clues that might lead to an understanding of the federal government's labor policy in the aftermath of Río Blanco, one finds that the regime tried various approaches to the labor problem, none of which were mutually exclusive. A hard-line policy on disorder was balanced somewhat by obvious efforts in mid-1907 to resolve the labor grievances of the more militant groups—Orizaba mill hands and railroad workers—by forcing the companies to implement reforms. Yet, by early 1908, the regime had withdrawn from active intervention into individual disputes, although it still kept its contacts with labor activities. Instead, it began working on broad federal legislation both to repress strikes, which Díaz and his advisors obviously feared for their political implications, and to pacify working-class demands through arbitration and, in the case of accident compensation,

99. Bernstein, *The Mexican Mining Industry*, pp. 82, 95.
100. Gov. of Coahuila (Valle) to Díaz, 5 October 1910, GPDC, 35:14935. An amendment governing accident compensation was added to the mining codes in October 1912 by the Madero government (Bernstein, *The Mexican Mining Industry*, p. 95).

through legislation. There the trail ends, however, in late 1908, leaving the researcher the impression that something had distracted the attention of the government just as it was about to make an effort to establish an extensive federal incursion into the field of labor-capital relations. If this is the case, the reason for this distraction could lie in a number of areas, ranging from a basic disinterest of the regime in doing anything more than defusing the labor problem to an open and effective opposition by powerful economic interests to government involvement in labor matters. The events themselves suggest an additional influence at work, however. It may well be that the labor question became submerged in broader questions of policy and political necessity after 1908, as intrigues and political maneuvering absorbed more and more of the attention of the regime's principal policy makers.

The Creelman Interview

In late February 1908, Mexicans were startled to read in several Mexico City dailies that Don Porfirio had indicated in an interview with a foreign journalist that he would step down in 1910 as president of Mexico. Díaz told the journalist, James Creelman, that Mexico had come of age and was now ready for the democracy for which he had been carefully grooming her over the years. Hence, he announced, he would retire at the end of the current term and allow the Mexican people to determine who should lead their nation after 1910. He even declared a willingness not only to tolerate but to nurture a loyal opposition. No one really knows whether the old *Caudillo* was "sincere but not serious," as John Womack puts it, or engaging in deliberate deception for some subtle political advantage.[101] If the latter was his motive, the old fox miscalculated, for the Creelman interview marks the beginning of the end of the long public career of Porfirio Díaz.

After a few months of speculation and maneuvering, many politicians, including both the *científicos* and their numerous enemies, came to the chilling realization that a free-for-all in 1910 might well

101. James Creelman, "Porfirio Díaz, Hero of the Americas," *Pearson's Magazine* 24 (March 1908): 241–77; *El Imparcial* published the full translation on 5 March 1908; Womack, *Zapata*, p. 11.

undermine the stability of the entire system, endangering them all. Representatives of various political cliques began to attempt to persuade the president to seek reelection in 1910. Perhaps that is what the old man wanted all along. Whatever the case may be, in October of 1908 Díaz let it be known that he considered talk of his stepping down "inopportune," stressing that his comments to Creelman had been only personal desire. He would do whatever his countrymen wished of him.[102] The message was clear. Don Porfirio would seek, and obtain, another six-year term at the age of eighty.

Had Díaz been as unequivocal about his vice-president, then the Porfirian system might have survived for a few more years before it collapsed. But Díaz failed to mention the vice-presidency, and former presidential ambitions were deflected toward that potentially critical position. The vice-president succeeds the president in the event of his death, and Díaz might not last another term.

In the waning months of 1908 and on into the new year, while workers and country people were struggling against the effects of an advancing recession, Mexican political clans and their retainers were preparing their campaigns for the vice-presidency. And a few at-odds sort of mavericks were actually considering an absurd contest for the presidency itself, regardless of the intentions of Díaz. Many more were engaged in regional contests against established house politicians, men hand-picked by Díaz or his associates. No one knew then that such traditional maneuverings would provide the fatal catalyst for the demise of the regime or that the political movements that were beginning in fashionable men's clubs or terraced town-houses would ultimately lead a meaner crowd—angry, embittered men from country villages and industrial *barrios*—toward unforeseen consequences.

102. Cosío Villegas, *La vida político interior*, 2:761–72; Taracena, *La verdadera Revolución*, pp. 23, 129; Limantour, *Mi vida pública*, pp. 162–65.

Chapter 6
Politics and the Mexican Industrial Worker

*". . . and we have come to believe that the Republic
of the Mexicans is playing out its final moments,
and in terrifying agony."*
—Workers of La Hormiga de Tizapán
to Díaz, 2 March 1909

In the months that followed the Creelman interview,
the labor question became lost to public view in the general excitement
that attended the newly revived political interest among middle- and
upper-class Mexicans. Newspapers that once carried labor grievances
turned their attention to politics, because for the first time in years
popular opposition candidates were appearing in state and local elections. In addition, the struggle between the supporters of Ramón
Corral and General Bernardo Reyes for the vice-presidency overshadowed all other contests for a time and divided Porfirian elites
along political lines. Eager politicians soon perceived, however, that
urban workers were a potential source of popular support. At the
same time, some Mexican workers saw in the opposition candidates a
possible means to resolve their problems. Neither group foresaw the
effect their alliance would have on the ultimate fate of the regime.
What role then did the Mexican workers play in the politics of the era?

First, how did each of the major political groups deal with the labor
question? Given the political necessities of the times, it was not possible for the *reyistas*, the reelectionists, or the antireelectionists to avoid
the number one social problem of the decade—the labor question.
Therefore, what promises did they make to the workers, and were
their appeals attractive and effective in gathering labor support?
What posture did the federal government take toward the workers'
demands now that other voices of discontent were beginning to be
raised in the land? How, for example, did the regime deal with the
increasingly serious railroadmen's agitation for equality on the na-

tional lines, and what was the government's response to the complex labor problems raised by the economic recession of 1909?

Did the *reyista* movement attract Mexican workers to its cause, or were workers by then unwilling to support Díaz no matter who his vice-president was? And when the Anti-Reelectionist Party finally rose in direct opposition to the continued rule of Don Porfirio, which way did Mexican workers go? Would they follow an unknown *político* from the north? And how many would see no alternative but the PLM under Ricardo Flores Magón? Whatever the answers, one thing became clear as the months wore on toward the elections in June 1910: the politicians of all factions would have to consider the men of Mexico's factories and shops as comrades or enemies, for they would no longer be ignored.

Industrial Unrest: January 1909 to June 1910

Although there was a slight increase in the number of strikes in the first half of 1909, the downward trend resumed during the second half of the year and the first six months of 1910. Most were of short duration, apparently designed to force the authorities' intervention in the hopes of obtaining a compromise settlement rather than to defeat the owners themselves. Times were hard, and few workers' associations had sufficient funds to support a long strike. "Workers do not like the strike," declared a letter from Río Blanco in May 1909, "they hate it because it means a lack of bread in their homes."[1]

The most outstanding characteristic of these conflicts is that twelve of the eighteen strikes in 1909 (and all four in the first half of 1910) took place in the textile industry, the largest surge of conflicts in that

1. *El Paladín*, 23 May 1909. For references to strikes see: *México Nuevo*, 27 April, 1, 4 May, 22 June, 18 July, 9 November 1909, 8 February 1910; *El Paladín*, 24 January, 2, 23 May 1909; Gov. of Jalisco to Díaz, 22 April 1909, GPDC, 34:5219; *jefe político* to Díaz, 2 February 1910, Orizaba, GPDC, 35:3762; *El Paladín*, 3, 10 February 1910; *jefe político* to Díaz, 4 March 1910, Orizaba, GPDC, 35:4039; Gov. of Puebla to Díaz, 3 June 1910, GPDC, 35:7719; *El Diario del Hogar*, 23 January 1910; Arturo Camarillo to Inspector General de C.R., 2 January 1909, AGN-Gob, leg. 852, and *Comandante* Méraz to I.G., 2 January 1909, (telegraph), Tehuacán, AGN-Gob, leg. 852.

industry since those bitter months after Río Blanco. Seven of the eighteen strikes in 1909 took place in the Federal District, where the governor of the District, Guillermo de Landa y Escandón, was conducting an active campaign to win the workers of the District away from affiliation with aggressive unionism and to his own mutualist organization. It may well be that the increased attention the textile workers were getting from the regime encouraged their walkouts. Of the strikes in the Federal District, the most important were a nine day strike at the Spanish-owned mill San Antonio Abad, an eighteen day strike at the large cotton mill La Hormiga, and a tobacco workers' strike.

The *Gran Liga de Torcedores de Tobacos* of the Federal District called a strike in January 1909 for the purpose of countering recent owners' efforts to destroy their organization. The strike spread to Puebla and was eventually broken by strikebreakers brought in with a police escort.[2]

The mill hands at La Hormiga struck in March over the issues of wages, fines, and mistreatment and immediately sent petitions to the prefect at San Ángel (Tizapán), to Landa y Escandón, and to Díaz himself. Their letter to Díaz spoke directly to the issues: "The worker is treated very badly in the mills, Sr. Presidente, and after being paid poorly for his work, he is fined without rhyme or reason." They went on to list their grievances, offering documentation for each—low wages, high quotas compared to those of other mills, outrageous fines, and contributions they were forced to make every week to feed the company dogs. They added a broader charge to the list, an indictment of the entire Porfirian structure: "It seems to us that in the land which saw our birth there are no longer any honorable men left who know how to enforce respect for the laws and guarantees of all the people. It just seems to us that everything is becoming a farce, and all that matters is who you know, and how easy you can make it for yourself, and we have come to believe that the Republic of the Mexicans is playing out its final moments, and in terrifying agony." Knowing how close they were to sedition, they also asked not to be treated as revolutionaries and sent to Quintana Roo or "other unhealthy places."[3]

2. *El Diario del Hogar*, 23 January 1909.
3. Workers of La Hormiga de Tizapán to Díaz, 2 March 1909, GPDC,

Workers on strike at the La Hormiga cotton textile mill, carrying signs and the Mexican flag.

Landa y Escandón wrote Díaz that he agreed with some of their complaints but that he could not interfere with the question of wages because it involved a private contract. The governor indicated that if the prefect of San Ángel could not work out an agreement with the directors of the mill that he would talk with them "to see what they will do for the operators."[4]

Whether the governor had a role in the settlement is not clear, but the workers returned to work on 22 March after arbitrary fines were abolished, discounts prohibited (especially for dog food), and an agreement reached that they were to be paid on Saturday early enough to end by 5:00 P.M. *El Diario del Hogar* announced that the prefect of San Ángel had authorized the settlement.[5]

34:4661. See also a copy of their appeal for aid from their fellow workers in Turner, *Barbarous Mexico*, pp. 180–81.

4. Landa y Escandón to Díaz, 5 March 1909, GPDC, 34:2984.

5. *El Diario del Hogar*, 10 April 1909.

Shortly after the end of the La Hormiga strike, the nation was shocked by the most widely publicized scandal since Cananea. Although it was not a labor issue, it involved a number of miners, and because of the arbitrary use of force by the political authorities, the press on several occasions compared the incident to Cananea and Río Blanco. The episode began when workers from the Velardeña Mine, near the town of Cuencame, Durango, were prevented by the local *jefe político* from holding a public religious procession during Holy Week. (Public religious activities were prohibited by the Reform laws, although the laws were sometimes overlooked in the *Porfiriato*.) The priest, a Father Valenzuela, protested vigorously and was forcefully restrained by the police. His outraged followers attacked the prefect's headquarters, forcing the prefect and his police to flee for their lives. The rioters burned the *jefatura*, looted several stores, and killed a night watchman at the mine. An all-night drunken *fiesta* ensued, according to official reports, ending abruptly early the following morning with the arrival of state *rurales*. Though accounts differ, official sources publicly admitted that anywhere from thirteen to eighteen "workers," as they were generally identified in the press reports, were rounded up and executed on the spot, with no pretense of due process.[6]

When word of the executions leaked out, the federal government was forced to acknowledge the incident. Ramón Corral ordered an investigation, admitting that illegal executions had taken place.[7] The usually moderate but very Catholic *El Tiempo* did not stop at demanding the punishment of those responsible but stated that "Velardeña is not an isolated case without precedents," and went on to point out the number of such incidents, including Río Blanco, and the "frequent application of the *ley fuga*."[8] The fact that the government was forced to conduct a public investigation clearly indicates that it believed that it could not afford another Río Blanco.

6. *El Tiempo*, 24 April 1909, carried official documents on the incident, including Corral's report, the *rurales'* report, and the governor of Durango's report.

7. *El Tiempo*, 19 April 1909. He noted that the president had agreed to the federal investigation.

8. Cited in *Regeneración* (PLM weekly), 10 September 1910, GPDC, 35:13338; *El Diablito Bromista*, 23 May 1909.

In contrast to the tapering off of strikes, working-class organization was on the increase. The Orizaba workers founded the *Sociedad Mutualista de Ahorros "Ignacio de la Llave."* Its president was Andrés Mota, charter member in the founding of the GCOL in April 1906. In addition, the following labor groups were organized in 1909 and 1910: *Unión de Linotipistas Mexicanos* (Mexico City), the *Gran Liga de Sastres*, the *Gran Liga de Electricistas Mexicanos* (Chihuahua), the *Círculo Libertario* and *La Confederación del Trabajo* (among Yucatán workers), and the *Asociación de Conductores y Maquinistas Mexicanos.* Among the more important labor organizations still active in 1909 were the *Alianza Obrera* of the Río Blanco mill, *La Unión de Mecánicos Mexicanos, La Gran Liga Mexicana de Empleados de Ferrocarril,* and *La Gran Liga de Torcedores de Tabacos.* In addition, a number of important worker or- ganizations were formed during the political campaigns of 1909–1910 and took an active part in the elections of 1910. The tobacco workers' slogan, "In the union there is strength," was beginning to take hold among Mexican industrial workers.[9] Their best opportunity, how- ever, would have to wait for other times.

As in the past, the issue that evoked the most complaints from the workers was mistreatment by their supervisors or foremen, who were more often than not foreigners. Beatings, unjust fines, extortion— these were the charges made by the increasingly bitter letters to *El Paladín* and *México Nuevo,* a new daily founded in late 1908 by Juan Sánchez Azcona. In only one case out of the seventeen or so recorded was there any attempt by the factory authorities to rectify the situa- tion. Close behind mistreatment complaints were wage-related grievances—increased work-load or piece-rate quotas, decreased wages, fines, or excesses of the company store. Workers from several mills in Tlaxcala complained that they were not allowed to read any newspapers but *El País* or other clerical papers. A worker was fired at the Río Blanco mill for reading *El Paladín,* and a typesetter and

9. *El Paladín,* 7 January, 11 March 1909; Peña, "Apuntes históricos," 5 August 1958; Petricioli, *La tragedia,* pp. 15, 59; Panfilo Méndez and Daniel L. Mendoza to Dehesa, 15 April 1908, SHUV-Gob, 1908, S-12; *México Nuevo,* 28 April 1909; Araiza, *El movimiento obrero,* pp. 10–11; *El Paladín,* 28 March, 13 May 1909; *México Nuevo,* 2 June 1909; *El Correo de Chihuahua,* 22 April, 5 October 1909. The *Liga de Tablajeros de la Ciudad de México* may also have been organized in 1909 (*El Diario del Hogar,* 31 October 1909).

member of the *Unión Linotipográfica* was fired for writing a letter to *México Nuevo*. An agent for *El Paladín* was threatened by the police, evidently because of certain unfavorable articles published by the paper on the quality of the local police.[10]

Despite the unresolved grievances, Mexican workers between January 1909 and June 1910 were moving ahead. They were actively pursuing their own betterment through organization and through participation in the political movements of the day. Not surprisingly, they managed to attract the regime's attention again, as the politics of the era forced the government of Porfirio Díaz to become involved in their problems.

Federal Labor Policy, January 1909 to June 1910

At some point early in 1909, the regime perceptibly altered its retrenchment policy of the previous year and moved again toward a more active confrontation of the labor question. The shift was closely related to the political events of the times. The campaign to reelect Díaz and Corral got underway in early April 1909 and needed working-class participation to give the appearance of public support. No documents directly link this revitalized concern for the workers with the immediate political needs of the administration, but it is much too direct to be coincidental. In addition, the bloody incident at Velardeña in March 1909 evoked widespread publicity on local abuse of power and may thus have encouraged the regime to give greater attention to the workers.

In any case, the regime's public relationship with workers entered a new phase. There seems to have been a conscious effort to acknowledge the existence of the workers and to appear among them. At a labor-sponsored celebration in honor of Jesús García, "the hero of Nacozari," President Díaz was only one of a number of top administration officials conspicuously present. He awed and charmed the workers that night, as he could, walking among them, talking of his youth when once he had worked as a carpenter. The occasion was an

10. For representative mistreatment cases, see *México Nuevo*, 8, 28 April, 9, 22 June, 6 July 1909; *El Paladín*, 28 January, 21 February, 11 March, 23 May, 10 June, 14 November, 23 December 1909.

important one because Jesús García had recently become a major folk hero. In November of the previous year in the copper mining town of Nacozari, Sonora, a train was being unloaded in the station when workers noticed smoke and flames spreading through several box cars filled with dynamite for the mines. A young railroad worker, Jesús García, jumped into a nearby engine and backed it up to the burning cars, coupled them, and began his slow assent out of town. He probably planned to jump when the train had gathered sufficient steam to carry it beyond the town, but he never got the chance. The dynamite exploded before he had gone half a mile. Twelve people including García were killed, and every window in the town was blown out. How many would have died had the train remained in the station one can only guess. The "hero of Nacozari" was hailed by the press and his sacrifice publicized at home and abroad.[11]

Díaz and Corral also headed a list of first-rank luminaries of the Republic at a celebration in February 1910 held by mutual societies of Mexico City as part of the Independence Centennial programs for that year. Special efforts were made to enlist workers' associations in the 1909 celebration of *Cinco de Mayo*, and there were many workers among the thirty thousand marchers who filed past the balcony of the National Palace on the fifth of May to be saluted by the old warrior. A similar demonstration had been planned in Orizaba, but at the appointed time no workers appeared, much to the disgust and apprehension of the public officials.[12] Undoubtedly, the managers of those events had hoped to promote Díaz's and Corral's reelections through the former's association with the heroic struggle against the French, in which he had played such an important role as a young Liberal general.

The Porfirian system at various levels evidenced a revitalized concern for *los de abajo*. In June 1909 the local authorities in Atlixco fined a Spanish foreman employed by the textile mill La Concepción 75 *pesos* for mistreating the workers under his control. The following January, the *jefe político* of Atlixco heard a Metepec workers' commission and offered to talk with the owners of the mill to resolve the grievances; the previous petitions to his office had gone unanswered.

11. *México Nuevo*, 18 November 1909.
12. *Obrero Mexicano*, 11 February 1910; A. Ortega to Díaz, 15 May 1909, GPDC, 34:10689.

Workers' commission posing with the president after delivering an invitation to attend their celebration in honor of the hero of Nacozari, Jesús García. Díaz is fifth from the right.

Miguel Gómez, the *jefe político* of Orizaba, met with the workers and administrators of the textile mill Santa Gertrudis to work out a new wage scale. When a strike took place at that same factory early in 1910, Gómez met with representatives from both parties to try to arrange a solution, the very thing he had said in October 1908 that he would not do. Although several Orizaba workers were consigned to Quintana Roo early in 1909, they were the last until the harassment of pro-Madero workers in 1910.[13]

Several state governors exhibited concern for the workers in their state or actively played a role in labor disputes. In Tlaxcala, Governor Próspero Cahuantzi intervened to settle several disputes in his states,

13. *México Nuevo*, 9 June 1909 and 30 January 1910; Gómez to Dehesa, 2 February 1910, GPDC, 35:3762; *El Paladín*, 24 January 1909.

although privately he continued to blame Mendoza as the instigator of many of the workers' grievances. Díaz paid no attention; Mendoza was proving useful. In February 1910 the governor of Querétaro made an effort to persuade the French owners of the textile mill Hércules not to lower the workers' wages in view of the rising cost of living. Two years before, during a similar conflict, he had been instructed by Díaz only to preserve public order. Indeed, Díaz ordered the governor to distribute corn and other necessities to the workers of the Hércules mill and made several unfavorable comments about the owners because of their labor practices and their attitudes toward the corn distribution program. In Coahuila, the governor attempted to force the mine owners to institute more safeguards against the accidents that regularly claimed the lives of coal miners in his state.[14]

Perhaps the most active Porfirian politician in this regard was Guillermo Landa y Escandón, governor of the Federal District, who had acquired the reputation of being sympathetic to the workers' problems. On a number of occasions he had offered his good offices to resolve labor conflicts, and occasionally he had intervened directly on the side of the workers. In May 1909 the governor arranged with textile mill owners of the Federal District to continue to advance partial wages to their workers, who had been temporarily laid off due to a power failure. The owner of one mill (La Carolina) refused to comply, but Landa y Escandón eventually persuaded him to conform with the request by personally guaranteeing to repay the owner any loss he might incur because of the arrangement.[15]

The governor conducted a formal walk-around tour of the District's factories and shops in the summer and fall of 1909, talking with workers and managers about their problems and setting up committees to bring the workers into his mutualist organization, the *Gran Sociedad Mutualista y Moralizadora de Obreros del Districto Federal*. The governor's mutualist society reflected his concern for the moral and intellectual uplifting of the worker and his preference for mutual

14. Gov. of Tlaxcala to Díaz, 28 July 1909, GPDC, 34:11681; Gov. of Tlaxcala to Mendoza in *La Lucha Obrera*, 11 July 1909, in GPDC, 34:13735. Gov. of Querétaro to Díaz, 19 February 1910, GPDC, 35:1423; Gov. of Coahuila to Díaz, 5 October 1910, GPDC, 35:14935.

15. González Navarro, *La vida social*, pp. 289, 304; *El Imparcial*, 27 May 1909.

self-help as opposed to forcing the owners to better the workers' material situation. The society encouraged the workers to attend special night classes, it established a theater group, and it talked of sponsoring a workers' park for recreation and family outings. It opposed strikes but substituted no alternative except the individual efforts of the governor. When the workers at the important textile mill San Antonio Abad struck over a pay decrease, the governor promised to see the owners but severely reprimanded the workers for striking.[16]

This kind of victorian paternalism was, at best, an honest and sincere effort by sensitive men to rationalize a system they were too much a part of to change, yet its exploitation of their fellow human beings was so obvious that they could no longer avoid acknowledging its inequities. The fatal weakness of paternalism as a solution to the problems of the working classes was captured by the satirical weekly *La Guacamaya*:

> With his fine manners
> he made sure that
> the children
> did not learn
> to drink *pulque*.
> Nor should they enter *cantinas*.
> But his divine laws,
> although an honorable and sincere man,
> were laws of Escandón,
> alone.[17]

The workers' opinions about the governor and the effectiveness of his efforts were divided. Some openly appreciated his work on their behalf. Workers from the *Compañía de Luz y Fuerza Matriz* sent *El Paladín* a letter thanking the governor for using his influence to settle a dispute. Some showed their support by enrolling in his mutualist society; by June 1910 the *Gran Sociedad* had enrolled five thousand workers from seventy-eight factories and shops, according to the official organ of the society.[18]

16. For a relatively favorable coverage of the governor's visits from a paper unfriendly to his *científico* political allies, see *México Nuevo*. On the strike, see *México Nuevo*, 10 November 1909.

17. *La Guacamaya*, 2 November 1904.

18. *El Paladín*, 27 May 1909; *Obrero Mexicano*, 3 June 1910.

Other workers, however, believed the governor to be sincere but doubted the effectiveness of his visits to the factories because, as Antonio Torres Gómez charged, only workers favorable to the firms were allowed to talk to him. Since it appears that the governor's itinerary was arranged in advance by the governor's aides and the factory administrators, the charge is probably correct.[19]

Some workers went further, seeing in the governor's labor programs an effort to keep the workers from challenging the capitalists or the state. "Sr. Escandón offers to help the workers on the conditions that they are good husbands and fathers," charged Alberto Palo in *México Obrero*, "while the official press maliciously inserts a second condition, that of 'being submissive and obedient to their patrons.' This would destroy the only freedom a worker has and make him into a slave; but do not count on it, Mr. Bureaucrat. We are continuing our task of freeing the people from your clutches; we are continuing so that the Mexican worker will know how to die of hunger but will never sell his precious freedom. Don't wait for it—the people have awakened!"[20] Some workers were clearly calling for action stronger than that of a mutualist, paternalistic approach.

On the federal level, Díaz and his ministers were active once again, intervening on an *ad hoc* basis and, in several important cases, attempting to provide some longer range, institutional solutions to the labor questions. In January 1909, for example, Pascual Mendoza wrote Díaz to discuss a project that would purchase politically safe reading materials for his workers. Evidently, Díaz had earlier agreed that the government would finance the project. Mendoza also met with the federal minister of development, Olegario Molina, to work out a wage scale acceptable to the textile workers in Puebla and Tlaxcala.[21]

Molina was a well-known *henequén* grower, a former governor of the state of Yucatán, and a political ally of the *científicos*. Nonetheless, he played an active role in the labor question for the Díaz regime, having accepted the ministry's portfolio sometime in 1907. Besides his work with Mendoza and his role in developing the revisions in the mining

19. Antonio Torres Gómez to Landa y Escandón, an open letter in *México Nuevo*, 21 December 1909; *México Nuevo*, 10 November 1909.

20. *México Obrero*, 1 September 1909.

21. Mendoza to Díaz, 20 January 1909, GPDC, 34:455; ibid., 22 February 1909, GPDC, 34:1439; *La Lucha Obrera*, 11 July 1909 in GPDC, 34:13735.

codes, Molina wrote a sharply-worded note to the owners of the Zacatecas mine, La Concepción de Oro, requesting an explanation to charges of mistreatment of their workers. The mine had a long history of disturbances, including a riot in 1908. When the company provided a report of its labor policies, he informed the owners that his information was not in agreement with their statement.[22]

In another incident, similar to one in mid-1906, an unpopular *rurales'* officer in the mill town of Río Blanco lost his post. Whether the action was labor-related was never officially verified, but the workers had made numerous complaints about the officer and were happy to see him go.[23]

The most obvious example of federal concern with the labor problem, however, was that of the railroads. The Mexican government controlled approximately two-thirds of the total track in the nation through a holding company in which it was the majority stockholder. The history of governmental involvement in the railroads went back to 1903 when, at the urging of Limantour, the Mexican government bought the majority interest in the Mexican National Railroad Company in order to avoid competing interests and to develop a more effective national transportation system. In 1906 the government acquired absolute control over the two major lines, the Central and the National, adding several smaller lines during the next four years. All these systems were nationalized into the National Railways Company. However, the former private companies retained their entire management structure under an executive president, E. N. Brown, with the government providing only broad policy guidelines. Employee practices remained the same.[24]

The grievances of the Mexican workers on the lines had been simmering for years. The strikes of 1906 through 1908 had publicized the workers' grievances but had not resolved them. By 1909 Mexican workers on the nationalized lines still complained bitterly of being discriminated against in wages, jobs, and promotions in favor of

22. Cosío Villegas, *Vida política interior*, 2:462, 464–66, 850, 853, 857. For the material on Concepción de Oro, see GN-Gob, leg. 582.

23. *México Nuevo*, 29 May 1909.

24. *Mexican Herald*, 14, 15 December 1906, in Thompson to Sec. of State, 14 December 1906, State, n.f.:3289, USNA; Consul General to Asst. Sec. of State, 28 December 1906, in ibid.; *El Economista Mexicano*, 28 November 1908.

American workers. Not only did Mexicans earn less than Americans doing the same job, but almost no Mexicans held administrative or supervisory positions, and very few held such white collar jobs as conductor. In addition, occasional charges were made that the American workers treated their fellow Mexican workers and even Mexican passengers with arrogance and contempt. There were other issues—long working hours, Sunday work, indemnification for accidents, wages—but none were as important to Mexican railroadmen as the foreign worker issue.[25]

Especially frustrating and galling was the use of English as the official language of the lines, thereby creating a major obstacle to the training and promotion of Mexicans to better positions. All the examinations for advancement were conducted in English. Alfredo Navarrete passed his exam to become an assistant brakeman on the Mexico-Puebla run of the Ferrocarril Interoceanico after studying two hours a day for four years. At seventy *pesos* a month, his pay was good in comparison to other jobs, but he later recalled his dissatisfaction: "It was a world dominated by foreigners, men with blond hair, white skin, blue eyes, almost all from the United States. These men monopolized all the important positions . . . A Mexican worker was a man condemned to stay on one level."[26] Although by 1909 about 96 percent of the brakemen and trainmen were Mexican and those positions were viewed as the next in the promotional sequence to that of conductor, only 14 percent of the conductors were Mexican. There were more Mexican engineers, some 32 percent of the 444 engineers. The influence of the American brotherhoods on promotion and examinations, as well as the hiring practices of the company, was responsible for this disproportionate representation of Mexican workers in those jobs.[27]

25. For examples of such complaints, see: Railroad workers from Gómez Palacio to *El Paladín*, 3 September 1908; *México Nuevo*, 1 May 1909; Miguel A. Iriarte to Díaz, 23 March 1908, GPDC, 33:3175, 3179; *Mexican Herald*, 17 November 1908, in Sands to Sec. of State, State, n.f.:3289, USNA; GPDC, 32:7307; see the program of the National Convention of the Mexican railroad mechanics held in July 1907, in GPDC, 32:7141; *Jalisco Libre*, 11 July 1907; Grisebelo González to *El Diario*, 17 May 1907.

26. Navarrete, *Alto*, p. 32.

27. Miller, "American Railroad Unions," pp. 244–48.

As early as the successful boilermakers' strike in June 1907, the Mexican government had indicated its support for the "mexicanization" of the nationalized railroads, promising better jobs for Mexican nationals. Later, Díaz had promised in an interview with Mexican railroad workers that they would not have to learn English to work on the lines, and Limantour as the cabinet officer responsible for the railroads had agreed.[28] Yet time passed, and few changes were made. Then came the political year of 1909 and with it a decided increase in federal attention to labor troubles on the lines.

The catalyst was a strike on 1 May by the American-dominated *Sociedades de Conductores y Maquinistas Americanos* over the issue of company inspectors. Within a week the Mexican conductors, dispatchers, and mechanics on the lines formed their own association, with the express goals of protecting the rights of Mexicans against discrimination in favor of the Americans. Prior to this time, only twenty-five Mexican conductors, dispatchers, and mechanics belonged to the American union, which had a membership of approximately four hundred railroadmen.[29]

Following the May strike, the government moved to enforce its proclaimed mexicanization policy, as it was officially called. On 1 July Limantour sent a directive to the executive president of the National Lines, rebuking him for moving too slowly on the mexicanization policy and specifically ordering him to implement a program guaranteeing equal treatment and job opportunity for Mexican employees. In order to implement the policy, Limantour ordered Brown to see that Spanish was the official language of the lines and that sufficient schools were established to train Mexican employees for better jobs.[30]

In compliance with the directive, the company issued an order to the dispatchers, predominantly Americans, to start training Mexicans in their positions. Rather than comply, the dispatchers called a strike,

28. *México Nuevo*, 1 May 1909.

29. *México Nuevo*, 9 May 1909, and *El Paladín*, 13 May 1909; Thompson to Sec. of State, 5 May 1909, State, n.f.:3289, USNA. See also a letter from a Mexican dispatcher describing the difficulties and sacrifices involved in a Mexican being promoted into a such a position, "Mexican dispatcher of trains" to Díaz, 9 June 1908, Puebla, GPDC, 33:250.

30. Limantour to Brown 1 July 1909, in Thompson to Secretary of State, 11 July 1909, State, nf.:5289, USNA.

supported a few days later by the American conductors' and mechanics' union. Complicating the issue were demands for increased wages, an eight hour day, and other benefits. The strike met with nearly uniform hostility in the national press. The company responded by using Mexicans to take over the jobs of the dispatchers, breaking the strike and fulfilling the government's directive at the same time.[31]

Following this action, the government carefully publicized Limantour's policy. First, it arranged for the publication in *El Imparcial* of his July first letter to Brown. Then, in another widely publicized policy statement, Ramón Corral wrote to the Board of Directors of the National Lines, requesting them in the name of the president to give careful consideration to the workers' petition for expanded hospital facilities, compensation for workers killed or injured on the job, and other policies to succor the workers' needs.[32]

At about the same time an incident took place which underlined the nationalist sentiment engendered by this issue. An investigation of a number of shortages that appeared from time to time in freight shipments resulted in the arrest and detention of several employees of the National Lines. They were accused of throwing goods off the slow-moving train to confederates along the lines. The main instigator was purported to be James A. Cook, an American conductor. The case was widely discussed in the press, generally featuring Cook as an American who was not satisfied with his large salary and his privileged position over Mexican workers, who had to rob as well. The American consul and the Order of Railway Conductors of America, Guadalajara branch, thought it unlikely that Cook would get a fair trial, given the "wave of anti-Americanism" that was centered on the railroads. The American ambassador noted significantly that it was not the railroad company that was prosecuting Cook, but the government. Cook was eventually tried and convicted.[33]

Despite public sentiment, the public position of the Díaz govern-

31. *México Nuevo*, 18 July 1909; *El Pueblo*, 20 July 1909; *El Diablito Bromista*, 29 November 1909; Thompson to Sec. of State, 11 August 1909, State, n.f.:3289, USNA.

32. *El Imparcial*, 11 August 1909; *México Nuevo*, 13 November 1909.

33. See documents in State, nf.:21980, USNA, and *México Nuevo*, 14, 15, 27 August 1909.

ment, and the efforts of the railroad workers themselves, by the beginning of the following year little had been done to implement the mexicanization program. A few token Mexicans were promoted to supervisory positions, but most of the latter and all of the superintendents' posts—the heads of the divisions of the National Lines—were still held by foreigners. One railroadman wrote Díaz that things had in fact worsened "because before, even though oppressed, we accepted it. We did not dream of ever getting out of our subservient condition and [therefore] had no ambition to do so. Since the initiation of the mexicanization of the railroads, the yankees' pride has turned to hate, and we are worse off than ever because we cannot count on any kind of protection, and our only recourse is silent desperation."[34]

Some Mexican workers were promoted to conductor and several even to engineer, and a few Americans were fired. The newly promoted Mexicans were subjected to special scrutiny and, according to one worker, were falsely blamed for accidents. A conservative Mexican daily even doubted the capacity of the Mexican workers to fill the positions of the foreigners. Meanwhile, Mexicans certified to run the trains in Aguascalientes, Guadalajara, and probably other depots found their way blocked, because the men who assigned the work were almost entirely Americans who saw that their countrymen retained the better jobs.[35]

Meanwhile, American conductors and engineers, fearing for their jobs, threatened a mass walkout, along with a boycott by their U.S. comrades of Mexican trains crossing the border, if the company did not agree to recognize the American unions as the bargaining agents for all the lines' conductors and engineers, and agree to its right to seat two of the four members on a board of examiners who were to

34. J. Trinidad Nav (last name indistinct) to Díaz, 10 March 1910, Guadalajara, GPDC, 35:4058. For other complaints of continued abuses by foreign workers and prejudice against Mexicans, see anonymous railroad worker to Díaz, 31 January 1911, GPDC, 36:999; *México Nuevo*, 9 April, 16 February 1910.

35. Anonymous railroad worker to Díaz, 31 January 1911, GPDC, 36:999; Sam E. Magill (Consul) to Asst. Sec. of State, 14, 23 December 1909, Guadalajara, State, n.f.:21980, USNA; see a letter signed by some fifty railroad workers in *México Nuevo*, 19 February 1910; J. Trinidad Nav(indistinct) to Díaz, 10 March 1910, GPDC, 35:4059.

test new employees after a two year apprenticeship. Such a policy would have further cemented the hold they had on the better jobs on the lines. The company held firm against those demands, however, and an appeal to the American government failed, so the American workers backed down from their threat of a strike.[36]

Meanwhile, Mexican railroad workers reorganized in an effort to strengthen their hand against the Americans and to force the government to carry through their policy of mexicanization. The largest union, *La Gran Liga*, had been weakened by its unsuccessful strike of 1908. Members of various of its branches wanted to join a federation of railroad unions, while others desired to maintain their autonomy. In February 1910 the *Conductores y Maquinistas Mexicanos*, the *Sociedad Mutualista de Telegrafistas Ferrocarrileros*, the *Alianza de Ferrocarrileros Mexicanos* and Branch Number 5 of the *Gran Liga* (Monterrey) called for a federation of various railroad unions. At a meeting in Mexico City in March, the effort of Mexican railroadmen to establish a federation met with only moderate success. Representatives of an estimated four thousand Mexican railroad workers signed a charter forming the *Confederación de Ferrocarrileros Mexicanos*.[37] The decision of Silvino Rodríguez's strong mechanics' union and of most of the branches of *La Gran Liga* to stay independent, however, considerably lessened the survival chances of the confederation.

In April 1910 delegates from various Mexican railroad unions met with Díaz in the Federal District in an effort to speed up the mexicanization program. There seemed to be little doubt that public feelings were strongly on the side of the Mexican workers struggling for equality on a railroad owned by their own government. The editor of *El Sufragio Libre*, writing on the railroad issue, demanded a "Mexico for the Mexicans."[58] Yet whatever the intention of the government, the

36. *El Paladín*, 6 February 1910; *México Nuevo*, 8, 10 February 1910; Miller, "American Railroad Unions," pp. 253–54.

37. Circular from Branch 8 of the *Gran Liga* in *México Nuevo*, 15 December 1909; *México Nuevo*, 16, 22, 25 February 1910; *El Estandarte*, 30 March 1910. Signing the charter were: *Alianza de Ferrocarrileros Mexicanos, Sociedad Mutualista de Telegrafistas Ferrocarrileros, Asociación de Conductores y Maquinistas Mexicanos* (formed after the May 1909 strike of American railroad workers), *Orden de Fogoneros de Guadalajara, Unión Jalisciense de Guadalajara*, and the *Orden de Fogoneros de Aguascalientes*.

American unions through various delaying tactics prevented any further erosion of their positions on the National lines and soon events in the north turned the regime's attention elsewhere.[38]

One area in which the government did succeed in acting to mitigate a serious complaint by Mexican workers was its corn distribution program. Food prices had been rising steadily during the decade but were aggravated by the severe frosts that hit many parts of Mexico in the fall of 1908, causing extensive damage to corn, barley, beans, and other crops throughout the nation. In some areas not a single ear of corn was harvested. Corn and beans were the major diet staples for most Mexicans, and by 1909 these two items alone were probably consuming more than 30 percent of the total weekly budget of urban working-class Mexicans.

The crisis finally forced the administration to act. The government lowered corn prices by law, and a special *junta* was empowered to spend one million *pesos* to buy foreign and domestic corn, selling it at reduced prices to the "poorer classes" in areas hit by the frost. José I. Limantour defended the program before the House of Deputies in December 1909, contending that the evils of disallowing free competition were offset by even greater evils if the interests of a few were allowed to triumph over the "otherwise defenseless masses." Indeed, he warned that "the progress achieved during the last quarter century runs the risk of being lost to a large extent, as far as millions of our wage-earners are concerned, unless a practical and permanent solution can be found for the problem of cheapening the staple food product of the people."[39]

The regime's program appeared to be at least partly successful, as the wholesale price of corn declined slightly in Mexican City in 1910, despite the continued increase in general prices. At least one Reelectionist party, the *Gran Partido Popular* (Pascual Mendoza was an officer), cited the corn program in the campaign of that year as evi-

38. Erasmo Martínez to Díaz, 24 April 1910, Laredo, Texas, GPDC, 35:4536; *El Sufragio Libre*, 9 February 1910; Miller, "American Railroad Unions," p. 254.

39. The speech is translated by Louis C. Simonds as "Financial Documents," in State, n.f.:8057, USNA; *The Mexican Daily Record*, 28 October 1909, in Thompson to Sec. of State, 28 October 1909, State, n.f.:22197, USNA.

dence of the Díaz administration's efforts on behalf of the common people.[40]

Yet neither the regime's corn distribution program nor any show of interest in the workers' problems could alter at this late date the regime's basic anti-worker image or allay many workers' increasingly obvious hostility to that portion of the Díaz regime dominated by what many workers perceived to be the *científico*–foreign capitalist alliance. The political activities during the years of 1909 and 1910 brought at last an opportunity for the Mexican worker to demand recognition; those were the years in which he sought his own deliverance. When Creelman issued the call, Mexican workers came forward like anyone else, without waiting to be asked. Indeed, many appeared on the verge of living up to José María González's prediction made over thirty years before: if they were not yet the lions he warned of, they were no longer sheep. "The people," as *Mexico Obrero* had declared, "have awakened."

Industrial Workers, *Reyistas*, and Reelectionists

Mexican working classes were not the only dissatisfied Mexicans and when serious politicking began in the early months of 1909, various factions were able to capitalize on widespread discontent which had been slowly gathering in all corners of the Republic. After nearly thirty years, the *Pax Porfiriana* was coming undone.

The peace imposed by Don Porfirio had not done away with partisan politics, as his early slogan of "poca política y mucha administración" had suggested. Rather it had been restructured, with the political elites being forced to acknowledge the rule of the central government and to accept Díaz as the ultimate political authority. Over the years of Porfirian rule an oligarchy developed, dominated by an elite made up of the major industrial, financial, and landed interests, along with the most important political families who had come to power with the old *Caudillo* or who had risen during the long years of his rule. Inevitably inter-elite rivalries developed, as often as not, subtly

40. *La Clase Media*, 24 October 1909, GPDC, 34:18050. See also *El Imparcial*, 4 November 1909.

fostered by Díaz as a means of strengthening his own hold as the arbitrator of such struggles and of keeping any potential competition divided among themselves. Such conflicts revolved around personalities but were based fundamentally on the need to wield political power in order to protect vital economic interests, as well as for the prestige that such power brought.

The *científico* group rose to top positions in the federal government and were the most important single clique. Their power lay in the control they exercised over national economic policy, and in the special relationship that this gave them with the major industrial and commercial houses. Moreover, they were often important men of business in their own right.

Opposition to the *científicos* centered among a loosely organized group of state governors and their supporters, most of whom were also well-known landholders and businessmen. Among the anti-*científico* politicians, Teodoro Dehesa in Veracruz and General Bernardo Reyes in Nuevo León were recognized as the informal leaders. Although the favor of the *Caudillo* was never given exclusively to one side or the other, the *científicos'* predominance in the national administration, particularly their control over *Hacienda, Gobernación*, and the vice-presidency, gave them at least the appearance of dominating national politics. But with the advancing age of Díaz, the possibility of his death could change the picture. That is why the question of the vice-presidency loomed so large to the great *políticos*. Díaz had made known his intentions to stay in the presidency for another term, but he had remained silent on his choice of the vice-president, or rather, about whether or not he would dump Ramón Corral.

Yet such factional disputes were part of the system, and business as usual might have continued had there not existed wide-spread discontent among the lower orders of the oligarchy—commercial farmers, medium-size domestic businessmen and merchants, and the significantly enlarged professional and intellectual classes—as well as among more marginal elements such as shopkeepers, retail merchants, and the group generally called the petite bourgeoisie. Their grievances were not with the system, necessarily, but with the operation of the system. Monopolistic pricing and political favoritism had hurt some from the very beginning of the *Porfiriato*. The cry against "caciquismo"—the political tyranny of a local *caudillo*—was a common complaint of the times. Yet most of the discontent appeared after mid-decade, when the system clearly was in economic trouble. The administration's switch to the gold standard in 1905 led to inflationary effects on the price of imported goods, adding to the already existing rate of inflation in the domestic market, which many merchants and businessmen found easy to blame on the administration's monetary reforms and on the monopolistic pricing practices of the foreign-dominated importing-exporting firms. Meanwhile the recession of 1908–1909 hurt many landowners and smaller businessmen, as the banks not only refused to extend short-term credit but recalled old loans and foreclosed on outstanding mortgages. And while the value of industrial production appeared to recover after it dropped in 1908, the value of commerce in the gross domestic product fell sharply in 1908 and failed to reach its 1907 peak by 1910. The Díaz regime could hardly escape the blame for the situation.

Coupled with recession, and aggravating it, was a long-term rising rate of inflation whose effects were felt by the urban professional classes and all intellectual elites dependent on wages or rents. Many of this group, as well as substantial portions from other middle- and upper-class sectors, believed that their troubles related to their nation's increasing dependence on foreign capital and foreign markets and chose to blame the regime's administrative directors—the *científicos*—for the overwhelming foreign influence. And so it was that when Mexican workers sought to obtain political resolution of their problems, they found themselves among strange bedfellows.[41]

The first national political movement to attract the attention of important groups of Mexican workers was the *reyista* party, whose paramount goal was to prevent the *científico* clique from dominating Mexican politics after the death of Díaz by forcing the president to choose General Bernardo Reyes as his vice-president. Reyes was not adverse to such a role. In August 1908 Reyes suggested that Díaz was still needed but hinted at the importance of the vice-presidency.[42] The

41. While a definitive study of Porfirian politics has yet to be made, the man best qualified at this moment to do such a study, Daniel Cosío Villegas, has put together two huge volumes in the Colegio de México series, *Historia moderna de México: El Porfiriato: La vida política interior, primera y segunda partes*.

42. Taracena, *La verdadera revolución*, pp. 176–77.

bluff, capable Reyes had built up a political following over the years as the most popular and prestigious anti-*científico* politician in the country. He left the actual politicking to others and gave no public sign that he was aware of the growing political controversy that was swirling around his name in the early months of 1909.

The *reyista* movement was made up of many and varied political groups, ranging from those who were intensely pro-Reyes to those who were intensely anti-*científico*, supporting Reyes out of political necessity rather than conviction. To include those various interests, a *Partido Democrático* was organized in late 1908 in Mexico City. At first its organizers officially supported no particular candidate, but the party soon openly became the main *reyista* national organization. In addition, many local *reyista* clubs, some loosely affiliated with the national party, others independent, were organized to campaign for Reyes as Díaz's vice-president.[43]

Opposing Reyes' ambitions and those of his followers were the *científicos*, their allies, and those who saw their political interests in the reelection of Corral. From those groups came the nucleus of the *científico*-dominated Reelectionist Party, founded in February 1909. The Reelectionist Party nominated Díaz and Corral in March 1909 and proceeded to send out speakers to the major state capitals to test the climate of opinion. It must have been disquieting; they were jeered wherever they went and even stoned in Guadalajara.[44] Understandably, then, the Reelectionists sought to build up their popular base by organizing support among the nation's workers.

In April 1909 the Reelectionists moved boldly to demonstrate their support among the workers of the country, arranging a pro-Díaz and Corral rally in Mexico City. The rally was attended by three thousand workers under the leadership of Pascual Mendoza. They were mainly from his Puebla and Tlaxcala mills. In conjunction with the rally, *El Imparcial* carried the names of thousands of workers on a petition supporting the reelection of Díaz and Corral. The leading *reyista* spokesman among the city's dailies, *México Nuevo*, immediately coun-

43. Ross, *Madero*, pp. 65–69; Cosío Villegas, *La vida política interior*, 2:822–31; Anthony T. Bryan, "Mexican Politics in Transition, 1900–1913: The Role of General Bernardo Reyes," (Ph.D. diss., University of Nebraska, 1970).

44. Ross, *Madero*, pp. 69–71; Cosío Villegas, *La vida política interior*, 2:840–62.

tered by denying that the petition represented the true feelings of Mexico's working classes. Instead, the paper charged that many workers had been forced to sign the petition by their bosses or lose their jobs. When questioned about the role that Mendoza played in the rally, one worker, who did *not* support Corral, replied that Mendoza was esteemed by many workers but that he must have been influenced by his nonworker friends.[45]

México Nuevo, whose editor was Juan Sánchez Azcona, a founder of the *Partido Democrático*, then proceeded to publish a number of interviews with workers, noting that most of them stated that they supported Díaz for president "in order to keep the peace" but preferred other candidates to Corral for the vice-president. The workers thought that Corral was too closely linked with foreign interests and a number of those interviewed even dared to suggest that he was responsible for the massacre of the textile workers at Río Blanco in January of 1907. The reporter noted, however, that Corral had a more favorable image among the workers' commissions that had worked with him on various matters. Those interviewed usually leaned toward General Reyes or Enrique Creel, governor of Chihuahua, as a running mate for Díaz. The paper acknowledged that although General Reyes had a large number of supporters, some workers feared that if he gained power he might establish a military regime, while others remembered the bloody events of 2 April 1903 in Monterrey when antigovernment demonstrators had been shot down without provocation.[46]

The day after the interviews in *México Nuevo*, posters appeared in various districts in Mexico City favoring the election of Díaz and Reyes and signed "The Working Class." Corral supporters promptly circulated a petition among the factories of the city protesting the use of the term "working class" in support of Reyes.[47]

45. *México Nuevo*, 27 April, 4 May 1909.

46. *México Nuevo*, 4 May 1909; *México Nuevo* soon became openly committed to the Reyes candidacy, as did other pro-labor papers: *El Paladín* (see 11 July 1909), *La Voz Popular* and *Pueblo Libre* (see 29 June 1909, and 20 August 1909 respectively), and *La Guacamaya* (see 14 May, 11 June 1908). Creel had earlier disavowed any higher political ambitions; Enrique Creel to Salvador Álvarez G., 8 April 1909, in GPDC, 33:4098.

47. Thompson to Sec. of State, 11 May 1909, State, n.f.:8183, encl. 245–46, USNA.

Nonetheless, Reyes was clearly the most popular vice-presidential candidate among the Mexican workers in the summer of 1909. *Reyista* clubs in Orizaba and Atlixco attracted support from the workers as did the *Club Democrático de Obreros "Porfirio Díaz and B. Reyes" de Jalapa.* In the Federal District the recently formed *El Gran Partido Nacional Obrero* announced in late June that it was supporting Reyes for the vice-presidency. Their reasons were that he was both a great patriot and a friend of the people. They noted in particular his accident compensation law, one of the very few in Mexico. The *Gran Partido* spokesman carefully pointed out that Díaz was unanimously acclaimed by the vote of the entire membership, some six hundred workers mainly from the craft and retail trades, while Reyes received a majority of the votes for vice-president. Their weekly paper, *México Obrero,* was an outspoken representative of the workingman's cause, attacking the poor living conditions in Mexico City, the rising prices, and the politicians responsible for their situation, the *científicos.*[48]

The *reyistas* not only accepted labor support, they actively sought it. For example, the *reyista* club of Torreón, Coahuila, put out a flier addressed to "The Working Classes of Torreón," inviting them to attend a political rally in support of Díaz and Reyes. A delegate was appointed by the Mexico City *reyista* club to solicit support for Reyes in various factories in that area.[49]

Despite these efforts, however, the *reyista* movement offered little to the workers in the way of concrete reforms. The Democratic Party of Mexico City favored accident insurance for the workers but said little else about the workers' problems. *Reyista* papers such as *El Paladín* and *La Guacamaya* were sympathetic to the workers but offered little in the way of concrete plans to solve their problems. The most important *reyista* spokesman, *México Nuevo,* followed the same pattern. It occasionally carried strong statements in favor of militant action to resolve the workers' problems, but its usual position was quite moder-

48. *México Obrero,* 1 September 1909. On worker support for Reyes, see *Archivo Espinosa de los Monteros,* 4:164, Fs 369; 93, Fs 158; 94; 20; 4:37; and 5:68; *El Paladín,* 24 June 1909; *México Nuevo,* 5, 22 June 1909. For correspondence of the president of the GPNO with Díaz, see GPDC, 34:8905, 8934, 9546.

49. Flier dated June 1909 from Felecitos F. Villarreal, president, AEM, 5:137; Heliodoro Villasena to sec. of *reyista* club, 25 June 1909, Mexico City, AEM, 4:113.

ate, obviously designed not to alienate the more conservative *reyista* followers. For example, the paper once carried an article which suggested that the best relationship between the worker and the capitalist should be paternalistic, like a father and son who respect and love each other. It recommended the *hacienda's patrón-peón* relationship as an instructive example.[50]

The *reyista* movement had begun to gather momentum in the spring and early summer of 1909 when it ran into trouble. After attracting impressive crowds in Veracruz, Orizaba, Guadalajara, and other cities, the Democratic Party ran up against the obvious displeasure of Díaz at having the choice of his running mate taken to the streets. On 28 July 1909 Reyes publicly disavowed any ambitions to serve as vice-president, despite the pleas of many of his followers, including the Federal District workers' *Gran Partido*. Any hopes his followers had of persuading him to change his mind were crushed in November 1909 when Reyes resigned as governor of Nuevo León to accept a military study assignment in Europe.[51] Whether for patriotism or political expediency, Reyes would not challenge Díaz and so left open the way for other men who were less closely tied to the regime.

For the Mexican worker, the demise of the *reyista* movement should have revealed that the regime had no intention of opening the political process to the public. Other incidents served the same purpose. In June 1909 an independent workers' club was founded in Mérida, Yucatán, in order to use political action to meet the growing economic crisis in that state. The next month the club's president, Gervasio Funtes, was arrested on the charge of sedition—the club had intended to run a presidential candidate of its own in the election of 1910. In August 1909 various Coahuilan workers' groups publicly thanked the legislature for appointing a popular interim governor after the resignation of the former governor. The interim governor, Venustiano

50. Manuel González, ed., *Manifiestos políticos, 1892–1912* (Mexico: Fondo de Cultura Económica, 1957), p. 57; for a relatively strong statement, see an article by "Pipila II," 4 May 1909 (before, however, the paper became clearly *reyista*). For the paternalism approach, see 7 November 1909. For other quite moderate positions on the labor question, see 24 April, 19 May, 5 November 1909.

51. Ross, *Madero*, p. 73.

Carranza, an acknowledged *reyista*, was cashiered not long afterwards. When the regular elections for governor were held, labor groups in Coahuila supported Carranza in his losing candidacy against the officially sponsored candidate, Lic. Jesús del Valle. Del Valle was preferred by both the former governor, Miguel Cárdenas, and by General Jeronimo Treviño, chief of the Third Military Zone and long personal associate of Porfirio Díaz.[52]

Toluca workers made a public appeal for a conference of Mexican workers to discuss their political rights and duties. Workers from the cotton mill La Carolina in the Federal District called for joint political action by all textile workers in the upcoming elections. A mason's brotherhood protested against the politically motivated arrest of Alfonso B. Peniche, editor of *La Redención*, accused of defamation of a treasury official. A group of Federal District retail clerks formed a mutual society for the purpose of involving other mutual societies in current politics. As late as June 1910 a retail clerks' group was installed within the National Democratic Party, a small Mexico City-based party that incorporated the surviving elements of the old *reyista* Democratic Party.[53] Politics seemed to many Mexican workers to be the logical medium for the resolution of their problems.

After the initial rally in April 1909, the Reelectionists continued to make efforts to attract working-class support. Except for Mendoza's mill hands, however, no large group of industrial workers were taken in by the Reelectionists. Díaz-Corral partisans in the north claimed to speak for the railroad workers of Monterrey, who they said supported the administration because of the government's railroad policies.[54] But given the slowness in implementing their current program of mexicanization, it hardly seems likely that the Reelectionists could have aroused much enthusiasm from the railroad workers.

Instead, the few Reelectionists who had contact with members of the working class were attempting to secure support from mutualist groups. By February of 1910, however, *El Obrero Mexicano*, a

52. *El Paladín*, 9 July 1909; *México Nuevo*, 28 June 1909; ibid., 12, 13, 14 August 1909; *El Diario del Hogar*, 14 August 1909.

53. *El Correo de Chihuahua*, 29 May 1909; *La Voz de Juárez*, 30 June 1909; *México Nuevo*, 2, 14 February, 12 June 1910.

54. See the official organ of the *Círculo Político Reeleccionista "José Yves Limantour." El Órgano de la Sultana del Norte*, GPDC, 34:18455.

mutualist spokesman for Landa y Escandón, was taking the position that mutualist workers should avoid all forms of politics, indicating, perhaps, that the reelectionists were not obtaining mutualist support and thus preferred their neutrality. On the other hand, *El Heraldo de Morelos*, the major mutualist organ in the Federal District, consistently supported Corral and Díaz throughout the electoral campaign.[55]

In September 1909 the Reelectionists made one last effort to organize a national drive to pick up working-class adherents. The *Club Electoral "Félix Díaz"* announced plans to form a *Convocatoria del Pueblo Obrero de la Nación*. Speaking as representatives of the working people and "with the unpolished but sincere frankness that characterizes us, the sons of labor," the group proposed to show their fellow workers "the benefits of the generous political and economic ideals . . . of the Supreme Magistrate of the Nation, C. General P. Díaz."[56] The organization appealed to the workers by painting an image of Díaz as a hero in war and a statesman in peace. Corral was praised for his intimate contact with the working classes and his other talents. Other workers' reelectionist's groups were formed, but they attracted few workers. The only major labor leaders supporting the reelection of Díaz and Corral were Pascual Mendoza and Roma de Vivar, the former president of the *reyista Gran Partido Nacional Obrero*, who defected to the Reelectionists after the collapse of the *reyista* movement.[57] Only Mendoza had a substantial labor following, and even his support fell away under the pressure of events in the months ahead.

While the politics of ambition and discontent were winding their way toward an uncertain end, Mexican workers were showing signs of

55. *México Nuevo*, 24 April, 3 May 1909, 14 February 1910; *El Imparcial*, 25 June 1909; *El Heraldo de Morelos*, 4 July 1909.

56. Circular, *Club Electoral "Félix Díaz,"* F. Spinosa, first secretary, 15 September 1909, GPDC, 34:14371; *El Imparcial*, 11 May 1909.

57. *El Imparcial*, 4 August 1909, 3 April 1910; see *Club Obrero Ramón Corral de Tacubaya* and *Club Obrero Ramón Corral de Mixcoac* at a public meeting on 15 November 1909: Gustavo Casasola, *Historia gráfica de la Revolución Mexicana 1900–1960*, 4 vols. (Mexico, 1965), 1:122; Francisco P. Molina to Díaz, 21 March 1910, Magdalena, Sonora, GPDC, 35:3234—petition of support containing about one hundred signatures of workers; González Navarro, *La vida social*, p. 352.

the emergence of a dangerous frustration built on feelings of angry helplessness about their situation—high prices, low wages, harsh treatment, and now the obvious unwillingness of the regime to listen to their political preferences as well. In particular, the issues over which the workers expressed their increasing anger were the injustice of the foreigners who controlled their lives and the worsening of the economy.

The economic problems were particularly frustrating because they could be blamed on no one in particular. Workers blamed the situation on poor management by the factories, or taxes, or Limantour's economic policies, or, most often, the speculators and monopolists. Someone was to blame! Even the proadministration and very mutualist *El Heraldo de Morelos* acknowledged a problem, saying as early as May 1908 that during the last three years it had become increasingly difficult to live in Mexico City on the wages paid to workers, blaming the "señores agiotistas" for artificially raising the prices of goods. In June 1909 the same paper ran articles about the "economic crisis" and gave examples of prices that had risen from 25 to 50 percent.[58] Wages had not kept up with prices, as the letters to *El Paladín* and *México Nuevo* pointed out time and time again. Even Pascual Mendoza's *La Lucha Obrera* complained of the situation. "The current state of our working classes could not be worse. They have always been poorly paid and what is more deplorable, the price of those articles of prime necessity have risen fantastically."[59]

While prices were going up, men were out of work. In the central states, industrial employment declined at least into 1910, while in the north the economic situation had been deteriorating since 1907. Work in the mines was scarce, the ranches were letting people go, and

58. Workers at the textile mill El Mayorazgo in Puebla to *México Nuevo*, 26 April 1910; skilled workers (carpenters, mechanics, blacksmiths, etc.), Mexico City, *México Nuevo*, 10 November 1909; ten workers to editor of *México Nuevo*, 7 June 1910; *El Paladín*, 13 May 1909; Juan Rendón, F. García, and other officers of Santa Rosa Labor Society to *El Paladín*, 6 January 1910; *El Diablito Bromista*, 29 November 1909; *El Heraldo de Morelos*, 24, 31 May 1908, 27 June 1909.

59. 11 July 1909, GPDC, 34:13735. Mendoza was also worried about the rumors of factories closing in his area; Mendoza to Díaz, 22 December 1909, GPDC, 34:18990.

the United States would permit no more *braceros* after 1908. It appears that certain sectors of the economy began to pick up by mid-1910, but for many workers, it was already too late.[60]

But the greatest public resentment, if not the hardest felt private deprivation, was increasingly directed toward the predominant role the workers believed that foreigners were playing in the life of the nation. In May 1909 mill hands at the foreign-owned Metepec factory struck in protest against lower wages and against treatment "insulting the dignity and honor of Mexicans."[61] Still the abuses continued. "What right," wrote Metepec workers indignantly in January 1910, "does a foreigner have to send a Mexican worker to the authorities for punishment?"[62]

Even Pascual Mendoza disparaged the "contemptible foreigners who only come to Mexico to rob the fruit of the workingman's labor under a wicked hypocrisy that makes them appear good when at the bottom of their soul they only carry the desire to annihilate our race, the heroic, a thousand times sainted race of Cuauhtémoc."[63] And the conservative *El Estandarte* of San Luis Potosí published a railroad workers' manifesto which reminded its readers that "our oppressors are foreigners; that they occupy our positions without any right whatsoever, snatching away from us that which we might have for our little children; that they humiliate and belittle us, offending our dignity as honorable men."[64] The editor of *El Paladín* expressed the belief that:

> Here in our country the truth is that up to now the exploitation
> of the mines, of the factories and a great portion of the
> industries has favored the foreigners as the owners, managers,
> directors and major employees, and not our compatriots, who
> occupy only the last place . . . and the truth is also that the
> foreigners are those who live much better, who live in beautiful
> mansions, while the crisis for the middle class and for our
> proletariat becomes more and more unbearable.[65]

60. Katz, "Labor Conditions on Haciendas," pp. 35–36.
61. *Mexico Nuevo*, 14 May 1909.
62. *El Paladín*, 1 January 1910.
63. *La Lucha Obrera*, 11 July 1909; GPDC, 34:13735.
64. *El Estandarte*, 10 March 1910.
65. *El Paladín*, 28 January 1909.

There was the bitter irony of the long letter from the Río Blanco workers, addressed to the "Honorable Congress of the Union," which told of their commissions to the factory manager being humiliated and thrown out. "And they treat us as if we were their children. What more could we want? And we say justice! Justice! Why don't they do us justice? . . . It should be understood that the workers are not asking for concessions but only justice, justice that will bring to an end all the arbitrary acts committed against us in our own country."[66]

The demands for justice and the bitterness over the economic situation and the foreign domination, these issues were unresolved by the political manuevering of the months after the Creelman interview and perhaps even accelerated during that time. In summing up the mood of Mexican workers, mill hands from the militant Santa Rosa mill, whose early leaders had died on the ashes of burnt-out company stores, charged that with "each passing day, life in this town is made more insufferable and unbearable."[67]

The potential for violence was great. Not everywhere, not to the same degree or at the same time, but among mill hands of the Puebla-Orizaba-Tlaxcala triangle and in other mills throughout the country, among the railroadmen, and in other pockets of discontent around the Republic, industrial workers were beginning to despair of obtaining justice under the present order of things. The swift end to the *reyista* movement must have added to their sense of hopelessness. Some began to hint of violence. One worker asked the rhetorical question as to whether the company wanted to bring back the days that produced the seventh of January.[68] In another oblique reference to Río Blanco, the president of the *Alianza Obrera* at the Río Blanco mill warned of the discontent at his factory, commenting that "painful experience has demonstrated that discontent among individuals of a community constitutes a danger to the public order." Then in a delicate balance between irony and menace he went on: "When the workers are treated to injustices they often lack the knowledge of their rights and duties, and blame the Government. This is an

66. Workers of the weaving department, Río Blanco mill, to *El Paladín*, 8 May 1910.
67. *El Paladín*, 14 April 1910.
68. Ibid., 30 September 1909.

error, no doubt, but on the other hand it is a fact that unfortunately follows . . . when their most just aspirations are thwarted."[69]

In the spring of 1910 one railroad worker wrote to Díaz about the situation of Mexican workers on the National Lines, describing the dominance of the foreign employees. Then in a thinly veiled warning, he said: "We hate any method that is not peaceful, but I fear that it is not possible to contain them [his fellow workers] much longer if things do not change. . . . Human patience has its limit, and this limit is now almost reached. Many, in their profound disgust, talk of a thousand things that are not worthy of us, and we have worked very hard to restrain them."[70]

If the Mexican industrial workers were feeling the frustration and bitterness that some of their fellows were expressing in their letters, they were, for a brief time, given an opportunity to vent their feelings. In the early months of 1910, Francisco Madero and the Anti-Reelectionist Party represented what hopes Mexican workers might have held for a political solution to their problems.

Mexican Workers and the Anti-Reelectionist Movement

On the eve of the great Mexican Revolution of 1910, industrial workers around the nation were largely pro-Madero. The reasons for their allegiance were clear to them at the time, and although historians have often treated Madero's social philosophy with scorn, to the tough, embittered millhands and factory workers in 1910, he was a *político* they could believe.

Francisco I. Madero, oldest son of a wealthy and prominent Coahuilan family, was everything that the workers were not. What bound them to him in this marriage of illusion was his sincerity and their needs, and the fact that there was no one else.

Disturbed by political conditions in his state of Coahuila, Madero entered politics in 1905 and soon became involved in various causes in opposition to the regime's political establishment. After aiding the

69. Reyes Moreno, "Ocurso al Gobernador de Veracruz," *El Paladín*, 1 August 1909.

70. J. Trinidad Nav(indistinct) to Díaz, 10 March 1910, Guadalajara, GPDC, 35:4062.

important opposition journalist Paulino Martínez, he commented that men such as Martínez were planting seeds of change and that "we will gather that harvest inside of five years."[71] Madero was an early supporter of Ricardo Flores Magón but disassociated himself from the PLM in 1906 when he became concerned that it was becoming a revolutionary party.

Encouraged by the Creelman interview, Madero became one of a growing cluster of independent politicians who hoped to use the opportunity to bring full political democracy to Mexico. In order to focus attention on the problem of democracy in Mexico under the Díaz regime, Madero began writing a book, *The Presidential Succession of 1910*. It was published in late January of 1909.

Madero opposed the Reyes boom then getting under way. He distrusted Reyes for many reasons, not the least of which was the latter's role in the slaughter of unarmed political demonstrators in Monterrey in April 1903. He was therefore unhappy over the extent of the *reyista* influence in the *Partido Democrático* and attempted to convince his friends of the necessity of forming an independent party to contest the presidency itself in 1910. He saw no purpose in supporting a man who had given little indication that his democratic convictions were any stronger than those of the man who held power.[72] In early 1909, the Anti-Reelectionist Center was established in Mexico City; it began its struggle against the Porfirian regime as a minor political party under the shadow of the *reyista* movement.

At the beginning of 1909, Madero was unknown to Mexico's *obreros*, except for those who remembered that he and his family had offered to employ striking workers on their lands during the great strike of December 1906. Even the publication of his book did not make him famous. However, his political activities in the spring of 1909, the press comments on his book, and the distrust of Reyes by some workers made him better known by that summer.[73]

Initially, the appeal of the Anti-Reelectionists to the industrial workers was blunted by the *reyista* movement. Yet by mid-1909 the Anti-Reelectionists were attracting the attention of the more disgrun-

71. Cited in Ross, *Madero*, p. 41.
72. Ibid., pp. 57, 65–69; Cosío Villegas, *La vida política interior*, 2:768–76.
73. *México Nuevo*, 23 May 1909; see also S. S. C. Solano (a worker from Orizaba) to *La Voz de Juárez*, 30 June 1909.

tled workers, like several mill hands from Nogales, Veracruz, who, after noticing a Reelectionist "Club Porfirista" sign in town, commented that "these people must be ignorant of the terrible conditions of the miserable outcasts under the present administration."[74] In June Dr. Carlos Ramírez and Gabriel Gavira, a cabinetmaker, organized the *Club Ignacio de la Llave de Orizaba* as the first step in attracting workers from the city and the surrounding mill towns to the Anti-Reelectionist cause. Ramírez had gained a local reputation as a *magonista* during the labor activities of 1906, and the local authorities were a little uneasy when he appeared at the head of the Anti-Reelectionists. As the *jefe político* said, there were sixteen thousand workers in the area, and he was afraid that the labor conflicts would become linked to political movements.[75]

During June of 1909, at the apogee of the *reyista* movement, the *Club Anti-Reeleccionista de Obreros Benito Juárez* was founded in the Federal District, followed in July by the *Club Anti-Reeleccionista de Obreros "Miguel Hidalgo y Costilla"* at the Concepción del Oro mine in Zacatecas, the *Club Anti-Reeleccionista de Obreros "Luz y Progreso"* in Puebla, led by Aquiles Serdán, and the *Club Anti-Reeleccionista "Ignacio Zaragoza"* in Puebla, with Agustín Díaz Durán as president.[76]

When Reyes withdrew his name as a candidate for the vice-presidency, many workers who supported him went over to the Anti-Reelectionist camp. Alfredo Navarrete was one. Reyes had been his first idol. A strong, independent statesman, a foe of the *científicos*, in Alfredo Navarrete's mind, Reyes stood for Mexico, a man who would put the foreigners in their place. But when the *reyista* movement failed, Navarrete joined the *Club Anti-Reeleccionista* which was recruiting workers from the railroadmen on his line. Their leader was

74. Letter to *El Paladín*, 13 May 1909.

75. *Jefe político* of Orizaba to Sec. of Gobernación, State of Veracruz, 15 June 1909, SHUV, Gob. 1911, 49-C; *jefe político* to Gov. of Veracruz, 13 June 1909, in *jefe político* of Orizaba to Díaz, n.d., GPDC, 34:3760; Gabriel Gavira, *General de brigada, Gabriel Gavira, su actuación político-militar revolucionaria* (Mexico: A. del Bosque, 1933), p. 9; Gen. Maass to Díaz, 19 June 1909, GPDC, 34:9801.

76. *México Nuevo*, 2 December 1909; GPDC, 34:12302; *El Diario del Hogar*, 23 July 1909. Both Puebla clubs initially had almost one hundred members each, including many textile workers.

Guadalupe Rojas, a foreman in the spinning room of a textile mill in the Federal District.[77]

The only major *reyista* defector to Corral was the president of the *Gran Partido Nacional Obrero* (GPNO), Abundio Romo de Vivar. The cofounder of the GPNO, Ignacio C. Castellanos, condemned Romo de Vivar for his support of Corral, because the *científicos*, said Castellanos, were attempting to enslave the Mexican people. "The people of Hidalgo de Zaragoza," he warned, "will prefer their complete destruction and ruin before tolerating such an affront."[78] Both *El Paladín* and *México Nuevo* were supporting Madero and the Anti-Reelectionists by the fall of 1909, undoubtedly with some influence on their working-class readers.

Anti-Reelectionist support among Mexican *obreros* slowly grew during the fall and winter months of 1909 and on into 1910. By June of 1910 at least thirty working-class groups opposing the reelection of Díaz and Corral had been formed in Orizaba, Atlixco, Puebla, Veracruz, Autlán (Jalisco), Aguascalientes, and Concepción del Oro (Zacatecas) and in various factories and shops of the Federal District. Orizaba mustered four clubs, three of them in the mill towns outside the city. The majority of the clubs were in the textile industry, but clubs also existed among railroad workers, commercial workers, miners, typographers, electricians, and others. Though undoubtedly some such clubs were initiated by nonworkers, it seems clear that most were organized by the workers themselves or by allies from craft and artisan occupations.[79]

Anti-Reelectionist strength among industrial workers can only be estimated, but indications are that it was high, ranging from 25 to over 50 percent active participation of workers in those mills and

77. Navarrete, *Alto*, pp. 37–40, 73.
78. See speech by Castellanos, 24 November 1909, AEM, 144:Fs285.
79. For workers' clubs in specific areas, see: Orizaba and Puebla—*El Paladín*, 17 February, 10 April, 29 May 1910; *El Constitucional*, 14 April 1910. For Orizaba alone, see Anti-Reelectionist poster in GPDC, 35:6601 and other correspondence in that *legajo*. For Federal District clubs, see *El Constitucional*, 24 March 1910; *México Nuevo*, 2 December 1909, 3 May, 8, 11, 12 June 1910; *La Evolución* (F.D. weekly), 1, 29 May 1910; Ana María Hernández, *La mujer mexicana en la industria textil* (Mexico: n.p., 1940), pp. 38, 49–50. For other areas, see *El Constitucional*, 14, 16 April 1910; GPDC, 34:12302.

factories with a history of labor problems. Four hundred eighty-nine members of the *Club Anti-Reeleccionista de Santa Rosa Necoxtla*, about one-fourth of the total workers employed by the mill, voted in the club's April caucus for their choice among the party's candidates for president and vice-president. The *Club Anti-Reeleccionista de Metepec "Guillermo Prieto"* attracted more than three thousand workers from the Atlixco area to their nominating convention, according to the Anti-Reelectionists' official organ, *El Constitucional*.[80] A rally on the first of May of pro-Madero workers in the Federal District drew five thousand demonstrators. Although no specific evidence is available, it should be assumed that at least a fair representation of workers were among the great numbers that greeted Madero or heard him talk in Veracruz (June 1909), Mérida (June 1909), Guadalajara (December 1909), Mazatlán and Culiacán (January 1910), Aguascalientes (March 1910), Guanajuato (April 1910), Guadalajara (May 1910), Puebla (May 1910), Jalapa (May 1910), and Orizaba (May 1910).

Madero's supporters in Puebla and Orizaba were particularly numerous and enthusiastic, probably numbering between twenty and thirty thousand each in those two important industrial towns. Pascual Mendoza tried to keep his workers from attending the rally Madero held in Puebla, but he was forced to admit to Díaz that he was not successful. Of the twenty-five to thirty thousand demonstrators in the 29 May Mexico City rally of Anti-Reelectionist clubs, a fair number were workers marching under the banners of their particular clubs. By May 1910 Madero was being referred to as "our candidate" by Orizaba workers, reflecting most likely the views of many of the Republic's industrial *obreros* and most of the politically aware and active workers.[81]

80. The Santa Rosa club submitted the following results of their caucus: For president, Madero, 458; Iglesias Calderón, 31; for vice-president, Lic. Toribio Esquivel Obregón, 248; Francisco Vázquez Gómez, 119; Iglesias Calderón, 80; Madero, 35; Paulino Martínez, 17 (*El Constitucional*, 14 April 1910). The Metepec club choose Madero and Paulino Martínez for vice-president (*El Constitucional*, 10 April 1910).

81. *México Nuevo*, 3 May 1910; Ross, *Madero*, pp. 81–94, 102–4. See photographs of the crowds—with many workers' wide-brimmed sombreros present—in *México Nuevo*, 30 May 1910, and Casasola, *Historia gráfica*, 1:157; Mendoza to Díaz, 18 May 1910, GPDC, 35:5984; *El Paladín*, 26, 29 May 1910; see letter signed by seventy-two workers, *México Nuevo*, 3 May 1910.

The workers of the Anti-Reelectionist clubs made a general appeal to their comrades for support, but they also appealed to specific ideas, ideals, and emotions. In a flier to Puebla workers, Aquiles Serdán invited to a meeting of the working class all those who agreed with the objectives of the *Club Anti-Reeleccionista de Obreros*, which were to throw off the hateful "tutelage" which weighed down the nation, and "to secure our constitutional rights, regaining the inherent freedom due every citizen."[82]

The *Club Anti-Reeleccionista "1910"* appealed to the workers and citizens of Tacuba, in the Federal District, for their support and active participation in the campaign. Their broadside appealed to the patriotism of those "that carry in their veins the blood of Cuauhtémoc, Hidalgo, and Juárez"; they were invited to march in the reconquest of their citizenship, but always within the law because peace was necessary for progress.[83] Speaking to an outdoor rally, one worker expressed the same theme in a poem written for the occasion:

Now that the fateful campaign approaches,
Do not wield the cruel sword
   even though the blood of our brothers
   has tarnished the glories of the
Statesman and the warrior.

Let us prove that in the century
   in which we live,
We are no longer what they imagine,
That in campaigns such as these
   we will not attack
With swords that wound or kill.

Instead, the poet went on, the workers would fight with the pen and the word to regain their "heritage from Juárez—the laws."[84]

In February 1910 the *Club Anti-Reeleccionista de Benito Juárez* organized an elaborate *fiesta* to celebrate the anniversary of the birth of their namesake. The fliers announcing the celebration called on the

82. This document is located among the exhibits of the Museo de Aquiles Serdán, in Serdán's house in Puebla.

83. Signed by Manuel Moreno, president, *El Club Constitucional Anti-Reeleccionista "1910"* dated 12 June 1910, GPDC, 35:18474.

84. Poem by Higinio C. Garcia, *México Nuevo*, 26 January 1910.

Anti-Reelectionist rally in Puebla during the campaign stop by Madero in May 1910. Among the banners in the crowd are those of the Atlixco workers' Club Anti-Reeleccionista Guillermo Prieto *and Aquiles Serdan's* Club Luz y Progreso. *The latter is represented by the white banner with the caption "No Reelección."*

workers to remember their history, how the working people had fought under General Juan Álvarez in defense of the principles of the Reform—justice, freedom, and equality.[85]

It is the appeal that Madero himself made to the workers, however, that reveals the compelling but paradoxical attraction that Mexican workers felt toward the man and his movement. This relationship between Madero and the nation's workers has often been ignored or misrepresented. Madero is usually portrayed as a political idealist unable to perceive that political reform would not solve the national problems, or worse, as a representative of discontented elements within the bourgeoisie, fundamentally at odds with a radicalized industrial working class. Both positions have some elements of the

85. *El Constitucional*, 6 February 1910.

truth, but nonetheless they distort Madero's social philosophy, and more importantly, they totally ignore the industrial workers' perceptions of Madero and of themselves.[86]

Madero's Orizaba speech is often the focus of his detractors. After a triumphant stop in Puebla, Madero was greeted in Orizaba on Sunday, 22 May 1910, by a huge, enthusiastic crowd, many members of which were undoubtedly workers from the mills and shops of the area. In his speech that afternoon, he alluded to the events which had taken place over three years before at Río Blanco, saying that in a democracy such a tragedy would not have happened. Then he went on to give a remarkably clear statement of his social philosophy, declaring:

> "Neither increases in wages nor decreases in working hours depend upon the government, and . . . we are not going to offer these to you because that is not what you want. You want freedom. You want your rights to be respected so that you will be able to form powerful associations in order that, united, you will be able to defend your own rights. You want freedom of thought . . . so that all those who sympathize with your sufferings will be able to show you the road to happiness. That is what you want, Gentlemen; . . . you do not want bread, you want only freedom because freedom will enable you to win your bread."[87]

At this point in his speech, according to *El Constitucional*, Madero was interrupted by cheers and prolonged applause from his audience. Perhaps it was not so much his rhetoric they were responding to, but the fact that he had come to them, that he obviously had listened to their grievances and sympathized with their suffering. From the nearby Santa Rosa mill just a few days before a worker wrote these words of hopelessness and despair: "Here in Santa Rosa it seems that oppression and despotism is growing stronger and that those who should eliminate this evil are deaf."[88] In a vague, undetermined way, those who heard Madero speak that Sunday believed somehow that things could be better now that they were being listened to. Many

86. In defense of Madero's awareness of the labor question, see Taracena, *La veradadera revolución*, pp. 138, 140, 156, 256, 267–68, and Ross, *Madero*, pp. 62, 82, 92, 103.
87. *El Constitucional*, 2 June 1910.
88. *El Paladín*, 19 May 1910.

certainly would have disagreed that the government had no responsibility concerning wages and working hours, but here, in the excitement of the moment, they heard what they wanted to hear.

Perhaps, however, the workers' belief in Madero has a firmer base than the excitement of the speech itself. They were also responding to such key words as "freedom," "rights respected," and "powerful associations," words that meant very specific ideas and ideals to them, evoking images of their rights fought for and won by the liberals of *La Reforma*, of their own associations formed to guarantee and protect their freedom. The workers were not dreamers like Madero; they were practical men. Yet they lived so close to the real world that they were as unaware as he himself was of the limitation of these ideals. Given their lack of experience in political democracy and their own assumptions about the social content of their political beliefs, their faith in Madero is not only understandable but, from their perspective, essential.

The vast majority of Mexico's industrial workers, having no viable ideological alternatives, reached back to a vague past of brave heroes and high words for their model of change. The appeals were to the Constitution of 1857, to liberty, to regaining their lost freedoms and having their rights respected. Although Madero's brand of liberalism did not turn out to be sufficient, most of the Republic's emerging industrial proletariat seemed disposed at this point to give it a try.

Madero's concepts on the proper means of resolving the labor question actually were broader than indicated in his Orizaba speech. He had said in his Puebla speech, for example, that his government would consider enacting "just and equitable laws which gradually improve the workers' situation, without attacking the industrialists' interests," maintaining that such interference by the government was necessary because capital "is always conservative and self-centered."[89] In March of 1910 Madero published a booklet, *El partido nacional Antireeleccionista y la proxima lucha electoral*, in which he promised to institute effective suffrage and expressed his position that democracy was only the means to "more transcendental objectives." Among these objectives was the vague but clear promise that "the government should be concerned with the improvement of the situation of the

89. *El Constitucional*, 2 June 1910.

workers," suggesting that a people could only be strong if the government were involved in elevating "its material, intellectual, and moral level."[90] Madero's failure was not that he believed solely in political reform or that he saw no role for government action in resolving social problems, but that his social concepts were ill-defined, lacking in depth and detail. He was, as were most men of his time, still unaware of the difficulty of the problems that faced them.

The labor platform of the Anti-Reelectionist Party was broader, although without any greater detail. The party's labor plank was revealed in its April 1910 Convention at which Madero and Dr. Francisco Vázquez Gómez were chosen as the candidates for the presidency and vice-presidency in the June elections. Article 6 of the Anti-Reelectionist's program pledged "to better the material, intellectual, and moral condition of the worker by establishing schools in the factories, promoting the passage of laws on indemnification for work-related accidents and combating alcoholism and gambling. . . . To accelerate the mexicanization of railroad personnel . . . instituting the centers of education that are necessary [to implement the program]."[91]

The official organ of the Anti-Reelectionists was more conservative in its approach to the labor question. *El Constitucional* occasionally carried such sections as "Pages for the Worker" but did not take specific stands on relevant working-class issues. Its one major article on labor praised mutualism as a solution to the workers' problems.[92]

Whatever the understanding and intentions of the Anti-Reelectionists toward the workers' problems, the workers clearly supported Madero's movement to oust Díaz and Corral. Whether they expected to succeed or not, Mexican workers were committed to the political struggle against the regime.

Among the Anti-Reelectionists who were concerned with the labor question, one of the most important was Juan Sánchez Azcona, editor of *México Nuevo*. After being forced out of *El Diario* in early 1908, he had helped form *México Nuevo* later that same year. As a *reyista*, Sán-

90. Cited in Ross, *Madero*, pp. 91–92.
91. *El Constitucional*, 29 April 1910.
92. See Jesús R. Oros, speech before the *Junta Directiva de la Sociedad Mutualista "Fraternal Hidalgo,"* in *El Constitucional*, 17 March 1910, and 30 January 1910.

chez Azcona printed an open letter to Madero in May 1909 in which he suggested that *"porfirismo* is currently the most effective force for national unity."[93] Yet when the Reyes movement died, he increasingly came to support the Anti-Reelectionists.

As an Anti-Reelectionist, his position on the labor question became less conservative than it had been as a *reyista*. For example, *México Nuevo* was more critical of Governor Landa y Escandón's paternalistic labor policies than it had been previously. At about the same time, *México Nuevo* gave considerable publicity to Andrés Molina Enríquez's *Los grandes problemas nacionales*, one of the very few of the numerous books and pamphlets appearing during those months that showed any depth and perception of social issues, including the labor question. By June of 1910 *México Nuevo* was even more critical of the regime's labor policies; an article by Cosío Robelo implied that Díaz had sided with the "plutocrats" against the workers and that the capitalists were enslaving the workers with their company stores. Its stand on strikes had changed considerably since November 1909, when it had opposed the use of the strike and suggested a paternalistic relationship between the workers and their employers.[94] Workers frequently wrote letters to the editor on political as well as job-related matters, and as events soon revealed, they considered the paper their major public spokesman.

In the two weeks following the huge 29 May Anti-Reelectionist rally in Mexico City, the workers' enthusiasm for the Madero campaign reached its peak. Three new worker Anti-Reelectionist clubs were formed among workers of the Federal District. One particular incident illustrates the involvement of Mexican workers in the Madero movement. In conjunction with the 29 May rally, Madero supporters posted broadsides around the city that promised wage increases if Madero were elected president. *El Imparcial* criticized the promise, arguing that wages could only be increased by increasing productivity, not through governmental intervention. In a series of articles, the

93. Díaz to Reyes, 6 June 1905, AGBR, "Correspondencia del Sr. Presidente, 1903–1909"; Sánchez Azcona to Díaz, 26 November 1905, GPDC, 30:14537; *México Nuevo*, 31 May 1909.

94. *México Nuevo*, 21, 22 February 1910; ibid., 8, 14 January 1910; see "Leonidades," 30 May 1910, "Pipila II," 2 June 1910, and Cosío Robelo's article, 2 June 1910; ibid., 2, 5, 7 November 1909.

semiofficial daily elaborated the advantages accruing to Mexico's workers because of the president's economic policies. Obviously designed to boost the administration's poor image among the Republic's *obreros*, the ploy backfired. Workers throughout central Mexico swamped *México Nuevo* with indignant letters, angrily condemning *El Imparcial* and decrying the "advantages" enjoyed by the workers. "I believe that those who have prospered most are the foreigners," wrote T. A. Oliveros, closing his letter with a plea for labor laws to protect the worker. One letter, signed by almost three hundred Federal District workers, doubted seriously that *El Imparcial* was the friend of the worker and angrily asked "Don't they [*El Imparcial*] understand that they have vilified our character?"[95]

The fury had not yet abated when *México Nuevo* was closed down by court order, charged with criminal libel. The response to *El Imparcial's* articles by the workers was simply one manifestation of the danger that the regime perceived in the Anti-Reelectionist movement. Juan Sánchez Azcona eventually was forced to join Madero in exile in the United States in attempting to bring down a regime that once they had tried to reform.[96] Efforts of the government to repress the movement simply drove it into open revolt.

During most of 1909, the Anti-Reelectionist movement appeared insignificant to the regime and was therefore relatively unharassed by the authorities. The exception was in Orizaba, where the *jefe político* feared the effect of the movement on the workers. The officers of the local clubs were under constant surveillance, and some were fired from their jobs. During Madero's spring campaign tour through the western and northern states, however, the general harassment of the movement increased. By June 1910 it was widespread and particularly oppressive against Madero's working-class followers.[97]

95. González Navarro, *La vida social*, p. 284; Oliveros, *México Nuevo*, 4 June 1910; workers from the *Palacio de Hierro*, the *Casa Pellandini*, the *Casa Mosler*, and San Antonio Abad to *México Nuevo*, 10 June 1910. Except for the last named, all were large, foreign-owned retail establishments.

96. *El Constitucional*, 15 June 1910. Sánchez Azcona pursued an active political and journalistic career until his death in 1938. He was a *carrancista* and remained an adamant antireelectionist, fighting Gen. Álvaro Obregón's reelection in 1928.

97. Ross, *Madero*, pp. 80–94; *El Paladín*, 11, 29 July 1909; Dr. Carlos

In Orizaba several leaders were arrested, and *rurales* were put on guard at the entrances of the Río Blanco mill during the hours when the workers were entering or leaving work to prevent their receiving "subversive literature." Striking workers at the Metepec mill shouted "vivas" for Madero, and immediately thirty were arrested. Sixteen were eventually consigned to the military. Madero protested to Díaz about the persecution of his working-class supporters, particularly in Puebla, Atlixco, Tlaxcala, and Cananea. He noted that the majority of the directors of the Anti-Reelectionist clubs in Puebla had been imprisoned, and some eighty workers in Atlixco were in jail because of their support of the Anti-Reelectionists.[98]

In May the *jefe político* of Orizaba, Miguel Gómez, refused permission for a rally by Anti-Reelectionist workers of the area, and when from three to five thousand workers gathered anyway, he broke up the demonstration with state *rurales*. The governor of the state, Teodoro Dehesa, kept close tabs on Gómez's policy toward the Anti-Reelectionists and suggested that he allow their demonstrations to take place because they were peaceful elsewhere.[99]

Such obstacles did not prevent Anti-Reelectionist sentiment from taking hold among the mill hands and factory workers. It only increased their frustration and determination. Madero warned Díaz that the persecution of the workers was only driving them toward violence, especially in Puebla, Atlixco, and Tlaxcala. The workers from the mills of Metepec and El León were more direct, calling on Díaz to halt the excesses of Governor Martínez and Macharro, the *jefe político* of Atlixco, or take the blame for the bloody fight that was certain to take place.[100]

Ramírez to Dehesa, 1, 11 June 1909 (telegrams), SHUV, Gob, 1911, 49-C; *jefe político* of Orizaba to Sec. of Gobernación, 15 June 1909, SHUV, Gob, 1911, 49-C.

98. *Jefe político* of Orizaba to Dehesa, 4 March 1910, GPDC, 35:3763 (Gómez sent Díaz copies of his important correspondence with Dehesa); *El Constitucional*, 2 June 1910; Gómez to Díaz, 11 March 1910, GPDC, 35:3758; Aquiles Serdán to editor, *México Nuevo*, 6 February 1910, and Serdán to Madero, 31 May 1910, in *México Nuevo*, 2 June 1910; Madero to Díaz, 26 May 1910, GPDC, 35:7738.

99. *Jefe político* to Dehesa, 8 May 1910, SHUV, Gob, 1911, S/N (40); Dehesa to *jefe político*, 13 May 1910, in ibid.

100. Madero to Díaz, 26 May 1910, GPDC, 35:7738; "Workers of Metepec and El León" to Díaz, 7 June 1910, GPDC, 35:8028.

However, some workers still did not see Díaz as the major oppo-
nent. Most were intensely anti-*científico* or anti-*corralista*, but many still
respected Díaz, remembering his past services to the nation. Pro-
Madero workers from a small shop in the Federal District made this
point when they praised Díaz as "peacemaker and statesman," attacking instead the "parasites who dishonor their Chief and devour the
Nation."[101] These workers believed that Díaz was a prisoner of his
advisors, the *científicos*, that he was misinformed and misguided rather
than being the one responsible for the government's repression or
inattention to the labor problem. "It is certain that you are not
aware of everything that goes on," one railroad worker boldly informed
Díaz, "and only hear what certain elements want you to hear."[102]

Díaz had stood for so long as the respected patriarch of his people
(an identification many workers undoubtedly accepted), that his
legitimacy in the eyes of the workers was still strong enough, even
during the campaign of 1910, to forestall personal attacks against
him. Rather the Porfirian system and its abuses were attacked, while
the legitimacy of Díaz himself was subtly preserved until after June
1910, when it became no longer possible to maintain such a fiction.

In 1908 a writer for a popular satire magazine probably expressed
how many workers felt toward the old *Caudillo*, when in epitaph form
he wrote:

Let passion be stilled! History
    will judge hard and true,
    and it will say that his name
    was Peace, Progress, and Victory;
    his work was not transitory,
    because as a statesman and warrior
    he put his homeland on course,
    and he made it great;
    but the Great Man died because
    of his love for the foreigner.[103]

101. "Workers from a small shop" to *México Nuevo*, 1 June 1910.
102. J. Trinidad Nav(indistinct) to Díaz, 10 March 1910, GPDC, 35:4058.
See also *México Nuevo*, 4 December 1909.
103. *El Diablito Rojo*, 2 October 1908.

The *Partido Liberal Mexicano* and Industrial Workers, 1909–1910

While the Anti-Reelectionists were winding their way slowly toward defeat and, eventually, revolt, their rivals on the left—the Mexican Liberal Party—appear to have been divided on what should be their relationship with the Madero movement. Samuel A. Ramírez shifted his allegiance to the Anti-Reelectionists, becoming their major organizer in the Orizaba area. On the other hand, Hilario C. Salas, PLM leader in the abortive 1906 revolts in Veracruz, was critical of Ramírez's activities, suggesting instead that the PLM should only conditionally support the Anti-Reelectionists' political efforts, contingent on their recognition of the PLM's July Program and their willingness to officially note the legitimacy of the PLM's own efforts against the regime. Salas doubted that Díaz would step down legally but saw the tactical advantage which would accrue to the PLM's revolutionary cause (as he saw it, the overthrow of the dictatorship) if Díaz were forced to repress the Anti-Reelectionist movement. Meanwhile Salas spent some time in Atlixco among the textile workers, and from there traveled to Puebla, Tlaxcala, and Veracruz in the spring of 1910, apparently attempting to encourage workers to revolt.[104]

Yet the textile workers in those areas appeared to have been solidly Anti-Reelectionist, not *magonistas*. Certainly they were not anarchist or socialist in any variety that would have been recognizable in Europe or the United States. The failure of the PLM to achieve any significant advantage from the workers' frustrations after 1908 needs to be analyzed.

First, after the failure of the 1908 revolts not only were many Liberals jailed, or driven out of the country, but those already in U.S. jails—including their most important leaders, Ricardo Flores Magón, Antonio Villarreal, Juan Sarabia, and Librado Rivera—were rendered incommunicado. Despite James Cockcroft's assertion that the remaining Liberals maintained an effective propaganda output to the workers through the PLM's organs, there is no indication that the

104. Salas to Ramón A. Sánchez (C. D. Padua), 7 July 1909, Atlixco, and 12 July 1909, in C. D. Padua, *El movimiento revolucionario de 1906 en Veracruz* (Mexico: n.p., 1936), pp. 34–36, 40–41.

Mexican worker received this material. *Reforma, Libertad y Justicia* was published only from June to September 1908 while *Revolución*, which replaced *Regeneración* in June 1907, was not being printed by mid-1909 and perhaps earlier. Praxedis G. Guerrero's anarchist weekly, *Punto Rojo*, was aimed at radicalizing Mexican workers but lasted only eight months, from August 1909 to March 1910. There were others but none was published for very long, or reached very far into Mexico.[105]

Furthermore, the PLM material which reached the workers in the central industrial areas seemed to have maintained the same progressive, but not radical, stance of the July 1906 program. A PLM flyer "Contra El Despotismo Mexicana," which circulated among the textile workers in May 1909, emphasized the July program. Members of the Orizaba Anti-Reelectionist club were arrested in June 1910 for reading PLM material to the workers, apparently also from the 1906 program. The material was certainly progressive and subversive; that is, it advocated revolution against the regime, but it did not contribute to the kind of atmosphere envisioned by Professor Cockcroft which would have given rise to a class-based revolutionary movement threatening Madero.[106] The workers were generally pro-Madero and propaganda from the PLM's 1906 program would hardly have changed this.

One explanation of the inability of the PLM to attract more workers, even as their disillusionment with the Díaz regime is shown by their support of Madero, might be that most PLM members and sympathizers in Mexico were not committed to a radical solution to the labor problem, but rather were simply progressive liberals, willing to use force to overthrow a dictatorship. This appears to have been the case of Samuel A. Ramírez, Dr. Carlos Ramírez, and Gabriel Gavira, all PLM supporters in earlier years who now headed up the Anti-Reelectionists in Orizaba. Even Salas, who never gave up in his belief that Díaz would have to be overthrown by force of arms, did not

105. Cockcroft, *Intellectual Precursors*, p. 153–55.

106. Gómez to Díaz, 11 June 1910, GPDC, 81:1644; Gómez to Díaz, 9 June 1910, GPDC, 81:1550; Ortega to Díaz, 28 January 1910, GPDC, 35:1299; Ortega to Díaz, 6 February 1910, GPDC, 35:1766. Sent to military prison in Veracruz were Ramírez, Gavira, Francisco Camarillo, and Ángel S. Juarico; see Gen. Maass to Díaz, 16 June 1910, GPDC, 35:7642. For flyer, see GPDC, 34:8880. Cockcroft, *Intellectual Precursors*, p. 156.

indicate any belief in social reorganization other than through reform. When the PLM floundered as an active revolutionary conspiracy after the failure of the 1908 revolts, the Anti-Reelectionists may have offered to a number of liberals the only significant, active movement opposing the regime of Porfirio Díaz.

Professor Raymond Buve offers a different explanation. His position is that although the PLM exercised considerable influence among workers and *campesino* groups in central Mexico, many PLM supporters joined the Madero cause in 1909 and 1910 for tactical or logistical reasons, just as Salas appeared to advise. The effect, according to Buve, was to confuse the ideological issues and moderate the goals of many PLM groups.[107]

The Liberal leadership issued a significant communication to its field staff just prior to the Madero revolt in November 1910. Recently released from an American prison, Ricardo Flores Magón acknowledged that many PLM members had allied themselves with the *maderistas*, thinking that was the wishes of the PLM's *Junta*. Instead the members were advised that while Madero's program was merely political, the PLM's was economic as well — that is, that the PLM advocated returning land stolen from the villagers, higher wages for workers and less working hours, and a reduced influence of the Church.[108] None of those goals were radical in the context of their times, and nothing was said to indicate that more radical programs separated themselves from the *maderistas*. Likely the *Junta* intended not to reveal their more radical orientation, not only because they themselves were divided on fundamental issues of policy but because they were not sure their rank and file activists *were* as radical as the *Junta* would have wished.

Several small PLM bands did in fact take the field in open revolt against the regime independent of the *maderistas*. Most members and sympathizers might have agreed, however, with one party member who rebuked the PLM-affiliated *Alba* for attacking Madero, maintaining that "Dr. F. I. Madero is the popular candidate of the nation . . . and as sincere liberals of principle we are not able to do more than to be satisfied with the worthy candidates presented to the

107. Buve, "Protesta de obreros," pp. 13–15.
108. Padua, *Movimiento revolucionario*, pp. 84–85.

nation by the Anti-Reelectionist Party, which is as liberal as ourselves."[109]

Whatever the case, by June of 1910 the regime was hardly making
any distinction between PLM revolutionaries and Madero's Anti-
Reelectionists. In mid-June the regime moved against the Anti-
Reelectionist leadership. On 14 June 1910 Madero was arrested, and
in the days that followed many Anti-Reelectionists joined him in
prison, or if they were not as lucky, in the pestilence-ridden cells of
Belem or San Juan de Ulúa or in military service in Quintana Roo.
Among those arrested were leaders of workers' clubs in Orizaba and
Cananea.[110]

Primary elections were held on 21 June and the secondary elections
early in July, both with the same results. Díaz and Corral were overwhelmingly reelected, aided by electoral fraud and the fact that a
great number of Madero supporters were unable to vote due to their
imprisonment or their flight to avoid prosecution. Formal protests of
election irregularities, including a petition from two hundred workers
at the Santa Rosa mill, achieved nothing. On 12 October the electoral
college officially declared Díaz and Corral reelected. A few days earlier Madero had broken his parole and crossed into the United
States.[111]

Many Mexican workers had chosen to support the Anti-
Reelectionist movement in its efforts to unseat Díaz by constitutional
means. Those efforts failed, further limiting the political options available for the resolution of their problems. One remaining option was
open revolt against the regime.

Díaz and Corral had been reelected for months when in the fall of
1910 rumors began to circulate among workers in Mexico's shops and
factories that Francisco Madero, safe for the moment in San Antonio,
Texas, was preparing to call them to arms. Certainly there were work-

109. Ignacio J. Mendiola to M. L. Escamilla, 10 May 1910, Brownsville,
U.S., in Gen. Villar to Díaz, 31 May 1910, Matamoros, GPDC, 35:7911. See
Alba, 3 April 1910, in GPDC, 35:4719.

110. *México Nuevo*, 2, 12 June 1910; *El Paladín*, 30 June 1910; *El Constitucional*, 5 July 1910; Gavira, *Su actuación político*, p. 21.

111. Cosío Villegas, *La vida política interior*, 2:893; *El Constitucional*, 3 July
1910; Ross, *Madero*, p. 111.

ers who must have felt that there was no recourse left but to break the peace that had become nothing but a guise for tyranny. Even then the workers had already heard there were *guerrilleros* in the backcountry of half a dozen states, although the official press called them bandits when they mentioned them at all.

Yet one cannot easily say how many factory workers, artisans, miners, or railroad hands were willing to take to the hills too, even when called to do so by Madero. Workers undoubtedly noticed the federal infantry units moving quietly into the industrial towns to reinforce the garrisons there. It was not likely that workers would face those troops again with only stones in their hands. And how could men who were barely able to feed their families find the money to buy weapons and ammunition? How many had a horse to take to the hills, much less a weapon with which to fight? Even with the weapons and the means to leave, how many workers could forget those dependent upon them to provide the food for the table? Those were hard questions, and many who might have wanted to go immediately when the insurgent standards were raised were not able or free to do so.

Nevertheless, some men in the fall and winter of 1910–1911 muttered hard things when they were safely past the arrogant *rurales* posted at the factory entrances. And a few workers would have had a horse or perhaps even a rifle, for many men still had ties with the land; a good horse and a rifle were valued possessions in the rural culture to which they belonged. A few then would have had the means to take to the hills in search of Juan Cuamatzi's band of ex-farmers and mill hands operating somewhere near the Puebla-Tlaxcalan border, or Gabriel Gavira's men near Jalapa, or any of the *jefes* whose names became known as revolt spread in late 1910 and on into 1911.

Whether the workers would fight, therefore, depended on many factors. But of those influences and circumstances, one was certain— few workers by the fall of 1910 had any hope left that Don Porfirio would help them achieve the justice they demanded. And likely even fewer had any affection for the old man they once respected. "Mula sin rabo," some workers had called him to his face, hurling other obscenities that a man would use only in a cold fury, ready to kill or be killed.[112] Whether they would or not was decided in the next few months.

112. "Un grupo de obreros" to Díaz, 11 July 1910, Puebla, GPDC, 35:10463.

Chapter 7
Mexican Workers and the Revolution of 1910

"... *a state of unrest exists in this Zone among the working mass.*"
—Miguel Gómez, *jefe político* of Orizaba, to Porfirio Díaz, in a telegram dated 27 July 1910.

Mexicans chose 20 November 1910 as the date marking the beginning of the Mexican Revolution, for that was the day which Francisco Madero set for his insurrection against the Díaz government. Men looking backward from later points in time have often found the Madero revolt an easy matter, one that quickly toppled a regime whose strength was largely illusionary. But the rebels themselves launched their revolt against no illusion. The Porfirian regime looked immensely strong to men of that day, on both sides, and only the very desperate or foolish, or brave, dared test its strength.

Thirty-five years of Porfirian rule had created the strongest central government in Mexico's history, from the rebels' perspective, one whose strength had been demonstrated all too clearly in bloody repressions of dissidents from Mayans to *magonistas*. They were well aware that the military was trained in the most advanced European tactics and equipped with modern weapons. Few had any special knowledge of its very real inadequacies. They were also aware that the government's railroad system could bring troop trains to even the most remote regions within hours after receiving word of an uprising. The rebels could not know that they were to be among the first men of the twentieth century to fight what would become a common pattern—an insurgent warfare of small, mobile bands successfully contesting a far larger, conventional military establishment. They only knew that the regime was strong. The confidence they may have felt was in their cause, but of their chances, "Quién sabe?" who could tell? As with most such movements, they began in darkness, with no certainty of victory, nor a clear view of the future.

As it turned out, the regime was not as strong as it appeared. The officer corps was generally competent but characterized by the same divisions that were in the society at large. The rank and file were often conscripted country people or convicted criminals, with little loyalty to the Porfirian system or to their officers. Yet whatever the condition of the military, the regime fell because it no longer commanded the support of the people themselves.

Of the elites of power and position who should have formed the bulwark of the regime, some were divided into bitter political factions, while many others found their economic interests threatened by the credit squeeze and general recession after 1907. More than a few wealthy Mexicans blamed their economic woes on the regime, casting particular guilt on the *científicos'* commercial policy. At a time when the government of Porfirio Díaz needed support from those who had benefited most from his rule, their neutrality or alienation was a hard blow.

The emerging middle-class groups owed their growth to the progress of the *Porfiriato*, but many had grievances with the system. Some chafed under the monopolization of power and status by new and old elites, whether local *caciques* or the few prominent families who often dominated individual states. Nearly all were hurt by the mounting inflation after 1900, and not a few felt humiliated by the predominance of foreigners in Mexico.

For the rural and urban popular classes, Porfirian progress had created a few opportunities, but mostly they were forced to pay a price for that progress, whether in material wellbeing or social disorientation. Of those men, most would have welcomed the fall of the regime, and some, indeed, were willing to take up arms against it. If most were not willing or able to risk their lives, their silent opposition to the regime counted for something because of their sheer numbers.

All those groups had some grievance with the regime. The promises of political reform explicit in the Creelman interview encouraged the belief that change could be implemented within the system, but the eventual repression of political opposition closed this avenue for redress of grievances and created a dangerous level of frustration among those groups most estranged from the regime. When revolution came, many were sympathetic to the call, and many others were indifferent to the fate of the regime the rebels sought to destroy.

The First Revolts

The first *maderista* revolt occurred six months before the actual call to arms, when in late May 1910, as Madero's Federal District supporters were preparing for the huge Anti-Reelectionist rally to be held at the end of the month, a small band of men attacked the Tlaxcalan *municipio* of San Bernardino Contla. The band, which included workers from Puebla and Tlaxcala mills, was led by Tlaxcalan Anti-Reelectionists Juan Cuamatzi, Marcos Hernández Xolocotzi, and Antonio Hidalgo, former leader of the Tlaxcalan textile workers during the conflicts in 1906. Numbering less than fifty ill-armed men, the rebels withdrew after the initial attack and dispersed.[1]

The motivation for the attack is obscure. One source maintains that the rebels were acting under orders from the Puebla Anti-Reelectionist Aquiles Serdán and that they called off their revolt when Serdán sent word that the uprisings scheduled for that night had been cancelled.[2] A second possibility is that the rebels were Anti-Reelectionists with PLM sympathies (or for that matter, PLM followers with Anti-Reelectionist sympathies), acting not on orders from Serdán but from H.C. Salas, the PLM's Veracruz chief. Salas had been in Tlaxcala in April and May 1910, attempting to persuade local men to revolt. When he left the state in late May, he wrote to Padua that he hoped to see Tlaxcala in revolt very soon. Exactly where he had been in Tlaxcala, and whom he had seen, he did not say, undoubtedly for reasons of security. Whatever the case I strongly suspect that Salas was involved in some way in the Contla uprising.

On the other hand, the governor of Tlaxcala, Col. Próspero Cahuantzi, believed that the incident was related to the efforts of Metepec workers to instigate rebellion among Tlaxcalan textile hands. According to his information, most of the attackers were workers. He ordered the execution of anyone involved in the uprising as an example to others.[3]

1. Gov. of Tlaxcala to Díaz, 28 May 1910, GPDC, 35:6641; Cuéllar, *Tlaxcala*, pp. 245–48.
2. Cuéllar, *Tlaxcala*, p. 246; see a number of letters from Salas to Padua during April and May in Padua, *Movimiento revolucionario*, pp. 41–42.
3. Gov. of Tlaxcala to Díaz, 28 May 1910, GPDC, 35:6641; Cuéllar, *Tlaxcala*, p. 248.

The discontent at the Metepec mill to which the Tlaxcalan governor referred had begun to escalate early that year. Workers at the mill struck, and unable to reach an agreement with the owners, they petitioned the authorities for land to colonize as farmers; many had come from small rural villages to work in the mill. It is not known when the workers returned to work, but they were denied the lands because the *jefe político* of Atlixco would not give them the required certificate of good conduct.[4]

Angered and frustrated by the refusal of the land, by the continued problems with the mill, and by the local authorities' repression of the Anti-Reelectionist movement, a group of workers began to prepare an attack against the nearby town of Atlixco. Although Atlixco was a well-garrisoned, important provincial town, the workers planned to take the army barracks and the *rurales'* post by surprise, offsetting their inferior weapons and scarce ammunition. Yet something about the whole idea was unreal, a valiant fantasy of desperate men. When the local political authorities received word of the uprising, they described it as "absurd," but as a precautionary measure they arrested all those they could find having any connection with it. Five of the leaders fled and were captured in Apizaco, Tlaxcala. Arms, ammunition, and explosives were recovered from the rebels.[5]

The incident created further trouble for the authorities when a rumor spread through the mill that the five men captured in Apizaco had been executed. Emotions ran high, and Governor Martínez felt compelled to inform Díaz that no one had been executed. The governor enclosed in his letter to Díaz several samples of obscene and threatening letters he had been receiving regularly from the workers because of the rumored executions.[6] After all the years of hostility and frustration, the mill hands of Metepec were on the verge of taking matters into their own hands.

4. *El Paladín*, 3, 6 February 1910; Emilio Vázquez to Díaz, 17 March 1910, GPDC, 35:3067 and 20 April 1910, GPDC, 35:4723; *México Nuevo*, 22, 29 April 1910.

5. Gov. of Puebla to Díaz, 3 June 1910, GPDC, 35:7719. There is no evidence connecting Salas with the unrest at the Metepec mill, but I suspect that such a connection is possible; see Salas to Ramón A. Sánchez (Padua), 12 July 1909, Atlixco, in Padua, *Movimiento revolucionario*, p. 36.

6. Gov. of Puebla to Díaz, 10 June 1910, GPDC, 35:7674.

In the early days of June, a number of the leaders of the Orizaba Anti-Reelectionist group were arrested on charges of fomenting rebellion in the mills.[7] Whether or not they were planning armed revolt, their arrests, along with the general harassment of the Anti-Reelectionist workers, increased the discontent among Gómez's sixteen thousand workers.

The environment of unrest throughout Mexico was affected by other events—the arrest of Madero and the imprisonment of many of his followers, the execution of the Sinaloan Anti-Reelectionist Gabriel Leyva, the bloodily repressed uprising at Valladolid in Yucatán, and the activities of the PLM *guerrillero* "Santanon" (Santa Ana Rodríquez) in Veracruz. In the north, rumors were spreading that Mexicans were buying large amounts of munitions on the American side of the border.[8] Nevertheless, by most appearances, the old *Caudillo* seemed firmly in control.

But a few disagreed, and their numbers were growing. Among them one must count José Guadalupe Posada. His cartoons, drawn mainly for the small circulation weeklies, had always been directed at the inequities in Mexican society, but during those months between Madero's arrest in June and the call to revolution in November, Posada's drawings began to incorporate harsher, more angry images of political and social injustice.

Posada published a cartoon in *El Diablito Rojo* in late June contrasting elections in the United States and Mexico. In the former they were fair and orderly, while in the Mexican elections, a man representing the Mexican people was getting a kick in the pants. In July another cartoon appeared in *El Diablito Rojo* on the election theme, this time showing a representation of democratic elections being carried for burial in a coffin. The various political factions were shown as children playing around the coffin without understanding the significance of what had happened.[9]

Then in August he began to get even tougher. One cartoon shows

7. *Jefe político* to Díaz, 9 June 1910, GPDC, 69:1550; ibid., 11 June 1910, GPDC, 69:1644.

8. Ross, *Madero*, pp. 107–8; John Foster to Col. Emilio Kosterlitsky, 14 June 1910, Bisbee, Arizona, GPDC, 35:10631.

9. 27 June, 25 July 1910.

José Guadalupe Posada drawing in El Diablito Rojo, 2 *November 1910.*
With permission of the Fondo Editorial de la Plástica Mexicana.

Díaz washing his hands in imitation of Pontius Pilate. In front of him
stands a condemned *campesino*, or in Posada's meaning, the Mexican
people. The caption read, "Comes the virile soldiery, and all are
united that once were journalists and today announce to the entire
country that now we are *guerrilleros*. Death to the *caciques! Mueran!*" [10]

At some point in the late summer or early fall, death symbols began
to appear in Posada's political drawings—they no longer can be called
cartoons. They were usually skeletons, dressed as if alive, with empty
skulls staring blankly out from under top hats and parasols, and they
remained associated with his work until his death in 1913. He had
used such symbols before, but eventually he became obsessed with
them. One cannot see them without being struck by their power. On 2
November, *Todos Santos* day, traditionally a holiday when skulls are
commonly displayed as bread and candy, *El Diablito Rojo* carried a full
page Posada drawing in which the devil is filling a huge pot with
skeletons, all well-dressed men and women with fashionable attire and

10. *El Diablito Rojo*, 8 August 1910.

top hats. The message was unmistakable even if the symbolism was obscure—something was wrong with Mexican society, and the resolution of what was wrong would require strong action.[11]

On the surface, July was a quiet month for Mexico's industrial workers. Worried reports arrived at the National Palace, however, indicating that the Anti-Reelectionist agitators were stirring up the workers of Orizaba and Puebla and telling of rumors that arms were being secretly stored in working-class *barrios* in preparation for an uprising *en masse*. Miguel Gómez refused Díaz's offer of additional troops for Orizaba but noted uneasily that a "state of unrest exists in this Zone among the working mass."[12] Governor Mucio Martínez of Puebla also reported those rumors and included the disturbing intelligence that "unfortunately" selective detention of workers in his state had confirmed the reports, although not in detail. He himself, however, refused to give credence to the story that Aquiles Serdán was distributing arms among the workers but promised that the Puebla Anti-Reelectionist would be kept under constant surveillance.[13]

In Orizaba an uneasy calm continued on into August with no abating of persistent rumors that workers in the nearby company towns would soon rise in revolt. Only the arrest of Enrique Bordes Mangel, however, provided any reason for Gómez to write to Díaz. Bordes had accompanied Madero on his trips to Veracruz and, so the authorities charged, had pronounced subversive discourses against the government. In addition, he continued to meet secretly with workers from Río Blanco and Santa Rosa, presumably for seditious purposes. Unfortunately Gómez was unable to provide any concrete evidence against him, causing Díaz to suggest, rather caustically, that if Gómez could not prove the charges against the prisoner "by any means," then the *jefe político* had the option of ordering him out of the area.[14] Whether Gómez took the hint is not known.

From the regime's standpoint, September should have been a

11. 2 November 1910.

12. Gómez to Díaz, 22, 23, 27 July 1910, GPDC, 35:9042, 9502 and GPDC, 69:2599; Díaz to Gómez, 25 July 1910, GPDC, 69:2600.

13. Martínez to Díaz, 25 July 1910, GPDC, 35:9317.

14. Gómez to Díaz, 8, 10 August 1910, GPDC, 69:2838, 2885; Díaz to Gómez, 9, 11 August 1910, GPDC, 69:2838, 2886.

month of patriotism when all Mexicans put aside their differences and celebrated the centennial of the *Grito de Dolores*—Padre Hidalgo's call to arms that began the struggle for Mexican independence from Spain. Commemorations were held in nearly every city and village in the Republic. In Mexico City representatives from all the important nations of the world came to honor the grim, dignified old man who had brought Mexico into the twentieth century, well on her way to becoming a modern, progressive nation. The Empress of China, soon to be removed from the throne by another great nationalist revolution, sent her representatives and a fine Ming Dynasty vase as a gift to the Republic. Spain sent the prince regent, don Carlos and his beautiful wife, who captivated the crowds lining the streets to view the famed royal couple. The mother country even returned to Mexico the sword and uniform of José Morelos, great hero of the war for independence, who had died before a Spanish firing squad.[15] Porfirio Díaz received them with tears in his eyes. He cried often now, people said, especially at times like these, when honoring the liberal *guerrilleros* he had outlived.

Yet the finely orchestrated pageantry could not quite hide the tones of anger and disgust that were heard when talk turned to the men who ruled the nation now. Dr. Frederick Starr, president of the University of Chicago and something of a scholar on Mexico, spent nearly a month wandering through the centennial crowds, talking with Mexicans from every class, and he encountered not one word of praise, he said, for the eighty-year-old man who stood for hours on the main balcony of the National Palace to review the marchers and the honor guards sent from foreign armies. "He surrounds himself with bad ministers," was the kindest comment he could obtain from his casual questions.[16] Alfredo Navarrete remembered it more bitterly. A "mundo doble," he called the celebrations, a two-faced or two-sided world, where misery existed side by side with the riches of a wealthy elite, displayed without reserve in the privileged boxes which lined the parade routes. Navarrete could attend the centennial celebrations and the parades, for he wore shoes and a presentable suit of clothes, not

15. See Casasola, *Historia gráfica*, 1:172–209, for excellent photographs of the centennial festivities.

16. Frederick Starr, *Mexico and the United States*, (Chicago: The Bible House, 1914), p. 290.

like the *patas rajadas*, as those without shoes were called, or the beggars that the Porfirian police kept out of downtown Mexico City; but he was not permitted to enter the forested grounds of Chapultepec Castle, for they were open only to the "gente decente."[17]

Looking back, one is struck by the colossal irony of the centennial—a celebration of pomp and ceremony, resplendent with visiting dignitaries in formal dress and their magnificently outfitted wives and ordered rows of uniformed soldiers and silver-studded *rurales* on prancing horses, all honoring Hidalgo's ragged troops of Indians and mestizos. Hidalgo had once threatened *gachupín* and creole society alike, yet their heirs and imitators still held sway, and Hidalgo's people waited for the rewards they had been promised. But now in many provincial villages and industrial towns there were some who would wait not much longer.

So Mexico was not a nation at peace with itself in September of 1910, and although there were still few *guerrilleros* in the hills, rumors of rebellion could be heard on any street corner. Public officials charged with maintaining order during the celebrations were apprehensive, for many of the most disgruntled citizens were the very workers scheduled to take part in the festivities. Earlier in the month, Miguel Gómez had nervously reported to his governor the rumor that the Orizaba workers were going to sabotage the city's electrical plant, cut the telegraph wires, loot the stores, and assassinate the public officials as their contribution to the centennial. Much to the *jefe político's* relief, however, the local festivities passed without incident, and he was able to note in his report to Díaz that "not a single disrespectful shout left the lips of the fifteen thousand people who waited to respond to my call for the independence cheer."[18] Elsewhere, Mexican workers were not as cooperative. In Puebla, on the night of the fifteenth, a large number of workers interrupted the celebrations with shouts of "Viva Madero" and "Muera Díaz." Over sixty were arrested, and thirty-six were ultimately assigned to military service in Quintana Roo.[19]

The following day an estimated one thousand men from the states

17. Navarrete, *Alto*, p. 34–35.
18. Gómez to Díaz, 19 September 1910, GPDC, 35:14434; Gómez to Dehesa in cover letter Dehesa to Díaz, 4 September 1910, GPDC, 69:3284; Díaz to Gómez, 5 September 1910, GPDC, 69:3284.

of Puebla, Tlaxcala, and Veracruz met at the town of Zacatelco, Tlax-cala, to celebrate the centennial. Much to the consternation of local authorities, many of the standards carried by the participants were openly seditious. "To die at the feet of Democracy," read one, while another even more directly proclaimed "Effective Suffrage." After listening to praises for the heroes of independence and condemna-tions of the regime, the crowd started for Atlixco on what was a peaceful if aggressive demonstration demanding their political rights. They were intercepted by Tlaxcalan state forces in the town of Santo Toribio and forcefully dispersed. Five persons were killed and fifty prisoners taken. An attempt was made that evening to free the pris-oners, but it failed and four more men died.[20]

That same month the PLM's *Regeneración* reappeared, after over four years of absence, calling on the Mexican workers to fight not simply to restore the political liberty of the Constitution of 1857 but to demand economic freedom as well, the right to share in the fruit of their production.[21] How much of *Regeneración*'s message got through to Mexican industrial workers is not known, but by then most workers were *maderistas*.

Following the September disturbances came reports in October of Tlaxcalan workers arming for revolt. In Orizaba, Gómez reported that an uprising was also being planned by the workers' associations and included people "from the outside."[22] October was important for one more reason: Madero escaped his house confinement and fled to the United States.

The Call to Arms

From his headquarters in San Antonio, Texas, in early November, Madero called upon the Mexican people to rise against the govern-

19. Martínez to Díaz, 23 September 1910, GPDC, 35:13123; unidentified writer to Díaz, 18 September 1910, GPDC, 35:13759.
20. Cuéller, *Tlaxcala*, pp. 249–50; Gov. of Tlaxcala to Díaz, 17, 21 September 1910, GPDC, 69:3539, and GPDC, 35:12955.
21. See *Regeneración*, 3, 10 September 1910; GPDC, 35:3333, 3338.
22. Gov. of Tlaxcala to Díaz, 13 October 1910, GPDC, 69:3923; Gómez to Díaz, 20 October 1910, GPDC, 35:15671.

ment of Porfirio Díaz. The call to arms was contained in his *Plan de San Luis Potosí*, a document which sought to justify the revolution because of the Díaz regime's abuse of the constitution, leaving no legal alternative for the expression of the political rights of the Mexican people. The uprising was to take place in the evening of 20 November, from six o'clock onward.[23] As various revolutionary leaders and their couriers were making their way southward to carry word of the revolt to their followers, an event took place which underlined the *inqueitud* of the times.

Antonio Rodríguez, a twenty year old Mexican, was killed by a mob in Rock Springs, Texas, on 3 November. Rodríguez was accused of murdering a rancher's wife and was awaiting trial in the Rock Springs jail when he was taken from his cell by an angry crowd of Rock Springs citizens, tied to a stake, and burned alive. The murder of Rodríguez touched off demonstrations and riots throughout Mexico, lasting nearly a week. In Mexico City the offices of the American-owned daily, *The Mexican Herald*, was demolished by a group of students, and in the days that followed American businesses were attacked in Guadalajara, Morelia, Oaxaca, San Luis Potosí, Tlaxcala, and other towns and cities of the Republic. Although the violence appears mainly to have been by students, other Mexicans, including workers, joined in the protests. Among them were employees of the Federal Telegraph Office in San Luis Potosí, railroadmen on various lines, workers in Aguascalientes, and the *Confederación del Trabajo* of the state of Yucatán.[24]

The protests and disturbances took on political overtones because inevitably from among the demonstrators would come cries of "Viva Madero." Even the offices of *El Imparcial* were attacked, presumably because it was the unofficial spokesman for the regime. The brutal death of a Mexican at the hands of foreigners was too closely related to domestic issues, and too close in time to political unrest to avoid the catalystic role that it played. Although the Mexican government ordered its Washington representatives to officially protest the incident, this action had little effect in quieting public outcry. When the local authorities used force to repress the violence and demonstrations,

23. Taracena, *La verdadera revolución*, pp. 306–12.

24. Ibid., p. 313–19; Manuel Ma. Escoffie, president of the *Confederación del Trabajo* to Díaz, 15 November 1910, GPDC, 35:17028.

various people were killed or injured, hardly helping the government's image.[25] As with Río Blanco and Cananea, the government of Porfirio Díaz appeared on the wrong side of popular opinion, and at the worse possible time for its own survival.

As 20 November neared, the government began to make preparations to crush the rumored revolt. Being well informed about many of the local revolutionaries, authorities arrested dozens of *maderistas* before they could answer their chief's call to arms. Federal troops were put on the alert in industrial centers throughout the Republic because of the rumors of worker uprisings. An informer had warned Díaz that workers from the Cocolapán and Cerritos mills in Orizaba would attack the barracks of the 15th Battalion on the night of the twentieth, "because Sr. Madero ordered them to," and federal troops were duly alerted. Governor Dehesa requested a small detachment for the state capital, Jalapa, because of the four textile mills there.[26]

A group of workers and townspeople numbering under two hundred men attacked the barracks of the 15th Battalion in Orizaba on the evening of the twentieth, as had been foretold. A band of fifty rebels came down from the hills out of the direction of Puebla-Tlaxcala but arrived too late to join the attack, because the first assault had already been driven back. No casualties were reported. One investigator told Díaz that although the officer in charge of the 15th Batallion reported a prolonged exchange of gunfire, he could find only one bullet hole in the side of the building where the attack supposedly took place. There was also an attack on the jail that same night, but again the investigator played it down, blaming it on workers attempting to release a drunken companion. Evidently the rebels were poorly armed, and the dynamite bombs they used failed to explode. At some point, perhaps later, the workers circulated leaflets among the soldiers stationed in Orizaba, asking them to defect to the revolution or at least not to fire on their brothers.[27]

25. Taracena, *La verdadera revolución*, pp. 313–19.

26. Ross, *Madero*, pp. 120–21; Vicente F. Sánchez to Díaz, 15 November 1910, GPDC, 35:16958; Dehesa to Díaz, 18 November 1910, GPDC, 69:4530.

27. *Jefe político* to Governor, 20 November 1910, SHUV, Gob, 1910, 46–R; *jefe político* to Gov., 21 November 1910, SHUV, Gob, 1910, 46–R; *jefe político* to Díaz, 22 November 1910, GPDC, 35:17210; Dehesa to Díaz, n.d., GPDC, 69:4632. Taracena reports that Juan Cuamatzi led fifty Tlaxcalan workers to

Leadership of the Orizaba workers' attempt at insurrection is usually attributed to Rafael Tapia, owner of a saddle and harness shop in town, and Gabriel Gavira, cabinet maker, who had been arrested and jailed in June for his activities as an officer of the Orizaba Anti-Reelectionist group. How Gavira left prison is not known. In addition, official reports listed a shoemaker and a Santa Rosa merchant as important accomplices. Gavira's house was searched immediately prior to the uprising, and several boxes of dynamite were found, but he had fled. Later, dynamite bombs were discovered near the home of Joaquín Oriza. His story was that Tapia had appeared early in the morning of 21 November, saying that everything was lost and telling Oriza to expect some boxes. Later that day Gabriel Gavira brought the boxes.[28]

In September Gómez had complained to Díaz about Rafael Tapia's agitation among the workers, but Dehesa personally vouched for Tapia, wiring Díaz that he was not a revolutionary, as he had been pictured, but a man of character and "sound" ideas. Tapia escaped from Orizaba and led a group of rebels in Veracruz until the fall of the regime.[29] Gabriel Gavira went on to become an important figure in the Revolution, accepting the governorship of San Luis Potosí during the Carranza period.

In the excitement of the revolt on 20 November many workers did not appear for work. The mills were kept open, however, and by 23 November all the workers had returned to their posts. That same day three workers were arrested and charged as leaders and participants in the abortive revolt; one had been an officer in the Nogales Anti-Reelectionist club. The Orizaba weekly *La Cosmopolita* ran the head-

---

aid in the Orizaba uprising; perhaps they were the group cited in the official report (Taracena, *La verdadera revolución*, p. 324); Gonzalo Luque, 22 November 1910, GPDC, 69:4826. Gómez to Díaz, 12 December 1910, GPDC, 35:20446.

28. Ross, *Madero*, p. 124; Taracena, *La veradadera revolución*, p. 324; Gavira *Su actuación revolucionaria*, p. 28; *jefe político* to Gov., 20 November 1910, SHUV, Gob, 1910, 46–R; Gómez to Díaz, 2 December 1910, GPDC, 69:5613; 10 December 1910, GPDC, 35:3009.

29. Gómez to Díaz, 19 September 1910, GPDC, 35:14434; Dehesa to Díaz, 23 September 1910, GPDC, 69:3609; Gen. Maass to Díaz, 10 January 1911, GPDC, 36:714; Gómez to Díaz, 21 January 1911, GPDC, 36:158; Gen. Maass to Díaz, 28 April 1911, GPDC, 36:6340.

line several days later, "Revolution Is Impossible in Mexico" and for some, it still must have appeared true.[30]

Several days before the Río Blanco revolt, Aquiles Serdán initiated an uprising in the city of Puebla. Aided only by his family and a few supporters, Serdán fought off Puebla police and *rurales* all day on 18 November. He had expected his followers to revolt in other parts of the city, but none did. Eventually, Serdán and nearly all his small force were killed. Among Serdán's lieutenants who did not rise that day was Samuel A. Ramírez, former leader of the Orizaba GCOL and currently at the Metepec mill. Ramírez evidently had the support of workers from various factories and mills, but with few arms and under close surveillance by suspicious local authorities, he was unable to aid Serdán.[31]

The death of Serdán and his followers gave the rebellion of Madero its first martyrs. The famous *zapatista* troubadour Marciano Silva sang these words: "Sons of Puebla, offer . . . homage on your knees to the workers and the students, who as glorious heroes fell with Serdán."[32]

On the surface, the regime seemed to have stood off rather easily these first attempts at revolt. The American ambassador Henry Lane Wilson, however, wrote to the State Department that there were strong feelings against Díaz's advisors, the *científicos*, and "it was only respect and fear of the President which restrains a formidable movement."[33]

Meanwhile, *maderistas* in the north were faring better under the leadership of such men as Pascual Orozco, Francisco Villa, and José de la Luz Blanco. The success of the revolt in the north relates to many factors, but for the purposes of this study the economic situation is the most relevant. The northern economy turned bad after 1906, and the resulting recession put many people out of work. Col. Greene's lumber mills near Madera, Chihuahua, closed down, as did his pulp plant, furniture shop, and lumber yards. The mills, the

30. 27 November 1910; Gómez to Díaz, 23 November 1910, GPDC, 69:4926; Gonzalo Luque to Díaz, 23 November 1910, GPDC, 69:4931. Those captured were Enrique Cipriano, Ventura Enríquez, Miguel Acevedo, and Onofre García.

31. Taracena, *La verdadera revolución*, p. 321; *El País*, 20 November 1910.

32. Cited in Simmons, *The Mexican Corrido*, p. 74.

33. U.S., Dept. of State, *Papers, 1911*, pp. 367–68.

mines, the railroads, the vast cattle ranches—all were letting people go. The fiber mill La Estrella in Parras, Coahuila, was closed down because of the decline in foreign markets and the "tremendous financial crises." Evaristo Madero, the owner, could not even pay his workers the money he owed them, although he noted that he was trying to find them jobs in the countryside.[34] But a succession of three bad harvests had brought financial ruin on many small and medium farmers in the north; even the big spreads were cutting back. The revolutionary chiefs' recruitment of followers was likely favored by the high unemployment resulting from these conditions. Many men simply had nothing to lose.

Pascual Orozco eventually became the head *maderista* general in the north. Operating mainly in Chihuahua, he defeated federal forces at Pedernales on 27 November and captured Ciudad Guerrero on 4 December, the first major victories of *maderista* forces. Later that month, however, Orozco's troops were forced to retreat by the federal general Juan J. Navarro after a battle southeast of Ciudad Guerrero. In a separate action that same month the *magonista* leader, Praxedis G. Guerrero, captured Casas Grandes, Chihuahua, site of an earlier PLM uprising.[35]

In attempting to reinforce Navarro, the federal army had encountered resistance on the part of the railroad workers, who refused to operate the trains that carried soldiers or supplies in support of the operation against the rebels. They pleaded that the rebels threatened to kill them if they aided the government, but the federal officer in charge of the reinforcements said his investigation revealed that the workers were actually rebel sympathizers.[36]

Other workers in the north evidenced pro-Madero sentiment as

34. Taracena, *La verdadera revolución*, pp. 324–29; GPDC, 33:8905. For a good discussion of the climate of unrest in Chihuahua and its economic origins, see William H. Beezley, *Insurgent Governor Abraham González and the Mexican Revolution in Chihuahua* (Lincoln, Neb.: University of Nebraska Press, 1973), pp. 35–37.

35. Michael C. Meyer, *Mexican Rebel: Pascual Orozco and the Mexican Revolution, 1910–1915* (Lincoln: University of Nebraska Press, 1967), pp. 20–23; Taracena, *La verdadera revolución*, p. 329; Cockcroft, *Intellectual Precursors*, p. 179.

36. Juan Hernández to Díaz, 16 December 1910, Chihuahua, GPDC, 35:20646; see also GPDC, 35:20634.

well. The *jefe político* of Casas Grandes, writing after Guerrero pulled his forces out of that town, said that the "working population" shouted for Madero and were waiting for the right moment to revolt. From Mapimí, near Torreón, came the *jefe político*'s evaluation that the revolutionary movement existed among the workers of some factories and among the greater part of the artisans.[37] The importance of these reports and the earlier rumors of workers arming is that the political authorities *believed* that various groups of workers were politically unreliable, a fact which complicated the regime's selection of tactics in dealing with the revolts.

Throughout most of the Madero rebellion, Díaz made no efforts to conciliate working-class opposition to his regime. Instead, he continually took a hard line. As early as June 1910, for example, Díaz supported Metepec mill owners in their dispute with their workers, despite the clear evidence that a number of Metepec's mill hands were on the verge of revolution. In response to the rumors of worker revolt during the summer of 1910, Díaz offered only troops and advised Orizaba's *jefe político*, Miguel Gómez, to take a strong stand in conserving the public order. Even when Gómez suggested to Díaz that he intercede on behalf of striking Río Blanco workers, the president demurred, not wanting, as he explained, to set a bad precedent.[38] Only in the late spring of 1911, when his regime was crumbling all around him, did Díaz attempt to pacify the workers. By then it was too late.

On the other hand, Gómez early began to show reluctance to crack down on anything but direct cases of rebellion. During most of his time as *jefe político* of Orizaba, Gómez had evidenced little interest in conciliating the workers, and on more than one occasion he had sent workers to an early grave in Quintana Roo. After the November revolts, however, he grew more reasonably disposed toward the workers and their problems. On several occasions he arrested workers suspected of *maderista* activities, only to release them for lack of evi-

37. F. Portillo to Alberto Terrazas, 19 December 1910, cited in Sandels, "Silvestre Terrazas and the Mexican Revolution," p. 205; *jefe político* to Díaz, 26 November 1910, Mapimí, Durango, GPDC, 35:16990.

38. Díaz to Martínez, 5 June 1910, GPDC, 35:7721; Díaz to Gómez, 25 July 1910, GPDC, 69:2600; ibid., 5 September 1910, GPDC, 69:3284; Gómez to Díaz, 1 March 1911, GPDC, 36:4704; Díaz to Gómez, 2 March 1911, GPDC, 36:4707.

dence or because they turned out to be "honorable workers" after all. By March Gómez was meeting regularly with officials of the workers' organizations to show his concern for their problems. Perhaps he was a *maderista*, as one of his political enemies implied.[39] More than likely, however, Gómez was shoring up his rather shaky relationship with the workers in case the rebellion succeeded. Undoubtedly, there were others like him in the winter of 1910–1911.

By the end of 1910 the regime still appeared to be in control of the situation. In late December federal forces repulsed an attack on the small town of Janos in Chihuahua, killing one of the PLM's ablest field commanders, Praxedis G. Guerrero. (Born of an old Creole family in Guanajuato, Guerrero could have lived an easier and longer life than the one he chose.) Although the guerrilla forces had not been crushed, they held no important territory even in Chihuahua, where the greatest number of rebels were. Indeed, General Navarro forced the rebel general Orozco to abandon Ciudad Guerrero early in January.[40]

With the coming of the new year, nonetheless, the old regime was in trouble. Not having crushed the rebellion in its earliest and weakest stage, the time was fast running out in which the government could be saved. Other men, seeing that the regime no longer was the invincible enemy it once seemed and driven by their own demons, began to take to the hills. Among these were Ramón F. Iturbe and Juan Banderas in Sinaloa, José Luis Moya in Zacatecas, Ambrosio and Romulo Figueroa in Guerrero, Ignacio Gutiérrez in Tabasco, and more. Then on 29 January, PLM forces captured Mexicali, capital of Baja California, and on 11 February, *magonista* troops under Prisciliano G. Silva occupied Guadalupe, Chihuahua. The red anarchist flag proclaiming *Tierra y Libertad* flew over both towns.[41] Although initially the PLM

39. Gómez to Díaz, 6 December 1910, GPDC, 69; Gómez to Díaz, 1 March 1911, GPDC, 70:4704; Aurelio Ortega to Díaz, 25 November 1910, GPDC, 35:16356.

40. Cockcroft, *Intellectual Precursors*, p. 179; Orozco withdrew from the city in preparation for his eventual attack on Ciudad Juárez (Meyer, *Mexican Rebel*, p. 24).

41. Alfonso Taracena, *En el vertigo de la Revolución Mexicana* (Mexico: Editorial Jus, 1936), pp. 109–14; Cockcroft, *Intellectual precursors*, p. 181; Blaisdell, *The Desert Revolution*.

had cooperated with Madero's forces, they withdrew their cooperation in the early spring of 1911 over both tactical and ideological
questions. Except for the capture of Tijuana, Baja California, in May
1911, the January and February victories were the highwater point
for PLM forces. They never were able to rally the broad support that
Madero attracted.

Throughout the Madero rebellion against Díaz, the president was
in frequent communication with the political authorities in states with
large working-class populations. In particular, the *jefe político* of
Orizaba, Governor Martínez of Puebla, and Governor Cahuantzi of
Tlaxcala reported directly to Díaz. In addition, the federal military
commanders and the *rurales* at the mill sites kept their respective
governors informed of all potentially dangerous situations as well.
Díaz obviously feared that the workers in these areas were politically
unreliable.

For the most part, this was true. However, except for the 20
November uprising in Orizaba, workers had not revolted as a group.
Individual workers undoubtedly joined the small rebel bands in the
hills, but most industrial workers kept to their machines prior to February 1911. Then, late in the evening of 5 February, a band of workers attacked the company store at the textile mill Los Molinos, near
Atlixco, Puebla, killing several *rurales* and looting the store. They fled
into the hills nearby, pursued by federal troops. Two days later, an
undetermined number of workers from the Metepec and La Carolina
mills also rose in revolt, killing four *rurales* and six other people. The
officer in charge of the *rurales* reported that they headed for Tlaxcala,
speculating that they would attempt to join the rebellious workers at
the Covadonga mill.[42]

42. *Comandante*, 9th *Cuerpo Rural*, to I.G., 6 January [*sic*, February] 1911,
Tehuacán, Puebla, AGN-Gob, leg. 824:52; Martínez to Díaz, 6 February 1911,
GPDC, 70:2509 and 8 February 1911, GPDC, 70:2724; Martínez (Gov. of
Puebla) to Díaz, 22 February, GPDC, 36:2144. The number of rebels at the
mill reported by the *rurales* was two hundred. The factory administrator
estimated one hundred rebels, and Martínez, from a source he considered to
be very reliable, estimated the number of insurrectionists to have been from
twenty to twenty-five. The attack may have been led by Juan Cuamatzi in
cooperation with several Puebla revolutionary leaders (Cuellar, *Tlaxcala*, p.
253). Martínez to Díaz, 8 February 1911, GPDC, 70:2724; C. Guerrero to
I.G., Tlaxcala, 7 February 1911, AGN-Gob, leg. 824:474.

The workers may well have done so, because the next day 415 workers at the textile mill La Covadonga on the Puebla-Tlaxcalan border left together for the rugged foothills of *La Malinche*, where rebel forces under Juan Cuamatzi were already gathering. The governor of the state reported several days later that other workers in other mills were not showing up for work and presumably were joining the rebels around *La Malinche*.[43]

A flyer circulated among the textile workers of Atlixco during these days, which read in part: "Comrades and citizens, now is the time to defend our homeland and to free it from slavery, to make the effort to emerge from under this infamous Government, a traitor to your fatherland. . . . Whoever accepts these sentiments can give proof that he is a real *maderista . . .* by putting his life on the line until death or victory over this infamous Government."[44] For Metepec mill hands, after all the years of abuse and disinterest, it was an appeal they could understand.

Those workers who joined Juan Cuamatzi's rebel band fought their first engagement in late February, when some 160 rebels clashed with Tlaxcalan state forces. Outnumbered, the rebels retreated leaving fifteen men dead on the field. Among those killed was their leader, Juan Cuamatzi, "the agitator" as he was called by the governor of Tlaxcala. The remnants of his band fled toward Cholula, Puebla, while others sought refuge in the factories near Panzacola.[45] Despite the setback, *maderista* forces in the Tlaxcala-Puebla area continued to increase in numbers throughout the late winter and early spring months.

Meanwhile, textile workers struck with greater frequency during the first five months of 1911 than at any time since the first half of 1907. Mill hands in Puebla and Atlixco struck in early February, at about the same time that the uprisings in the mills took place, causing

43. Cruz Guerrero, *Comandante* 9th *Cuerpo Rural*, Tlaxcala, 11 February 1911, AGN-Gob, leg. 824:475; Gov. of Tlaxcala to Díaz, 9 February 1911, GPDC, 36:3226; Gov. of Tlaxcala to Díaz, 9 February 1911, GPDC, 36:3226; Cuellar, *Tlaxcala*, p. 253.

44. From a circular dated 7 February 1911, AGN-Gob, leg. 824.

45. Gov. of Tlaxcala to Díaz, 26 February 1911, GPDC, 36:3147. According to Cuellar, Cuamatzi and four companions were taken alive after their ammunition ran out and later executed on the orders of the governor, Col. Próspero Cahuantzi (Cuellar, *Tlaxcala*, p. 253).

the authorities to fear additional worker violence. Although no Puebla strikes turned into armed revolt, this was not the case in Orizaba. Río Blanco weavers struck late in the morning of 28 February, and as they left the mill, cries of "Viva Madero" were heard. Two days later a group of workers broke into the company store, firing on the *rurales* who had been summoned to the scene. The latter returned the fire, ending the disturbance and taking thirty-six prisoners. Several days later the workers returned to their machines without settling their grievances. Río Blanco workers struck again in April, this time staying out until June.[46] There were eight textile strikes in all from January to the end of May 1911, although none were recorded in other industries. At least for the textile workers, strikes were one way to show their discontent without actually taking up arms against the regime.

By March the *maderista* revolt was making headway, despite a defeat at Casas Grandes early that month. In state after state, new rebel groups were taking to the field. Orozco's forces were well placed for their planned feint against Chihuahua City and then their surprise movement against Ciudad Juárez, across the border from El Paso. Perhaps equally important, Madero arrived in Mexico in February, giving the revolt a focal point.[47]

In mid-March the government acknowledged the extent of the revolution by suspending constitutional guarantees and providing for summary execution for those who attacked trains, cut telegraph wires, set fire to establishments, or engaged in violence against place or person. The decree, however, only formalized a practice already engaged in by various federal commanders.[48]

Also in March an assortment of Anti-Reelectionists, Madero sym-

46. Martínez to Díaz, 8 February 1911, GPDC, 70:2738; ibid., 9 February 1911, GPDC, 70:2803; ibid., 13 February 1911, GPDC, 70:3238. On strikes, see Ignacio Macharro, *jefe político* of Atlixco to Gov. of Puebla, 27 November 1910, GPDC, 35:17917; *El Obrero Mexicano*, 25 November 1910; Gómez to Díaz, 28 February 1911, GPDC, 70:4621; Martínez to Díaz, 8, 9, 13 February 1911, GPDC, 70:2738, 2803, 3238; Gómez to Díaz, 28 February 1911, GPDC, 70:4621; ibid., 1 March 1911, GPDC, 70:4704; Luis Amezquita, 2nd Lt., Río Blanco, to *comandante*, 8th C.R., 4 March 1911, AGN-Gob, leg. 824; ibid., 4, 6 March 1911, AGN-Gob, leg. 2226; Yamada, "The Cotton Textile Industry," p. 120.

47. Ross, *Madero*, pp. 148–49.

48. Gildardo Magaña, *Emiliano Zapata y el agrarismo en México*, 5 vols. (Mexico, 1934), 1:117–20, 122–24.

pathizers, and members of other discontented groups, under the general leadership of the former PLM leader, Camilo Arriaga, began to plot a joint, pro-Madero uprising. The revolt was to take place in various states, but the plot was centered in Tacubaya in the Federal District and came to be known as the "Tacubaya Conspiracy." Included among the conspirators were workers from the La Hormiga mill in Tizapán and workers from other factories and shops of the Federal District. Among the leaders of the conspiracy were three well-known textile workers from the early phase of the GCOL of Orizaba—Porfirio Meneses Córdova, José Neira, and Samuel A. Ramírez. The uprising had its own program, including articles that called for increased wages (as profits increased), a workday of not less than eight and no more than nine hours, foreign firms to employ Mexicans in at least half their positions at all levels, and housing and rent regulations covering the working classes. In addition, the conspirators' program also contained articles on political and intellectual freedom, land redistribution, and abolition of monopolies and the centralized educational system.[49] Their program, although under the banner of the Madero movement, was obviously more radical than anything yet proclaimed by the *maderistas*. Although not as advanced as the PLM program of the day, their proposals foreshadowed the difficulties that Madero later had in uniting the various factions of his movement once he came to power. The conspiracy never had a chance, however, to raise its banner in revolt. It was discovered and a number of its members arrested.

Late in March 1911 Pascual Mendoza wrote Díaz to inform him that his workers would no longer listen to him and to request an audience to discuss the matter. Díaz wrote back, asking Mendoza to write instead, since there was "so little time."[50] He did not know how little.

The Last Days of the Old Regime

The Revolution turned the corner in April, as the extent of rebel advances and advantages became apparent. Rebel strategy in

49. The conspirators were from the Federal District and the states of Puebla, Tlaxcala, Guerrero, Campeche, and Michoacán.
50. Mendoza to Díaz, 21 March 1911, GPDC, 36:5217. Mendoza stayed in

Chihuahua was working well. The troops that might have rescued the sorely beleaguered town of Ciudad Juárez had been pulled back to guard the state capital from the rumored *maderista* attack that never came. Rebel commanders in a dozen states were attacking small outposts, threatening the larger towns, and successfully eluding their pursuers. They were winning the war by avoiding defeat.[51]

On 28 April 1911, General Joaquín Maass, the military commander of the Veracruz area, wrote to Díaz a detailed report that illustrates the kinds of problems the government was having in coping with the rebel guerrilla tactics. The dispatch reported the deployment of the troops under Maass's command. The village of Santa Ana, near Orizaba, he noted, had been attacked by a group of fifty rebels whom he identified as workers. The attackers then joined the rebel commander Rafael Tapia, who was leading his men north toward Coscomatepec, a town situated perhaps forty miles northeast of Orizaba along the twisting route that wound slowly through numerous valleys on its way toward the state capital, Jalapa. Tapia's force was pursued by auxiliary troops under the command of a regular army officer and supported by a small squad of regulars from the 16th Battalion of federal infantry stationed in Orizaba. Tapia took his men through Coscomatepec and then turned westward toward the rugged foothills skirting the eighteen thousand foot extinct volcano Citlaltepetl, known as the "peak of Orizaba." The area was perfect to elude pursuers, both difficult of access and far from the sources of logistical support needed by the regular army.[52]

Meanwhile, another band of four hundred insurgents attacked the town of Zongólica, approximately thirty miles due south of Orizaba over rough terrain. Maass ordered the 19th Battalion, which was also stationed in Orizaba, to march in relief of Zongólica. He had first obtained the permission of the secretary of war in Mexico to move those troops and assured Díaz that they were prepared to return at any time if they were needed to protect Orizaba itself. He added parenthetically that he could not send Colonel Llave and the remain-

the labor movement even after the fall of his protector. See a complaint that he was agitating the Orizaba workers in sub-sec. of gobernación, Veracruz, July 1911, SHUV, Gob., 1911, L–10.

51. Ross, *Madero*, pp. 150–53.

52. Maass to Díaz, 28 April 1911, GPDC, 36:6340.

der of his 16th Battalion after the Zongólica rebels, because they had just been ordered to advance to the town of San Andrés Tuxtla, under heavy siege by yet another group of *maderistas*. In addition, troops which might have aided the *federales* in relief of San Andrés Tuxtla were concentrated around Jalapa because of the threat posed by Gabriel Gavira's rebels operating in that area.[53]

Tied down by the necessity of following the chain of command to Mexico City itself before anything but minor troop movements could be made, forced to defend the more populated areas against *potential* attack, and lacking the mobility which the rebels had because of their tactical independence and their smaller size, federal forces were constantly on the defensive, unable to bring their superior numbers and weaponry to bear. Whatever its other weaknesses, the Mexican military was not prepared to fight a popular insurgent movement of the kind that was opposing it.

Díaz did not give up easily, despite the usual claim that he was growing senile by the time of the Revolution. One cannot review the thousands of documents that passed through his hands during those days without acquiring some measure of respect for the old man's ability to stay informed. If he attempted to centralize too much control in his own hands in fighting the rebels and gave his field commanders too little leeway, it was most likely a mistake, but it is hardly a symptom of senility.

Toward the end of March, having failed to crush the rebellion, Díaz attempted to placate public opinion with last minute political reforms. He requested the resignation of six members of his cabinet on 24 March and forced the removal of the most unpopular governors, including Terrazas in Chihuahua, Martínez in Puebla, Muñoz Arístegui in Yucatán, and Pimentel in Oaxaca.[54] The latter's removal was met with jubilation. One ecstatic letter to Díaz declared that "the working people, the humble people, the people who have suffered, lift their heads and raise their voices in exultation to praise their *caudillo* on this memorable date."[55] In a ploy to win the support of the *reyistas*,

53. Ibid. San Andrés Tuxtla was eventually taken by the rebels; Ross, *Madero*, p. 152.

54. Ross, *Madero*, p. 153.

55. A number of signatures to Díaz, 2 April 1911, Oaxaca, GPDC, 36:6738.

Díaz was apparently considering asking Reyes to return from Europe to serve as his minister of war or as minister of *gobernación*.[56]

Then, on 1 April, the old *Caudillo* offered to the Congress a far-reaching reform program that included the prohibition of reelection, important judicial reforms, and even the division of the large, rural estates. At the same time, Díaz resumed the policy of direct intervention into labor disputes and showed considerable interest in workers' grievances. For example, he agreed to talk directly with an Orizaba workers' commission, something he had not done since the Río Blanco strike over four years before. Pánfilo Méndez, a leader from the old *Gran Círculo de Obreros Libres*, and Guadalupe Pastrana were named as the commissioners to present the workers' grievances to the president.[57]

But too much time had fled since the *Caudillo* was master, and too many men had compromised their ambitions and their lives to oppose him. More important, the people of Mexico no longer considered Porfirio Díaz the right and lawful ruler of their nation. Once they had believed that he deserved to govern them, that he was their legitimate ruler despite the fact that he would permit no serious opposition to contest his rule. But somewhere on the road from Cananea in June of 1906 to Ciudad Juárez in May of 1911, this critical sense of legitimacy was tarnished beyond recall for a significant portion of the Mexican people. The motivation and timing differed from group to group, but by the spring of 1911 the process was nearly complete.

Rebel forces in the field mirrored this condition. Contrasting the fact that the Díaz regime could get few volunteers for their auxiliary forces despite high inducements, rebel units expanded in manpower and scope of operations throughout the month of April 1911. Indé and Mapimí in Durango fell to *maderistas*. Agua Prieta was taken in Sonora. By the end of the month insurgent forces held nearly all the state of Chihuahua except the capital itself. The critical rail center of Torreón on the Durango-Coahuila border was nearly cut off from the surrounding countryside, and San Andrés Tuxtla, in Veracruz, had fallen to rebels despite the efforts of General Maass to relieve it. In Sonora and in the Yucatán, in Guerrero and in San Luis Potosí, and in

56. Ross, *Madero*, p. 154; Cosío Villegas, *La vida política interior*, 2:905–6.
57. Ross, *Madero*, p. 154; Gómez to Díaz, 23 April 1911, GPDC, 36:6170.

nearly every state in the Republic, rebel forces were operating at will, as state and federal forces barely held on to the major cities and the state capitals. And across the Río Bravo from El Paso, nearly three thousand men led by General Pascual Orozco and under the personal command of Francisco Madero were besieging Ciudad Juárez.[58] The end was in sight for the regime of Porfirio Díaz.

In mid-April Lt. Gómez, the officer in charge of the *rurales* defending the walled and fortified Metepec mill, informed his superior that the mail was no longer getting through to his outpost. Although the rebels had not taken the company town that lay close by the walls of the mill, Lt. Gómez estimated the number of *maderistas* in the area at six thousand men. How many of these were Puebla mill hands cannot be said, but at about this time Fortino Ayaquica, a young textile worker from Atlixco, gathered a band of men from his area, presumably including other workers, and took them over the state line to Emiliano Zapata's camp in Morelos.[59] Remembering the Metepec workers' demand for land to colonize, it is hardly inconsistent that Ayaquica and his men should join forces with the man who was fighting for land.

Ciudad Juárez fell to a determined rebel assault on 10 May, and within days the *maderistas* had captured nearly a dozen state capitals. The government of Porfirio Díaz now only functioned in the very largest cities. Even then the stubborn old man could not be persuaded to resign until 25 May. He had left Mexico for exile by the end of the month. The same week that Madero entered Ciudad Juárez, fifty-three workers from Pachuca, capital of the state of Hidalgo, wrote an open letter to Díaz, asking him to resign in order to reestablish peace in the land.[60] And after all the years of anonymous letters they dared to sign their names.

58. Ross, *Madero*, pp. 150–58; Taracena, *La verdadera revolución*, pp. 360–78.

59. A. Gómez to *comandante* 9th C. R., 18 April 1911, AGN-Gob, leg. 824:160; Womack, *Zapata*, p. 81. Ayaquica developed into one of Zapata's major commanders.

60. *El Estudiante y El Obrero*, 14 May 1911. They described themselves as mechanics.

Chapter 8
Conclusion

*"OF ALL I HAVE DONE, OF ALL
    I HAVE LOST,
of all I have won unexpectedly,
in bitter iron, in leaves; I can offer a little."*
—"Bruselas," Pablo Neruda

The resignation of Porfirio Díaz on 25 May 1911 does not mark the death of one era and the birth of another; the *Porfiriato* was history, but the old regime lived on in institutions and ways with roots too deep and influences too pervasive to fall with the old *Caudillo* who had so long kept them secure. Certainly for Mexican industrial workers the struggle had only begun. The Madero administration would attempt to resolve the labor question with perhaps greater sincerity than had Díaz and his advisors but with no greater understanding or success. Yet the events of the years that follow the *maderista* triumph belong to another history. The story of the Mexican worker in the fierce, combative times of the Mexican Revolution awaits its chronicler.[1]

As the historian interprets his facts, he is also explaining human behavior in an historical setting. Despite the charges of his critics and even his own occasional denials, the historian in this century not only has sought to provide the facts but generally has attempted to give them meaning, either to explain in a limited sense the motivation, timing, or process of historical events or to provide broad generalizations of how and why groups of human beings think and act. Implicitly or explicitly, this study has interpreted the nature of the labor conflicts during the *Porfiriato*. I would like to review these explanations in order to clarify certain points of interpretation which seem to me to be particularly important.

1. See Salazar, *Pugnas de la gleba*, and Marjorie Ruth Clark, *Organized Labor in Mexico* (Chapel Hill: University of North Carolina Press, 1934).

A Curious Paradox—Labor Policy and the Porfirian System

Emerging from the growth of the administration's labor policy from 1906 to 1911 is what appears to be a curious paradox. At first glance, Díaz's reaction to the labor problems supports Daniel Cosío Villegas's contention that the *Porfiriato* was an era of extreme centralism.[2] The president himself directed the administration's labor policy, keeping in personal contact with the most critical trouble spots. Yet, paradoxically, Díaz was rarely able to institute effective reforms. Even on the government's own railroad lines, the regime appeared unable to carry out its widely publicized mexicanization program. It can be argued that Díaz was a reluctant actor in the struggles between capital and labor, preferring to let the workers find their own way. Certainly it is true that he would much rather have encouraged the industrial growth that had made him an elder statesman, benevolently presiding over the modernization of Mexico. Yet given clear indications of the political dangers hidden in the frustrations of restless workers, Díaz moved almost instinctively along familiar pathways in order to maneuver into position to dominate the problem, to render it politically manageable.

The cotton textile workers provide the best case study of the Porfirian system in action. During the 1906 labor problems Díaz not only worked with the Veracruz state and local authorities, he set the policy direction for other states, particularly Puebla and Tlaxcala. When this level of politics failed to establish a balance and the Puebla textile strike of December 1906 took place, Díaz increased his involvement, agreeing to arbitrate the dispute. The resulting *laudo*—entered into by the industrialists only after what must have been strong pressure from federal authorities—made certain concessions to the workers, cost the owners relatively little, and contained articles designed to further both the industrialists' control over their workers and the government's control over the workers' political activity. When the *laudo* failed to pacify the Orizaba workers, the public order was restored with force, and Díaz decreed harsh punishment for those responsible for the violence.

2. Cosío Villegas, *La vida política interior*, 2:xx–xxii, 940.

poor working conditions, and, as the nineteenth century drew to a close, the complaint of ill-treatment became more and more significant.

None of these issues was totally new, and indeed all had roots in the old ways as well as in the changes brought by Porfirian economic progress. What was new was the deterioration of many of the social and cultural mechanisms that had previously enabled Mexican workers to cope with their inferior position in life. Whatever the living and working conditions in the villages and towns of pre-Porfirian Mexico, and they were hardly a paragon of traditional virtue and peace, men were generally able to ignore or deal with the inequities and the personal miseries because they either appeared to be a part of the way life was expected to be or because for many people, the rural community provided a sufficient cultural buffer to enable the individual to survive. There was a balance, however tenuous and shifting, between the *peón* and *patrón*, the villages and the *haciendas*, the artisans and their *maestros*.

But in the 1870s and 1880s Mexico began to undergo economic and social changes, changes that were accelerated in the 1890s. Population grew as medical advances, improved economic conditions, and political peace lowered the death rate and increased the life expectancy of many Mexicans. Population pressure on the available land, together with the expansion of *haciendas* attracted by the profits to be made in domestic and foreign markets, began to destroy the ancient villages, forcing more men and women to seek means of livelihood elsewhere. Meanwhile, competition from industrial products was slowly undermining many artisan trades at the same time that most industrial workers were encountering a more stringently enforced work discipline. The latter was true particularly after 1890, when many of the smaller, older plants tightened up production and personnel procedures. Older, more relaxed work habits and routines, personal relationships between workers and their bosses, face-saving courtesies between inferior and superior—all were modified or eliminated as many aspects of the old world became unbalanced in the face of relentless economic pressures. It happened neither all at once nor to each worker in the same way, for the timing and the extent of the changes depended on many different and complex factors. Yet wherever industrial forces brought both economic misery and social dislocation, closing options that might otherwise have absorbed the shock, men protested their fate. Somewhere in the years surrounding the turn of the century lies the watershed of modern Mexican labor history.

The turn of the nineteenth century marked the beginning of the last phase of the Porfirian labor problem. A short recession lasted until 1902, and although there were recoveries in a number of industries through to 1907 or 1908, the plants that survived the crisis, particularly in the textile industry, were encouraged to rationalize production methods and employment practices still further. Although strikes were less frequent in most of the years from 1900 to 1906, the issues of low wages, fines, company stores, and mistreatment gathered greater force; the effects of economic forces that had been building up over the years shortly presented Mexico with a full-fledged social problem.

Industrial strife increased significantly after 1905. Research for this study recorded 117 strikes from January 1906 through May 1911, compared to 29 in the previous five years.[3] What are the possible explanations for the increased tempo of industrial unrest after 1905?

First, one may look at the strikes from the point of view of the workers involved: what reasons did they give at the time for striking? Over the five and a half year period covered by this study, grievances connected with wages were the number one cause of strikes, followed closely by grievances related to personnel practices (workday, overtime, changes in quotas, firing for union activity and others), and finally by mistreatment. González Navarro gives wages as the number one issue in Porfirian labor conflicts with mistreatment as second. The difference between the two studies on this question lies mainly in the

3. These are unofficial statistics. Undoubtedly I have overlooked various strikes during this period, but I feel the number is small. On the rare occasion when two shops of the same owner went out at the same time (e.g., Hércules and La Purísima cotton mills in Querétaro), I counted it as one strike. I also considered as one strike those called by the same union at the same time, including railroad strikes joined by various branches of the same union. The most significant example was the Puebla-Tlaxcala strike in December 1906 involving nearly forty mills. I was unable to determine the number of working days lost or the number of workers involved in a sufficient number of cases to warrant inclusion of those statistics..

fact that I used only three categories, while Professor González Navarro used a number of others.[4] Indeed, mistreatment was a major grievance which, along with poor working conditions, undoubtedly contributed importantly to the environment of discontent which gave rise to the strikes, whatever the stated grievances were. Yet given the reasons to strike, what explains the timing of the conflicts?

First of all, industrial unrest from 1906 to 1911 appeared generally to have followed the business cycle, increasing in times of rising production and employment and falling as the economy worsened, particularly after 1907. The peak in strike frequency was between 1 June 1906 and 30 June 1907, corresponding to the peak in the value of manufacturing production for that decade. The decline in manufacturing production for the next two fiscal years corresponded roughly to the decline in the frequency and duration of strikes. The relationship can be seen even more clearly in the textile industry, where twenty-one strikes were declared between 1 June and 31 December 1906 (including the GCOL strike involving nearly forty mills, counted here as one strike), while fourteen strikes occurred between 1 January and 30 June 1907. Strikes then fell off to three in the following six months, and never rose to more than six in any half year period after that. The net value of textile production by mid-1909 had fallen 26 percent from the peak reached during the fiscal year 1906–1907 (the peak also for strike activity) and rose only slowly after that.[5]

The obvious conclusion is that strikes took place in times of general economic expansion, while a downswing in the business cycle discouraged strikes; jobs were scarce, men were out of work, and a larger pool of surplus labor could be drawn on to replace striking workers. A letter written in 1909 by several mill hands noted that strikes were currently rare "because it means a lack of bread in our homes."[6] This characteristic has been common historically in industrial societies until the era of strong trade unions. Selig Perlman noted that in the United States, union activities expanded in times of prosperity and con-

4. See Appendix A.7–8. I counted two grievances per strike where applicable, but in various cases the issues at stake were indeterminable. Hence the number of grievances does not coincide with the number of strikes. González Navarro, *La vida social*, p. 299.

5. El Colegio de México, *Estadísticas económicas*, p. 106.

6. *El Paladín*, 23 May 1909.

tracted during recession, when American workers turned more to "panaceas and politics."[7]

Yet if the business cycle explains much of the timing of the conflicts from 1906 to 1911, and this is still only an hypothesis, what explains the heavy concentration of strikes in the textile mills of Orizaba, Puebla, Atlixco, and the Federal District? Furthermore, what explains the fact that, while only the large, relatively modern plants in Orizaba, Atlixco, and the Federal District were struck, many of the smaller ones were struck in Puebla? And why smaller mills in Puebla and not similar plants in the northern states or Jalisco, or Michoacán, or Oaxaca? For example, there were ten mills in the Federal District. Of the eleven strikes from 1906 to 1911 in the cotton mills there, all but one were at the largest three plants, La Magdalena, La Hormiga, and San Antonio de Abad. These three accounted for approximately 75 percent of the sales of all the cotton mills in the Federal District for the fiscal year 1905–1906. Of the seventy-six textile strikes from 1906 to 1911, all but eighteen were in mills with a 1906 tax quota of 10,000 *pesos* or more. Although the selection of 10,000 *pesos* is arbitrary, it would seem to represent an acceptable cutoff between the small plants and the larger, more efficient ones. Of the 125 factories listed in the 1906 tax quota for the cotton textile industry, the 37 mills with over 10,000 *pesos* sales tax accounted for nearly 70 percent of total production.[8]

In any case, although answers to these questions will have to await more detailed industrial and regional studies, I would like to explore several tentative explanations. First, militancy among Puebla textile hands after 1905 may well relate to the fact that the internal markets of the generally smaller, less efficient mills in both Puebla and Tlaxcala forced them to compete with the more efficient, foreign-owned mills of Orizaba, Atlixco, and the Federal District.

This had not always been the case. During the industrial expansion of the last half of the 1890s, the market was sufficient for all existing mills. Competition among the mills—at least in Puebla—was kept to a minimum through informal agreements. Modernization of equip-

7. "Upheaval and Reorganization," in John R. Commons et. al., *History of Labor in the United States*, 4 vols. (New York: Macmillan Co., 1921–35), p. 472.
8. *La Semana Mercantil*, 25 June 1906, pp. 301–3.

ment and general production technology, and corresponding changes in personnel policies, took place in the next decade. Meanwhile there were few or no industrial strikes during the 1890s in Puebla, while from 1895 to 1900 the industrial and agricultural labor force in that state grew in absolute numbers faster than that of almost any of the other central states (see Appendix Table B.4). The inference is that jobs were plentiful, and hence, I suspect, turnover rates were high in many industrial jobs, permitting discontent to be diluted through the alternatives available to workers unhappy with their jobs. I also suspect that the recruitment of workers from a growing body of rural landless *campesinos* meant that industrial work was probably viewed by them as a temporary job until they could get back to the land or into some more rewarding work than factory employment. Perhaps some went to find jobs in the growing states of the north or even into the United States as *braceros*.

The hard times at the beginning of the century, however, combined with: (1) establishment of such additional major competitors as Santa Rosa (1898) and the huge Metepec mill (1902); (2) greater relative increase in population between 1900 and 1910 in the state of Veracruz and the Federal District compared to Puebla; and (3) absolute decline in the economically active population in the state of Puebla as opposed to increases in Veracruz and the Federal District between 1900 and 1910. These developments encouraged the Puebla-Tlaxcala mills to modernize their plant and equipment as well as their production and sales procedures. Such changes undoubtedly produced hardships for the workers, both in wages and in a more strict enforcement of industrial discipline. The partial recovery of the industry after 1902 and the good times from 1905 through 1907—including expanding jobs—provided an improved environment for the development of labor organization. Simultaneously, the workers' grievances increased, both because their actual conditions were worsening and because they now had a means to make known their grievances.[9]

9. For population, see El Colegio de México, *Estadísticas económicas*, pp. 26, 38; on price fixing, see Fernando Rosenzweig, "La industria," p. 333; on modernization of the industry, see Keremitsis, *La industria textil*, pp. 105, 110–15 and Rosenzweig, "La industria," pp. 333–38.

Another factor which likely made life more difficult for some workers in the Tlaxcalan-Puebla area is that because of both state policy and private initiative, the rural communities in both states were contracting, leaving less opportunity for workers to return to the land if factory work became too oppressive. Raymond Buves's work indicates that textile mill hands in Tlaxcala were close to the village *comunidad* and probably reacted to factory work more as peasants (*campesinos* would perhaps be more accurate) than as urban workers. Before the Díaz regime took power, many had been part-time farmers who engaged in part-time occupations as artisans, mule skinners, etc. Many, especially the artisans, were forced into the factories after 1880, while state fiscal measures hurt the position of the villages. Hence they were being hurt from both sides, especially after 1900. Their involvement in the labor conflicts and their later support of revolutionary groups clearly was affected by both the industrial and the rural situation.[10]

In support of the Buve thesis is the fact that on a number of occasions, textile workers at the Metepec mill (which appeared to recruit from the rural villages) as well as at mills in Puebla and Veracruz, requested the government to give them land to colonize as *campesinos* if their conflicts with the industrialists were not resolved.[11]

On the other hand, industrial strikes increased in the Federal District during the 1890s (Appendix Table A.5), and although they rose again in the 1906 to 1911 period, there were less than half as many textile strikes as in Puebla or Veracruz, and hardly more overall industrial strikes. Although the owners of the Federal District mills did not modernize their production facilities to any great extent in the 1890s, they did institute changes in personnel policies designed to increase worker productivity and efficiency. Thus there was a significant increase in strikes due to changes in factory regulations during this decade, particularly in the textile industry. Exactly why those various pressures are applied to Federal District workers in the 1890s and why they reacted as strongly as they did is still not clear to me. Perhaps it was due to the nature of the industrial competition in the District, or to the social character of the workers (second-

10. Buve, "Protesta de obreros," p. 13.

11. González Navarro, *La vida social*, p. 306, and "Las huelgas textiles," p. 517; Emilio Vázquez to Díaz, 17 March 1910, GPDC, 35:3067.

generation urban workers), or to the presence of an expanding job market, which gave workers more opportunities to work should strikes take place or should they lose their jobs because of the strike. The recruitment of industrial workers for the Federal District, therefore, may well have been from more urbanized workers, less willing than Puebla workers to seek work in the countryside when the conditions of their industrial employment turned against their liking. Only further research will clarify these questions.

Strikes may have taken place at the larger cotton mills around Orizaba, as well as Metepec, because the greater number of workers made replacement by strikebreakers more difficult and because the number of potential union members increased through the development of a feeling of solidarity from their common work and their close proximity in the company towns. Maurice Zietlan's study of Cuban workers suggests that work at the larger plants tended to encourage worker consciousness and militancy. Mutsuo Yamada contends that the large, impersonal work environment was unsettling for many Orizaba mill hands because most were ex-*campesinos*, recruited from the countryside with no previous industrial work experience. In Orizaba, Yamada shows that industrialization and urbanization occurred simultaneously, in contrast to the "core" cities such as Puebla and the Federal District, where factories could draw on a more docile, adapted labor force. In addition, there is no doubt that industrial discipline at the larger plants was strictly enforced by the predominately foreign supervisors, adding yet another ingredient to the environment of discontent. An officer of the *rurales* investigating discontent at the Metepec mill in 1903 blamed the problem on the poor treatment of the workers by the administrators and other mill employees, many of whom were foreigners, as they were in Orizaba.[12]

While wages appear higher in the larger mills than in the smaller ones, it was in the former that wages were more likely to be reduced by fines, extortion by foremen, rent paid for company housing, and discounted script redeemable only at the company store. The Puebla

12. Yamada, "The Cotton Textile Industry," p. 87. Maurice Zeitlin, *Revolutionary Politics and the Cuban Working Class* (Princeton, New Jersey: Princeton University Press, 1967), p. 282. Yamada, "The Cotton Textile Industry," pp. 127–29. For the *rurales'* report, see AGN-Gob, leg. 824.

and Tlaxcalan mills only became centers of unrest after the turn of the century, when economic conditions forced mill owners to introduce harsher personnel policies, including such practices as fines and payment for broken equipment.

A distinction should be made between the Orizaba mills (and Metepec) and those of the Federal District. Although factory regulations and personnel practices may have been the same by 1906, the Orizaba mills were still larger and more modern. Moreover, it is likely that the worker recruitment was still fundamentally different in the two areas, making it difficult to differentiate between the ways the workers reacted to similar work experiences.

In the numerous smaller mills in other regions of the Republic, however, shortages of skilled personnel may have led to higher wages and better working conditions, while the lack of large, efficient competitors may have encouraged the owners not to enforce industrial discipline to the detriment of their relations with the workers. And the availability of jobs in the north, where labor was relatively scarce compared to the center, as well as the opportunities for work over the border, gave workers alternatives that were not available elsewhere, thus encouraging job turnover rather than conflict in cases of job discontent.

After 1905, however, the reverse appears to have been true, particularly in the north, where economic hard times began to set in. Among the four northern states of Coahuila, Chihuahua, Durango, and Nuevo León, the number of workers in the textile mills declined significantly after their peak during fiscal year 1904–1905. Also in the north, the major textile state of Coahuila, with 11 mills in 1906, reached its peak in sales in 1904–1905 rather than in 1907–1908, as did Veracruz and states of the center in general. The same that is true of Coahuila is true of the states of the south, particularly Oaxaca.[13] Labor conflicts during those years of economic hardships would have been few, as in fact they were.

This study has not attempted an in-depth account of the labor market or the regional variations in the business cycle, so that the above statements represent simply possible or alternative explanations. More systematic studies of these problems are needed to pro-

13. El Colegio de México, *Estadísticas económicas*, pp. 108, 112.

vide answers to these questions, especially investigations of regional variations in the labor market and of the relationship between labor unrest, the size of the industrial plant, and the condition of competition in regional markets. In addition, the concentration of work stoppages in the textile industry is not easily explainable, even though it is a common pattern in industrial labor history.[14] With the possible exception of the railroad industry, textile plants had the greatest number of industrial workers working under modern, industrial factory conditions. In addition, along with the railroads, it is the industry with the longest history in the use of what can be called industrial machinery. The latter combined with the former are conditions likely to encourage the development of organizational efforts among the workers, a movement unwittingly facilitated by the development of the company towns servicing the newer and larger mills. In those towns, a greater number of workers were brought together at work and at home, facilitating at least the development of a group consciousness, a unity in adversity that can only help to encourage organization and to enforce group decisions. However, since similar conditions were present in such plants as the Monterrey Iron and Steel Works, the Mexican National Dynamite and Explosives Co., the Monterrey Mining, Smelting and Refining Co., why was there no conflict in those plants, and others like them? The answers to these questions and more await further study.

The objective of what I have done is to show "how men made history as they really and bravely made it, without knowing beforehand how it would turn out."[15] To the workers of that time, the origins of their frustration and anger were obvious: they were underpaid, overworked, mistreated, discriminated against in favor of foreign workers, and humiliated by all these conditions; their children

14. See Clark Kerr and Abraham Siegel, "The Inter-industry Propensity to Strike—An International Comparison," in Arthur Kornhauser, Robert Dubin, Arthur M. Ross, eds., *Industrial Conflict* (New York: McGraw-Hill Co., 1954), pp. 189–212.

15. John Womack, Jr., "Mexican Political Historiography, 1959–1969," in *Investigaciones contemporáneas sobre historia de México: Memorias de la tercera reunión de historiadores mexicanos y norteamericanos* (Mexico: Universidad Nacional Autónoma de México, El Colegio de México, The University of Texas at Austin, 1971), p. 487.

lacked opportunities for education; if injured on the job there was little or no compensation; and when they were old, they could expect to be turned out with no consideration for their years of work and with few resources to maintain themselves; and, what galled them even more, their government, which they believed should have been the source of their deliverance, had fallen into the very hands of those who were oppressing them.

Despite the bitterness with which the workers expressed their discontent, little evidence has been uncovered which indicates that the workers wanted anything but to be admitted to national society if not on equal terms with other classes, at least respected as workers and citizens. They were sensitive to the charges of drunkenness, improvidence, and vice. Workers admitted that those vices existed but denied that they were characteristic of all working men, blaming them instead on poor living and working conditions.

A search for the origins of Mexican industrial unrest, then, ultimately comes back to its beginnings. Mexican workers *acted*, they created their own history, and the explanations they themselves offered of their behavior are the only sure guideposts we have to the writing of history as it seemed to those who lived it. If their viewpoint is only one of several possible explanations of historical reality, it is a viewpoint that deserves to be respected.

The Politics of Industrial Conflict

Given the economic environment in which the labor conflicts took place, how did the workers propose to resolve their problems? What general ideological framework did they favor, what strategies did they use to promote the long range success of their movement, and what tactics were they willing to employ to achieve their immediate objectives and their short range goals?

The narrative of this book has suggested certain answers to the above questions, but I would like to here make clear my interpretations of these problems, adding certain additional materials not found in the text.

One noted historian of Latin American labor movements asserts that in Latin America labor movements "spring from an essentially ideological base."[16] He is supported by other general studies on Latin American workers which maintain that the various labor movements got their start through contact with anarchist, socialist, and syndicalist ideologies imported from Europe, particularly France and Spain.[17] Even if this thesis were generally true, which I doubt, it was not so in the case of Mexico. Nonetheless, scholars of Mexican history have come to accept the thesis that the ill-fated but valiant *Partido Liberal Mexicano* (PLM), aided by Spanish anarchism already influential among Mexican *obreros*, guided the workers' effort into a struggle not only against the Díaz regime but, ultimately, against the capitalist system itself.[18]

The Spanish anarchist thesis is the weakest, although it cannot yet be discarded. A number of different sources mention such influences, it is true, but specific details are rare. Vicente Fuentes Díaz holds that a group of Catalán workers spread the anarchist ideas of Bakunin, Prouhdon, and Kropotkin in the textile industry prior to the Mexican Revolution. Luis F. Bustamante maintains that various Spanish radicals came to Mexico between 1905 and 1910 and that Juan Francisco Moncaleano, a socialist from Venezuela, helped found the *Sindicato de Canteros* and the *Federación de Trabajadores de Artes Gráficas*. Rosendo Salazar mentions eight Spanish anarchists who were members of the *Casa del Obrero Mundial* in 1912, although none are described as playing a role in the Porfirian labor movement. He does give the name of Jacinto Huitrón, a Colombian anarchist, who worked among Mexican construction workers at the first of the century. John Hart in his study on Mexican anarchism notes that Spanish immigration to Mexico increased from 9,533 in 1887 to 16,258 in 1900, suggesting that, given the persecution of anarchists in Spain at the time, many might have

16. Victor Alba, *Politics and the Labor Movement in Latin America* (Stanford: Stanford University Press, 1960), author's note.

17. See Robert J. Alexander, *Organized Labor in Latin America* (New York: Free Press, 1965), p. 15; Moisés Trancoso Poblete and Ben G. Burnett, *The Rise of the Latin American Labor Movement* (New Haven: Yale University Press, 1960), pp. 97–98.

18. Clark, *Organized Labor in Mexico*, pp. 6–14; López Aparicio, *El movimiento obrero*, p. 136; Cockcroft, *Intellectual Precursors*, pp. 48, 134–56, 161–63, 168; Blaisdell, *The Desert Revolution*, p. 8; Montes Rodríguez, *La huelga de Río Blanco*, pp. 68, 89; Salazar and Escobedo, *Pugnas de la gleba*, p. 26; Cline, *The United States and Mexico*, p. 117.

chosen to leave the country for Mexico. The documents which were reviewed for this study, however, did not reveal any such influence. That there were Spanish anarchists in Mexico is certainly probable. What is lacking is evidence directly linking any such radicals to the labor unrest.[19]

The governor of the state of Yucatán deported two journalists he called anarchists and warned Díaz that Spanish anarchists from Catalonia were agitating the Republic's workers. He could give no details, however. Another presumably Spanish anarchist, Andrés Sanz Coy, wrote or edited *El Mauser* in Orizaba, Veracruz. In addition, Díaz received a report that certain Cuban anarchists were considering coming to Mexico, possibly to assassinate him. Yet without more hard data to go on, and given other evidence which indicates no such influence, the conclusion has to be that it is unlikely that foreign radicals were influential in the Mexican labor movement in the last decade or so before the fall of the regime.[20]

The most difficult problem to resolve is the question of the extent of the influence of the *Partido Liberal Mexicano* on the industrial labor force. Professor James Cockcroft's study of the PLM shows that after 1906 the PLM moved away from democratic liberalism toward anarchism, and in doing so, placed greater emphasis on the role of Mexican workers and peasants in the inevitable revolution against the Díaz regime and on the economic and social changes which would accompany the revolution. He then argues that, at the same time,

19. Vicente Fuentes Díaz, *Los partidos políticos en México*, 2 vols. (Mexico: n.p., 1954), 1:87. Luis F. Bustamante, "La huelga de Cananea hace 28 anos," *CROM* (Mexico City), 1, 15 July 1934, p. 11. (Other proponents of the role of the Spanish anarchists are: Clark, *Organized Labor*, p. 6; Poblete Trancoso and Burnett, *Latin American Labor*, pp. 97–98; Buve, "Protesta de obreros," pp. 7–8, 14; Jean Meyer, "Los obreros en la Revolución Mexicana: Los 'Batallones Rojos'," *Historia Mexicana* 20 (July–September 1971), p. 3. Salazar, *Líderes y sindicatos* (Mexico: T. C. Modelo, 1953), pp. 17–20, 40. John Hart, *Los anarquistas*, pp. 29–30.

20. Gov. of Yucatán to Díaz, 3, 31 December 1907, GPDC, 32:14297, 15486; ibid., 22 January 1908, 33:1414; *México Nuevo*, 21 April 1909; unidentified writer to A. Reynaud, 4 November 1906, Río Blanco, AGN-Gob, leg. 817; Gov. of Yucatán to Díaz, 4 February 1908, GPDC, 33:1430; Agüeros (editor of *El Tiempo*) to Díaz, GPDC, 33:5653; José Rente de Vales, 15 May 1908, Habana, Cuba, GPDC, 33:5687.

PLM popularity was increasing among the workers and peasants. Indeed, he maintains that the major labor conflicts from 1906 through 1908 were inspired by the PLM's appeal to the workers, and that "the main political force behind these strikes was the PLM." Cockcroft further contends that the Orizaba area continued to be a center of PLM plotting after the repression of the Río Blanco strike, but that "strong government surveillance prevented any further outbreaks of violence during the Precursor period." Cockcroft goes on to suggest that the PLM-worker-*campesino* alliance formed in the Porfirian era ultimately threatened the bourgeoisie-based Madero movement, forcing subsequent moderate political groups to undercut PLM's radical influence on labor before such groups could consolidate power after 1915.[21]

Whatever the ideological character of the labor movement after Madero's victory over Díaz in May 1911, the influence of the PLM on Mexican workers before that time appears to be doubtful, and at best inconclusive. Certainly no working-class group rose in the name of the PLM, either in 1906, 1908, *or* 1910. One might maintain that had not the Díaz regime so closely watched the workers, had it not used such harsh repression, the workers might have shown greater affinity for the Liberal cause.

Yet the problem of why Mexican workers did not more openly and actively support the PLM's revolutionary efforts cannot be resolved simply by reference to the regime's use of repression and close surveillance to prevent such influence from being effective. Certainly the same government policies did not stop various groups of Mexican workers from joining the *maderista* revolt in 1910 and 1911. Moreover, the existence of surveillance and repression is not *prima facie* evidence that the workers were repressed PLM adherents or that they would have been had they received the PLM's propaganda or had they been able to listen to the PLM agents. Rather, the extent of PLM influence among Mexican workers should be posed not as a problem in the PLM's desires or efforts, but as a question of the workers' ideological perspective.

From this perspective the Mexican industrial workers' struggle for

21. Cockcroft, *Intellectual Precursors*, pp. 134, 145; 157–69; ibid., p. 140; ibid., pp. 156, 169, 228–35.

justice in the late years of the *Porfiriato* was not "inspired" by the PLM, as Cockcroft asserts and others assume. The workers in the mines and factories of Mexico needed no inspiration from middle-class intellectuals to protest their conditions; working men and women in Mexico were sufficiently aware of their conditions and sufficiently desirous of changing them to provide the major impetus themselves. What evidence there is about the PLM's relationship to Mexican workers suggests that the PLM was a marginal factor in their existence, a vaguely known, sympathetic, but distant force, not central to what they did or thought about their problems. Undoubtedly there were workers who were *magonistas*, and no doubt there were PLM activists who were influential among certain groups of workers. But the available evidence clearly points out that most industrial workers were not ideologically radical, nor were they politically committed to the overthrow of the Díaz regime by force. Like most groups in 1910 and 1911, they were driven to revolution.

In the first place, except for the Cananea strike in 1906, and the early phase of the GCOL, there is no evidence that the PLM was a significant force, or even an element, in the labor unrest of the period. During the most militant phase of the GCOL—June to December 1906—the organization avoided any association with the PLM. Although the PLM still maintained contacts in the area, only a few of these can be definitely identified as workers.[22] Although it is commonly said that the PLM July Program of 1906 influenced the labor movements of that year and provided guideposts for their demands in the years that followed, why might not one also assume that the influence was really the reverse—that the workers influenced the PLM's July Program?

One important study which deals indirectly with the PLM influence in Tlaxcala, particularly, is that of Raymond Buve, a Dutch scholar. Buve has provided certain important hypotheses concerning rural-urban relations which bear directly on the labor problem. He suggests that traditional patterns of interlocking regional markets and long-standing job mobility between rural villages and urban areas, com-

22. Besides the captured PLM documents which list their contacts in the Orizaba-Puebla area, there is some evidence of a PLM faction at the Santa Rosa Mill (see Peña, "Apuntes históricos," 4 November, 2, 9 December 1958).

bined with the population pressure and the hacienda expansion of the *Porfiriato*, gave rise to an urban work force with strong ties to the countryside. As a result, villages—particularly in the states of Tlaxcala, Puebla, and Mexico—made important contacts with radical doctrines through these ties. Besides contacts with socialist and collectivist doctrine in the 1870s and 1880s, Buve specifically maintains that the *Partido Liberal Mexicano* was influential in this regard, both on urban workers and, through their ties with the villages, on the discontented *campesinos*.[23] He bases part of his evidence on an interview with Antonio Hidalgo, former GCOL leader in Tlaxcala.

Although I find his argument on urban-rural contacts persuasive, whether or not they affected labor unrest is another matter. Certainly he makes a strong case for this to have been true in Tlaxcala, where the textile mills were often located near small villages in essentially rural areas. There also is evidence that the workers of the Metepec mill near Atlixco were often ex-*campesinos* and maintained close contact with the nearby villages.[24]

The influence of the PLM may have been greater in the north, where fairly easy contacts could have been made with PLM members and their numerous supporters in the Mexican-American communities along the border. Certain evidence points to the middle and lower middle class people—professionals, small shopkeepers, muleteers, artisans of all kinds—as more likely PLM supporters in the north than industrial workers. One list of PLM members and supporters in the Monterrey area, identified by their contributions of money or their subscription to *Regeneración*, contained the names of fifty-one individuals. Of those named, only seventeen were specifically noted as having a working-class occupation, and most of those were artisans. Only three were industrial workers. The rest were classified vaguely as "gente del pueblo," or, for the most part, were obviously

23. Buve, "Protesta de obreros," pp. 2–3, 8, 11–15.
24. Ibid., pp. 11, 13. For a similar thesis on rural-urban contacts, see Jean A. Meyer, "Historia de la vida social," in *Investigaciones contemporáneas sobre historia de México*, p. 383. Moore, *Industrialization and Labor*, pp. 285–95. Even as late as the 1940s, 18 percent of the Metepec workers' mother tongue was an Indian dialect, and 21 percent was bilingual (ibid., p. 288, tables 21, 23).

middle class, being either professional people or property owners.[25] Whether this characteristic holds true for other areas is difficult to say. I suspect it does, but at this point the evidence is lacking.

In any case, after the failures of the PLM's 1906 revolts, and certainly after the mid-1908 uprisings, what Liberal influence there was among the various groups of Mexican workers was declining, not increasing. The reasons for this are many. For one thing, the PLM itself was increasingly under attack, both in the United States and in Mexico, with more and more of its personnel behind bars or in hiding. It is doubtful that those who were left were able to maintain contact with many working-class supporters, particularly after 1908. In some cases the PLM operators themselves moved toward a more moderate opposition to the government—Dr. Carlos Ramírez, Gabriel Gavira, and Samuel A. Ramírez are examples of PLM activists who supported the Anti-Reelectionist movement more avidly than their critics within the PLM thought wise.

From the workers' perspective, armed revolt against the regime would not have been attractive. By mid-1908 the Mexican economy was in the first stages of a full-scale recession, and more than a few workers were worried about keeping their jobs. Many would have been too preoccupied with sheer survival to consider revolt. Moreover, whatever their ideological beliefs, I suspect that until quite late in the decade, most workers believed that the regime was too strong to bring down by force and that revolt would only invite even greater repression than they had already experienced. Some workers were no doubt still harboring illusions about the possibilities of governmental intervention to resolve their problems. At least the records show that many efforts were made to obtain such support.

On the other hand, after 1908 the actions of a number of the most militant workers' groups—especially those in Orizaba, Tlaxcala, and Puebla, where PLM influence was supposedly the strongest—were in support of a political, not a revolutionary, solution to their demands. Having failed to gain the support of the Díaz administration, many workers were attracted by the post-Creelman interview political movements, hoping to improve their situation by an alliance with

25. Sub-secretary of Gobernación (Miguel S. Macedo) to Gen. Bernardo Reyes, 27 February, 5 April 1907, AGBR, Correspondencia ministeria, 1903–1909.

dissidents from other classes. Their willingness to ally themselves with political movements that spoke only briefly and vaguely to their own interests appears sufficiently unlikely that historians have overlooked or disregarded the evidence of such an alliance. The key to understanding the Mexican workers' political choice and actions, their strategy and tactics, is seen in who they thought to be their enemies, as well as in who they believed could be their friends. It is seen particularly in their short- and long-term objectives and in how they viewed themselves and their place in their society. One needs to see the basic ideological perspectives which linked various groups of Mexican workers and which separated them from European ideologies or the more radical Mexican movements such as the PLM.

The social complexity of the *Porfiriato* creates enormous difficulties in generalizing about Mexican industrial workers. In a country undergoing rapid industrialization and consequent rapid social change, the Mexican labor force undoubtedly reflected those changes in the manner in which various sectors of the labor force reacted to their problems. The critical problem, and one which lies essentially outside the scope of this study, is to differentiate between and among the various types of social responses to industrial work and to relate those different responses to the origins of industrial conflict in Mexico.[26] Until future studies deal with job mobility, social origins of factory workers, etc. within individual factories, we can only speculate as to the effect such differences must have had on the nature of the industrial conflicts in Mexico.

No doubt many workers reacted to their problems (both on and off the job) by the usual symptoms of personal disequilibrium—alcoholism, desertion of family, psychotic behavior, and other forms of escape or "coping." For example, although one need not consider

26. For a sociological perspective, see Neil J. Smelser, *Theory of Collective Behavior* (New York: Free Press of Glencoe, 1963), pp. 47–66, and his earlier important study, *Social Change in the Industrial Revolution. An Application of Theory to the British Cotton Industry 1770–1840* (Chicago: University of Chicago Press, 1959), pp. 402–8. See also an interesting study by Samir Khalaf, "Industrialization and Industrial Conflict in Lebanon," *International Journal of Comparative Sociology* 8 (March 1967): 89–98, which emphasizes changing role expectations as causal factors in industrial conflict among first generation industrial workers.

evidence of alcoholism among Mexican workers as a direct factor in industrial unrest, it may indicate the insecurity and harshness of their life and work, and, in general, provide evidence of the psychological environment of unrest.[27] Translated into political terms, such means of coping with problems may not lead to unrest at all but to apathy and resignation.

Of those who did protest their working conditions, some were no doubt fighting to retain the social benefits of the old society, their traditional relationship with the owners, their sense of acceptance within their shop instead of competition, their freedom as free artisans rather than factory workers or day laborers. Others, whose roots were in the land and the rural villages, were factory workers by necessity; for these workers labor conflicts may have been a last resort effort to retain certain aspects of the agrarian society they grew up in or simply their efforts to make the best of a bad situation, that is, to make industrial work bearable. Yet still others, perhaps second generation industrial workers or second generation urban dwellers, were struggling to achieve for themselves a respected, accepted role in the new order—the industrial, national society. It would have been this latter group particularly that saw themselves as part of the prevailing order of things, a poorer part, certainly, and a part that was being deprived of its share of the wealth and progress of its nation, but a part of it nonetheless. What they were demanding is that the industrial system be made to work for them as well as for the rich and powerful.

Those various and different workers were linked together by their common goals and aspirations: their demands to be respected and to improve the material rewards of their work; the feeling of being exploited by foreigners and their domestic allies; their sense of being

27. For alienation from work as a causal factor in industrial conflicts, see Daniel Katz, "Satisfactions and Deprivations in Industrial Life," in Kornhauser, Dubin, and Ross, *Industrial Conflict*, pp. 88–94, 98–106; Philip M. Hauser, "The Social, Economic, and Technical Problems of Rapid Urbanization," in *Industrialization and Society*, eds. Bert F. Hoselitz and W. E. Moore (Paris: UNESCO, 1963), pp. 199–217 and his discussion of the literature of the effects of urban living, pp. 209–11. In contrast to this position, dissident scholars doubt the significance of the process of modernization on industrial conflict (see Henry Bienen, *Violence and Social Change. A Review of Current Literature*. (Chicago: The University of Chicago Press, 1968), pp. 100–105).

"Mexican" (rather than being "workers"); and their faith in the promises held out by the *Reforma* of the previous century. Moreover, they were also united by their common demand for a governmentally imposed solution to their problems. Whatever the pressure of the situation which encouraged this tactic, the underlying "ideological" basis for it lay in the long established, traditional source of such solutions—the *patrón*. As the owners and entrepreneurs became more modernized, they failed to perform this traditional role, forcing the workers to seek aid and comfort elsewhere, in other words, from the government.[28]

That most Mexican workers chose to remain within the existing political system, both as it then operated and as it was traditionally constructed, can be seen in the way those workers expressed their goals and demands. In what they said, as well as in what they did, one can clearly see the political perspectives of most Mexican industrial workers. Most workers commonly expressed their goals in terms of fair treatment from the capitalists, respect from their foremen and from society at large, aid and justice from their government, and equality with other classes.[29] "Those who have raised their voices to demand justice," asserted a textile workers' flyer, "do so because they consider Capital and Labor to be equal."[30] It was equality, respect, and justice they wanted, and although it may seem clear to later generations that new institutional arrangements were needed before these needs could be met, there is no inherent reason why workers in the *Porfiriato* should have believed this.

Particularly significant is the insistent demand for justice that appeared in nearly everything they wrote. "And it should be understood," declared one particularly bitter letter to the editor of *El Paladín*, "that the workers are not asking for concessions but only justice, justice that will end the arbitrary acts that are committed against us."[31]

28. Meyer, "Batallones Rojos," p. 32, suggests a similar cultural influence on the workers' faith in government intervention to resolve their problems.
29. For representative statement of those goals, see: a flier from the workers of El Dique, 31 May 1906 (Jalapa, Veracruz), GPDC, 31:5889; workers' letters to *El Paladín*, 7 January, 14 May 1909; *México Nuevo*, 13 June 1909; *El Diablito Rojo*, 7 February 1910; workers of the Santa Rosa factory to Ramón Corral, 19 October 1906, AGN-Gob, leg. 817.
30. The industrial workers of El Dique, 31 May 1906, GPDC, 31:5889.
31. Workers in the weaving department of Río Blanco to *El Paladín*, 8 May

The workers from the La Hormiga mill pleaded with Díaz for help, threatening that "if the justice of our nation sleeps in the far off, dusty past, we will awaken it with our message in order to force it to finish its sacred mission."[32] The Mexican workers defined justice both as a moral and a legal right. Certain old weavers from Río Blanco wrote that it was "an injustice to be considered even worse than an outcast in our own land, being that our laws protect us."[33] A Mexico City *obrero* declared that they, the workers, must strive for the "TRIUMPH OF THE LAW."[34]

Their demand for justice under the law was not a naive belief that the Porfirian judicial system might come to their aid by enforcing certain specific statutes of the legal codes. Rather it was essentially a strong, stubborn faith in the basic law of the nation, the Constitution of 1857. The evidence for this can be seen in the expressions characteristically used by Mexican workers to justify their grievances. Their demands for justice were often phrased with references to the past, linking their struggle with the great liberal movements of the nineteenth century. The textile workers at the San Bruno mill in Jalapa struck for nearly half a year rather than permit the firing of a number of their comrades who refused to work on the anniversary of Padre Hidalgo's birthday. In the last days of their strike they issued a proclamation proudly declaring: "We have fought tirelessly, bearing our shield of reason and justice ever before us, the fundamental basis for every individual who would claim their rights. . . . We have not wavered in defending our sacred rights."[35] They believed that their rights were directly related to the political and social struggle began by the man whose birthday they celebrated.

When Flavio R. Arroyo spoke to fellow textile workers during the great strike of December 1906, he referred to the "Constitution of Benito Juárez" as the hard rock of their goals.[36] Workers from Santa

1910; for similar demands, see *El Paladín*, 12 August 1909, 8 May, 12 June 1910.

32. Workers of La Hormiga to Díaz, 2 March 1909, GPDC, 34:4661.

33. *El Paladín*, 13 March 1910.

34. "La unión es fuerza," article by Cruz Villafranca in *México Nuevo*, 19 April 1910.

35. *El Paladín*, 7 January 1909.

36. Cited in *La Lucha Obrera*, 16 December 1906. See also "Los obreros en huelga," *El Paladín*, 7 January 1909. John Womack, Jr. points out a strong

Rosa protested to Ramón Corral that the mill owners had violated "our reform laws that cost so much shedding of blood by our heroes, who defended them with justice and loyalty."[37] A railroadman wrote Díaz to request justice in the name of the liberals who fell in battle during the struggles of the Reform, giving "their blood and their life on the altar of . . . liberty."[38] From the workers' perspective, then, what they needed was not a new social order but a *restoration* of the rights granted them by the liberal reform movements of the nineteenth century.[39] They did not know that Article 4 of the Constitution of 1857 on freedom of labor had often been used against workers to prevent them from organizing or striking.[40] They were basing their appeals not on a legal interpretation of the Constitution but on what the Constitution stood for in their own minds.

For one thing, the Mexican industrial workers identified the Constitution of 1857, and the liberal movement in general, with nationalism and patriotism because of their long struggles against the Spanish, the North Americans, and the French. This identification of liberalism with patriotism was one important step in the development of a working-class political ideology during the *Porfiriato*. The workers identified with liberalism and the Constitution because they themselves were patriots and nationalists, and their nationalism helped give shape and form to their political perspectives.

It is hardly news to scholars of Latin American labor movements that working-class protests have tended to be nationalistic in tone.[41] This is clearly the case in Porfirian Mexico. The most convincing

feeling among the country people of Morelos for the Constitution of 1857 and a faith that what was needed to solve their problems was to carry out the laws, honestly and justly (*Zapata*, p. 71). See similar sentiments in two Posada cartoons in *El Diablito Rojo*, 8 February 1909.

37. Letter dated 29 October 1906, AGN-Gob, leg. 817.
38. J. Trinidad Nav(indistinct) to Díaz, 10 March 1910, GPDC, 35:4058.
39. For references to restoration of rights see: Ignacio C. Castellanos, AEM, 144:280, 24 November 1909; "Convocatoria a la clase obreros," Aquiles Serdán, flyer, from the Serdán museum, Puebla; Juan Ramírez, *México Nuevo*, 6 August 1909; "Old weavers from Río Blanco," *El Paladín*, 13 March 1910; a flyer, "The workers of the Republic," from the GCOL, Río Blanco, 6 November 1906, AGN-Gob, leg. 817; T. E. Paniagua, *El Correo de Chihuahua*, 22 April 1909.
40. González Navarro, *La vida social*, p. 298.
41. See Alexander, *Organized Labor*, pp. 6–7.

evidence of the workers' nationalism is their obvious belief that they *were* Mexican patriots, that in fighting their battles with the industrialists they were fighting the nation's battles as well. When striking Metepec textile workers proudly wrote to *México Nuevo* that "Mexicans, no matter how humble, will not permit their own dignity to be insulted, much less that of their fatherland," they were identifying their struggle with that of the nation.[42] José Neira, leader of the GCOL in its radical phase in 1906, sought support from his fellow mill hands by relating his fears that "soon we are going to see our race disappear and be destroyed, losing forever our beloved homeland."[43] In fact, several accounts of the early meetings of the group of mill hands who eventually formed the GCOL mention that one motivating factor in their impulse to come together was a common indignation against Francisco Bulnes's controversial book disparaging Juárez, *La verdadera Juárez*, published in 1904.[44] Bulnes and his fellow *científicos* seemed to those men to be tearing down everything that was Mexican.

In the rhetoric and actions of the Mexican industrial worker—in his references to the great heroes of the *Reforma*, in his hatred of the *científicos* and their foreign friends and European ways, in his support of General Bernardo Reyes because of Reyes's known patriotism, in his bitter denunciation of the foreign influence in his land—the Mexican worker was expressing his consciousness of being Mexican. For whatever the reason, he saw his own fate bound up with the larger fate of his nation.[45]

The workers' faith in the justice of the *Reforma* is not only based on that era's struggle for national independence but also on their perception of the social content of the liberal movement. Historians commonly interpret nineteenth century liberalism as the ideology of an emerging bourgeoisie and point to the liberal regimes' general inability or unwillingness to deal with social issues. This thesis is no doubt

42. *México Nuevo*, 16 May 1909.
43. "In the Arena," in *Revolución Social*, Peña, "Apuntes históricos," 19 August 1958.
44. "Breve historia de un crimen. 7 de enero de 1907," CROM, 15 January 1927, p. 18; Peña, "Apuntes históricos," 29 July 1958.
45. Zietlan in his study of post-1959 attitudes of Cuban workers states that the workers' sense of work exploitation "was inseparable from the national colonial status" of their country (*Revolutionary Politics and the Cuban Working Class*, p. 287).

true. Looking backward, however, to industrial workers in the first decade of this century the liberal movements appear to be a quest for social justice within the framework of national independence. It was the workers' belief that the Reform movement had defeated not just Maximilian's foreign rule, or the clerics and the conservatives, but *gachupinismo*—a native creole society ruling as if they were foreign masters dominating an indigenous population.

I have no proof of this, of course. Rather I offer it as a partial explanation of the workers' obvious identification with the liberals of the previous century. Exactly why they should have believed in the social justice of liberalism is not clear to me. Perhaps because of the role played by such low-born men as Morelos, Guerrero, Juárez, and Juan Álvarez, perhaps also because the concept of *la raza*, with its inherent collective overtones, linked up in the minds of many workers the great struggles of the past with the workers' own struggle for well-being and dignity. A textile workers' leader reminded his men that they were "descendents of the indomitable race of Cuauhtémoc, Hidalgo, and Morelos."[46] Puebla mill hands were challenged to "prove that you are Mexicans worthy of the blood of Cuauhtémoc, Juárez."[47] Those were appeals to cultural pride in which the fate of all classes were bound together and were important in enabling Mexican workers to identify their own cause with that of their country.

Mexican workers demanded justice from their society and supported those demands by referring to the nation's past commitment to social justice, as they perceived it. Their patriotism, therefore, emerges as neither naive nor calculating. It was what they wanted to believe about their nation and what they needed to believe about themselves—that they were the legitimate heirs of the patriots and reformers of earlier times. Their nationalism did not dilute their demands for social justice; it stimulated them, giving them form and strength. In effect it legitimized the workers' demands in their own eyes, casting their movement as patriotic, not revolutionary, and placing their cause squarely in the mainstream of Mexico's historical development.

One may argue, of course, that the workers' efforts to identify their

46. Flier "A los proletarios del Segundo Círculo de Obreros Libres," Puebla, 11 November 1906, AGN-Gob, leg. 817.
47. Cited in Martínez to Díaz, 21 December 1906, GPDC, 31:16370.

movement with the nation's historical struggle for justice were based on tactical considerations; i.e., that they were motivated by the workers' belief that only by appealing to the nationalist sentiments of other Mexicans would they be successful in their efforts to gain allies against the industrialists, particularly when the latter were often foreigners. If true, the workers' nationalism becomes opportunism, explaining little (or much) about the nature of their movement. I choose, however, to accept the workers' apparent nationalism at its face value because it appears to me to be the most reasonable explanation of what was a widespread and consistent characteristic, and because I have no evidence that suggests the workers were not sincere. What we know at this point, both through what they said and what they did, is that Mexican workers considered themselves to be working Mexicans fighting for their self-betterment within the traditional system of justice.

Industrial Workers and Mexican Nationalism

A *chicano* student of mine once brought to class a quotation from an article he had read. "To be Mexican is not to have a nationality," the quote read, "it is to be addicted."[48] Recognizing the ambiguity of such a statement, it still can hardly be denied that the development of Mexican national identity has been one ingredient in the modern history of the Mexican people. In the most ambitious attempt yet by a non-Mexican to define Mexican nationalism and analyze its growth, Frederick C. Turner, in his book *The Dynamic of Mexican Nationalism*, asserts that Mexico's nationalism "has given the Mexican national community a particular cohesiveness and flexibility," resulting in a remarkable sense of national consensus about social and economic goals.[49] Furthermore, Turner suggests that the Mexican Revolution gave many Mexicans a new sense of social injustice. He quotes Profes-

48. From Abel Quesada, "Dime que comes y te dire quien eres," in *Hoy*, 10 May 1969, p. 15.

49. *The Dynamic of Mexican Nationalism*, (Chapel Hill: North Carolina University Press, 1968), p. 4. See also his explanation of the concept of Mexican nationalism, pp. 4–21.

sor C. Trejo Lerdo de Tejada, who wrote in 1916 that the Revolution had "transformed the national conscience" and had created "a demand, a reality, a new and indisputable tendency of justice and equality," for Mexico's "subjugated majority."[50]

Although I suspect that Turner has overstated his case—that nationalism is a kind of all-purpose miracle salve for the pains of nation-building—the relationship between Mexican nationalism and the country's particular approach to its problems deserves serious study. It certainly appears, for instance, that some Mexicans viewed the labor problem in the late *Porfiriato* in a nationalist context, a connection which grew out of Cananea, Río Blanco, and the general struggle of Mexican workers against foreign employers in the factories and mines and on the railroad lines owned by their own government.

Beginning with the national outrage that accompanied the Cananea strike, the grievances of Mexican workers became subtly but inextricably linked with the questions other Mexicans were raising concerning the privileges foreign capitalists appeared to have in their country. Given the failure of the regime to condemn the actions of Governor Isábel at Cananea, the rumored slaughter of the Río Blanco workers must have shocked Mexican nationalists into asking themselves how many Mexicans the regime was willing to kill in behalf of foreign interests. The railroad question, especially after 1908, continually raised the image of arrogant foreigners depreciating everything Mexican, even on railway lines owned by their own government. The labor press, the sympathetic weeklies, and even a few important dailies continued to print letters from workers detailing charges against foreign supervisors and foreign bosses, who were at best uninterested in Mexican tradition and history and who all too often were scornful of their host nation and its people. The image that foreigners presented to many Mexicans was succinctly stated in an antiforeign political cartoon published in *El Diablito Rojo*: "We enjoy the privileges of the laws and legal codes," say the foreigners in the cartoon, "and you greasers get the penalties."[51]

Meanwhile, post-Creelman political movements provided the envi-

50. Cited in ibid., p. 130.
51. "The Latest Plebisite," 22 June 1908.

ronment in which the workers' plight and the government's supposed
sympathy for the foreigners became issues used against the regime.
The manner in which the workers' problems were handled by the
administration was one of the clearest evidences of its strong ties with
foreigners, men whose presence in Mexico was increasingly becoming
a source of indignation and even a threat to many Mexicans. When
the regime of Porfirio Díaz fell in May 1911, its defeat was due in an
important way to the Mexican worker.

Postscript

In the green refuge of Chapultepec Park in Mexico City, close by the Castle itself, is a museum of Mexican history. This modern, round-shaped building features famous scenes from Mexican history done in three-dimensional relief. On any day of the week excited bands of school children with their slightly harried teachers invade the grounds, and among the historical scenes at which they stare intently are two events described in this study—the strikes of Cananea and Río Blanco. Both show Mexican workers angrily confronting their oppressors—soldiers in the case of Río Blanco and U.S. "Rangers" at Cananea. At the entrance to the museum, just inside the door, is a large stone plaque, telling its readers that this museum is dedicated to "The Struggle of the Mexican People for their Freedom." It continues:

> Mexican: Understand, appreciate, and respect the efforts of all
> those who lived their lives in order to make their nation great.
> The example of men, women, and even the children who
> fought to obtain your freedom, to defend your land, and to
> affirm justice among your brothers will guide you in your life as
> in the halls of this building. Be influenced by this example and
> endeavor always to be worthy of the heroes of the Inde-
> pendence, the Reform, and the Revolution.

For the Mexican people, Cananea and Río Blanco are not only historical events, they are social myths; that is, they are national symbols which transcend class to provide a common identity, binding the Mexican people together as a nation. They are not myths simply because all that is popularly believed about these events did not really happen; they are myths because those who came afterwards chose to give to these events a social truth rather than an historical one. To do so does not render them a lie. It is the right of a people to transform their history from the level of historical reality to that of mythology just as much as it is the right of an artist to call an arrangement of colored paint "An Old Man Sitting In A Chair." Both create their own reality as they interpret what they see and feel. If the story that has been told in the pages of this book contradicts the accepted mythology of Cananea and Río Blanco, it should not be concluded that one is "right" and the other is "wrong." Historians have a professional responsibility to recreate the past as they believe it was lived, out of respect for the men and women who lived it. Yet for as long as it will be needed, the Mexican people will most likely honor "los martires de Río Blanco" and remember them as brave men facing death to stand up against tyranny and greed.

Appendix A
Strike Tables, 1865–1911

TABLE A.1
Strikes By Industry, 1865–1905

Year	Total	Textile	Railroad	Tobacco	Mines	Craft	Trolley	Misc.
1865	2	2						
1868	2	2						
1872	1				1			
1873	4	3			1			
1874	3	1			2			
1875	1					1		
1876	2	2						
1877	4	4						
1878	3	1						2
1879	3	1			1			1
1880	2	1						1
1881	7	2		2		1		2
1882	4				1			3
1883	7	3	1		1			2
1884	13	8		1	2			2
1885	4	2		2				
1886	4	1			1	1		1
1887	1		1					
1888	3	1		2				
1889	10	7		2			1	
1890	4	1	1	1	1			
1891	5	1	1		2			1
1892	5	4	1					
1893	3	1	1		1			
1894	4	1	2	1				
1895	10	4	1	1	1	2		1
1896	5	3	1			1		
1897	1		1					
1898	7	5	1				1	
1899	1		1					
1900	4	4						

TABLE A.1 (CON'T)

Year	Total	Textile	Railroad	Tobacco	Mines	Craft	Trolley	Misc.
1901	10	2	6		1		1	
1902	4	1	3					
1903	4	2	1		1			
1904	1							1
1905	6	1	2	3				
Sub-totals:								
1865–1879	25	16	0	0	5	1	0	3
1880–1889	55	25	2	9	5	2	1	11
1890–1899	45	20	11	3	5	3	1	2
1900–1905	29	10	12	3	2	0	1	1
Total:								
1865–1905	154	71	25	15	17	6	3	17

Source: Compiled by the author from various primary and secondary sources. See especially Moisés González Navarro, "Las huelgas textiles en el Porfiriato," *"Historia Mexicana*, 6 (October–December 1956):204–10 and his *El Porfiriato, la vida social*, in Daniel Cosío Villegas, ed. *Historia Moderna de México*, vol. 4.

TABLE A.2
Strikes by Industry, 1906–1911

Year-Month	Total	Textile	Railroad	Tobacco	Mines	Craft	Trolley	Misc.[1]
1906 January–June	8	5			1			2
1906 July–December	19	17	1		1			
1907 January–June	20	14	3				1	2
1907 July–December	15	3	3		2	3	3	
1908 January–June	15	5	1	1	1	1	4	2
1908 July–December	8	4	1	1	2			
1909 January–June	11	6	1	2	1			1
1909 July–December	7	6	1					
1910 January–June	4	4						
1910 July–December	4	4						
1911 January–May	8	8						
Total	117	76	11	4	8	4	8	7

Source: Compiled by author from primary and secondary sources, especially newspapers.
1. Includes strikes by longshoremen, linotype operators, construction workers, and metal workers.

TABLE A.3
Geographic Origins of Industrial Strikes: 1865–1905

States	Total 1865–1905	1865–1879	Sub-totals 1880–1889	1890–1899	1900–1905
Federal District	61	16	17	22	6
Veracruz	21		11	4	6
Puebla	9	2	5		2
San Luis Potosí	8		3	3	2
México	3		2	1	
Jalisco	3		1	1	1
Tlaxcala	3		3		
Nueva León	3		1		2
Sinaloa	3	1	2		
Querétaro	2	1		1	
Hidalgo	2	2			
Guanajuato	2	2			
Colima	2		2		
Chihuahua	1		1		
Aguascalientes	1			1	
Sonora	1			1	
Total	125*				

*Of the 154 strikes noted in Appendix Table A.1, only 125 were identifiable as to state of origin.

TABLE A.4

Geographic Origins of Industrial Strikes: 1906–1911[1]

States	Total 1906–1911	Totals by Industry Tex-tiles	Steet-car[2]	Mining	Misc.[3]
Puebla	31	27	1	0	3
Veracruz	28	24	1	0	3
Federal Dist.	19	11	2	0	6
Jalisco	6	2	3	0	1
Tlaxcala	5	5	0	0	0
Querétaro	4	4	0	0	0
México	4	4	0	0	0
Hidalgo	4	0	0	4	0
Aguascalientes	1	0	0	0	1
Chihuahua	1	0	0	0	1
Coahuila	1	0	0	1	0
Sonora	1	0	0	1	0
Zacatecas	1	0	0	1	0
Totals	106	77	7	8	15

1. The total does not include railroad strikes because of the difficulty in determining location of strikes.

2. The total of streetcars is minus one strike noted in Appendix Table A.2 because origin could not be determined.

3. Includes strikes noted in Appendix Table A.2, note 1, as well as strikes by various groups of artisans and tobacco workers.

TABLE A.5
Geographic Origins of Textile Strikes: 1865–1905

States	1865–1905	1865–1879	1880–1889	1890–1899	1900–1905
Federal District	35	12	7	14	2
Veracruz	15	0	8	3	4
Puebla	7	2	3	0	2
Jalisco	3	0	1	1	1
Tlaxcala	3	0	3	0	0
México	3	1	1	1	0
Querétaro	2	1	0	1	0
Totals	68	16	23	20	9

TABLE A.6
Geographic Origins of Textile Strikes: 1906–1911

States	1906–11	1906[1]	1907[2]	1908	1909	1910[3]	1911
Veracruz	24	10	6	2	1	3	2
Puebla	27	9	3	4	2	3	6
Federal District	11	2	1	1	6	1	0
Tlaxcala	5	1	1	1	2	0	0
Querétaro	4	0	3	1	0	0	0
México	3	0	3	0	0	0	0
Jalisco	2	0	0	0	1	1	0
Totals	76	22	17	9	12	8	8

1. The GCOL strike of the Puebla and Tlascala mills in December are counted as one strike for each state.

2. The three strikes noted for Querétaro in 1907 included as one strike the simultaneous work stoppage at the Hércules and the Purísima mills.

3. The strike of the fiber (jute) mill Santa Gertrudis in Orizaba is included here, under textiles. The mill, owned by British investors, was an important one, employing just over one thousand men.

TABLE A.7

The Grievances: 1865–1905[1]

Grievances	Total	1865–1879	1880–1889	1890–1899	1900–1905
Wages[2]	78	14	37	14	13
Regulations[3]	36	4	9	16	7
Treatment[4]	17	0	7	6	4

1. Where the information was available, a maximum of two grievances were included for any one strike. In a number of cases only one grievance was noted and in a few cases none at all.

2. Grievances over wages included either the lowering of wages or workers' desire to increase wages, as well as protests of fines, wage discounts, and the use of company script in payment of wages.

3. Grievances over regulations included the issues of hiring or firing, length of workday or workweek, firing for union activity, work on holidays, or miscellaneous company regulations.

4. Grievances over treatment involved mistreatment such as beatings or insults by supervisors or owners.

TABLE A.8

The Grievances: 1906–1911[1]

Grievances	Total 1906–1911	1906	1907	1908	1909	1910	1911[2]
Wages	45	15	17	3	5	4	1
Regulations	42	12	11	12	5	2	0
Treatment	14	3	6	2	2	0	1

1. Where the information was available, a maximum of two grievances were included for any one strike. In a number of cases only one grievance was noted and in several cases none at all.

2. Only January through May.

TABLE A.9

Strike Totals: 1865–1911

By Industry:

Years	Total	Textiles	Rail-roads	Mines	To-bacco	Trolley	Crafts	Misc.
1865–1905	154	71	25	17	15	3	6	17
1906–1911	118	76	11	8	4	8	4	7
Total	272	147	36	25	19	11	10	24

By Issue:

Years	Wages	Regulations	Treatment
1865–1905	78	36	17
1906–1911	43	41	13
Totals	121	77	30

By Geographic Origin:

Years	Federal District	Vera-cruz	Puebla	San Luis Potosí	Méx-ico	Jalisco	Tlax-cala	Que-rétaro	Hidalgo
1865–1905	61	21	9	8	3	3	3	2	2
1906–1911	19	28	31	0	4	6	5	4	4
Totals	80	49	40	8	7	9	8	6	6

By Geographic Origins, Textile Industry:

Years	Federal District	Vera-cruz	Puebla	Jalisco	Tlax-cala	México	Que-rétaro
1865–1905	35	15	7	3	3	3	2
1906–1911	11	24	27	2	5	3	4
Totals	46	39	34	5	8	6	6

Appendix B
Work Force Tables

TABLE B.1

Work Force in the Textile Industry: 1897–1911

States/Years	1897–1898	1898–1899	1899–1900	1900–1901	1901–1902	1902–1903	1903–1904
MEXICO - Totals	21960	19406	27677	27767	28617	26149	27706
Veracruz	3537	3537	4992	4992	5409	5232	5390
Puebla	3037	3037	3987	3987	3884	4282	5196
México	2012	2012	2154	2154	2199	1945	1805
Federal District	1863	1863	2487	2487	2717	2021	2311
Coahuila	1548	1548	1892	2051	1993	2068	2082
Tlaxcala	1324	1324	1549	1549	1632	1416	1420
Querétaro	1230	1230	1320	1320	1350	1200	1280
Guanajuato	994	994	1316	1316	1248	1041	1196
Jalisco	990	990	1726	1726	1962	1707	1780
Durango	923	923	1191	1191	1066	830	940
Oaxaca	785	785	765	765	705	670	640
Nuevo León	742	742	781	781	824	852	740
Michoacán	689	689	738	738	780	669	884
Tepic (Nayarit)	590	590	590	590	590	320	320
Sinaloa	398	398	412	412	399	332	197
Hidalgo	318	318	361	361	443	301	341
San Luis Potosí	266	266	331	331	300	250	250
Guerrero	242	242	162	162	162	162	162
Colima	170	170	176	163	163	147	144
Sonora	150	150	160	160	168	248	208
Chiapas	100	100	100	100	120	130	130
Chihuahua	52	52	437	437	453	320	290

Source: El Colegio de México, *Estadísticas económicas*, p. 108.
*Figures for 1901–1902 are from Matías Romero, *Los jornales en México*, p. 405 in López, *Historia económico de México*, p. 308.

TABLE B.1 (CON'T.)
Work Force in the Textile Industry: 1897–1911

States / Years	1904–1905	1905–1906	1906–1907	1907–1908	1908–1909	1909–1910	1910–1911
MEXICO - Totals	29464	31096	33132	35866	32209	31953	32147
Veracruz	5876	6160	7056	6975	6824	7213	7194
Puebla	5679	6351	7520	8549	7859	8074	8142
México	1831	1897	1925	1843	1774	909	1542
Federal District	2802	2705	3339	4670	4090	4717	5088
Coahuila	2105	2054	1570	1546	996	1833	1007
Tlaxcala	1434	1395	1835	1870	1932	1988	1668
Querétaro	1260	1220	1175	1175	972	901	765
Guanajuato	1245	1274	1390	1474	1222	1106	1000
Jalisco	1219	1880	1848	1848	1714	910	1538
Durango	1030	1062	852	1060	520	351	628
Oaxaca	570	570	570	570	490	250	250
Nuevo León	877	813	829	860	857	958	945
Michoacán	885	892	727	616	739	787	556
Tepic (Nayarit)	605	605	320	320	280	280	280
Sinaloa	304	348	180	300	307	301	139
Hidalgo	388	391	434	450	37	37	345
San Luis Potosí	250	250	250	300	300	145	N.A.
Guerrero	162	259	288	419	419	432	432
Colima	122	129	90	105	102	60	N.A.
Sonora	244	244	264	236	220	216	180
Chipas	150	160	157	160	150	150	150
Chihuahua	426	437	513	520	425	335	311

TABLE B.2
Work Force in Mining: 1898–1907

States / Years	1898	1899	1900	1901	1902	1903	1904	1906*	1907
MEXICO-									
Totals	89072	106539	95523	98196	85333	86815	81368	72023	97288
Guanajuato	13000	11886	17683	8053	8474	9165	5062	6912	11005
México	11908	1757	2576	3423	4130	3622	5192	—	6697
Jalisco	8686	2359	2629	2419	3433	1520	2554	1801	2996
Zacatecas	8089	17818	9850	21847	21842	8726	7108	3895	9670
Durango	7658	8310	7048	8500	8000	10721	8468	7226	5741
Sonora	4982	5519	4104	3569	6006	7255	6824	4747	7124
Chihuahua	4852	9692	6350	6357	2630	6287	6434	8564	7673
San Luis Potosí	3989	3915	7646	10768	6623	5559	8189	9989	8618
Oaxaca	3529	2525	2726	2477	1702	1751	1816	1326	2291
Nuevo León	3483	9158	3520	3310	4387	4157	3457	2131	9935
Hidalgo	3434	9498	9406	8759	—	8644	9725	9895	10037
Sinaloa	3210	4265	4411	4572	3964	3475	2509	3243	4016
Coahuila	2843	7361	3885	2869	3817	6177	1700	2605	2180
Baja California	2400	2553	2903	2777	2130	2383	2344	4374	2028
Michoacán	2144	2441	3640	2832	2954	1992	5700	—	1700
Guerrero	1675	3405	1776	1257	993	1070	1021	683	1167
Aguascalientes	753	762	2257	1159	1529	1584	1143	1460	1828
Querétaro	745	599	633	—	329	267	514	584	198
Tepic	740	1161	1268	1528	1278	1232	906	635	875
Chiapas	340	290	437	262	345	170	—	—	—
Tamaulipas	300	185	398	612	202	202	37	373	—
Puebla	192	949	355	385	399	732	602	1396	1373

Source: El Colegio de México, *Estadísticas económicas*, p. 131.
* No figures available for 1905.

TABLE B.3
Mexican Work Force: 1895–1910

	1895	1900	1910
Total	4761914	5131051	5337889
Agricultural	2976128	3177840	3584191
Industrial	692697	803294	803262
Manufacturing	554555	624039	613913
Extractive	88548	107348	104039
Transport	55678	59666	55091
Construction	49594	62997	74703
Electrical	——	8910	10553

Source: El Colegio de México, *Estadísticas económicas*, pp. 39, 45–50.

TABLE B.4
Mexican Work Force: 1895–1910, by State

	1895		1900		1910	
	In-dustry	Agri-culture	In-dustry	Agri-culture	In-dustry	Agri-culture
Jalisco	72736	278854	84525	277044	62985	301154
Guanajuato	64918	299989	66946	241748	66528	243425
Oaxaca	54032	243237	65845	259104	57428	274310
Puebla	50268	224073	60846	236714	63097	241584
Veracruz	28314	229976	29522	245529	44273	315052
Michoacán	41731	210639	45482	242932	41835	262562
México	27137	195573	32448	226826	43868	234464
San Luis Potosí	22958	101918	25553	139138	26021	154200
Federal District	65752	33019	70610	44999	92009	52035
Hidalgo	24424	117471	36771	138586	30092	148125
Querétaro	12711	63805	12058	61528	10761	65782
Zacatecas	32431	94182	30026	99192	22060	104315
Chiapas	37847	75243	30934	92624	22587	107610
Nuevo León	12744	69892	15872	54169	17835	81921
Guerrero	7357	106490	7641	120996	9192	160077
Yucatán	12880	83428	13771	81633	21941	77079
Sinaloa	14013	66284	24750	69263	13666	84076
Durango	13704	74763	23847	71821	23503	125227
Chihuahua	13566	64293	17108	78972	24333	86721
Coahuila	10448	54073	41056	58797	30950	77638
Sonora	9854	47132	13419	52033	18662	57621
Tamaulipas	4865	45653	6064	54574	5993	63407
Tepic	8923	29481	7060	37993	6726	46849
Tlaxcala	16550	29005	8697	38729	10599	41871
Morelos	4189	43031	4418	42887	5739	49963
Aguascalientes	8734	24241	9726	22117	11300	24869
Tabasco	3372	29828	4784	38747	4412	44366
Campeche	9468	19094	5894	21977	5522	23499
Colima	3314	12967	3343	16804	4816	19799
Baja California	3452	8494	4258	10364	3929	12181

Source: El Colegio de México, *Estadísticas económicas*, pp. 39, 45–50.

Appendix C
Factory Regulations Proposed by the *Gran Círculo de Obreros Libres* of Puebla, December 1906

The workers of the factories "Mayorazgo," "Amat-lán," "Molino de Enmedio," "La Teja," "San Alfonso," "El Carmen," "Hilandera," "Economía," "Beneficencia," "Santo Domingo," "Inde-pendencia," "La Constancia," "San Diego," "Santa María," "La Covadonga," "Santa Cruz Guadalupe," "La Josefina," "La Tlax-calteca," "San Manuel," "La Trinidad," "La Estrella," "Elena," "San Luis Apizaquito," "San Juan Pautzingo," "San Damián," "El Carmen" (Atlixco), "El Volcán," "El León," and "Guadalupe Analco," in view of the regulations issued by the "Centro Industrial Mexicano" whereas which are highly prejudicial to the interests of the working commu-nity inasmuch as they limit the freedom of the home, and which attempt in such a way to reduce the workers' wages, already greatly diminished, and in response to the prevailing general discontent among the workers, and to the end of restraining subsequent conflicts, we have resolved to propose to the industrialists the follow-ing

REGLAMENTO:

1. Working hours shall be from 6:00 A.M. until 8:00 at night, minus 45 minutes for lunch and the same for dinner. On Saturday, work shall be suspended at 5:30 P.M. The fifteenth of September and the twenty-fifth of December shall be half days of work.

The work whistle [*toque de llamada*] shall be sounded five minutes before the hour that work begins. In the morning in addition to the work whistle, two warning whistles shall be sounded: one at 5:30 A.M. and one at 5:45 A.M.

The night shift shall enter the factory only after the day shift has left.

2. Workers coming to work in a state of drunkenness shall not be admitted to the factory.

3. Payday for all workers shall be on Saturdays, without exception. Paying shall be completed by 6:00 P.M., and the method of paying should be changed so as to effect this.

4. No one employed by the factory shall mistreat workers by word or deed, as this, besides being a violation of the law, is an act of savagery repudiated by all civilized nations. The workers demand to be respected and in turn shall show respect for their superiors.

5. Foremen and supervisors shall continue to be forbidden to charge fees for the allocation of work to the workers, the violation of which will result in the firing of the offender.

6. The foremen (*maestros*), as delegates of the administration and acting under authority and instructions as such, shall deal directly with the workers of the section to which they [the foremen] were appointed. They [the foremen] shall take care that the machines of their sections are in perfect order, giving notice of any defects that are observed in these machines.

7. The workers shall take care of the machinery and tools under their charge, as well as pick up the bobbins, spools, and other objects that fall near their machines, but they shall not be responsible for any accident that such machinery or tools suffer due to the frequency with which they are used.

8. As it is arbitrary to prohibit the reading of newspapers, the workers are obligated only to forego reading when such interferes with their work.

9. The supervisors of the departments shall deal with all acts of disorder that arise in the factory.

10. There should always be paper in the washrooms in order to avoid having the workers use cotton or yarn in these places.

11. Workers shall not be deprived of any personal papers that they might carry with them when they enter the factory.

12. No worker shall suffer unjust deductions [from his pay] for the purpose of paying the factory physician, for store debts, or other reasons.

13. Workers on legal [union] commissions shall not be fired for such activity. Each factory shall have two representatives from our Society whose purpose will be to report immediately any disorder to the fac-

tory administration or to the authorities and to the officers of our Society.

14. The administration is prohibited from admitting apprentices or workers under the age of 14, in conformity with the public education law.

15. All shuttles which, on the judgment of the foreman, had deteriorated because of constant use, shall be changed immediately.

16. In the case of defective fabric, the worker shall be responsible for payment of the value of the damaged cloth only, and not the value of the labor. The payment shall be made on the judgment of a permanent commission in each factory.

17. All fabric that is not included in the above regulation (#16), as well as additional manufactured products of the factory, shall remain as previously agreed upon.

18. As it is publicly and widely known that in all the factories of the Republic there are company stores which exercise a monopoly, we ask that they be officially prosecuted both because they are unconstitutional and because they are very prejudicial to the working class.

19. All workers returning to work [after the settlement of the strike] shall be given the same position they held previously.

20. When there are differences between workers concerning the changing of yarn or fabric and there is not sufficient agreement between the foremen and the Society, outside experts shall be brought in.

21. The owners, administrators, managers, and supervisors of all the factories of the Republic shall be forced, without exception, to obey articles five and thirteen of the Constitution.

22. All workers who because of the lack of assistance have to perform the work usually done by these assistants shall be paid the fees usually received by the same. This shall apply in all departments except weaving.

23. Workers who because of the lack of physical ability do not meet the [excessive] demands of the job shall not be fired from their positions, since it is not possible for each worker to have the same ability. The same shall apply to older workers, who have worked in the factory all their lives and who for this reason alone should be worthy of every consideration.

24. Workers that are disabled on the job shall be pensioned at half wages for as long as they stay at the factory.

25. The firm shall pay to have binders [*atadores*], and any worker who performs this work shall receive the corresponding remuneration. When two or three reams [of fabric] are involved, the workers shall be paid a moderate amount for the loss of his regular work time.

26. The night shift shall receive an increase of 25 percent over the regular wages, because night work is more demanding on the worker.

DÍAS FESTIVOS

First of the year, 6 January, 2 and 5 February, 19 March, Monday and Tuesday of *carnival*, Thursday, Friday, and Saturday of the Holy Week, 5 May, *Corpus* Thursday, 24 and 29 June, 15 August, 8 September (in Puebla and Atlixco), 1 and 2 November, 8, 12, and 25 December.

TRANSITORIO. Reserving the rights of this Society that pertain to it at all times, toward whatever eventuality or unforeseen occurrence, and basing all [this document] on the laws of our fundamental charter.*

Puebla de Zaragoza, 9 December 1906. (Signed by Pascual Mendoza, Adolfo Ramírez, and Antonio Espinosa.)

Source: Fernando Rodarte, *7 de enero de 1907*, pp. 10–17. Not included in the above translation of the *Reglamento* were the detailed wage and piece-work suggestions, pp. 14–16.

* The original "nuestra carta fundamental" presumably referring to the Constitution of 1857.

Appendix D
Workers' Anti-Reelectionist Clubs

I. Federal District:
Club Político Obreros "Benito Juárez"
Obreros de Tacubaya
Femenil Hijas de Anáhuac
Club Constitucional Anti–Reeleccionista "1910" de Tacubaya
Constitución y Reforma
Mártires de Padierna
Miguel Hidalgo
José María Morelos
Cuauhtémoc
Club Anti–Reeleccionista de la Fábrica Linera
Club Anti–Reeleccionista de Artes Gráficos
Clubes Anti–Reeleccionistas en Tlalpan

II. Orizaba:
Ignacio de la Llave
Mártires de Río Blanco
Club Anti–Reeleccionista de Obreros de la Fábrica de Yute
"Mariano Escobedo" de Nogales
Club Anti–Reeleccionista de Santa Rosa
"Sebatian Lerdo" de Río Blanco

III. Other:
"Miguel Hidalgo y Costilla" (Concepción del Oro, Zacatecas)
"Guillermo Prieto" (Atlixco)
Club Anti–Reeleccionista de Obreros de Autlán (Autlán, Jalisco)
Club Anti–Reeleccionista de Obreros "Luz y Progreso" (Puebla)
"Ignacio Zaragoza" (Puebla)
Club Anti–Reeleccionista de Fábrica de Hilados y Tejidos de Lana "Soria" (Empalme Escobedo, Guanajuato)
Club Anti–Reeleccionista de Fábrica de Colchas 'La Providencia' (Celaya, Guanajuato)
Héroes de Chapúltepec (location not known)
"Carlos Pacheco" (location not known)
Libertad (location not known)

Obreros Libres (location not known)
"Nicolas Bravo" (location not known)
"Melchor Ocampo" (location not known)

Source: Compiled by the author. Several other clubs are known to have been
established (e.g., in the city of Veracruz, Aguascalientes, and among
various artisan groups in Guanajuato) but have not been listed here for
lack of a name or more specific information.

Appendix E
History and the "Inarticulate": A Personal Note

In recent years historians have begun to write about the "inarticulate," meaning ordinary men and women who silently pass through life, leaving few traces of their existence and making no impact on their times. Without power or position, the "inarticulate" have supposedly lacked the necessary opportunities to leave as their historical legacy the documents which are indispensable for the writing of a true and proper account of the past. Hence, history has tended to be written about the elites of society because the historian has been largely unable to recover the facts which might illuminate the lives of most of mankind.

Certainly much of the thesis of the "inarticulate" is true, and the effort to write history from the perspective of common men and women is long overdue. Yet once serious scholarship is directed toward the problem of the "inarticulate," it becomes rather obvious that the term is misleading. Jesse Lemisch, for example, became so concerned about the inappropriateness of its use that he began placing quotation marks around the word, and I have copied the practice here to emphasize the point.[1] The problem with the use of the term to describe ordinary people throughout history is, in the first place, that men are not rendered historically inarticulate because they are illiterate, a prime and obvious assumption of the doctrine of the inarticulate. Illiteracy is not necessarily the same thing as ignorance or apathy. Men *act* and leave evidence of their actions in the documents and chronicles of others, and the historian's training should be sufficient for him to recover this information.

Also modern technology enables quantitative data to be used to answer broad questions about large bodies of people. A whole new

1 See Jesse Lemisch, "The American Revolution Bicentennial and the Papers of Great White Men," *American Historical Association Newsletter* 9 (November 1971): 7–21; and Lemisch and John K. Alexander, "The White Oaks, Jack Tar, and the Concept of the 'Inarticulate'," *William and Mary Quarterly* 29 (1972): 109–34.

branch of history is evolving, based on such sources as tax lists, election roles, church records, municipal archives and the like. In addition, such statistical sources can be given flesh and blood through the use of materials ignored or ill-used by previous generations of historians—popular verse and song, oral traditions, records of workingmen's societies and their journals, autobiographical materials, and letters to the editor of newspapers are only a few such sources.

Furthermore, I believe that since the eighteenth century many people without position or wealth have been literate or have had access to writing through literate members of their own class and through public scribes (*escritores*) for almost as long as literacy has been common among their social betters. This fact has been demonstrated in American labor history by Professor Lemisch and Herbert G. Gutman, and by the British historian Edward Thompson in his pioneering work *The Making of the English Working Class*, to name a few. My own research clearly indicates that Mexican working-class people at the turn of the century, for example, were far more literate and articulate than has been assumed by historians.

It is hard to deny that the low socio-political profile of the great majority of people in all civilizations throughout human history has determined the lack of impact they have had on the writing of history, but I suspect that the neglect has resulted as much from the interests and prejudices of the historian as from a fundamental "inarticulateness" of the common man. Too often, ordinary people have been rendered inarticulate by the historians themselves, some of whom, like Professor Charles F. Mullett, consider that the writing of the history of "dirty people with no names . . . must be left to God."[2]

This historical disenfranchisement may be as seemingly deliberate as Professor Mullett's insult, or it may be an inevitable oversight in a profession dominated until recently by the John R. Commons school of labor history. Commons, the great University of Wisconsin economic historian, emphasized wage demands and working conditions, institutional developments within the labor movement, and the

2. *Journal of Southern History* 35 (1969): 78. Professor Mullett's remark was made in a review of an article by Jesse Lemisch, "The American Revolution Seen from the Bottom Up" in Barton J. Bernstein, ed., *Towards a New Past: Dissenting Essays in American History* (New York: Pantheon Books, 1968).

economics of trade unionism. These problems are important, certainly, but in adhering too narrowly to the field which Commons established, many of his followers lost sight of the socio-cultural milieu of the rank and file worker and in doing so have failed to appreciate and explore the complex varieties of the historical experience of American working men and women. In recent years, the works of Lemisch, Irving Bernstein, Herbert Gutman, Eli Ginzberg and Hyman Berman, Studs Terkel, Staughton Lynd, Stephan Thernstrom, and others have helped remedy what is still a major deficiency.[3]

Likewise, in the past writers and scholars of Latin American labor history have followed similar paths, or they have been too outraged by the obvious injustices or too wedded to ideological commitments to engage in the difficult and often frustrating basic research that needs to be done. Recent historiographic surveys have suggested that the writing of Latin American social history and labor history in particular has expanded significantly in the last decade or so, contesting and even displacing the essentially elitist concentration on diplomatic, biographical, political, and military history that once characterized the great bulk of Latin American historical writing, both in English and Spanish. Charles Bergquist sees in this trend a movement toward "mass-oriented versus elite history," noting that while social and economic history combined made up only one-quarter of the articles published by the *Hispanic American Historical Review* in its first thirty years, it made up 38 percent in an eight year period from 1965 to 1972. In a nearly exhaustive survey of studies dealing with Latin American working classes in the ABC countries, three labor scholars suggested that there is "a substantial and growing body of literature on labor and the working class."[4]

Much of this work is useful, some even outstanding. Yet all too

3. Robert H. Ziegler, "Workers and Scholars: Recent Trends in American Labor Historiography," *Labor History* 13 (Spring 1972): 254–60.

4. Bergquist, "Recent United States Studies in Latin American History: Trends Since 1965," *Latin American Research Review* 9 (Spring 1974): 3–35. Kenneth Paul Ericson, Patrick V. Peppe, and Hobart A. Spalding, Jr., "Research on the Urban Working Class and Organized Labor in Argentina, Brazil, and Chile: What Is Left To Be Done?" *Latin American Research Review* 9 (Summer 1974): 115–42.

often the Latin American worker, his beliefs and needs, his response to industrial work, and his place in the history of his nation are as uncertain as before. With important exceptions, studies that propose to raise the worker from the obscurity of the past have treated him as if he were inarticulate, like the ancient worker in Pablo Neruda's "Alturas de Macchu Pichu"—mute, imprisoned in the depths of the earth, unable to express the essence of his own historical experience.

Peter Stearns in his study of French syndicalism noted that while historians are committed to writing history "from the bottom up," they ironically fail to apply this principle to their own work. He suggests that perhaps the reason is that "historians, being to some degree intellectuals, too often look at the expressed ideas of a movement or organization without checking the extent to which the ideas were held by participants or manifested in their behavior."[5]

Fundamentally and essentially, history is written not by individuals but by generations and by special intellectual classes within each generation. American historians, regardless of their class origin, bring to their work certain assumptions about the historical experience of working people. Despite the tradition, however, that the American people value hard work and respect those who work with their hands, I fear that for American historians, and intellectuals in general, this is a myth. Instead I believe that what most intellectuals respect and honor are the abilities and opportunities that provide mobility *out* of the working class into what they consider to be more rewarding work and a more meaningful existence. They may sympathize with the workingman's experience, but they do not respect it. In turn, they may romanticize the workingman's past struggles, but they neither understand nor are able to relate to his contemporary existence. I suspect that most historians and perhaps most scholars—conservative, liberal, or Marxist—by virtue of their occupation and social training, are elitist, not democratic, in their fundamental outlook on life. It is this basic value that is the origin of many historians' assumption that the common man is fundamentally inarticulate, or worse, that his past could hardly matter.

5. Peter Stearns, *Revolutionary Syndicalism and the French Worker, 1890–1914* (Rutgers, N.J.: Rutgers University Press, 1973), p. 1.

Bibliographical Comments

The following is a discussion of the sources and materials used in this study and of several points of methodology. For more detailed discussion of particular sources, see Manuel Carrera Stampa, *Archivalia mexicana* (Mexico: Universidad Nacional Autónoma de México, 1952) and Agustín Millares Carlo, *Repertorio bibliográfico de los archivos mexicanos y de los europeos y norteamericanos de interés para la historia de México* (Mexico: UNAM, 1959). A valuable guide to research in Mexico is Michael Meyer and Richard Greenleaf, eds., *Research in Mexican History: Topics, Methodology, Sources, and A Practical Guide to Field Research* (Lincoln, Neb.: University of Nebraska Press, 1973).

Primary Sources

ARCHIVO GENERAL DE LA NACIÓN

A number of important documents are found in the *Ramo de Gobernación*, legajos 12, 718, 817, 824, and 2226, including *rurales'* materials on labor disturbances and documents connected with the ministry's role in the government's efforts to deal with the labor unrest. Unfortunately, a number of other relevant legajos and boxes that I consulted in my dissertation research have been recatalogued since then, and a cross index of new and old legajos is not available. A discussion of the contents of each such legajo can be found in the dissertation, available from the University of Michigan, abstract published in 1969. For references to other labor-related *gobernación* materials that were also subsequently renumbered, see Manuel González Ramírez, *La Revolución social de México*, vol. 1, *Las ideas y la violencia*, pp. 73, 76, 79, 81.

The Ministry of *Fomento, Colonización, e Industria* handled industrial affairs during this period. (It was not until 1912 that the *Dirección de Trabajo* was established in this ministry, giving labor official representation for the first time.) The archive for this ministry was, at last report, located in the Casa Amarilla, in Tacubaya, an extension of the

AGN but with no facilities for research. The secretary of this ministry, Olegario Molina, became officially involved in several labor questions. In addition, a thorough search of this archive through 1911 might well reveal badly needed basic data on industrial workers. Of value for the post-1911 period is caja 30, legajo 6, expediente 40 of the *Dirección de Trabajo*, containing a list by state of labor societies active in 1912, and caja 30, legajo 7, expediente 68, which contains a list of cotton textile mills operating in Mexico as of September 1914.

In 1917 this ministry became the *Secretaría de Industria, Commercio y Trabajo*, and under Cárdenas the labor section became an independent ministry. At least part of its archive—those labor materials prior to 1917—went to the Casa Amarilla instead of to the new ministry, but it is possible that some Porfirian documents are housed in the present ministry's *archivo (Secretaría del Trabajo y Previsión Social)*, to which I did not have access. In addition the *Secretaría de Economía Nacional* may have materials pertaining to the *Porfiriato* in its archives. Neither ministry is easily accessible to researchers.

ARCHIVO GENERAL DE LA SECRETARÍA DE RELACIONES EXTERIORES

This archive was used for its materials on the *Partido Liberal Mexicano* (PLM) in the *Ramo de Ricardo Flores Magón*, L–E–918 to 954, thirty-six volumes in all. This ramo is also available, bound and copied, at the *Biblioteca de la Secretaría de Hacienda y Crédito Público*. Only a few of the documents of this *ramo* were directly applicable to the study of Porfirian labor, but a more systematic use of these materials in answering such questions as the extent and geographic origins of working-class contributors to the PLM might further clarify the relationship between the Liberals and Mexican industrial workers.

ARCHIVO GENERAL DEL GOBIERNO DEL ESTADO DE VERACRUZ-LLAVE

Selected ministerial materials from this archive for the 1906–1914 period are copied, in full or in part, and available at the Seminario Histórico de la Universidad Veracruzana in Jalapa, Veracruz, Prof. David Ramírez director. Its value to this study is primarily for the correspondence between the *jefe político* of Orizaba (Carlos Herrera, 1906, and Miguel Gómez, 1907–1911) and the state government.

An undetermined amount of personal papers belonging to the governor of the state, Teodoro A. Dehesa, are held by Lic. Leonardo Pasquel, director of the Editorial Citlaltepetl in Mexico City. I saw only several folders (dealing mostly with the political activities of Dehesa following the Creelman interview), but it is possible that there are more documents. Pasquel noted in one of his publications (*Mátalos en caliente*, Mexico, 1965, p. XVII) that he would at some future date publish the "Dehesa Memorias."

See also María Elena Sodi de Pallares, *Teodoro A. Dehesa: Una época y un hombre* (1959). Sodi de Pallares had access to an extensive repository of documents, on loan from the Dehesa family. Her book contains many of these documents, poorly used. An unconfirmed report is that the bulk of the Dehesa archive was destroyed by fire, presumably after the book was written.

EL CENTRO DE ESTUDIOS DE HISTORIA DE MÉXICO

Located in the Fundación Cultural de Condumex, S.A., this repository contains a few materials of interest, including *memorias* of various ministries, a number of copies of *El Hijo de Ahuizote*, and the important literary journals *Revista Azul* and *Revista Moderna*, drawings and cartoons by José Guadalupe Posada, and the published census of 1910.

U.S. NATIONAL ARCHIVES

With few exceptions, the materials consulted from this source concerned the PLM. Examined in the U.S. Department of State records, Record Group 59, numerical file 1906–1910, were volumes 22, 186, 353, 430, 512, and 594. Also seen were Record Group 84 containing consular post records for 1906–1911; the U.S. Department of Justice records, Record Group 60, files nos. 90755, sections 1–23, boxes 717–20, and 43718, box 148; and the U.S. Supreme Court records, Appellate Case no. 21153, relevant to the appeal of the Liberals convicted of violating U.S. neutrality laws. Of marginal value, mainly for reports of worker involvement in the Revolution of 1910, is "The

State Department Papers on Internal Affairs of Mexico, 1910–1929," political file 812, nos. 534, 1110, 1160, 1300, 1381, 1399, 1884, and 5045.

ARCHIVO ESPINOSA DE LOS MONTEROS (AEM)

This archive is located in the History Annex of Chapultepec Castle and is well organized. It contains important *reyista* materials from the Mexico City movement, along with documents from other *reyista* organizations. Labor-related materials are few but throw some light on General Reyes's appeal to workers.

ARCHIVO GENERAL BERNARDO REYES (AGBR)

This fairly extensive archive is located in Mexico City in the building that houses the "Capilla Alfonsina," a private library and literary society dedicated to the works of Reyes' famous literary son Alfonso. It contains numerous documents to and from Díaz and such ministers as Ramón Corral but is only of minor interest for labor matters.

EL MUSEO NACIONAL DE ANTROPOLOGÍA (MNA)

Though only several series of documents were consulted for this study, undoubtedly more information lies in the various state materials contained in this repository.

JOSÉ Y. LIMANTOUR PAPERS

The only significant Limantour papers available to historians are located in the Latin American Collection of the University of Texas Library in Austin and consist mainly of personal financial data. See "José I. Limantour Correspondencia 1848–1911," folder 87A. Limantour's financial interests were widespread, and he was, undoubtedly, one of Mexico's richest men.

GENERAL PORFIRIO DÍAZ COLLECTION (GPDC)

This enormous collection, housed in the library of the University of the Americas in Cholula, Puebla, proved to be extremely important for this study. The collection is organized chronologically within broad categories of materials, the most extensive of which are the over 500,000 letters and 161,000 telegrams covering the years from 1876 to 1911. Although there is no subject index available as of yet, the material is organized by the year and by the month and by general chronological order within each month. Most of the letters and telegrams from early 1905 to June 1911 were reviewed in the course of this study. Important telegrams were sent in code but can often be decoded without reference to the code books (which are available but difficult to use) by either searching for the precoded copy of the telegram or one that had been decoded upon arrival.

This collection was opened to researchers in 1970. Previously it had been made available to Alberto María Carreño by Col. Porfirio Díaz, son of the president. Carreño brought out thirty volumes of the archive between 1947 and 1961 (published as *Archivo del General Porfirio Díaz: Memorias y Documentos*), covering only selected documents relating to the years up to 1880. With the death of Carreño, as well as Col. Díaz and his son Genaro Díaz Raygosa, the papers came back into the possession of the family. Their guardian and widow of Díaz Raygosa, Mrs. Marie Therese Gatouillat, eventually reached an agreement with the University of the Americas to make the collection available to historians. At that point the archive came under the care of Prof. Laurens B. Perry of the University of the Americas, whose work in organizing, numbering, and microfilming the documents reduced to months a task that might have taken years to accomplish. All the legajos, except miscellaneous pamphlets and newspapers, and code books, are now available on microfilm for consultation at the University of the Americas. Eventually the University will house the originals themselves, which as of 1973 were still at the family residence in Mexico City.

Though the collection is of special interest for historians of politics in the *Porfiriato*, scholars concerned with social and economic problems will find considerable materials there. The greater number of documents reveal more about state or local situations, however, than about federal policy or Díaz's personal designs. Díaz generally said little in his correspondence with either officials or private citizens, often simply acknowledging receipt of the original letter or telegram, noting its basic content. One learns much more from letters to Díaz (or correspondence of a third party sent to Díaz as part of the "rules of the game," to use Cosío Villegas's phrase). Nonetheless, here and there hints of Díaz's ideas and intentions are found, and in conjunction with other sources, they add up to an historical portrait of Porfirio Díaz more accurate than anything yet revealed.

Like most historians, I suspect that the most useful sources were the ones I did not use or those which lie unknown in regional archives or factory and union hall repositories. Indeed, from the perspective of this study, the most useful would be the letters, diaries, journals, and personal reminiscences of workers of the era that must exist and that someday will be used to clarify, or contradict, many of the assumptions and interpretations I have made here.

Although the general assumption might be that such sources are limited, the first-hand evidence uncovered for this study would indicate that many more still remain to be utilized. The concentration of this study on sources available in Mexico City, for example, suggests that regional studies would be fruitful in this regard, especially for such cities as Orizaba, Puebla, Monterrey, Guadalajara, and others, where local sources would likely yield information not available in the research centers of Mexico City.

Even where there exist few first-hand reports by the workers themselves, the historian has other materials waiting to be of use—government statistics on health and migration, factory records dealing with worker turnover, previous occupation, etc., and newspaper evidence giving incidents of working-class attitudes and showing actual group action such as strikes and petitions, to name a few. A more careful study of strike patterns than attempted here undoubtedly will reveal much about the problems Mexican workers faced as perceived in the factory and the shop, about the goals and needs of the various movements, and about the broader question of origins and timing in industrial conflicts. Regional and local comparisons need to be made, for the Mexican workers were no more of one mind than were their contemporaries at large.

In the search for a clearer image of Mexican workers, local city government records need to be more thoroughly explored. An examination of the holdings of the Ayuntamiento of the City of

Mexico will almost certainly reveal data on working conditions of that city, material almost totally ignored by historians (including this writer) heretofore. See Manuel Carrera Stampa, "Guía del archivo del antiguo ayuntamiento de la ciudad de México," in *Los archivos nacionales de la América Latina*, edited by Roscoe R. Hill (Habana, Archivo Nacional Publicaciones), no. 23, pp. 1–53.

If in the process of reconstructing the past of working men and women in Mexico one should not concentrate on leaders and organizations, one can hardly ignore them either. Pascual Mendoza's personal papers, certainly, if they exist, would be extremely interesting, as would those of José Morales and José Neira. The papers of the latter were reported to be in Orizaba by José Ortiz Petricioli in his 1940 pamphlet on Río Blanco, although he was not able to see them at the time. It may well be that Hubierto Peña Samaniego's newspaper series (in *El Clarín*, Orizaba weekly) on the 1906–1907 Orizaba textile workers' movement utilized Neira's papers, since the details presented in Peña's articles were from an obviously informed source.

The files of the labor unions of the day are likely scarce, if any survived the unsettling events in the decades that followed. Luis Araiza in his *Historia del movimiento obrero mexicano* cites certain documentary materials held by the *Sindicato de Obreros y Artesanos de la Industria Cervecera y Conexos*, in Orizaba. In addition, Mutsuo Yamada's thesis "The Cotton Textile Industry in Orizaba," noted below, contains labor materials drawn from private archives in the area.

NEWSPAPERS

Mexico City dailies, proworker weeklies, and provincial newspapers are a major resource in the study of industrial workers in the *Porfiriato*. Carefully used, they not only yield otherwise unobtainable facts about the various labor movements and conflicts but reveal much about the working-classes' own view of their problems through the numerous letters to the editor, petitions, and flyers published in the Mexican press. *El Paladín* (1906–1911), *El Diario* (1907–1908), and *México Nuevo* (1909–1910) carried the greatest number of such documents, especially letters. Textile workers were the most vocal, but over the years letters appeared from workers in various industries and occupations located throughout the central states. Other sources documenting worker complaints were the Mexico City weeklies *La Guacamaya* (1902–1908), *El Diablito Bromista* (1906–1908), *El Diablito Rojo* (1908–1910), and *La Palanca* (1904–1905). Papers carrying the most reports on the labor movements, besides the above, were the Mexico City dailies *El País*, *El Tiempo*, *El Diario del Hogar*, *El Imparcial*, and the *Mexican Herald*. Provincial dailies and weeklies with consistant coverage of labor problems and developments were *Jalisco Libre*, *La Revista de Mérida*, *El Correo de Chihuahua*, *El Estandarte* (San Luis Potosí), *El Cosmopolita* (Orizaba), and *El Dictamen* (Veracruz).

In addition, the best sources of business viewpoints are the weekly journals *El Economista Mexicano* (pro-*científico*) and *La Semana Mercantil*. The latter, edited by Everardo Hegewish, was the official organ of the Industrial and Commercial Confederations of the Republic and the Chamber of Commerce of Mexico City. It took a relatively more moderate and independent position on the labor question than did *El Economista Mexicano*. An interesting commercial paper with a subtle antiforeign and anti-*científico* bias is *El Progreso Latino*. All were published in Mexico City. *El Imparcial* is a good source of probusiness opinion, although its position as the unofficial administration spokesman places it in a different category from all three of the above.

Most of the above papers are available at the Hemeroteca Nacional. Of the weeklies, *La Guacamaya*, *La Bromista*, and *La Palanca*, along with a few issues of a number of other weeklies, are held by the University of Texas library. Single copies of such worker papers as *Revolución Social* and *La Lucha Obrera*, as well as other useful newspapers, are available in various archives (especially the GPDC) and are identified with these archives when used in the notes for this text. The Bibliography lists the names of all prolabor or labor newspapers during this period known to this writer, whether or not they were consulted for this study.

The use of this kind of historical evidence presents several methodological problems. First, one must deal with the particular bias of the paper, separating fact from editorial fancy or prejudice. Once identified, however, such positions become evidence in and of themselves, representing a range of nonworking-class social attitudes toward the workers. Without a doubt, newspapers are one of the best available indications of how the new industrial classes were regarded by their fellow citizens.

The most difficult methodological problem lies in the verification of the evidence found in these papers, as well as verification of similar evidence from other sources. Many of the over three hundred working-class documents I reviewed were unsigned except anonymously such as "various workers from Río Blanco," or "old weavers." The problem is whether it can be assumed that such letters were actually written by members of the working classes, and, if so, whether it should be assumed that they were representative of their own class.

I attempted to verify the working-class origins of the documents by comparison with other documents that I knew to be written by workers, and by ascertaining the accuracy of their evidence as attested by other, known reliable sources. The representativeness of such documents is clearly the most difficult and important problem, because such interpretations as that of the workers' political attitudes and ideological orientation are partly dependent on such evidence. Lacking quantitative data on working-class attitudes, I tested the representativeness of my evidence through the traditional methods of my profession—by using my judgment as to whether or not the available evidence was from a reasonable number of sources and whether or not my interpretation of this evidence provided an adequate explanation of the known behavior of a sufficiently broad stratum of Mexican industrial workers.

POST–1911 NEWSPAPER SOURCES

Of the literally hundreds of newspaper and journal articles on Porfirian labor published since the fall of the old *Caudillo*, most are about the Cananea and Río Blanco strikes, and very few are useful for historical purposes. There are exceptions, usually accounts by participants or witnesses. See such examples as articles in *La Opinión* (Veracruz), 21 February 1912; *El Democrática*, 29 August to 30 September 1924; *Mañana*, 18 November 1944; *El Universal* (Mexico City), 7 January 1954; and *El Clarín* (Orizaba), July 1958 to December 1960. An excellent source of such articles is Stanley R. Ross, ed., *Fuentes de la historia contemporánea de México: Periódicos y revistas*, 2 vols., (Mexico, 1965–1967), 1:3–232, especially pp. 15–98.

PUBLISHED DOCUMENTS AND SOURCES OF STATISTICAL
AND DESCRIPTIVE DATA

Governmental documents published during this period were generally of little value for this study. The *Diario de los Debates de la Cámara
de Senadores del Congreso de los E.U.M.* and the corresponding *diario* for
the House of Deputies give some feeling for the attitudes of the political elites, but for the most part little attention was given to the workers
or their problems. For example, during the critical textile strike-
lockout in December 1906, the debates in Congress made no mention
of the crisis.

The available sources of statistical and descriptive socio-economic
data are few. The pamphlet *El Florecimiento de México* (1906) contains
useful information on textile mill ownership, and the various yearly
issues of *The Mexican Year Book* give valuable economic data for various firms in a variety of industries. The journal *México Industrial* contains articles of a general nature on industrial and commercial
technology, giving some insight into the optimism of the era.

Sources of statistical data are few. The most reliable for social statistics such as birth rates, education, etc. is Moisés González Navarro,
Estadísticas sociales del Porfiriato, 1877–1911; for economic statistics including production by industry, wages, and prices, etc., El Colegio de
México, *Estadísticas económicas del Porfiriato: Fuerza de trabajo y actividad
económica por sectores*. For economic analysis and description, see the
two volumes in the Colegio series *Historia Moderna de México*, dealing
with economic life in the *Porfiriato*, and the *Porfiriato* section of Clark
Reynolds, *The Mexican Economy: Twentieth Century Structure and Growth*.
Materials direct from the census of 1910 were used only sparingly in
this study, although they are available in published form.

Contemporary sources of interesting statistical and descriptive information on economic and social conditions are: Julio Guerrero, *La
génesis del crimen en México* (1908); Alberto J. Pani, *Hygiene in Mexico*
(1917); E. D. Trowbridge, *Mexico: Today and Tomorrow* (1919); and
Wallace Thompson, *The People of Mexico* (1921). Thompson's book,
though patronizing and subtly biased against hispanic culture, contains useful descriptions of social conditions in Porfirian Mexico. His
statistical analysis of the labor force is helpful, given the difficulty of
arriving at adequate definition of "industrial labor."

Secondary Sources

A successful revolution calls forth its own history of the old regime, inevitably tied to the politics of the new situation. In the decades that followed the overthrow of the Díaz government, the development of the historical image of the *Porfiriato* was determined by the necessity not only to legitimize the victors but also to play a role in the political struggles of the times. With the emergence of a labor movement as a participant in those struggles, the history of the Mexican workers' experience in the *Porfiriato* was slowly reconstructed to fit the ideological and political needs of the workers and their leaders, both within and without the labor movement.

The essence of what came to be the mythology of the Porfirian labor movement acquired its original shape and form in the years immediately preceding the *maderista* revolt against Díaz, with the publication of the works of Rafael de Zayas Enríquez (1908), Carlo de Fornaro (1909), and John Kenneth Turner (1909–1910), all of whom exaggerated the political character of working-class protests. When the great Mexican labor historian and labor leader Rosendo Salazar began his long and sometimes stormy career with the publication of *Las pugnas de la gleba, 1907–1922* (1923), he effectively canonized the myth of class-consciousness among prerevolutionary workers and its corollary, their adherence to the *magonista* cause.

Such myths prospered in the late 1920s and 1930s with the publication of various popular or semipopular histories treating the prerevolutionary labor movements, works which in effect and in some cases by design served as ideological adjuncts to the rise of a politically-oriented industrial labor movement. Among those were books and pamphlets by Salazar, Manuel Maple Arce, Teodoro Hernández, the brothers Germán and Armando List Arzubide, León Díaz Cárdenas, Juan de Dios Bojórquez, Luis Chávez Orozco, Manuel Díaz Ramírez, and others. At the same time numerous articles and pieces appeared in such diverse sources as *El Nacional*, *El Popular*, *Universal Gráfico*, *Últimas Noticias*, *CROM*, and *Excelsior*. Some of the latter particularly contained valuable information in the form of *memorias* which would otherwise have been lost to the historian. Generally, however, the scholarship was weak and the facts too often unreliable.

During the presidency of Lázaro Cárdenas, particularly, the government sponsored the publication of a considerable amount of such works. For example, the Ministry of the National Economy published Luis Chávez Orozco's important eleven-volume series of documents on the economic history of the country, mostly for the colonial period and the nineteenth century. The Ministry of Education under Gonzalo Vázquez Vela established the series *Biblioteca del Obrero y Campesino* to publish popular works dealing with social themes, the stated goal being to encourage socialist education in Mexico. Among the works published in this series were Germán and Armando List's pamphlet on Río Blanco and León Díaz Cárdenas's work on Cananea. The ministry even published a series of interesting essays by secondary school students on the Río Blanco and Cananea strikes. Introducing the short pamphlet, Vázquez suggests that "Socialist Education sponsored by the Government of the Revolution is grounded on the foundation of productive and socially useful work." In essence, under Cárdenas the great events of Cananea and Río Blanco became evidence of a revolutionary heritage designed to support the legitimacy of the workers' demands for social justice and to justify the regime's efforts in fulfilling them.

American readers had no reason to doubt such accounts. Marjorie Ruth Clark's work, *Organized Labor in Mexico* (1934), while providing important information on the post-1911 labor movement, perpetuated the same myths concerning the ideological nature of the Porfirian labor unrest. Her study became the classic English language work on Mexican labor and hence the authority most American authors cited on labor problems under Díaz, although that was hardly the emphasis of her study. Such texts or general studies as Henry Bamford Parkes, *A History of Mexico* (1938), Howard Cline's *The United States and Mexico* (1953), and Charles C. Cumberland's *Mexico: The Struggle for Modernity* (1938), all followed the same line, as did such overall surveys of Latin American labor as those by Moisés Trancoso Poblete and Ben G. Burnett (1960), Victor Alba (1960), and Robert Alexander (1965). Only Cumberland added anything new to our knowledge of Porfirian workers, making various materials available in English for the first time. Charleton Beals's *Porfirio Díaz: Dictator of Mexico* (1932) has some interesting details, but its comments on labor are useless.

In Mexico the election in 1940 of General Manuel Ávila Camacho as president brought a changed political climate. Economic development became the new national goal, and there was little desire to encourage a militant class-consciousness among Mexican workers. Three useful pamphlets on the Porfirian textile labor movement were published in 1940, although none with state funds: Fernando Rodarte reproduced several important documents on the crisis of 1906–1907; Ana María Hernández gave important details concerning women in the labor movement; and José Ortiz Petricioli published his interviews with surviving participants of the labor conflicts of 1906–1907 in Orizaba, probably the most important source on Porfirian labor to that date. Rafael Ramos Pedrueza's marxist book *La lucha de clases a través de la historia de México* was published in 1941 by the government press, but it was the last of its kind with official sponsorship.

Nonetheless, beginning in the 1940s more objective and scholarly treatments of the *Porfiriato* began to appear, the most important being José C. Valadés's three volume work (1941–1948) *El porfirismo: historia de un régimen.* By the 1950s various general and specialized works on Mexican labor were available, more objective than the earlier studies but often no less committed to the goals of social justice for the Mexican people.

Two such general studies of the Mexican labor movements stand out. Alfonso López Aparicio's *El movimiento obrero en México* (1945) is careful and dispassionate and is still the best general narrative of the Mexican labor movement available. His section on the *Porfiriato* is weakened by an overemphasis on the role of the *Partido Liberal Mexicano*, but it is a necessary study. Moisés González Navarro's contribution to the Colegio de México's series *Historia moderna de México* stands as the seminal scholarship on Porfirian workers. In his study, *El Porfiriato: la vida social* (1957), Professor González Navarro utilized mainly published sources, especially newspapers and government documents, but the breadth of his treatment of issues, organizations, and conflicts and his feel for the material will make this work the point of departure for research on Porfirian labor for years to come.

Following the first edition of López Aparicio's survey came four less successful attempts to cover the same field: Alberto Trueba Urbina, *Evolución de la huelga* (1950), Roberto de la Cerda Silva, *El movimiento obrero en México* (1961), Luis Araiza (himself a trade unionist from the revolutionary period), *Historia del movimiento obrero mexicano* (1965), and Leonardo Graham Fernández, *Los sindicatos en México* (1969). More specialized were: Esteban B. Calderón, leader of the copper workers during Cananea, and his *Juicio sobre la guerra del Yaqui y génesis de la huelga de Cananea* (1956), Lyle C. Brown, "The Mexican Liberals and Their Struggle Against the Díaz Dictatorship" (1956), Manuel González Ramírez's edited monograph on Cananea for the *Fondo de Cultura Económica*'s series on the Mexican Revolution (1956), Ezequiel Montes Rodríguez, *La huelga de Río Blanco* (1965), Angel J. Hermida Ruiz's *Acayucán y Río Blanco: Gestas precursoras de la Revolución* (1964), and Alfredo Navarrete, *Alto a la contrarrevolución* (1971).

Of those, Araiza, González Navarro, Calderón, Brown, and Navarrete offered new materials but only González Navarro, and Brown (on Cananea) offered new interpretations and perspectives. Alfredo Navarrete's work is autobiographical in nature with a close feeling for the late *Porfiriato*, as well as some new information on the labor movement. González Ramírez made more convenient documents already available, including an interview with Esteban B. Calderón which more or less summarized the material contained in his *Juicio*.

In the past few years new interpretations have come to the forefront as research on Porfirian topics has increased on a broad front. Most notable are Raymond Buve's article "Protesta de obreros y campesinos durante el Porfiriato" (1972); Jean Meyer, "Los obreros en la Revolución mexicana" (1971), an article in *Historia Mexicana* which deals more with the decade of the Revolution but contains several interesting theses on Mexican labor in the *Porfiriato;* Stephen R. Niblo's doctoral dissertation "The Political Economy of the First Díaz Administration" (1972) with important material on the early years of the Díaz regime; John M. Hart's *Los anarquistas mexicanos, 1860–1900*, a revisionist study on the early labor movement; and James D. Cockcroft, *Intellectual Precursors of the Mexican Revolution, 1900–1911* (1968). Although I disagree with a number of Professor Cockcroft's hypotheses concerning the PLM and the labor unrest of the late *Porfiriato*, his study is a very important contribution to our understanding of the origins of the Mexican Revolution.

Other sources which should be mentioned are: Matt Meier, "Industrial Unrest in Mexico 1876 to 1911" (1947) for his early synthesis of Porfirian labor conflicts; Mutsuo Yamada, "The Cotton Textile Industry in Orizaba: A Case Study of Mexican Labor and Industrialization During the Díaz Regime" (1965), a quite important economic history of that industrial town; Dawn Keremitsis, *La industria textil mexicana en el siglo xix* (1973), a careful study with useful materials on labor in the cotton textile industry; Marcelo N. Rodea's early study of the railroad workers, *Historia del movimiento obrero ferrocarrilero en México, 1890–1943* (1944), contains documents and other material of value.

Bibliography

Primary Sources

ARCHIVES AND MANUSCRIPTS

Archivo Espinosa de los Monteros (abbreviated AEM). Located in the Museo Nacional de Historia, annex to Chapultepec Castle.

Archivo General Bernardo Reyes (abbreviated AGBR). Held by the family, Mexico City.

Archivo General de la Secretaría de Relaciones Exteriores, Ramo de Flores Magón et al (abbreviated Rel-RFM).

Archivo General de Gobierno del Estado de Veracruz, Ramo de Gobernación. Copies of documents located at the Seminario Histórico de la Universidad Veracruzana, Jalapa, Veracruz (abbreviated SHUV).

Archivo General de la Nación (abbreviated AGN).

Archivo General de la Nación, Ramo de Gobernación (abbreviated AGN-Gob).

General Porfirio Díaz Collection (abbreviated GPDC), University of the Americas, Cholula, Puebla.

"José I. Limantour, Correspondencia 1848–1911." Manuscript collection at the University of Texas library, Austin, Texas.

Museo Nacional de Antropología (abbreviated MNA).

U.S., Department of Justice, Record Group 60 and U.S. Supreme Court records, National Archives, Washington, D.C.

U.S., Department of State, Record Groups 59 and 84 (abbreviated State, USNA), National Archives, Washington, D.C.

PUBLISHED DOCUMENTS

El Colegio de México. *Estadísticas económicas del Porfiriato. Fuerzo de trabajo y actividad económica por sectores*. Mexico: El Colegio de México, n.d.

Carreño, Alverto María, ed. *Archivo del general Porfirio Díaz: memorias y documentos*. 30 vols. Mexico City: Universidad Nacional Instituto de Historia, 1947–58.

González Navarro, Moisés. *Estadísticas sociales de Porfiriato, 1877–1910*. Mexico: Secretaría de la Economia Nacional, 1956.

González Ramírez, Manuel, ed. *La caricatura política. Fuentes para la historia de la Revolución Mexicana*, vol. 2. Mexico: Fondo de Cultura Económica, 1955.

———. *Epistolario y textos de Ricardo Flores Magón*. Mexico: Fondo de Cultura Económica, 1964.

———. *Manifestos políticos, 1892–1912*. Mexico: Fondo de Cultura Económica, 1954.

OFFICIAL PUBLICATIONS

Great Britain. Foreign Office. Diplomatic and Consular Reports. "Report on the Cotton Manufacturing Industry in Mexico," prepared by Lionel E. G. Carden (Miscellaneous Series no. 453), London: Harris and Sons, 1898.

Mexico. Congreso de los Estados Unidos Mexicanos. *Diarios de los debates de la Cámara de Diputados.* Congreso 18, vol. 3. Mexico: Talleres gráficos de la Nación.

Mexico. *Diario oficial del supremo gobierno de los Estados Unidos Mexicanos.*

Mexico. Secretaría de Agricultura y Fomento. *Tercer censo de población de los estados unidos mexicanos.* Mexico: Talleres Gráficos de la Nación, 1918.

Mexico. Secretaría de Fomento. *Boletín de la secretaría de fomento, colonización e indústria de la República de México, 1902–1912.*

Tlaxcala. *Diario oficial del estado de Tlaxcala.*

U.S. Congress, House, Rules Committee, *Alleged Persecution of Mexican Citizens by the Government of Mexico,* 61st Cong., 2d sess., 1910.

U.S. Congress, Senate, Subcommittee of the Committee on Foreign Relations, *Investigation of Mexican Affairs,* 3 vols. 66th Cong., 1st sess., 1919.

U.S. Department of Commerce and Labor. Monthly Consular Reports, no. 331, March 1908, *Cotton and Products,* prepared by A. B. Butman. (Washington, D.C.: Government Printing Office, 1908), pp. 60–64.

U.S. Department of Commerce and Labor. Monthly Consular Reports, vol. 75, no. 285, June 1904 (Washington, D.C.: Government Printing Office, 1904).

U.S. Department of State, *Papers Relating to the Foreign Relations of the United States, 1877* (Washington, D.C.: Government Printing Office, 1862–).

U.S. Department of State, *Papers Relating to the Foreign Relations of the United States, 1878–1879* (Washington, D.C.: Government Printing Office, 1862–).

U.S. Department of State, *Papers Relating to the Foreign Relations of the United States, 1880–1881* (Washington, D.C.: Government Printing Office, 1862–).

U.S. Department of State, *Papers Relating to the Foreign Relations of the United States, part II, 1906* (Washington, D.C.: Government Printing Office, 1862–).

U.S. Department of State, *Papers Relating to the Foreign Relations of the United States, 1911* (Washington, D.C.: Government Printing Office, 1862–).

Veracruz. *Diario oficial del estado de Veracruz-Llave.*

Newspapers and Journals*

MEXICO CITY DAILIES

El Correo Español, January–June 1906.
El Diario, January 1907–June 1908.
El Diario del Hogar, July 1906–October 1909.
El Imparcial, January 1906–May 1911.
The Mexican Herald, December 1906–November 1909.
México Nuevo, February 1909–June 1910.
El País, August 1906–December 1910.
El Paladín, (three times weekly) February 1906–June 1910.
El Popular, June 1906.
El Tiempo, January 1906–April 1909.
La Voz de México, January 1907.

MEXICO CITY WEEKLIES

El Chile Piquín, August 1904. (Univ. of Texas–Austin.)
El Colmillo Público, January–July 1906.
El Debate, 1909–1910.
El Diablito Bromista, February 1906–November 1909. (Univ. of Texas–Austin.)
El Diablito Rojo, February 1908–November 1910.
La Guacamaya, July 1902–August 1908. (Univ. of Texas–Austin.)
El Morrongo, July 1903. (Univ. of Texas–Austin.)
La Palanca, October 1904–January 1905. (Univ. of Texas–Austin.)
El Pinche, July 1904. (Univ. of Texas–Austin.)
La Protesta, December 1902. (Univ. of Texas–Austin.)
La Reelección, August 1909–July 1910.
El Sufragio Libre, January–December 1910.
El Vulcano, December 1909. (Univ. of Texas–Austin.)
La Voz de Hidalgo, February 1910.

PROVINCIAL DAILIES

El Contemporáneo (San Luis Potosí), July–December 1906.
El Correo de Chihuahua (Chihuahua), September 1906–July 1910.
El Dictamen (Veracruz), January 1906–January 1907. (Univ. of Texas–Austin.)
El Estandarte (San Luis Potosí), February 1906–March 1910.
Jalisco Libre (Guadalajara), January–September 1906, June–December 1907.
La Revista de Mérida (Mérida), April–June 1909.

*All are available at the Hemeroteca Nacional unless otherwise noted. The dates given in the entries are those issues reviewed by the author.

PROVINCIAL WEEKLIES

El Clarín (Orizaba), January 1957–December 1960.
El Correo de Zacatecas (Zacatecas), January–December 1906.
El Cosmopolita (Orizaba), January 1906–December 1910.
La Democracia (Toluca, México), August 1908–July 1910.
El Obrero de Tepic (Tepic [Nayarit]), January–December 1906.
El Observador (Guanajuato), January 1905–June 1908, January–December 1910.
El Universo (Chihuahua), January 1906–December 1907.

WORKER AND OPPOSITION PRESS (WEEKLY OR PERIODICAL)

Alba (*Magonista*), April 1910. (GPDC, 35:4719.)
La Bandera Roja (*Magonista*). Not reviewed; for reference see AGN-Gob, leg. 12 ("Sec. de Gob. asuntos diversos magonistas y revolucionarios 1907–1908"), Juan Olivares to Rafael Rosete, 2 September 1906, El Paso, U.S.
El Constitucional (Anti–Reelectionist), December 1909–September 1910.
El Defensor de Obrero (*Magonista*, Laredo, Texas). Not reviewed; see reference in AGBR, 1906.
Democracia (*Magonista*). Not reviewed; for reference see AGN-Gob, leg. 12 ("Sec. de Gob. asuntos diversos magonistas y revolucionarios 1907–1908"), Juan Olivares to Rafael Rosete, 2 September 1906, El Paso, U.S.
El Esfuerzo Obrero (Mutualist, organ of the *Centro Obrero Mutuo Cooperativa de la República*), 1910.
El Ferrocarrilero (Organ of the *Gran Liga Mexicana de Empleados de Ferrocarril*, Mexico City). Not reviewed; see reference Rodea, *Historia obrero ferrocarrilero*, p. 103.
El Guía del Obrero (Organ of the *Liga Esteban de Antuñano*, Puebla), 1906. Not reviewed; for reference, see AGN-Gob, leg. 12.
El Heraldo de Morelos (Mutualist, organ of the *Centro mutualista de la República Mexicana*, Mexico City), January 1908–June 1909.
El Hijo de Azujote (Mexico City), April 1903.
La Libertad (Organ of the *Club Democrático de Guadalajara*), July 1909.
La Lucha Obrera (Organ of the *Liga Esteban de Antuñano*), 1906–1911.
El Mauser (Orizaba). Not reviewed; see reference in AGN-Gob, leg. 817.
El México Obrero (Mexico City), September 1909. (Univ. of Texas–Austin.)
El Obrero (Guadalajara). Not reviewed; for reference see *Jalisco Libre*, June 1906.
El Obrero Mexicano (Mutualist, Mexico City), December 1909–November 1910.
El Obrero Socialista (Mexico City), 1906. Not reviewed; for reference, see Clark, *Organized Labor*, pp. 9, 298.

Punto Rojo (*Magonista*, Los Angeles, U.S.), Aug. 1909.

La Reforma Social (*Magonista*). Not reviewed; for reference see AGN-Gob, leg. 12 ("Sec. de Gob. asuntos diversos magonistas y revolucionarios 1907–1908"), Juan Olivares to Rafael Rosete, 2 September 1906, El Paso, U.S.

La Regeneración (*Magonista*, Los Angeles, U.S.).

La Rendención del Obrero (Orizaba). Not reviewed; see reference AGN-Gob, Leg. 817, November 1906.

Revolución (*Magonista*, Los Angeles, U.S.). Not reviewed; see reference in GPDC, 32:7255.

Revolución Social (Organ of the *Gran Círculo de Obreros Libres*, Orizaba), June 1906. Not reviewed; see copy in GPDC, 31:6373.

La Tierra (Anarchist (?), Mérida), 1908–1909 (?). Not reviewed; see reference in Navarrete, *Alto a la contrarrevolución*, p. 65.

La Unión Obrero (Organ of the *Gran Círculo de Obreros Libres*, Orizaba), September–December 1906. Not reviewed; see reference in Peña Samaniego, *El Clarín*, 4 November, 9 December 1958.

La Unión Social (Mutualist, organ of *Sociedad Mutua Fundadora "Unión y Amistad" del Ramo de Panadería*), 1910. Not reviewed; see reference in AGN-Gob leg. 817.

La Voz de Cepeda (Monthly organ of the *Sociedad Mutualista de la Gran Círculo de Obreros "Victoriano Cepeda,"* Saltillo), February 1908.

INDUSTRIAL AND COMMERCIAL JOURNALS

El Economista Mexicano (Mexico City weekly), April 1906–March 1910.

México Industrial (Mexico City), 1905–1906.

El Progreso (Tabasco weekly). Not reviewed; Hemeroteca Nacional has years 1905–1913.

El Progreso Latino (Mexico City weekly), June–December 1906.

El Progreso de México (Mexico City weekly). Not reviewed; Hemeroteca Nacional has 1895–1911.

La Semana Mercantil (Mexico City weekly, organ of the *Confederaciones Industrial y Mercantil de la República y de la Cámara de Comercio de México*), January 1906–December 1910.

MISCELLANEOUS JOURNALS

Revista Moderna (Mexico City literary). Located in the *Fundación Cultural de Condumex, S.A.*

Revista Azul. (Mexico City literary). Located in the *Fundación Cultural de Condumex, S.A.*

Revista Positiva. (Positivist, Mexico City monthly), January 1906–May 1911.

Secondary Sources

BIBLIOGRAPHIES AND GUIDES

Brown, Lyle C."Guide to Ramo de Ricardo Flores Magón et. al." (L-E-918 only). Unpublished. Baylor University, Waco, Texas.

Brown, Lyle C. "A Magonista Bibliography." Unpublished. Baylor University, Waco, Texas.

Millanes, Augustín Carlo. *Repertorio bibliográfico de los archivos mexicanos y de los Europeos y Norteamericanos de interés para la historia de México.* Mexico: Universidad Nacional Autónoma de México, 1959.

Ross, Stanley R., ed. *Fuentes de la historia contemporánea de México: periódicos y revistas.* 2 vols. Mexico: Colegio de México, 1965–1967.

Ulloa, Berta. "Guía al ramo de Flores Magón, et. al. en El Archivo de Secretaría de Relaciones Exteriores de México, 1963." Unpublished. El Colegio de México.

Uribe de Fernández de Córdoba, Susana. "Ciencias auxiliares de la historia." In El Colegio de México, *Veinticinco años de investigación histórica en México.* Mexico: El Colegio de México, 1966.

Zavala, Silvia Arturo and Castelo, María. *Fuentes para la historia del trabajo en Nueva España.* Mexico: Fondo de Cultura Económica, 1939.

Carrera Stampa, Manuel. *Archivalia mexicana.* Mexico: Universidad Nacional Autónoma de México. Instituto de Historia, 1952.

BOOKS AND PAMPHLETS: GENERAL STUDIES

Alexander, Robert Jackson. *Labour Movements in Latin America.* London: Fabian Publications and V. Gollancz, 1947.

Allen, V. L. *The Sociology of Industrial Relations: Studies In Method.* London: The Longman Group, 1971.

Aragón, Agustín. *Porfirio Díaz.* 2 vols. Mexico: Editora Intercontinental, 1962.

Aronson, Robert L. *Labour Commitment Among Jamaican Bauxite Workers.* Reprint Series, no. 108. Ithaca: New York State School of Industrial and Labor Relations, 1961.

Baerlein, Henry Philip Bernard. *Mexico, the Land of Unrest: Being Chiefly an Account of What Produced the Outbreak of 1910 Together with the Story of the Revolutions Down to this Day.* Philadelphia: J. P. Lippincott; London: Herbert and Daniel, 1913.

Balán, Jorge; Browing, Harley L.; and Jelin, Elizabeth. *Men in a Developing Society: Geographic and Social Mobility in Monterrey, Mexico.* Austin: University of Texas, 1973.

Bancrott, Hubert H. *The Works of Hubert H. Bancroft.* 10 vols. Vol. 2, *History of Mexico.* San Francisco: The History Co. Publishers, 1888.

Barrera Fuentes, Florencio. *Historia de la Revolución Mexicana; la etapa precur-*

sora. Mexico City: Biblioteca del Instituto Nacional de Estudios Históricos de la Revolución Mexicana, 1955.

Beals, Carleton. *Porfirio Díaz: Dictator of Mexico*. Philadelphia: J. B. Lippincott Co., 1932.

Briggs, Asa. *Victorian Cities*. London: Odhams Books, 1965.

Brown, John William. *Modern Mexico and its Problems*. London: The Labour Publishing Co., 1927.

Cabrera, Luis. *Viente años después*. Mexico: Ediciones Botas, 1930.

Cerdo Silva, Roberto de la. *El movimiento obrero en México*. Mexico: Instituto de Investigaciones Sociales, U.N.A.M., 1961.

Chaplin, David. *The Peruvian Industrial Labor Force*. Princeton: Princeton University Press, 1967.

Chapoy Bonifaz, Dolores Beatriz. *El movimiento obrero y el sindicato en México*. Mexico: no publication information available, 1961.

Chesneaux, Jean. *The Chinese Labor Movement 1919–1927*. Stanford: Stanford University Press, 1968.

Chevalier, François. *Land and Society in Colonial Mexico: The Great Hacienda*. Translated by Alvin Eustis. Berkeley: University of California Press, 1963.

Clark, Marjorie Ruth. *Organized Labor in Mexico*. Chapel Hill: University of North Carolina Press, 1934.

Cline, Howard F. *The United States and Mexico*. Cambridge, Mass.: Harvard University Press, 1965.

Commons, John R. et al. *History of Labor in the United States*. 4 vols. New York: Macmillan, 1921–1935.

Cumberland, Charles C. *Mexico: The Struggle for Modernity*. New York: The Oxford University Press, 1968.

Davis, Harold Eugene. *Latin American Social Thought: The History of its Development Since Independence with Selected Readings*. Washington, D.C.: The University Press of Washington, 1963.

Diccionario Porrúa: historia, biographía y geografía de México. 2d edition. Mexico City: Porrúa, 1964.

Ginzberg, Eli, and Berman, Hyman. *The American Worker in the Twentieth Century, a History through Autobiographies*. New York: Free Press of Glencoe, 1963.

Graham Fernández, Leonardo. *Los sindicatos en México; antecedentes, estructuración, funcionamiento, objeto, y fines*. Mexico: Editorial Atlamiliztli, 1969.

Gruening, Ernest Henry. *Mexico and its Heritage*. New York: Appleton–Century–Crofts, 1928.

Gurr, Ted. *Why Men Rebel*. Princeton: Princeton University Press, 1970.

Ingersoll, Ralph McA. *In and Under Mexico*. London: T. Werner Lavrie, Ltd., 1924.

International Bureau of American Republic, Washington, D.C. *American Constitutions; a Compilation of the Political Constitutions of the Independent Na-*

tions of the New World. Washington: Government Printing Office, 1906–1907.

Jayawardena, Visakha Kumari. *The Rise of the Labor Movement in Ceylon.* Durham, N.C.: Duke University Press, 1972.

Jones, Chester Lloyd, *Mexico and its Reconstruction.* New York and London: D. Appleton & Co., 1921.

Kornhauser, Arthur William; Dublin, Robert; and Ross, Arthur M., eds. *Industrial Conflict.* New York: McGraw-Hill, 1954.

La Force, James Clayburn, Jr. *The Development of the Spanish Textile Industry 1750–1800.* Berkeley: University of California Press, 1965.

Langer, William L. *Political and Social Upheaval: 1832–1852.* New York: Harper & Row, 1969.

Leyva Velázquez, Gabriel. *Resonancias de la lucha; ecos de la epopeya sinaloense, 1910.* Mexico: Imprenta mundial, 1945.

López Aparicio, Alfonso. *El movimiento obrero: Antecedentes, desarrollo y tendencias.* Mexico: Fondo de Cultura Económica, 1945.

López Rosado, Diego G. *Historia y pensamiento económico de México: Communicaciones y transportes: Relaciones de trabajo.* Mexico: Universidad Nacional Autónoma de México, 1969.

Mair, Norman Raymond Frederick. *Psychology in Industry; a Psychological Approach to Industrial Problems.* Boston, New York: Houghton Mifflin Co., 1946.

Martin, Percy Falcke. *Mexico of the Twentieth Century*, vol. 1. New York: Dodd, Mead, and Co., 1907.

McCaleb, Walter F. *The Public Finances of Mexico.* New York and London: Harper Brothers, 1921.

McLaurin, Melton Alonza. *Paternalism and Protest; Southern Cotton Mill Workers and Organized Labor, 1875–1905.* Westport, Conn.: Greenwood Publications Corp., 1971.

Mendizábal, Miguel Othón de. *Obras completas.* 6 vols. Mexico: no publication information available, 1946–47.

Moore, Wilbert E. *Industrialization and Labor: Social Aspects of Economic Development.* Ithaca: Cornell University Press, 1951.

Moore, Wilbert E., and Feldman, Arnold S., eds. *Labor Commitment and Social Change in Developing Areas.* New York: Social Science Research Council, 1960.

Morris, Morris David. *The Emergence of an Industrial Labor Force in India; A Study of the Bombay Cotton Mills, 1854–1947.* Berkeley: University of California Press, 1965.

Motolinía, Toribio. *History of the Indians of New Spain.* Translated and edited by Elizabeth Andros Foster. Berkeley, Calif.: Cortés Society, 1950.

Murray, Paul V. *The Catholic Church in Mexico; Historical Essays for the General Reader.* Vol. 1, *1519–1910.* Editorial E.P.M., 1965.

Padden, R.C. *The Hummingbird and the Hawk: Conquest and Sovereignty in the*

Valley of Mexico; 1503–1541. Columbus: Ohio State University Press, 1967.

Payne, James L. *Labor and Politics in Peru: The System of Political Bargaining*. New Haven: Yale University Press, 1965.

Pope, Liston. *Millhands and Preachers, a Study of Gastonia*. New Haven: Yale University Press, 1942.

Poblete, Troncoso Moisés, and Burnett, Ben G. *The Rise of the Latin American Labor Movement*. New Haven: College and University Press, 1960.

Prescott, W. H. *Mexico and the Life of the Conqueror Hernando Cortés*. 2 Vols. New York: P. F. Collier and Son, 1900.

Prieto, Guillermo. *Memorias de mis tiempos*. Mexico: Editorial Patria, 1948.

———. *Breves nociones de economía política, o sean principios elementales de esta ciencia: Para los primeros estudios escolares*. Mexico: Oficina Tipografía de la Sec. de Fomento, 1888.

———. *Lecciones elementales de economía política dadas en la escuela de jurisprudencia de México en el curso de 1871*. Mexico: Imprenta del Gobierno en Palacio, 1871.

Rabasa, Emilio. *La constitución y la dictadura; estudio sobre la organización política de México*. Mexico: Editorial Porrúa, 1956.

Redford, Arthur. *Labour Migration in England, 1800–1850*. Manchester: Manchester University Press, 1926.

Reyes Heroles, Jesús. *El liberalismo mexicana*. 3 vols. Mexico: Universidad Nacional de México, Facultad de Derecho, 1957–1961.

Romero Flores, Jesús. *Del porfirismo a la revolución constitucionalista: Anales históricos de la Revolución Mexicana*, vol. 1. Mexico: Libro Mex Editores, 1960.

Rudé, George. *The Crowd in History: A Study of Popular Disturbances in France and England 1730–1848*. New York: Wiley and Sons Inc., 1964.

Silva Herzoy, Jesús. *Breve historia de la Revolución Mexicana*. Mexico: Fondo de Cultura Económica, 1960.

Simmons, Merle E. *The Mexican Corrido as a Source for Interpretive Study of Modern Mexico (1870–1950)*. Bloomington: Indiana University Press, 1957.

Stromberg, Roland N. *European Intellectual History Since 1789*. New York: Appleton-Century-Crofts, 1968.

Thompson, Edward P. *The Making of the English Working Class*. New York: Pantheon Press, A Division of Random House, 1964.

Urrutia Montoya, Miguel. *The Development of the Colombia Labor Movement*. New Haven: Yale University Press, 1969.

Valdés, José C. *El porfirismo: historia de un régimen*. 3 vols. Mexico: Antigua librería Robredo, de J. Porrúa e hijos, 1941–48.

Vera Estañol, Jorge. *La Revolución social de México*. Editorial Porrúa. 1956.

Wagner, Henry R. *The Rise of Fernando Cortés*. Los Angeles: The Cortés Society, 1944.

Wells, David A. *A Study of Mexico.* New York: D. Appleton & Co., 1887.
Woodward, Ralph Lee, Jr., ed. *Positivism in Latin America, 1850–1900: Are Order and Progress Reconcilable?* Lexington, Mass.: Heath, 1971.
Zavala, Silvio. *Ensayos sobre la colonización española en América.* Buenos Aires: Emecé editores, 1944.

BOOKS AND PAMPHLETS: SPECIAL STUDIES

Abad de Santillán, Diego. *El apostal de la Revolución social mexicana.* Mexico: Grupo Cultural, "Ricardo Flores Magón," 1925.
Alba, Victor. *Las ideas sociales contemporáneas en México.* Mexico: Fondo de Cultura Económica, 1960.
Araiza, Luis. *Historia del movimiento obrero mexicano.* 4 vols. Mexico: no publication information available, 1964–65.
Baca Calderón, Esteban. *Juicio sobre la guerra del yaqui y génesis de la huelga de Cananea.* Mexico: Ed. del Sindícato Mex. de Electricistas, 1956.
Baranda, Joaquín. *Recordaciones históricas.* 2 vols. Mexico: "La Europea," 1907.
Beezley, William H. *Insurgent Governor Abraham González and the Mexican Revolution in Chihuahua.* Lincoln, Neb.: University of Nebraska Press, 1973.
Bejar Navarro, Raul, and Álvarez, Francisco Casanova. *Historia de la industrialización del estado de México.* Mexico: Biblioteca Enciclopédica del Estado de México, 1970.
Bernstein, Marvin D. *The Mexican Mining Industry, 1890–1950; A Study of the Interaction of Politics, Economics, and Technology.* Albany, N.Y.: State University of New York, 1964.
Blaisdell, Lowell L. *Desert Revolution: Baja California, 1911.* Madison: University of Wisconsin Press, 1962.
Bojórquez, Juan de Dios. *Directorio de asociaciones sindicales de la República.* Mexico: N.P.A., 1936.
Bulnes, Francisco. *El verdadero Díaz y la revolución.* Mexico: Editora Nacional, 1952.
Calderón, Esteban B. *Juicio sobre la guerra del yaqui y génesis de la huelga de Cananea.* Mexico: Edición del Sindicato Mexicano de Electricistas, 1956.
Calderón, Francisco R. *La república restaurada: la vida económica.* Vol. 2 of *Historia moderna de México,* edited by Daniel Cosío Villegas. 10 vols. Mexico: Editorial Hermes, 1956–1971.
Carrera Stampa, Manuel. *Los gremios mexicanos; la organización gremial en Nueva España, 1521–1861.* Mexico: Edición y Distribución Ibero Americana de Publicaciones, 1954.
Carrillo, Rafael. *Ricardo Flores Magón: Presidente de la junta organizadora del Partido Liberal Mexicano.* Mexico, 1945.
Casasola, Gustavo. *Historia gráfica de la Revolución Mexicana, 1900–1960,* vol. 1. Mexico: Editorial F. Trillas, 1965.

Castillo, José R. del. *Historia de la revolución social de México*. Mexico: no publication information available, 1915.
Chávez Orozco, Luis. *Agricultura e industria textil de Veracruz, siglo XIX*. Xalapa: Universidad Veracruzana, 1965.
Cockcroft, James D. *Intellectual Precursors of the Mexican Revolution, 1900–1913*. Austin: University of Texas Press, 1968.
Cosío Villegas, Daniel, ed. *Historia moderna de México*. 10 vols. Mexico: Editorial Hermes, 1956–71.
———. *El Porfiriato: La vida política interior*. Vols. 9 and 10 of *Historia moderna de México*, edited by Daniel Cosío Villegas. 10 vols. Mexico: Editorial Hermes, 1971–72.
Díaz Cárdenas, León. *Cananea, primer brote del sindicalismo en México*. Mexico: Departamento de Bibliotecas de la Secretaría de Educación Pública, 1936.
Díaz Dufoo, Carlos. *Limantour*. Mexico: Eusebio Gómez de la Puente, 1910.
d'Olwer, Nicolai. *El Porfiriato. La vida económica*. Volume 7 of *Historia moderna de México*, edited by Daniel Cosío Villegas. 10 vols. Mexico: Editorial Hermes, 1956–71.
Esquivel Obregón, Toribio. *Mi labor en servicio de México*. Ediciones Botas, 1934.
El Floriciemiento de México. Mexico: no publication information available, 1906.
Flores Magón, Enrique. *Combatimos la tiranía*. Translated by Jesús Amaya Topete. Edited by Samuel Kaplan. Mexico: Tallares Gráficos de la Nacion, 1958.
Flores Magón, Ricardo. *Batalla de la dictadura textos políticos*. Vol. 3 of *El liberalismo mexicano en pensamiento y en acción*, edited by Martín Luis Guzman. Mexico: Empresas Editorales, 1948.
Florescano, M. Enrique. *El algodón y su industria en Veracruz, 1800–1900*. Jalapa, Veracruz: Editorio del Gobierno de Veracruz, 1965.
Fornaro, Carlo de. *Díaz, Czar of Mexico*. New York: International Publishing Co., 1909.
Fuentes Díaz, Vicente. *Los partidos políticos en México (1810–1911)*, vol. 1. Mexico: no publication information available, 1954.
García Cantú, Gastón. *El socialismo en México, siglo XIX*. Mexico: Ediciones Era, 1969.
García Granados, Ricardo. *Historia de México desde la restauración de república en 1867, hasta la caída de Porfirio Díaz*. Mexico: Editorial Andrés Botas e Hijo, 1923.
García, Rubén. *El anti porfirismo*. Mexico: Talleres gráficos de la nación, 1935.
Gavira, Gabriel. *General de brigada Gabriel Gavira, su actuación politicomilitar revolucionaria*. Mexico: Talleres tipográficos de A. del Bosque, 1933.
Genin, Auguste. *Les français an mexique de xvie síecle á nos jours*. Paris: Nouvelles editions Argo, 1931.
Gibson, Charles. *The Aztecs under Spanish rule; A History of the Indians of the*

Valley of Mexico, 1519–1810. Stanford, Calif.: Stanford University Press, 1964.

González y González, Luis. *La república restaurada: la vida social.* Vol. 3 of *Historia moderna de México,* edited by Daniel Cosío Villegas. Mexico: Editorial Hermes, 1956–71.

González Navarro, Moisés. *El Porfiriato: La vida social.* Vol. 4 of *Historia moderna de México,* edited by Daniel Cosío Villegas. Mexico: Editorial Hermes, 1957.

González Ramírez, Manuel. *La huelga de Cananea: Fuentes para la historia de la Revolución Mexicana,* vol. 3. Mexico: Fondo de Cultura Económica, 1956.

————. *La evolución social de México,* vol. 1. Mexico: Fondo de Cultura Económica, 1960.

Grupo Cultural "Ricardo Flores Magón." *Ricardo Flores Magón, vida y obra.* 9 vols. Mexico: Grupo Cultural "Ricardo Flores Magón," 1923–25.

Gutiérrez de Lara, Lázaro, and Pinchón, Edgcumb. *The Mexican People: Their Struggle for Freedom.* Garden City: Doubleday, Page and Co., 1914.

Guerrero, Julio. *La génesis del crimen en México; estudio de psiquiatría social.* Mexico: Vda de C. Bouret, 1901.

Hale, Charles Adams. *Mexican Liberalism in the Age of Mora, 1821–1853.* New Haven: Yale University Press, 1968.

Hart, John M. *Los anarquistas mexicanos, 1860–1900.* Translated by María Elena Hope. Mexico: Secretaría de Educación Pública (SEP/SENTENTAS), 1974.

Hermida Ruiz, Ángel J. *Acayucán y Río Blanco: gestas precursoras de la Revolución.* Jalapa, Mexico: Gobierno del Estado de Veracruz. Dirección General de Educación, 1964.

Hernández, Ana María. *La mujer mexicana en la indústria textil.* Mexico: Biblioteca Universidad, 1940.

Hernández, Teodoro. *Los precursores de la Revolución.* Mexico: no publication information available, 1940.

————. *La historia de la Revolución debe hacerse.* Mexico: no publication information available, 1950.

————. *Las tinajas de Ulúa.* Mexico: Editorial "Hermida," 1943.

Iturribarría, Jorge Fernando, *Porfirio Díaz ante la historia.* Mexico: Carlos Villejas García Condor 100, 1967.

Keremitsis, Dawn. *La industria textil mexicana en el siglo XIX.* Mexico: Sec. de Educación Pública, 1973.

Limantour, José Ives. *Apuntes sobre mi vida pública.* Mexico: Editorial Porrúa, 1965.

List Arzubide, Germán y Armando. *La huelga de Río Blanco.* Mexico: Dept. de Biblioteca de la Secretaría de Educación Pública, 1935.

Lister, Florence C., and Lister, Robert H. *Chihuahua: Storehouse of Storms.* Albuquerque: University of New Mexico Press, 1966.

Magaña, Gildardo. *Emiliano Zapata y el agrarismo en México.* 5 vols. Mexico: no publication information available, 1934.

Manero, Antonio. *El antiguo régimen y la Revolución.* Mexico: Tipografía y Litografía "La Europea," 1911.

Maples Arce, Manuel. *El movimiento social en Veracruz.* Jalapa, Veracruz: Tallares Gráficos del Gobierno del Estado, 1927.

Martínez Nuñez, Eugenio. *Perfiles revolucionarios: La vida heroica de Parxedis G. Guerrero.* Mexico: Biblioteca del Instituto Nacional de Estudios Históricos de la Revolución Mexicana, 1960.

Martin, Percy Falcke. *Mexico's Treasure House (Guanajuato): An Illustrated and Descriptive Account of the Mines and Their Operations in 1906.* New York: The Cheltenham Press, 1906.

Medina Hoyos, Francisco. *Cananea, cuna de la Revolución Mexicana: en el cincuentenario de la primera gran huelga proletaria de México.* Mexico: CTM, 1956.

The Mexican Yearbook, vols. 1 and 2. London: McCorguodale and Co., 1908, 1910.

Meyer, Michael C. *Mexican Rebel: Pascual Orozco and the Mexican Revolution, 1910–1915.* Lincoln: University of Nebraska Press, 1967.

Molina Enríquez, Andrés. *Los grandes problemas nacionales.* Mexico: Impr. de A. Carranza de hijos, 1909.

Montes Rodríguez, Ezequiel. *La huelga de Río Blanco.* Mexico: Sindicato de Trabajadores en General de la CIDOSA, 1965.

Mota, Gonzalo, and Morales, Ignacio. *El general Esteban Baca Calderón: sus rasgos biográficos; su actuación revolucionaria.* Mexico: no publication information available, 1917.

Muñoz Cota, José. *Ricardo Flores Magón, corridos.* Mexico: Editorial Castalia, 1962.

———. *Ricardo Flores Magón; un sol clavado en la sombra.* Mexico: Editores Mexicanos Unidos, 1963.

Navarrete, Alfredo. *Alto a la contrarrevolucion.* Mexico: Editorial Libros de Mexico, 1971.

O'Connor, Harvey. *The Guggenheims; The Making of an American Dynasty.* New York: Covic Friede, 1937.

Ortega, C. Rafael [Agetro Leafar]. *Las luchas proletarias en Veracruz; historia y autocrítica.* Jalapa, Ver., Mexico: Editorial "Barricada," 1942.

Ortiz Petricioli, José. *El compañero Morones: biografía de un gran líder.* Mexico: B. Costa-Amic, 1968.

———. *La tragedia del 7 de enero.* Mexico: Casa del Obrero Mundial, 1940.

Padua, C. D. *El movimiento revolucionario de 1906 en Veracruz.* Mexico: no publication information available, 1936.

Pani, Alberto J. *Apuntes autobiográficos,* vol. 1. 2d rev. ed. Mexico: M. Porrúa. 1950.

———. *Hygiene in Mexico: A Study of Sanitation and Educational Problems.* Translated by Ernest L. de Gogorza. New York: G. P. Putnam and Sons, 1917.

Pletcher, David M. *Rails, Mines, and Progress: Seven American Promoters in Mexico, 1867–1911*. Ithaca, New York: Cornell University Press, 1958.

Quirk, Robert E. *The Mexican Revolution and the Catholic Church: 1910–1929*. Bloomington: Indiana University Press, 1973.

Ramos Pedrueza, Rafael. *La lucha de clases a través de la historia de México revolución democrático burguesa*. Mexico: Ediciones "Revista Lux," 1941.

Reyes, Rodolfo. *De mi vida-memorias políticas 1899/1913*. Madrid: Biblioteca Nueva, 1929.

Reynolds, Clark W. *The Mexican Economy: Twentieth Century Structure and Growth*. New Haven: Yale University Press, 1970.

Richard, Thomas A. *Journeys of Observation*. San Francisco: Dewey Publishing Co., 1907.

Rodarte, Fernando, *7 de Enero de 1907*. Mexico: A. del Bosque, 1940.

Rodea, Marcelo N. *Historia del movimiento obrero ferrocarrilero en México, 1890–1943*. Mexico: no publication information available, 1944.

Romero, Matías. *Mexico And The United States; A Study of Subjects Affecting Their Political, Commercial, and Social Relations, Made With A View To Their Promotion*, vol. 1. New York: G. P. Putnam and Sons, 1898.

Ross, Stanley R. *Francisco I. Madero, Apostle of Mexican Democracy*. New York: Columbia University Press, 1955.

Salazar, Rosendo. *La casa del Obrero Mundial*. Mexico: Costa–Amic, 1962.

———. *Lideres y sindicatos*. Mexico: T. C. Modelo, 1953.

Salazar, Rosendo, and Escobedo, José G. *Las pugnas de la gleba, 1907–1922*. Mexico: Editorial Avante, 1923.

Sánchez Santos, Trinidad. *Obras selectas*. Puebla: Linotipografía "Primavera," 1945.

Sierra, Justo, ed., *Mexico: Its Social Evolution*. 2 vols. Trans. by G. Sentiñon. Mexico: J. Ballesca & Co., 1900–1904.

Sodi de Pallares, María Elena. *Teodoro A. Dehesa: Una época y un hombre*. Mexico: Editorial Citlaltepetl, 1959.

Tapia Quijada, Cesar. *Apuntes sobre la huelga de Cananea*. Sonora: Universidad de Sonora, 1956.

Taracena, Alfonso. *La verdadera Revolución Mexicana, primera etapa (1909 a 1911)*. 2d ed. Mexico: Editorial Jus, 1965.

Thompson, Wallace. *The People of Mexico: Who They Are and How They Live*. New York: Harper and Brothers, 1921.

Trowbridge, Edward D. *Mexico: Today and Tomorrow*. New York: The MacMillan Co., 1919.

Trueba Urbina, Alberto. *Evolución de la huelga*. Mexico: Ediciones Botas, 1950.

Turner, Ethel Duffy. *Ricardo Flores Magón y el Partido Liberal Mexicano*. Translated by Eduardo Limón G. Morelia. Mich: Editorial "Erandi," 1960.

Turner, John Kenneth. *Barbarous Mexico*. New ed. Austin: University of Texas Press, 1969.

Uriostegui Miranda, Pinadaro. *Testimonios del proceso revolucionario de México*. Mexico: Impreso en los Tallares de ARGRIN, 1970.

Vizcaya Canales, Isidro. *Los orígenes de la industrialización de Monterrey: una historia económica y social desde la caída del Segundo Imperio hasta el fin de la Revolución (1867–1920)*. Monterrey: Publicaciones del Instituto Technológico y de Estudios Superiores de Monterrey, 1969.

Womack, John. *Zapata and the Mexican Revolution*. New York: Alfred A. Knopf Inc., 1968.

Yarlez, Agustín. *Don Justo Sierra, su vida, sus ideas y su obra*. 2d ed. Mexico: Universidad Nacional Autónoma de México, 1962.

Zavala, Silvio. *Ordenanzas del trabajo, siglos XVI and XVII*. Mexico: Editorial "Elede," 1947.

Zayas Enríquez, Rafael de. *Porfirio Díaz*. Translated by T. Quincy Browne. New York: D. Appleton and Co., 1908.

———. *Porfirio Díaz, la evolución de su vida*. New York: D. Appleton y companía, 1908.

ARTICLES IN COLLECTIONS

Bazant, Jan. "Estudio sobre la productividad de la industria algondonera mexicana en 1843–1845." In *La industria nacional y el comercio exterior (1842–1851)*. Mexico: Banco Nacional de Comercio Exterior, 1962.

Belshaw, Cyril S. "Adaptation of Personnel Policies in Social Context." In *Labor Commitment and Social Change in Developing Areas*, edited by W. E. Moore & Arnold S. Feldman. New York: Social Science Research Council, 1960.

Brown, Lyle C. "The Mexican Liberals and Their Struggle Against the Díaz Dictatorship." *Antología*. Mexico: Mexico City College Press, 1956.

Calderón, Francisco R. "Los ferrocarriles." In *El Porfiriato: la vida económica*, edited by Nicolan d'Olwer et al. Vol. 7 of *Historia moderna de México*, edited by Daniel Cosío Villegas. 10 vols. Mexico: Editorial Hermes, 1956–71.

Chávez, Ezekiel A. "Science in Mexico." In *Mexico: Its Social Evolution*, translated by G. Sentiñon and edited by Justo Sierra. Vol. 1. Mexico: J. Ballesca & Co., 1900–1904.

Díaz Dufoo, Carlos. "Industrial Evolution." In *Mexico: Its Social Evolution*, vol. 2, translated by G. Sentiñon and edited by Justo Sierra. Mexico: J. Ballesca & Co., 1900–1904.

d'Olwer, Luis Nicolan, "Las inversiones extranjeras." In his *La vida económica*. Vol. 8 of *Historia moderna de México*, edited by Daniel Cosío Villegas. 10 vols. Mexico: Editorial Hermes, 1955–65.

Elkan, Walter, and Fallers, Lloyd A. "The Mobility of Labor." In *Labor Commitment and Social Change in Developing Areas*, edited by Wilbert E. Moore and Arnold S. Feldman. New York: Social Science Research Council, 1960.

Germani, Gino. "Inquiry Into the Social Effects of Urbanization in a Working Class Sector of Greater Buenos Aires." In *Urbanization in Latin America*, edited by P. M. Hauser. New York: Columbia University Press, 1961.

Kerr, Clark, and Siegel, Abraham. "The Interindustry Propensity to Strike—An International Comparison." In *Industrial Conflict*, edited by Arthur Kornhauser, Robert Dubin, Arthur M. Ross. New York: McGraw-Hill Co., 1954.

Landsberger, Henry A. "The Labor Elite: Is it Revolutionary?" In *Elites in Latin America*, edited by Seymour Martin Lipset and Aldo Solari. New York: 1967.

Macedo, Pablo. "Commercial Evolution." In *Mexico: Its Social Evolution*, vol. 2, edited by Justo Sierra. Mexico: J. Ballegas and Co., 1900–1904.

Meyer, Jean A. "Historia de la vida social." In *Investigaciones contemporáneas sobre la historia de México: memorias de la tercera reunión de historiadores mexicanos y norte americanos*. Mexico: Universidad Nacional Autónoma de Mexico, 1971.

Morris, Morris David. "The Labor Market in India." In *Labor Commitment and Social Change in Developing Areas*, edited by Wilbert E. Moore and Arnold S. Feldman. New York: Social Research Council, 1960.

Nava Oteo, Guadalupe. "La Minería." In *La vida económica*, edited by Nicolan D'Olwer et al. Vol. 7 of *Historia moderna de México*, edited by Daniel Cosío Villegas. 10 vols. Mexico: Editorial Hermes, 1956–1971.

Pearse, Andrew. "Some Characteristics of Urbanization in the City of Rio de Janeiro." In *Urbanization in Latin America*, edited by P. M. Hauser. New York: Columbia University Press, 1961.

Rontondo, H. "Psychological and Mental Health: Problems in Urbanization Based on Case Studies in Peru." In *Urbanization in Latin America*, edited by P. M. Hauser. New York: Columbia University Press, 1961.

Rosenzweig, Fernando. "El comercio exterior." In *La vida económica*, edited by Nicolan D'Olwer et. al. Vol. 7 of *Historia moderna de México*, edited by Daniel Cosío Villegas. 10 vols. Mexico: Editorial Hermes, 1956–1971.

Rosenzweig, Fernando. "La industria." In *La vida económica*, edited by Nicolan d'Olwer et. al. Vol. 7 of *Historia moderna de México*, edited by Daniel Cosío Villegas. 10 vols. Mexico: Editorial Hermes, 1956–1971.

Singer, Milton. "Changing Craft Traditions in India." In *Labor Commitment and Social Change in Developing Areas*, edited by Wilbert E. Moore and Arnold S. Feldman. New York: Social Science Research Council, 1960.

Zamora, Gloria Peralta. "La hacienda pública." In *La vida económica*, edited by Nicolan d'Olwer et. al. Vol. 7 of *Historia moderna de México*, edited by Daniel Cosío Villegas. 10 vols. Mexico: Editorial Hermes, 1956–1971.

ARTICLES IN PERIODICALS

Albro, Ward S. "El secuestro de Manuel Sarabia." *Historia Mexicana* 18 (1969): 400–407.

Anderson, Rodney D. "Mexican Workers and the Politics of Revolution, 1906–1911." *Hispanic American Historical Review* 54 (1974): 94–113.

Bazant, Jan. "Evolución de la industrial textil poblana (1554–1845)." *Historia Mexicana* 13 (1964) 4: 473–516.

——. "Industria algodonera poblana de 1800–1843 en numeros." *Historia Mexicana* 14 (1964) 1: 131–43.

Briones, Guillermo. "Training and Adaption of the Labour Force in the Early Stages of Industrialization." *International Social Science Journal* 15 (1963): 571–80.

Buve, R. Th. J. "Protesta de obreros y campesinos durante el Porfiriato: unas consideraciones sobre su desarollo e interrelaciones en el este de México Central." Translated by Anneke Roos. *Boletín de Estudios Latinoamericanos* 13 (1972): 1–25.

Cadenhead, Ivie E., Jr. "The American Socialists and the Mexican Revolution of the 1910." *Southwestern Social Science Quarterly* 43 (1962): 103–17.

Castillo, Daniel. "Apuntes de un obrero." *El Clarín* (Orizaba weekly), 7 June 1959.

Cumberland, Charles C. "Precursors of the Mexican Revolution." *Hispanic American Historical Review* 22 (1942): 344–56.

Díaz Dufoo, Carlos. "El teatro español contemporáneo—Juan José." *Revista Azul* 5 (1896): 26–27.

H. G. Elwes. "Points about Mexican Labor." *The Engineering and Mining Journal* 90 (1910): 662.

Florescano, Enrique and Moreno Toscano, Alejandra. "Historia económica y social." *Historia Mexicana* 15 (1965–66): 310–78.

Foster, Alice. "Orizaba: A Community in the Sierra Madre Oriental." *Economic Geography* 1 (1925): 356–72.

González Navarro, Moisés. "La huelga de Río Blanco." *Historia Mexicana* 6 (1957): 510–33.

——. "Las huelgas textiles en el Porfiriato." *Historia Mexicana* 6 (1956): 201–16.

Gurr, Ted. "Psychological Factors in Civil Violence." *World Politics* 20 (1968): 245–78.

Hahn, Otto H. "On the Development of Silver Smelting in Mexico." *Institution of Mining and Metallurgy Transactions* 8 (1899–1900): 267–68.

Hale, Charles A. "José María Luis Mora and the Structure of Mexican Liberalism." *Hispanic American Historical Review* 45 (1965): 196–227.

Hart, John. "Nineteenth Century Urban Labor Precursors of the Mexican Revolution: Development of An Ideology." *The Americas* 31 (1974): 298–318.

Jones, C. K. "Recent Acquisitions of the Library of Congress Mainly Treating of Mexico in Revolution." *Hispanic American Historical Review* 1 (1919): 480–81.

Katz, Friedrich. "Labor Conditions on Haciendas in Porfirian Mexico: Some Trends and Tendencies." *Hispanic American Historical Review* 54 (1974): 1–47.

Keesing, Donald B. "Structural Change Early in Development: Mexico's Changing Industrial and Occupational Structure from 1895–1950." *Journal of Economic History* 29 (1969): 716–38.

Medina Salazar, Lino. "Albores del movimiento obrero en México." *Historia y Sociedad* 4 (1965): 56–68.

Meyer, Michael C. "Habla por ti mismo, Juan: una propuesta para un método alternativo de investigación." *Historia Mexicana* 22 (1973): 396–408.

Mignone, Frederick A. "A Feif for Mexico: Colonel Greene's Empire Ends." *Southwest Review* 44 (1959): 332–339.

Neymet, Marcela de. "El movimiento obrero y la Revolución Mexicano." *Historia y Sociedad* 6 (1967): 56–73.

Peña Samaniego, Hubierto. "Apuntes históricos de Río Blanco." *El Clarín* (Orizaba), August 1958–December 1960.

Potash, Robert A. "The Historiography of Mexico since 1821." *Hispanic American Historical Review* 40 (1960): 383–424.

Powell, T. G. "Mexican Intellectuals and the Indian Question, 1876–1911." *Hispanic American Historical Review* 48 (1968): 19–36.

Prida, Ramón. "Los sucesos de Río Blanco en enero de 1907." *Suplemento al Boletín de la Sociedad Mexicana de Geografía y Estadística, Conferencias de Caracter Histórico* (1935): 87–103.

Priestley, H. I. "Mexican Literature on the Recent Revolution," *Hispanic American Historical Review* 2 (1919): 286–311.

Quirarte, Martín. "Historia política: siglo XIX." *Historia Mexicana* 15 (1965–66): 408–424.

Raat, William D. "Leopoldo Zea and Mexican Positivism: A Reappraisal," *Hispanic American Historical Review* 48 (1968): 1–18.

Rogers, Allen H. "Character and Habits of the Mexican Miner." *The Engineering and Mining Journal* 85 (1908): 700–702.

Rosenzweig Hernández, Fernando. "Las exportaciones mexicanas de 1817–1911." *Historia Mexicana* 9 (1960): 395–411.

Ross, Stanley R. "Cosío Villegas' *Historia moderna de México*." *Hispanic America Historical Review* 46 (1966): 274–82.

Schmitt, Karl M. "The Díaz Conciliation Policy on State and Local Levels 1876–1911." *Hispanic American Historical Review* 40 (1960): 513–532.

Solís Martínez, Vicente. "Como surgio la lucha obrera mexicana en Río Blanco." *El Clarín*, 7 June 1959.

Tays, E. A. H. "Present Labor Conditions in Mexico." *The Engineering and Mining Journal* 84 (1907): 621–624.

UNPUBLISHED MATERIALS

Albro, Ward S., III. "Ricardo Flores Magón and the Liberal Party: An Inquiry into the Origins of the Mexican Revolution of 1910." Ph.D. dissertation, The University of Arizona, 1967.

Álvarez, Lynne. R. de. "The Río Blanco Strike and the Díaz Regime." Mimeographed seminar paper. The University of Americas, Cholula, Mexico, 1972.

Bryan, Anthony I. "Mexican Politics in Transition, 1900–1913: The Role of General Bernardo Reyes." Ph.D. dissertation, The University of Nebraska, 1970.

Burkes, David D. "The Dawn of Manufacturing in Mexico, 1821–1855." Ph.D. dissertation, University of Chicago, 1952.

Chambers, Ron. "Cananea, 1906: A Harbinger of Warning." Mimeographed seminar paper. The University of the Americas, Cholula, Mexico, 1972.

Crosman, Herbert A. "The Early Career of José Ives Limantour, 1854–1886." Ph.D. dissertation, Harvard University, 1950.

Delorme, Robert Lee. "The Political Basis of Economic Development: Mexico, 1884–1911, A Case Study." Ph.D. dissertation, University of Minnesota, 1968.

Doty, Richard G. "Mexican Industry under Porfirio Díaz, 1876–1911." Ph.D. dissertation, University of Southern California, 1967.

Gómez–Quiñones, Juan. "Social Change, Intellectual Discontent and the Growth of Mexican Nationalism, 1890–1911." Ph.D. dissertation, University of California at Los Angeles, 1972.

Jenkins, Myra E. "Ricardo Flores Magón and the Mexican Liberal Party." Ph.D. dissertation, University of New Mexico, 1953.

Meier, Matt S. "Industrial Unrest in Mexico, 1887–1910." Master's thesis, Mexico City College, 1949.

Michaels, Albert A., and Bernstein, Marvin. "The Modernization of the Old Order: Organization and Periodization of 20th Century Mexican History." Paper presented to the IV International Congress of Mexican Studies, Santa Monica, California, 17–21 October 1973. Mimeographed.

Miller, Richard U. "The Role of Labor Organization in a Developing Country: The Case of Mexico." Ph.D. dissertation, Cornell University, 1966.

Niblo, Stephen Randall. "The Political Economy of the Early Porfiriato: Politics and Economics in Mexico, 1876–1880." Ph.D. dissertation, Northern Illinois University, 1972.

Raat, William Dirk. "Positivism in Díaz Mexico 1876–1910: An Essay in Intellectual History." Ph.D. dissertation, The University of Utah, 1967.

Roehl, Charlotte. "Porfirio Díaz in the Press of the United States." Ph.D. dissertation, University of Chicago, 1953.

Romney, Joseph Barnard. "American Interests in Mexico: Development and Impact During the Rule of Porfirio Díaz, 1876–1911." Ph.D. dissertation, University of Utah, 1969.

Ruiz, Ramón Eduardo. "Madero, the Apostle and the Worker." Paper presented to the IV International Congress of Mexican Studies in Santa Monica, California, 17–21 October 1973.

Sandels, Robert L. "Silvestre Terrazas, The Press, and the Origins of the Mexican Revolution in Chihuahua." Ph.D. dissertation, University of Oregon, 1967.

Sujer, Ray J. "The Mexican Labour Press, 1880–1884: The Editorial Positions of *El Socialista* and *El Hijo de Trabajo*." University of the Americas, 1973. Mimeographed.

Vanderwood, Paul. "The Rurales: Mexico's Rural Police Force, 1861–1914." Ph.D. dissertation, University of Texas at Austin, 1970.

Yamada, Mutsuo. "The Cotton Textile Industry in Orizaba: A Case Study of Mexican Labor and Industrialization During the Díaz Regime." Master's thesis, University of Florida, 1965.

INTERVIEWS

Nicolas T. Bernal (Mexico City), 1966, 1969.

Gabriel Cházaro (Mexico City), 1966.

José Ortiz Petricioli (Mexico City), 1966.

Ethel Duffy Turner (Mrs. John Kenneth Turner) (Cuernavaca), 1966.

Index